The Art of Bamboozling in plain sight...what white people do to cover their asses

(and one man's experience of 'working while Black' in social care in the United Kingdom)

VOLUME 1

D.Eric Lawrence

This is a work of nonfiction.

Ordering Information:

Prime Seven Media
518 Landmann St.
Tomah City, WI 54660

Printed in the United States of America

Volume 1: **The Art of Bamboozling in plain sight...**what white people do to cover their asses (and one man's experience of 'working while Black' in social care in the United Kingdom)

Bamboozled

1 : to deceive many by underhanded and or toxic methods: dupe, hoodwink I got **bamboozled** by an unethical legal system to help a variety low life's and unworthy human beings. 2 : to confuse, frustrate, or throw off press and media thoroughly and or by completely ignoring human rights and British Law as a 'defence' as well as an 'offence' in plain sight of many.

The memoirs of D.Eric Lawrence that covers the period of his work life from 2015-2016 and beyond.

Written by: D. E. Lawrence

Edited by: Patrick Jellow

Warning: There are limits to D.Eric Lawrence's memoirs. He is only writing about himself and highlights the interactions with the diverse 'Collection of Toxic Actors' that decided to either drag him into something that was really none of his business, and or repeatedly threatened him for information and or protected others that created and or perpetuated 'the big lie' for reasons only known to themselves about incidents that occurred during 2015-16 and beyond.

The author's use of phrases such as 'white privilege' and 'white male privilege' are based on their personal and professional experiences. They are all aware that there are and have always been human beings that describe themselves as 'white', that can and have been absolutely magnificent human beings, ones that are allies, ones that are often generous with their time and energy (including walking 'shoulder to shoulder' with others during periods of societal stress).

A prologue:
People that I met along the way

> "...The devil likes to make you feel that it's only you that's been hurt, only you that's scapegoated and left alone to cope...then he's winning and laughing.
>
> Luckily, the universe she provides unplanned and unexpected reminders to show that we are definitely not alone... scapegoating, bystanders, victims and survivors are too too many. Meeting other victims and survivors can be humbling and healing...the devil does not want you to know this...run baby run!

I initially thought that I would be one *angry, disappointed* and *frustrated* brother for my memoir period and beyond.

Angry at myself for being picked out to be the 'scapegoating target' of my 2015-16+ lived experiences, angry for a large part of the development of my memoirs, *angry* that I thought that I had literally had no legal and or human rights support and *angry* because I felt quite literally stuck.

Disappointed at the lack of support from those around me and or nothing coming from the wider public, some that were on the receiving end of my large body of work and contributions to the care sector going back to the 70s in the USA, UK, EU and the Caribbean. Especially *disappointed* with local public health authorities who did not seem to question the authenticity of the evidence that they were presented with in 2018-19. You'd think someone taking their own life would deserve the upmost reverence and quality consideration...especially when looking at 'what went wrong' and what can be learned from such a sad death.

Frustrated for reasons listed above, the 'gridlock' was real and seemed endless, like a satanic never ending video game.

I had felt so alone at times and only thought I had two choices... get cleared or stay 'branded' as the guy the deprived that poor family information about their poor daughter's passing in 2016.

The universe as she always does, she had other plans for me. She had me speak with over 100 survivors and victims, ones that cared deeply within a social care setting and ones that cared deeply in settings such as teaching, youth work, social work, etc..

Ironically, every one that I met in my writing journey they genuinely had their own stories and they all seem to relate to some type of loss such as potential loss of liberty, being scapegoated by a senior manager, a loss of career, loss of professional associations/affiliations, loss of family, loss of relationships, loss of self- esteem and identity, loss of dreams and goals...wow, an amazing amount of pain and anguish, and drama for people that just wish to help others.

For me, it made me feel quite insignificant in my 'me me me' memoir zone time period and focus.

Because I was very deeply touched by my 'human to human' contact, I decided to add three anonymous stories to my memoirs, they genuinely redirected the path that I was on, in this book and in life in general.

I laid them out in similar ways to how my spirit was trying to make sense of things in and around me.

- Who are you?
- What happen?
- Why you?
- Where was the truth?
- Why didn't those around you come forth and tell the truth?
- Where are you now?

_____

Who are you?

'Crystal and John'

What happen?

"...My wife was accused of sexually grooming one of her pupils..."

"...It was proven that the head had coached a young person to say that I had singled him out a lot and that he liked it ...".

Why you?

"...Parents and students seemed to really like my teaching and most knew I would go the extra mile...."

Where was the truth?

"...A group of young boys confessed that I was just a nice teacher and did nothing wrong. The school unfortunately had a lot of 'staff burn out' and often we treated our pupils quite poorly. Our head was over her head, unhappy and very stressed out. Ofsted inspection showed parents and young people really enjoyed my team's work and my head did not like this...we were clearly not on the same page....".

"...We have two young children and I worried about my wife being struck off and going to prison, I was really afraid, did not know who to turn to..." .

Why didn't those around you come forth and tell the truth?

"...Some were afraid that they'd lose their jobs too just by helping me out.

There were some that were jealous because they thought I was the pupil's favourite teacher, not true though, some were genuinely appreciative of their teachers and assistants...".

Where are you now?

"...She is too afraid to go back, that she's lost her edge and would only cry all day...".

"...I am not sure I can be around others, especially my white colleagues without having negative feelings...that would put me off my caring nature and would probably be paranoid and think that everyone is watching me, waiting for me to trip up...".

"...I haven't worked for a while, I have no confidence. This impacts all areas of my life. My friends always thought I was the strong one, not now!...".

Who are you?

'Theo'

What happen?

"...I was accused of supplying young adults with alcohol from the shops...".

Why you?

"...I was a very popular and caring school care taker. I worked at the school for over 20 years. These particular group of young people always wanted to smoke and I was the one to catch them...".

Where was the truth?

"...Not sure, I always tried to keep everyone safe and always always always stopped young people from smoking...maybe this was the reason...".

Why didn't those around you come forth and tell the truth?

"...At times I thought it was because I tried to help teachers by trying to cut through red tape. I often opened up for the teachers for free, during my own time...".

Where are you now?

"...I became a hermit, and did not go out. I am sure everyone knew that I was sacked and lost my pension. I grew up in the same area that I was a caretaker.

Don't get me wrong, teachers and families brought me food in the early days but I was not used to being someone's charity...I worked since I was 15 and now I am on benefits.

My children tell me to take my school to court but I know not many of us (West Indians) that ever win against racism and I am too old and ill now to fight. I take a truck load of pills each day...you tell me what would you do?..."

Who are you?

'Winston' and 'Princess Gloria'

What happen?

I had a multicultural children's home a while back in South London. It was small but it grew and improved steadily each and every year. I thought that I had a very close staff team and with good relationships with all of our children and young people.

I took on a Nigerian business partner after a few years, I really looked forward to her joining me, she was a Christian, she was well educated and a great cook. I was born in Jamaica but always wanted a black business partner for my UK business ventures.

Problems started to arise when little by little the service users started to ask could they have her to be their cook instead of their current cook. Then our new staff as well started to complain that my business partner was more experienced than me and "...why can't she lead us...". This wasn't true, I was not really sure but it was very hurtful because it seemed to come out of the blue.

The crazy thing was that myself and my business partner we never actually argued...not even once.

The truth soon came out when after only five months of being joint CEOs, she then asked could she buy me and my debts out...after three years of me building up the home with its good reputation...she wanted to take it all away after not really bringing much to the table...I worked day and night to make this business grow and neglected my family at times... ahhhhhhhhhh!!!!

Why you?

I think she may have seen me as a soft touch, one that would not fight to keep his own business, even one that I made many sacrifices for...you'd need to ask her.

No one did this to me, I lived in 'a dream world of my own' at times. Even when there are no 'white people' around to screw you up, not even one, then we always seemed to find a way to kill each other off. Shame really.

White people must think we are bat shit crazy at times.

Where was the truth?

Dreams, hope and working with 'your own' was never something that I took lightly.

I guess I was a bit like a stereotype.... took the first bit of money that was offered to me (to pay off my large bills) and never even thought to seriously vet a business partner.

Why didn't those around you come forth and tell the truth?

Some weren't really my friends as I had thought, they were more of "...I told you so..." people. Some seemed happy because I seemed happy.

Where are you now?

I moved into my childhood home in Kingston Jamaica. I own part of an American bar with my cousin. I try not to think about the home.

Conclusion

Meeting and experiencing so many interesting individuals during the years of developing my memoir manuscript was very humbling and, in some cases, made me feel that my life was trivial, especially if I heard that people had passed away, or that some were physically and legally struggling in the end...some clearly find ways to get 'moments of joy'.

Even though I initially had no plans to speak about (in this memoir) views gathered from the majority of individuals, couples and families that spoke to me, if I could sum up some of their words of wisdom, maybe they tell my 'me me me self' something like "...D.Eric Lawrence, please don't shut us down..."('these voices') ...their voices ...some are louder than others and some are very very clear thoughts and reflections that belong here, 'in this moment' (part of the memoir introduction) and not anywhere else ..."just say it D.Eric Lawrence !!!, don't explain it to make others comfortable like you always try to do...leave that to a keen post-graduate university student to follow up, not you!...". Get on with it brother!

I am sure these reflections (from my 'people to people' interviews) would make an interesting research paper and documentary and or spoken word book...*most of us ('people of colour') do not have 'uneventful' social care careers/work histories.* In this instance I am also referring to those working in education, children's homes, probation, prisons, SEND projects, adult care homes, community health care, drug and alcohol rehab, community mental health centres, women's health centres, men's health centres, training centres, funders, children and family mental health programs, human rights programmes, criminal justice, etc...*without at least one major interpersonal challenge lasting say longer than one year (e.g., disciplinary, termination, etc.).*

Maybe the research question then could be something like "...do people of colour[1] experience a higher rate of interpersonal challenges while in social care field (this would include volunteers and interns and included areas such as internalised sexism, internalised racism, white male privilege, absence of human rights, etc.) at main grade up through senior grades? I was stumped when asked to "...literally think of one person who had one long 'social care' career where they felt productive and did not experience moderate to severe work challenges that were related to race, racism, internalised racism, sex, sexism, internalised sexism, privilege, white male privilege, bias, etc...".

The secondary research question could relate to what 'things did respondents do to themselves and 'others' (e.g., other people of colour, work colleagues, family, friends, service users, etc) just to 'survive in the work place'?

---

[1] those that describe themselves as non-black/ not a person of colour, etc..

Of course, there are other areas such as 'physical and mental health impacts' that could directly relate to their work places too. And finally, a research question around 'loss' could be useful too... "do they think that they 'lost something' by being people of colour in their social care careers?" ...interesting!

I am very grateful to the universe for regularly bringing confusing thoughts, inspiration, and hope into my consciousness from time to time.

In recent months however, especially when thinking about applying for work, this is when the expression 'a lived experience' keeps knocking around in my head and in my heart.

Initially I rejected what I thought was another 'PC expression' that meant 'a lot of nothing' and because I was feeling quite self-centred at the time, I felt that everywhere I turned, it seemed like I was getting blocked from having someone to objectively and honestly review my experiences from 2015 and beyond, and then make a legal comment for example.

To be honest I was getting very frustrated with constant blocks and denials that my world perspective even existed... gas lighting 101.

It seemed like some friends and associates were forever making excuses for not making brave and honest 'human to human' comments to show me that 'they felt me' and that they could 'understand where I was coming from'. They usually only ended up telling me how they would feel and what they might do if they were me...crazy I know, hence my ambivalent thoughts about this phrase.

The words below reflected some of my early thinking around this topic;

Throughout my life I have seen and have participated in various protests to get others, primarily the white majority to understand the impact of their actions and inactions on American, British and European institutions such as family, friendships, carers, health, welfare, criminal justice, financial systems, political systems, arts and entertainment, the acknowledgment of indigenous peoples, sports, education, careers and science...these social action activities were viewed as 'positive' and or 'negative' by academics and local members of society, this was dependent upon what side of 'the fence' that you were standing on[2] politically, financially, socially, culturally, racially, etc..

I guess what I am trying to say here is that 'the choices' in our lifetimes seems limited to;

Who are you?

What happen?

Why you?

Why didn't those around you come forth and tell the truth?

Where are you now?

During this memoir period, 2015 and beyond, my consultation work seemed to pick up (especially after the 2007 financial

---

[2]   In some cases, actually 'standing on the fence'.

crash) in areas where I have lived experiences that were not directly related to 'racism'. Yes, this is very ironic because it has been widely known that at times I was called 'the nice race guy'. I now have learned to make better use of 'work creation opportunities' and now help my potential customers in ways other than just those areas that they have gotten used to with me over the years such as racism, criminal justice, education ...I may have lived and contributed to these latter areas in the US, UK, EU and the Caribbean ... and I certainly did not 'just know people' who were involved and or living in these areas...I was 'deep within' these areas for myself too.

'Living and working with white people'...
something to consider?

I know there are many hundreds of different groups around the world that have long talked about and or have developed creative, impractical and perhaps practical 'reparations' frameworks for addressing slavery and the long term 'impact of privilege' generally and the impact of 'white male privilege' especially upon 'minority and the majority groups'...living and working with white people is definitely 'a thing' and a major influential life factor in the same way perhaps as are medical challenges, war, racism, religious persecution, islamophobia, conflict, natural disasters, climate change, social upheavals, sexual harassment and violence.

I was always told as a young person "...mind your own business and usually 'they' will let you get on with your work and if you are lucky they will forget you are even there too!...".I did not really understand it then but as I grew into adolescence it was as clear as a laser beam what this phrase meant.

Certain people of colour may have even colluded at times but this by no means should discount its position (white people) as indeed 'a lived experience trigger'. Denying its existence does not simply make you a racist, and more rigorous study is definitely needed in this area.

...I wonder would any of them have stepped up and done something 'different' if they had known that their silence and or lies/false narratives would lead to (only) me going to prison and not ' the others'.

The people that I met along the way however...as a tribute to them I will promise to assertively struggle in the following memoirs to move through anger, through disappointment and through frustration...to struggle with the universe to be a survivor regardless of what anyone else does around me.

From those that I met along the way ... from the individuals and the institutions that have worked very hard to keep the truth away, why should I be the exception...just need to take time to breathe each day...and survive, the devil can wait!

- *Who are you?*
- Why you?
- Where was the truth?
- Why didn't those around you come forth and tell the truth?
- Where are you now?

Figure 1 Dave, D.Eric Lawrence and Jean...playing Latin jazz at the London Metropolitan Police Black History Event

Table of Contents

Dedicated to the joys, hope, wisdom and 'the quiet' that come from still moments...incredibly grateful...to Udish, a lovely human being, one that always had an 'idea or two on the go'...I am glad that you made it to Sri Lanka and may you now rest in peace brother!

Also dedicated to Dave, my long time friend and music and creative partner... "...we keep doing it our way brother!...".

And finally, to Patrick, my long-suffering friend and editor... this memoir was long and not easy to write and you read every new version without complaint.

Some thoughts about the memoir delays

For the most part, the bulk of these memoirs was ready to go in 2022 and had a signed publishing contract...I was very happily hyper and raring to go too! There was even some emerging thoughts of developing my memoirs into a podcast series and or an audio book. To be honest I still like the audio book idea!

There were unexpected but 'regular' external roadblocks, and it was at these 'low times' that I would wonder if there was 'collusion' going on somewhere within international publishers, especially if and when my name came up. But most of the time I was pulled back from my irrational conspiracy theories and just realised that lateral thinking and having other creative art projects to keep me and my spirit busy was the best path for my well-being, all with practical outcomes. I have written and published two small books while awaiting the memoirs publication.

Unfortunately, the universe, she had other plans for me and 2025 it was...the birth of my memoirs!

If I am really honest here, I worried that the people that really to needed to read this and or the other toxic actors, and 'minor toxic extras', that they might have passed away and would never ever read this (and then perhaps even less of them would never be able to attempt to make things right if they wanted to).

Some of my forever hard-working focus group reminded me that 'Trump' is now in the White House and the challenges and 'the straight out lies in plain sight' that I faced could easily have (and do) exist across the pond too.

Who are you?

1. **Getting sucked in**... the lure of Health and Social Care/The Actors and Winter 2015-Working for RPFI

Some Reflective thoughts from D.Eric Lawrence

> **Bamboozled Wisdom** (Number 1) Working for the devil does not mean you know his/her secrets, no matter how long you have worked for them...only the devil can speak their truth if cornered and or desperate enough.

Some would say and have said that my recent life is more like a novel or a play...to me, at times it felt like this as well although I might have described it as an "...*an adventure of truth into fiction and back out again...loads of adventure and intrigue, people die, people lie...this is very much and 'audience participation' book...what do you believe??? ... you decide...*".

The main 'influential character' of this 'social care story' besides myself is **Elly Jansen** (also goes by 'Nelly' too I recently found out).

How 'influential' is she I hear my readers ask? She founded the Social Care organisation that I worked for during late 2015-16, she has an OBE, she owned the three social care homes that made up the social care organisation that I worked with and provided support for[3] and she had a vast career internationally in the 70s and 80s developing 'therapeutic community model' in areas such as mental health, drug and alcohol dependency, etc.(where service users are supported to develop their voices, and influence where and how they live and how they can participate more in their care). A few years back she lost her organisation, *readers will have to do their own research to become more aware of this particular scandal.*

Finally, had she been truthful and not have been so heavily protected, most of us would have never have been fined, blacklisted, decimated by the press/social media or even sent to prison. She is definitely the star of my memoir drama!

On 14 February 2018 at 22:52, Elly Jansen <elly.jansen@rpfi.org> wrote:

GEOFF AND I INTERVIEWED YOU AND WERE SATISFIED THAT YOU WERE ABLE TO HELP US, AND MY OPINION DID NOT CHANGE.

I AM NOW ASKED TO PRODUCE YOUR CV AND ESPECIALLY YOUR QUALIFICATION AS A THERAPIST. I believe you ARE QUALIFIED AT A MUCH HIGHER LEVER THAN VINCENT AND THAT ROHIT HAD NO RECOGNISED CERTIFICATE, BUT NEVERTHELESS ACTED AS IF HE WAS A THERAPIST.I AM SORRY TO HAVE TO ASK YOU TO PROVIDE THE ABOVE. I STILL HAVE NO FILING HELP AND STILL WORK PRO DEO 70 HOURS PER WEEK WITHOUT COMPENSATION. MUCH OF IT HAS BEEN IN VAIN.

IN RESPONSE TO YOUR SUGGESTIONS TO CLOSE L.L. WE WOULD NOT HAVE BEEN ABLE TO FILL IT AGAIN AS EVERYBODY WOULD HAVE BELIEVED VINCENT BUT - IN RETROSPECT - IT WOULD HAVE SAVED YEARS OF TORTURE!

YOURS SINCERELY,

ELLY--Elly Jansen, OBE, Consultant to RPFI

---

[3] She had other homes that she was trying to rent out to other providers and during my time had a unit that the Chair-Geoff Benton (RIP) and her were trying to get another children's home up and running.

Other 'Supporting Toxic Actors' included:

Elly/Nelly Jansen: Richmond Psychosocial Foundation International Charity founder/Lead in 2016: stood by and let press/court hurt D.Lawrence for her actions/co-actions after adult service user took her own life 3 months after he had already left her organisation.

Geoff Benton: Ex-Chair of the Trustees (RIP): He was and is a very decent human being, unfortunately he had a severe heart attack before the Coroner's Jan 2019 Inquest. I can guarantee (I think) that he would not have let anyone be scapegoated.

Assistant Coroner: for some reason didn't believe D.Lawrence 13.12.18 Witness Statement/Exhibits at initial coroner inquest and was manipulated by other interested stakeholders against D.Lawrence to show bias, misrepresentations, racism and outright lies to the coroner process, to the legal system and to the public and press/media. He needs to be legally held accountable for his actions. He was presented 'additional DL 2016 emails' in August 2019 from D.Lawrence (as was the court clerk and prosecutor) and kept quiet about it to the public and the media/press. His treatment of me was a true reflection of the chaos at the West London Coroners Court...the police, CPS, Prosecution, press and public were carefully guided away from hearing about this vital piece of information.

Senior Coroner: Had the opportunity to read RPFI charity emails[4] between all senior staff and the charity founder/lead

---

[4]   He was given about 70% of this books worth of evidence to review!

advisor from key moments in Feb 2016 that were presented to him via D.Lawrence in Feb 2020. After reading these, he chose to say nothing whatsoever about their content, even when they clearly casted doubt upon the Assistant Coroner's unprofessional and bias treatment of D.Lawrence and Inquest Outcome. He could have at least detailed in writing what evidence that D.Lawrence provided to him and how he considered or not considered this same substantial evidence. He had a very tumultuous work history at the West London Coroners Court and was finally sacked in 2023. He too could have easily kept those that he supervised from pushing false lies and narratives about me or anyone else in 2019...in 2020...why not? There were rumours that too many of his colleagues had too much on him for him to be an effective leader.

Chief Coroner: after several email letters from D.Lawrence in 2019/2020 he asked the Senior Coroner to do an 'internal investigation' of my concerns/evidence in Feb 2020(but because of Covid-19 it was delayed several months). Once he was made aware in spring 2020 that the Senior Coroner did not even come close to reviewing and or discussing the issues and evidence that D.Lawrence presented, he did nothing. In his position, this was totally unacceptable, especially after he himself knew there were problems but kept quiet. Upon reflection, I was very surprised that he referred him to the chaotic West London Coroners Court to review D.Lawrence case.

MET: Voluntarily interviewed D.Lawrence in June 2019, primarily about spring/early summer 2019 when D.Lawrence was in regular communication with assistant coroner, but allowed him to be given a charge by the CPS with a ' charge period' that began on 10 June 2018 when he did not even know the Assistant Coroner until 30 August 2018(via an email attachment letter from the RPFI's charity solicitor). D. Lawrence was never questioned about the summer of 2018, nor was he asked about any summer 2018 contact with the coroner. D.Lawrence provided work emails and email correspondence between himself and the charity founder/ lead advisor well in advance of the MET interview, yet these were never presented in court. He was regularly asked by D.Lawrence to clarify the charge dates and only blamed others.

CPS: allowed D.Lawrence to be charged for a period in 2018 that he was not in contact with the Assistant Coroner and allowed prosecutor to use D.Lawrence interview statements as if they covered the summer 2018 period too(and not just the actual spring/early summer period of 2019 that he and the Assistant Coroner were actually in contact).The 'confusing charge' allowed the court to not be specific about their false accusations, especially when withholding D.Lawrence four email letters to the court which would added a factual narrative to the court proceedings. After over a years' worth of chasing up, the CPS has yet to take responsibility for the inappropriate charge period dates, the unanswered court letters, inappropriate judge and prosecutor behaviours, manipulation of the media/press(that D.Lawrence was somehow withholding information from the Bennett family since 10 June 2018...total false narrative)and allowing a 60 y/o to go to prison with no prior criminal record, one with 40+years of public service.

Was sentenced 30.10.19 to four months after previously fining him £650 in May 2019 for not attending the Coroner's Inquest, the 'Double Jeopardy' rules ignored.

Kingston Crown Court: was meant to be the court where D.Lawrence appeal was to be heard. The judge (HHJ Barklem) for reasons only known to them refused numerous and reasonable requests to comment about the legal status of D.Lawrence four original unanswered court letters, especially the 24.10 Application to change his plea, request to submit witnesses and evidence. Instead, they fined him twice 23.7.2020(£330 both times) with no explanation or warning. It is clear this judge does not appreciate assertiveness from citizens. They also refer to D.Lawrence in a 'negative manner' and referred to something that they saw within 'file' that they had on him(I have not seen this file).

Press/Media: Regularly unleased untruths, examples of racism, bias, etc. and non-factual narratives without speaking to D.Lawrence even once for a quality interview.

BACP: I went from being immensely proud of my contributions and associations going back decades, to now feeling humiliated and disregarded by the same organisation. From my perspective, they have been one of my major hindrances to clear my name. It seems like they thought that they were doing their civic duty by trying to kick me out of the association and the more 'publicly' the better. I provided them with ample email evidence and example pathways to be my Ally. I have given years to this organisation and they wished get me away from them as if I was shit.

I can imagine the 'investigation panel' and the composition of the panel members assigned to get me out, they thinking that they were really only 'following the rules'. Crazily enough they would not even let me resign in 2020, they only wanted to let me out on their terms e.g., more public decimation, misrepresentation and never once attempting a 'public challenge' of what they were reading or hearing about me. I was in no mood to see them face-to-face and provided their panel with more than enough evidence to 'do something different' from afar.

I will later in Volume II share some of my example energetic responses that I used trying to get them to be fair and for them to critically evaluate anything they saw in the press and review anything from the coroner process in order make sure that it was fair, accurate and just. They caused me many sleepless nights, I just kept imagining the press headlines that I was kicked out of one of my 6 fellowships. I tried so so hard to resign my membership in 2019 - to make it easier for both of us...they were not having any of it and just ploughed through. I really could have used their support.

D.Eric Lawrence: The 'coroner process' of 2018+ and English Legal System separately (2019-2020) and together regularly violated D.Lawrence's Human Rights, especially as it related to Article 6.They both blatantly misrepresented him often, were racist and inaccurate in their charge and conspired to send him to prison. Mr Lawrence was never included in the legal process in a transparent manner, all decision making processes were kept away from him and the legal actors, the press and media actors regularly tried to decimate his decades of public and voluntary service to the US, UK, and EU in the areas of education diversity and inclusion, social care, mental health, young offenders, black offenders, criminal justice, research, well-being, SEN, etc as group worker, practitioner, trainer, manager, consultant/advisor, content provider, sport and music professional...it was as if they wished D.Lawrence's contributions, skills, knowledge, and contributions to the 'wider body of knowledge' had never actually happened and or were always of a 'lower quality' and 'based upon inexperience'.

Moving on...'Social Care' is generally an easy accessible vocational field to come in to ...volunteers often can just start doing positive activities in their communities, some with rigid security screening and some can enter with just a good heart. Interns can join in to develop their specific skills and insights usually with no hassle at all.

Modern social care workers often can join with little or no qualifications and just get either on-the-job qualifications, or on-the-job experiences and then top these up in further education or university. Owners of social care facilities, investors of social care facilities, etc. have entered via various pathways such as officially 'registering their interests', some hire 'front people' that easily link with the 'official bodies', some just keep quiet, and some are 'protected from scrutiny' in very creative ways.

D.Eric Lawrence and his 'Road to Health and Social Care'

I was always very fortunate, 'the universe' she seemed to have her own plans for me and most of the time I made myself available to her ultimate wisdom and vast opportunities.

Growing up, my only career dreams (*I think*) focused on either being a Professional American Football player, a jazz funk artist or join the military and being a career man like my father. Working in the UK and the EU was never a dream, nor was it ever an expectation for if things went wrong, and never ever in my wildest dreams would I have thought that there would be people trying to 'cancel me out', with a very toxic attempt to hide and or decimate my career choices and experiences, while others simply watched[5].

I was the one that organisations brought in when there were 'internal problems. I think being an introvert helped, along with my 'coaching style' of management and my sense of loyalty to whoever I was working for. Often working for cheaper rate than a lot of comparable consultants didn't hurt either.

There were those in unfair privileged positions, those that did not know a thing about me personally and or professionally, just actively trying 'in plain sight' to wipe out my in-depth

---

[5]   Since my 'post 2019' self-awareness was heightened, I now realise that I am prone to make 'younger workplace men generally' and 'some white men' specifically very envious and or threatened of my talents at times just by being around and or being effective, where I as a person that loves to observe others, I can be easily in awe of talents in others and have no desire whatsoever to mess with them, where with me, others at times want to find a reason to down play my diverse offerings and push me out. It is usually my women colleagues that point this observation out to me... amazing!

range of social care contributions in the 'world of work', a whole body of international work, hundreds of children, young people, families, carers, individuals, organisations, etc., just simply wipe everything away and keep things hidden just to justify a false narrative that protected some and 'created new villains'. I am very confident, if my experience was known...at least see the 'light of day', at least there might have been a fair and ethical public opinion debate about my fitness to be Elly Jansen's Consultant.

In the early 80s I came to UK as a tourist because I felt like I was getting 'too old before my time' and thought I would try to live the life of a musician/composer for a while and just 'see what happens'. I started my 'UK adventure' with an alto saxophone, a bass guitar and a ton of resumes. Playing gigs in places that I had only previously saw on album covers as a teenager ... meeting so many diverse individuals and artists and my confidence as 'shy guy' grew in leaps and bounds during these days. After about six months I decided to extend my UK stay because I really felt London, at least musically it reminded me of a 'small New York' at times and Europe was just so amazing too, it had many places that I would soon get to know my way around in just by walking. For my first 'non music' job abroad, I even worked in a petrol station in northwest London for about a year too, just to top up my income. I always smelled like gas but I really needed the money.

In some ways I wish I had been more mature in my early romantic adventures, to me they were remarkable but I only focused more upon the music career which felt a bit selfish at times but didn't allow myself to slow down. I am definitely grateful and very undeserving at times for meeting some of the greatest people that I have ever known and some that clearly have left positive marks on my soul! My daughters were and continue to be a great motivation to me as a man, as a person and as a father. I will always want 'the best D.Eric Lawrence' for them and I am very lucky to be called 'DD', 'dad' and 'daddy granddad'.

Along the way and in the very real world of sport, arts, music, criminal justice and social sciences I have met some of the most amazing human beings and their families, just through carrying out our daily work and creative activities!

I was once described as a 'willing multi-tasker'. As my musical adventures started to slow down, my social care adventure began to grow, *it was that damn universe pushing me ever further to non-artistic opportunities*....I was introduced to loads of interesting charities that asked me to provide content, asked me to do training and staff/team mentoring, to support individuals and their families, and represent them at times at local meetings, national meetings and conferences. I even supported some local politicians. Ironically, my very 'first ever social care job' in the UK came about as a result of a random discussion with an Alcohol Charity Manager in a coffee bar. He was an American from NYC, but had lived in the UK for several years.

One job led to another, although most of my jobs for several years related to 'race and culture'. For example, in my early days I did 'race' and criminal justice, 'race' and young people, 'black people' and mental health, working with 'black managers' and their 'black teams', etc...can you see 'the trend'? Because I needed to pay the bills and desperately wanting a 'work permit', I became 'a diversity consultant/ trainer'[6].These in-depth and life changing experiences can't be erased. In a lot of cases, they provided me with incredible learning and development opportunities and the people that really know me will often hear me say "...*I will do anything once, especially if you buy me a drink or feed me...*".

My first 'European job' was working in Utrecht, Netherlands. I was hired to support a large and diverse community group, more of a 'creative teambuilding session', so that they could learn to work together rather than fighting over limited funding for those considered as racial and or cultural and or language minorities. They asked me back quite a few times over the years. These trips filled my heart...my soul and my passion for diversity and inclusion issues that first began in the Arctic Circle, these just continued to grow and grow, and still is very much a deep passion today.

Believe me, even though young in age I was always a lifetime student and a 'forever inquisitive creative young man', the one that would 'look under the rocks', often when no one was looking. There were also several times that I really thought that I would have had a genuine heart attack at times (due to 'work excitement') and so I meditated and 'negotiated' many many times with the universe for her to keep me alive and well a little while longer...I was so excited just to be involved

---

[6]   Although in the mid 80s, the phrase "...the EOPS guy..." was banded about

'in the London Life', in the 'Euro Life' and I had to regularly remind myself that I was really here in the UK.

I have been a trainer, a consultant, an artist, an external and internal moderator, a senior researcher, a content provider, a business and sports coach and an Ally for hundreds of charities, statutory bodies and the private sector all before the age of 45. I was one 'very blessed brother' that also presented papers in five countries and usually got asked back to participate. It seemed however, that as my 'circle of positive colleagues' and I grew older, we were replaced, no one except for perhaps our students/ex-students, young people and their parents and carers seemed to want to hear our stories any more.

Working as a consultant...what does this mean?

This phrase, 'consultant' reflects my 30 + years work and publications at least on a continuous part-time basis as a 'consultant'(UK, EU and the Caribbean).

I realised that, using the 'internet definition of D.Eric Lawrence', where this term describes me/my past work, was a 'cancelling out term', one that purposely sets out to minimalize my experiences/talents/body of work and drastically misrepresents how I describe myself.

I was in 2015 and am still a Fellow within several professions such as education, leadership, sport, etc. *In my multi-layered 'professions'(refer specifically to the above term), we use the term 'consultant' to mean;*

Management consulting is working with businesses to identify solutions to problems to maximize business performance, improve business processes, and increase revenue. A management consultant can cover a range of areas including business management, marketing, business strategy, supply chain, and employee productivity.

Diversity consulting is the branch of professional consultancy that supports organisations, in the area of diversity and inclusion. The provision of consultancy can take several tailored forms and includes both advisory and the implementation of services, training, projects and other initiatives.

As a **social care consultant**, you will be responsible for a wide range of tasks, including developing and implementing policies, implementing national guidelines, designing and delivering training programs, conducting audits, and advising on best practices in social care.

For most jobs from the 2000s I am usually getting interviewed by people half my age and they seem to care less at times about my interesting and vast work experience from the 80s and 90s and what it could bring to an organisation like theirs...was like the lyrics to a Janet Jackson song, "*...what have you done for me lately...*". During these years I was very very fortunate because I had regularly met world class and pioneering theorists at conferences and social events, ones that my students and their lecturers had only read about. When I mentioned this at a job interview in Guildford (UK) in 2014, a very insecure interviewer didn't believe me and treated me as if my experience 'brought no value' to her and to her courses whatsoever...this is only one example from many of when my vast 'work experiences' that to someone else were potentially seen as 'a threat', and or 'a trigger for professional jealousy', and or 'non-existent value' to the interviewer and their organisations. These experiences did not just happen to me and I have talked through them with 100s of people and professionals of colour, but I am still not always sure if these experiences just related to racism, agism, anti-Americanism, jealousy, white male privilege and or just plain foolishness of other insecure professionals.

Modern curriculum vitas[7] are meant to just be two pages but for years I used to have 3-5 page resumes with several dozen past and present organisations listed throughout each page. There were organisations that appreciated my track record, the skill and the perseverance that it took to develop new business relationships...these are 'far and few in between' in modern times however.

There are a few of us around still and where we can(then and now), we use each other for work, friendship and content development...getting older doesn't always mean you have to be pushed aside.

I think 'my career peak' was when I was simultaneously involved in various action research projects, actively working for 'The National Probation Service' as it was called back then(e.g. 'Insight Project', 'Black Offenders Group Work', 'racially motivated offenders' assessment, groupwork

---

[7]   A 'resume'...

programme for at-risk, etc.), worked for an innovative European counselling award body with a diversity and inclusion brief, and supporting (and learning from),worked with four lovely black pioneering women and humans, they were the early London social workers, especially concerned with supporting and empowering black children, young people, families and carers...I learned and contributed so much during this period and had very interesting national and international travel as well related to these parts of my work. I met so many lovely people along the way and began to write chapters and articles at the urging of one of my very learned and respected department heads and friend.

Life was not always a 'total summer breeze' though, I had to experience my own immaturity growth spurts (like they say, "...youth is often wasted on the young(er)..."), internalised racism situations which to me are much worse than racism ever could be (e.g. things that we do to each other, things that might have their roots within white privilege, but can only be squarely put upon our own door steps). It was also during this period that I first met Elly Jansen and co-managed one of her homes in Northwest London. Even Elly Jansen herself told me once in the 80s, "...it is not what you ('Duncan') do, It's what you can do to empower the therapeutic community to do for themselves...", amazing! I guess people stopped listening to her along the way too...she has created organisations in her name all over the UK yet almost no one knows about or cares about her contributions any more regarding social care, mental health, alcohol addiction and 'on-the-job training'. Maybe these factors added to her increased toxicity over the years...shame really.

It was also during this time period that I became aware that loads of people were making money from children's homes, from semi-independent units and from social care homes. I was not really interested in owning a home myself but really enjoyed supporting them along with their young people, their families/carers and their staff.

When social work started to dry up the universe, she redirected me back to my roots, education and sports.

After over 100s of charities, statuary groups and private sector organisations, this was when I was re-introduced to Elly Jansen, during the Winter of 2015. She had three social care homes that made up 'RPFI'.

'Peggy', 'Duncan' and ' Elly' in the winter of 2015

Even though there was a serious relationship breakdown between Elly, the current CEO (and ex-CEOs) and the original charity's adult social care home staff teams and its manager,

the Lancaster Lodge, I went to work for her anyway ...".... universe where were you then!!!!...".

This was 2015-2016, at the time where I was involved with several professional associations and had started and or completed and or was soon to complete several CPD courses:

> *2014 to Present: Fellow-Institute for Leadership and Management Number :0010140325*
>
> *2008 to Present: Fellow-Society for Education and Training Number: AB044611*
>
> *2009 to Present: Fellow- Royal Society for the encouragement of Arts, Manufactures and Commerce (RSA) Fellowship Number: 6010878*
>
> *1990-Present: Fellow-Retired Member British Association for Counselling and Psychotherapy (one of the founding members of the RACE division)- Members Number:505455*
>
> *2016-Present: Aspiring Manager Member -The Chartered Institute for the Management of Sport and Physical Activity (formerly known as the Register of Exercise Professionals-UK) Number:382608*

2015-16 CPD Activities included:

- *Level 3 Award in Equality and Diversity (UK*
- *Level 4 Certificate Managing Equality and Diversity in an Organisation (UK)*
- *Level 3 Diploma in Fitness Instructing and Personal Training[8]*
- *SEN (Special Education Needs) Diploma[9]*

---

[8] Began this programme in 2015
[9] Began SEN training in 2015-16

- *Boot Camp and Circuit Training Award*
- *2014 England Basketball Level 1 UK Coaching Certificate (UKCC L1)(UK)/Basketball Activators Award (UK)*

These all 'added value' to my business clients at the time (2014-16) in social care, education, leadership, special education, sport, etc.. The 'added value' would have also included:

- *Diversity and inclusion management*
- *Health and nutrition*
- *Group and individual fitness*
- *Leadership and management*
- *Team Building*
- *Well-being considerations*

I had a variety of tasks and roles within the RFPI such as trainer, content provider, non-management supervision and team and management mentoring, staff debriefing, senior management team, management support etc... this was across all three of the charities group homes. Most companies that hire me it is usually because I am considered 'a multi-tasker' and that I have been and am always involved in related and interesting national and international CPD activities my entire adult life. Since that 2016 period, my CPD has included:

- *2018 Level 2 Certificate in Understanding Behaviours that Challenge.*
- *2019 Level 2 Certificate in Understanding Autism*
- *2021 SENCO – Special Educational Needs Coordination*
- *2021 Corona virus (COVID-19) Awareness Course*
- *2021 Exercise Referral Diploma*
- *2021 Digital Marketing Associate (Digital Marketing Institute)*
- *2022 L5 Certificate in Sports Leadership and Management (CMI)*

Conclusion

"...social care does not really care about its workers or its clients..." (this quote is spoken at least weekly within every social care agency within the UK, and usually by a professional of colour).

BLAME from within the senior management teams seems to be the default setting at times of stress in social care and this can be very contagious and lead to needless calamities that impact good people[10] physically, emotionally and financially at times.

I often experienced social care as a place where leaders and founders usually' get shot' (literally, losing their own charity or lose their inspirational leadership at times), a place where the truth, bravery, compassion and courage often go amiss.

In my memoirs I try to explain why I think organisations hire someone like me for consulting, writing, training, leadership etc..

There were four key individuals responsible for me arriving at RPFI and supporting that organisation, one more so than the others.

Two of the four senior managers either hired me previously in one of their various charity units, and or knew me since the late 80s/early 90s as a distant but professional colleague.

Coming out of 2015-16 however I never once publicly and or privately really heard of organisations like RPFI, nor the

---

[10] And often spread to their families, friendships, etc..

people that brought me in to them,ever *explain why they did it(brought me in)* nor did they ever explain their own individual challenges within the RPFI charity and say *what their reflections and insights were before, during and after any interventions from me?*

From 'the talkers', and 'in the shadow hiders' of this group of four, what would have been amazing, would been to have you to also have shown the courage to publicly and honestly explain "...*how RPFI was before I arrived, why was I brought in, what did you expect me to do at RPFI that you yourselves could not do at that point and or what you did not wish to do...*" (I did not even know that RPFI existed before I worked there).

It would also be helpful to explain for example; *when was I valuable, when was I not, when were my efforts generally supported and when were they not*, especially during the period leading up to the young woman taking her own life.

From an 'I 'perspective, these same questions could and should have been asked of every staff, every shift leader, every senior manager, Trustee Chair, trustees, Charity Founder, ex-CEOS, the family, etc..

I never heard even a hint of factual POV narrative in court and or in the press/media about 'these questions and their answers'.

Keeping the focus unfairly upon me while everyone else was 'silent' (although still in plain sight) and or covering their own asses shows 'a wicked intention', 'institutional and character flaws', ones which then led to professional bodies, parents/

carers, the public, coroners, police, courts, press, etc. all being BAMBOOZLED!

Note to Actors: If you are finally ready to tell your truth, from an 'I' perspective please write to the Assistant Coroner, to the CPS, to the London Metropolitan Police, to the press, etc.. I wouldn't even waste your time on me knowing in advance what you might do, for me 'actions' always speak much louder than 'words'. But after 'the doing', ahhhhh, I would genuinely love to sit over a nice glass of Chardonnay and celebrate our joint bravery together!

The ways that the court, the press, and the media picked on the 'clinical lead role' was very racist, misleading, and misrepresented the depth and scope of my work at the charity. I have had no medical training whatsoever. The Charity Trustees, the external HR [11] , the Charity founder/advisor wrote the job description not me and it was not based upon me having a 'medical role' or a 'medical degree', something that I have never had.

---

[11]   Heather Grant
      Senior Employment Law Adviser
      Ellis Whittam Limited
      Tel: 0845 226 8393
      Web: www.elliswhittam.com

      Ellis Whittam is proud to support North West Air Ambulance and NSPCC. To learn more click here Ellis Whittam Limited. Woodhouse, Aldford, Chester, Cheshire, CH3 6JD.Registered in England, company number 04382739. Authorised and regulated by the Financial Conduct Authority. Copyright in this message and any attachments remains with Ellis Whittam Limited. This message is confidential and may be legally privileged. If this message is not intended for you it must not be read, copied or used by you or disclosed to anyone else. Please advise the sender immediately if you have received this message in error. Although this message and any attachments thereto are believed to be free of any virus or other defect that might affect any computer system into which it is received and opened it is the responsibility of the recipient to ensure that it is virus free and no responsibility is accepted by Ellis Whittam Limited for any loss or damage in any way arising from its use.

The assistant coroner picked on and demeaned my 1994 DPA CPD award, where in reality this was a great CPD opportunity for me in the early 90s and it gave me an opportunity to write and complete research papers. Going onto belittle the training provider and the quality of my CPD award was again very unfair, racist and it had nothing whatsoever to do with my work within the charity. The university did not exist in 2019 and could not defend itself.

It seems like it was more consistent with the toxic energy arising out of the Assistant Coroner process, the court, media etc. and their attempt to decimate me as a human being and as a valued international professional and content provider.

The charity, especially the original Lancaster Lodge Unit had a turbulent history of some of its service users self-harming on a daily basis. Even during my brief time, there were young women that regularly jumped (or tried to jump) into the Thames and or would regularly jump out into traffic and use other forms of self-harm. These occurrences happen so often that the Police at times would just call the unit and the unit staff would simply collect the young women and return them to the unit...often without even documenting the incident(s) into their service unit notes. It was these types of things that the founder/lead advisor and Trustee Chair (RIP) hired me to get a handle on too...anyone that was actively self-harming and or had suicidal ideation were not actually meant to stay at the unit and were meant to be referred onto a more appropriate organisation.

Certain ex-staff and current staff during that period, as part of covering up their own issues 'let the false narrative' develop and run wild, lying that these things only began as a reaction to the 2015/2016 'transformation efforts' that I was involved with...total lies and mis-directions, the neighbours knew, the charity trustees knew...a clear cover up...Bamboozled!

Records from this period were never produced and were never referred to within the court, nor ever mentioned in the press/media. These acts must have taken their toll on the staff, the service users of the time and upon their parents and carers... how much, we will never know because 'the questions leading to the facts, these were never legally or publicly asked'.

On one of the last days of the charity for me involved a CQC inspector showing up for 'surprise visit' to Lancaster Lodge. The charity founder/advisor always complained that he graded this unit and its management too highly every year during his annual inspections, this was made especially confusing to the founder/advisor when they/the unit wanted nothing to do with her 'therapeutic community' theories.

Conclusion Part 2(Regarding the 'Actors'):

'A Perfect Storm': Unfortunately, as soon as I told the charity senior managers that I probably would not be able to attend the initial Assistant Coroner Inquest during Jan/Feb 2019...I am confident that some of them were incredibly happy and started to consider 'the opportunities available to then to rewrite history', especially if there is no email back up to challenge their false narratives... 'new emerging charity narratives'. Continuing, once 'the other actors' heard that I was not attending 'false narrative storm clouds' started to brew...

With every one present at the coroners hearings (although not the founder/lead advisor and not relevant senior managers that were working on the day of the service user May 2016 death), without written evidence, just oaths/statements... some found it relatively easy to try to 'decimate me' personally and professionally (especially with an Assistant Coroner whose bias towards me grew every minute it seems) on the way to get the CEO and Founder/Lead Advisor and on the way to some a potential future cash pay-out . Because the Chair of the Trustees sadly passed away before the 2019 coroner sessions, I was elevated to 'main player status'... **now, the perfect storm was in full fury!**

Poem:

*Dear Social Care...I still got love for you...**2020***

Dear Social Care,

I still got love for you even though over the past few years I have seen you stomp out loads of dreams from good, decent and hopeful people.

Dear Social Care,

My parents took us around house to house offering warm food and clothing to those in need, yet you let me be scapegoated by a woman that got away with owning houses then renting them out to her service users and yet you let others get struck off for doing the exact same thing.

Dear Social Care,

Why did let people think that I'd known something about a period of time...three months after I had already left a job and was kept out of the loop after that...you knew it, the stakeholders knew this and my memoirs have detailed emails showing that I tried to 'stop the rot' in this little social care charity almost daily...were you yourself as an 'institution' trying to hide something too? ... I wonder.

Dear Social Care,

I could not grieve, two parents that passed away approximately a year apart from each other...they each gave more to you than me....

Dear Social Care,

During university you have me in a theatre group that went to dozens of elementary schools exploring 'good touch and bad touch'...not naturally something an introvert would do.

Dear Social Care,

Why so many charities, churches, prisons, probation offices, schools, young offender institutions, youth clubs, children's homes, drug and alcohol rehab, therapy clinics, mental health facilities, classrooms, universities, training police, creating projects from scratch, inspectors, monitors, etc.... when years later you watched me being publicly scapegoated and told "... not enough experience to be a social care consultant...?"

Dear Social Care,

Why couldn't you just be an ally when I got dragged into things that had nothing to do with me.

Dear Social Care,

You confused me when you sent me to work all over the world with talented beautiful human beings and then allowed me to be disrespected by toxic and pathetic assistant coroners, magistrates, prosecutors, probation staff and the press/ media within the UK...why?...I will never understand this one.

Dear Social Care,

Why do you allow toxic actors to lie, demean and decimate good people in public, in the press and on the internet...was this your master plan here all along for those that enter social care?

Dear Social Care,

Do insecure white men and or 'guru types' make better leaders than emotionally healthy and humble managers?

Dear Social Care,

Don't you believe in fair fights?,...

*You allow insecure and or toxic leaders to libel and slander their own teams ...why not have CEOs, and managers and any other type leaders to just openly ask their staff teams "...**what do you think about me as a person...as a leader...am I fair and decent?...".***

Dear Social Care,

Do you enjoy watching people of colour hurt each other just to protect themselves and their egos... what should we fear from you when we are being truthful even during times of stress and strain?

Dear Social Care,

Sometimes you encourage others to value my heart, my hard work, my experience, my creativity and flexibility and yet at other times I am encouraged to keep my mouth shut and just follow instructions or get the sack. Usually in those latter situations I am managed by people 'young enough' to be my children and or 'old enough' to know better.

Dear Social Care,

What do you want my family, my friends, my past and present associates and the general public etc. to feel...how do you want them to see me ...as 'cautionary tale', as a victim, or a symbol of strength and inspiration...you tell me.

Dear Social Care,

Will I ever 'get my roses' in my life time?

Dear Social Care,

Why not encourage bystanders and colluders to show bravery instead of allowing them to join toxic activities against others, ...did you take holiday leave when you saw me coming?

Dear Social Care,

Can you explain in detail what you allowed me to be prosecuted for?

Dear Social Care,

As a hard worker, when was it never enough for us 'to be protected' and or simply just left alone to get on...You are 'a career' as well as an' institution' but often when bravery and truth are needed you often allow 'less than' to rule the day... this scene is repeated over and over again unfortunately.

Dear Social Care,

I still got love for you even though at times you suck... sometimes quite a lot!

Thought Questions:

?=What do you think about D.Eric Lawrence's work experiences leading up to his three month role at RPFI?

?=Did D.Eric Lawrence do 'too much race related work' to ever really be accepted and or respected by 'white mainstream'? Y/N Explain

?=What is your initial thoughts about the 'social care' sector?

What Happen?[12]

---

[12] The upcoming chapter is personally a messy one for me (emotionally and physically). I had my lovely father that recently passed away and a sweet mother that was mentally and physically gravely unwell (and soon to pass away) ...this man never once showed compassion to me not even once, especially when leaking crazy things to the press about me...I continue to refuse to put much time into writing and editing this chapter, one that reflects upon him!

2. **First Contact** with the Assistant Coroner, Senior Coroner, United Kingdom's Chief Coroner…the long journey to nowhere

Some Reflective thoughts from D.Eric Lawrence

Bamboozled Wisdom: (Number 2) Rule makers will only 'listen' so long before their words become 'laws of the moment'…but who reviews the rule makers and the rule hiders?

Bamboozled Wisdom: (Number 2.1) When someone sadly passes away, who is really worthy to 'the investigation' of the history of life(and death)…those with unclear commitment to the truth, or the group of stakeholders asking to help you with your investigation, they too at times come with unclear commitments to the truth…these are the things that make you go 'humph' and should keep you up at night…"

Bamboozled Wisdom: (Number 2.2) "…He got away with it because he could…he never saw D.Eric Lawrence as a 'human being' and got away with it(treating him 'as less than') in plain sight…because he could".

Initially I thought that the Assistant Coroner would have left me alone after fining me £650 late spring of 2019 for not attending the inquest. He was ultimately a very toxic and obsessive person, one that I could not shake off (and I really really tried!) and he seemed incredibly determined to 'teach me a lesson' for not attending the initial inquest and potentially coming across as too cocky.

Between 10/06/2018 and 04/02/2019, within the jurisdiction of the Central Criminal Court, Duncan Lawrence failed to provide documentation as directed by the coroner for the purposes of an investigation, with the intention to have the effect of preventing that evidence, document or other thing from being given, produced or provided for the purposes of such an investigation, contrary to paragraph 7(1)(b) of Schedule 6 of the Coroners and Justice Act 2009.

This is one of the chapters that I often give to potential employers when I am applying for jobs... the part of the memoir draft that is dirty and messy (at least to me), I do this for them to get some glimpse of what it was like during the period, say from my perspective.

Sometimes, maybe two out of ten times after reading this chapter some very learned people knock me off my feet by saying something like "...hey Duncan something is very wrong here...how could one 'small guy' like you brought in assist a small but problematic social care organisation, then be held with 'absolute responsibility', absolute accountability when sadly, a service user took her own life??? "...Where was the 'duty of care to him...to Duncan...".

I don't ever think this crazy toxic person will ever admit that he got me so so wrong, as much as he wanted to get to the charity, the charity founder and its CEO and then blame them for the poor service users passing, things never really worked out for him. He even thought that with ex-staff members, ex-managers, service users, service user parents/ carers, volunteers/students etc. ...that I'd be 'icing on the cake of narrative that he and others created'.

Sadly, the Trustee Chair passed away, I remember him as having a great memory and where I had old emails to rely upon, he had a memory full of Charity stories. I do not really remember seeing any Trustee Meeting minutes but I really do remember that the meetings could get very hot, especially with Elly Jansen always taking unforgiving digs at her enemies such as current managers and senior staff of the various units...she too had a great memory going back and was an excellent 'story teller', with her always being the 'star of the show, the lead victim'.

I have no idea how she wangled out of attending the coroner sessions, she could have given the assistant coroner everything he wanted, but as she at the time good at scapegoating me and others, I guess I was the only one left for this toxic actor to go after.

I guess he thought that if he twist and twist me during my vulnerable state (with my father recently passing and my mother gravely ill at the time) that I'd say something about the charity that I hadn't said in the past...".....You need to ask the Trustee Chair...ask the Trustees, ask the charity founder/adviser...".I continually voiced these unanswered suggestions to him.

Because he never answered any of my questions,I had no idea if he or the Metropolitan Police ever followed up anything that I ever said.

Even in later months when the charity and the CEO got fined in another court, he never came back to apologise, was like he got his 'pound of flesh and moved on'.

'Social Care' used to have Trustees and Management Committees to keep them 'supported and out of trouble' in the areas of programme development, staffing, finance, management, service users, diversity and inclusion, etc.. In those days they were also 'legally responsible' for their social care project too. Where were they during any investigations" ...who gave brother Duncan some support???...".

What about the external HR that the organisations used [13], why weren't they key to any coroner inquiry and any related legal investigation.

What about the charity's own solicitors...going on the 'Internet' and reading about the coroner's investigation lacks so many important stakeholder perspectives and there is no one responsible or brave enough to ensure that I do not take

---

[13]   Heather Grant Senior Employment Law Adviser Ellis Whittam Limited
        Tel:
        0845 226 8393
        Web:
        www.elliswhittam.com

        Ellis Whittam is proud to support North West Air Ambulance and NSPCC. To learn more click here Ellis Whittam Limited. Woodhouse, Aldford, Chester, Cheshire, CH3 6JD.Registered in England, company number 04382739. Authorised and regulated by the Financial Conduct Authority. Copyright in this message and any attachments remains with Ellis Whittam Limited. This message is confidential and may be legally privileged. If this message is not intended for you it must not be read, copied or used by you or disclosed to anyone else. Please advise the sender immediately if you have received this message in error. Although this message and any attachments thereto are believed to be free of any virus or other defect that might affect any computer system into which it is received and opened it is the responsibility of the recipient to ensure that it is virus free and no responsibility is accepted by Ellis Whittam Limited for any loss or damage in any way arising from its use.

the heat for the organisation's short comings...ironically, I shared similar concerns to the assistant coroner at times but always tried to put them in writing.

The assistant coroner in a quiet space, say with his best friend would probably admit that he 'wanted to teach me a lesson' and that it was not his job to clear me, not his job to answer my questions to him in 2019 and or to even check out if what I was saying was true... on some level I could even see him saying "... it's his employer's job to protect him not mine...".

Even when I showed him proof about my father 's passing and my mother' s physical and mental fragility he didn't even acknowledge that I had sent him anything.

I'd quickly saw him as toxic racist bully, one with a fragile ego and an arrogant white privileged backbone. He had no ethical filter to make himself self-regulate what he says, what he writes and what he allows the media and the criminal justice sector to say in his name...then he goes away with 'clean hands'...somewhat.

The senior coroner, the assistant coroner's boss and the Chief Coroner...I would love to know what they really felt about the information that I presented to them. They both never even ever described the range of information that I presented to them...I assumed my information if they admitted that they had it and read it, then perhaps they would be then forced to do something about it.

I went to the highest (at least I thought so at the time) Coroner in the UK and it took several emails to get any action from his post, but *I can almost guarantee that even with my case and the intrenched chaos arising from West London Coroner's Office, can guarantee that there have been no safeguarding improvements, especially those that stop one person from writing narratives that are unsafe and far from the truth, one that tried to regularly bully me and then weaponise coroner process into a legal charge...the first ever in the UK.*

Going back to my initial comments about applying for jobs, only two (of many) actually said something like " *...wait, didn't I just read a witness statement from you, dated before the coroner's inquiry? In his reports and leaks to the press he made it seem like you gave him nothing ...rest assured working for us, keep your paperwork 'fit for purpose' and like a collective we will always share the burden in the good times and especially during the bad times...".* Employers definitely are not doing their 'due diligence' using one 'unsafe source' before deciding whether or not to hire someone or not.

If I can create an ally within one or all of the UK institutions (health, education, welfare, law, press etc), and to encourage them to just be brave and curious enough to investigate any 'unsafe areas' ... I will then promise to give you any materials, Interviews etc and then get out of your way.

There are so so many stakeholders that 'make me guilty' and keep me in this difficult place by the lies and their lack of bravery . Some potential employers even make me feel like I was on trial...I provide them my memoir draft and they think lazily only 'watching and reading from the internet sources', that this will give them what they need and then never seem to consider what they have 'missed' from not reading my memoirs and or what damage that inadvertently do when they 'project onto me' when they resume their job selection activities with me.

I would really like anything related to this coroner's case (on the internet) to be revised and have links to this book's contents, especially any letters received before and after, as well as adding magistrate court summary from the social care charity and ex-CEO case where both being found guilty and being fined two years after me.

Without a more well-rounded and less 'D.Eric Lawrence centre narrative', the public and related professionals e.g. law, public health, social care, police etc will not really realise how unsafe the initial assistant coroners inquiry really was.

I was completely shocked when the CPS and the Met charged me for a period that I did not even know the Assistant Coroner... from this moment onward I went into 'self-protection mode' and urgently looked for individuals and organisations to make complaints to about this dangerous and crazy person that would not let go of me and had too much power and control.

To this day, I am so so disappointed by the lack of bravery shown by so many stakeholders...I told anybody and everybody"... I was not there when the young woman took her own life and I did not even know that the assistant coroner even existed...".

I found out in the same way that the press could have, that my professional associations could have, that the CPS could have, that my various employers could have, that the London Metropolitan Police could have,etc....they could have asked the charity 's own solicitors, they all could have asked for proof from the West London Coroner's court, the one with a serious chaotic history[14], one well and truly with a messed up path before they even started to mess with me. "*...Did you really know Duncan Lawrence for the period of time that you said you did? ...*".

And to the Senior Coroner, the one that was meant to 'objectively review' my case and check for any bias "*...were you under pressure to be so useless in reviewing my case materials ...the easiest thing that you could have done in 2020 is to honestly clarify on whether or not I even knew who the assistant coroner was...*". Once that lie was debunked then everything else said by this lying unethical assistant coroner would have, or at least should have come into question...*but no, no such luck and you kept quiet*!

I used to read about different people trying to get information from the West London Coroner's Court offices and being blocked and some even tried using 'the freedom of information Act ' and still getting blocked.

It only dawned on me after I heard that the Senior Coroner was recently sacked, that maybe now someone could now finally and objectively review any cases that the Senior Coroner had direct involvement in and or those cases that he supervised...including mine from 2019-2020.

---

[14]   https://www.standard.co.uk/news/london/chinyere-inyama-coroner-bully-sacked-alice-gross-b1059812.html

The rumour has been that he was compromised for a long time from doing his job because too many of his colleagues had information on him and he had to tread carefully.

I am surprised that the Chief Coroner of the UK did not even know this guys 'checkered past' when he referred him to review my case, to do an 'objective review' and comment about any potential bias...could have been so simple and one large step toward getting my life back.

They definitely did not 'police themselves' at the West London Coroners Court, especially when they let an assistant coroner initiate a criminal charge against me for a large period of time, a false period of time that he did not even know me. The charity's own solicitor even put this in writing to show when and how I was introduced to the Assistant Coroner[15].

---

[15] **From: Kate Fawell-Comley <Kate.Fawell-Comley@hilldickinson.com>**
Date: Fri, 14 Oct 2022 at 16:49
Subject: RE: Various related with: Request for assistance concerning a coroner's inquiry. [HD-UKLIVE.12014150.1]
To: Duncan Lawrence <diversitymanagementlcl@gmail.com>
Dear Mr Lawrence,
I write further to your below email.
I have reviewed our file in relation to this inquest. I can confirm that the email and letter from Julie Ford to you (dated 31 August 2018 and referred to in your below email) was the first communication from Hill Dickinson LLP to yourself in relation to the inquest touching upon the death of SB.
Yours sincerely,
Kate Fawell-Comley
Solicitor-Advocate
Senior Associate – Healthcare & Public Law
Hill Dickinson LLP
The Broadgate Tower, 20 Primrose Street, London, EC2A 2EW
Offices in London, Monaco, Piraeus, Singapore, Hong Kong, Liverpool, Manchester, Newcastle and Leeds
D: +44 (0)20 7280 9197
T: +44 (0)20 7283 9033
hilldickinson.com
Privacy notice

I have asked a particular news investigator (2023) to see if there can be a review of the West London Coroner Court Cases from that period of time, including my case.

From my first contact on the last day of August 2018 (when the charity solicitor introduced me to the coroner process), until 13 December 2018 when the charity solicitor submitted my substantial witness statement and exhibits, the Assistant Coroner was not chasing me for any information, and I was quite confused with my crazy charge of 'withholding information'.

From mid December 2018 until 4 Feb 2019 was just the three-way discussions (between the charity solicitor, the coroner team and myself) about how and if I could attend the hearings. There was no information related to the Bennett death that I was additionally asked for during this period.

The Jan-4 Feb 2019 Inquests dates, I naïvely assumed that my substantial witness statement and exhibits would be a useful submission in my absence and even thought that those in attendance would actually 'say thanks' to me, knowing how difficult it was after losing my father and having a mentally and medically fragile mother that was homeless at times... wow was I wrong!

*I still think it quite amazing having a large portion of charge dates against me when I did not even know of the Assistant Coroner. **Even as of today's date** (14th October 2022) the Charity solicitors confirmed that they first contacted me about the Assistant Coroner's existence on 31.8.18.*

From: Kate Fawell-Comley <Kate.Fawell-Comley@hilldickinson.com>
Date: Fri, 14 Oct 2022 at 16:49
Subject: RE: Various related with: Request for assistance concerning a coroner's inquiry. [HD-UKLIVE.12014150.1]
To: Duncan Lawrence <diversitymanagementlcl@gmail.com>

Dear Mr Lawrence,

I write further to your below email.

I have reviewed our file in relation to this inquest. I can confirm that the email and letter from Julie Ford to you (dated 31 August 2018 and referred to in your below email) was the first communication from Hill Dickinson LLP to yourself in relation to the inquest touching upon the death of SB.

Yours sincerely,

Kate Fawell-Comley
Solicitor-Advocate
Senior Associate – Healthcare & Public Law
Hill Dickinson LLP
The Broadgate Tower, 20 Primrose Street, London, EC2A 2EW
Offices in London, Monaco, Piraeus, Singapore, Hong Kong, Liverpool, Manchester, Newcastle and Leeds
D: +44 (0)20 7280 9197
T: +44 (0)20 7283 9033
hilldickinson.com

Privacy notice

Note: I had to go way outside the sentence charge date areas when looking through over hundreds of old smart phone files, files inside of files, searching old Cloud photos, so compiling these notes continues to concern me, that potentially it was a very bad move, being told by the charity solicitor in Autumn/Winter of 2018 (although I never saw it in writing), to only confine my witness statements for the coroner, to primarily January, February and March of 2016.

As I stated in 2019, but in not strong enough language obviously, the RPFI charity had interpersonal issues that must have had an impact upon their service delivery, especially with the Lancaster Lodge staff versus the 'charity'(founder/lead advisor, ex-CEO, some ex-Chair and Trustees) going back a few years. The Lancaster unit was Elly Jansen's first unit when she founded the 'Richmond Fellowship' all those decades ago.

Just primarily only discussing three months (for example) in a Coroners Witness Statement was never going to yield the truth and potentially keep some of my contributions 'out of context'.

I realise from organising my emails and illustrations for my original coroner inquest and legal case evidence, that 'my truths' will only be seen for what they truly are if others in and around the charity are expected to tell 'their truths' too (hence me regularly referring the coroner process to speak to the charity founder-lead advisor, the ex-chair of the Trustees/Trustees and the ex-CEO and not put so much unrealistic expectations upon me (to be 'everyone's evidence').

I seemed to have been used as a distraction leading up to the assistant coroners' processes, during and after (e.g. him regularly taking my suggestions out of context, with misrepresentations of me and my actions within the charity, over a short space of time etc) rather than keeping my short time within the charity reflections just that...a short time period (rather than leading to the nasty and unfortunate caricatures presented in the media and press).

My truths only work 'in context'(talking a bit about 2016 and beyond) e.g., illustrating as best as I can my time and my real and hardworking connections with others within the small charity.

This includes even trying to 'tell my truths' to the charity solicitors when they were developing my 2018 coroners witness statement, but upon reflection, I am sure that they only wanted my statement to not cast any doubt or negativity upon my old charity senior colleagues and founder (and had no care and concern for me).

I hope these emails, that while they 'bring others into my story ', that they also force the various courts to re-examine their misrepresentations about me and the outright lies too...I was just as I am, a hard-working nice human being. I have always tried to answer and help the charity founder, the charity solicitors (even though they only used a relatively small part of what I gave to them) and or the coroner process anytime that I was asked, even when not even legally liable to do so. I am not a 'human memory stick' and these emails and illustrations are not complete by any means but hopefully show a pattern of my continuous intention of trying to be helpful when asked. I sure hope other past Charity senior staff, advisors, Trustees etc. are being looked at in this way as I am within their written evidence etc. ...I have never seen any evidence of this.

Conclusion

This coroner for whatever reason has some very powerful people holding him up with his outrageous narrative about me...the London Metropolitan Police, The Crown Prosecution Services, The Senior Coroner, the judiciary, the probation service, the press...the list is endless!

This was the chapter that I have always hated the most, sometimes I even got physically sick doing my updates. This guy wrote to so many of my professional associations trying to decimate my reputation. I am sure that I was always more qualified than him, contributed more to the UK society than him, yet I was additionally very clear that he was definitely 'the toxic press leak' and that every time I refused to meet with him, that there would be hell to pay in the press/media almost immediately as a result. I was also clear, that the press would get me going and coming, so staying home was the safest place I could be.

The idea that I would get a white guy to pretend that they were me for a coroner video practice session, one of the most absurd things I ever heard. If I was a blond-haired white guy with blue eyes probably would have taken some of the sting away from this toxic actor that got me so so wrong.

In our Spring/Summer 2019 'back and forth emails', he never once let me know if he ever followed up any of my suggestions such as going back to the charity founder/advisor, the charity Trustees [16] etc, in order to check out my statements...just a straight

---

[16] I did not know that Geoff Benton had passed away, he was very 'clued up and hands on' Chair of the Trustees.

on bully with me. I was very slow to submit any qualifications or CPD documents to him because I had no confidence in his ethics and I knew the press/media would soon be discussing anything that I gave to him. I was correct in every sense.

The 'real crazy shit show' seemed to be at the inquest where varied stakeholders were trying to cover their own asses and shift blame to others, while also playing to the press (go back and check the internet related to the coroner inquest, it was like a circus for those seeking their '15 minutes of fame'!).

If I had the Assistant Coroner in front of me in court or and legal tribunal or similar, I would want to ask:

1. What was it about me that caused you (and or who told you) not to believe my witness statement and exhibits submitted to you December 2018?

2. The above comments cover the 'charge period dates' on the charge dates given by you to the CPS...how and when did you actually first contact me...what information (within these dates) did I withhold and when...does this really justify me being sentenced and or going to prison?

3. Did you ever admit to anyone formally and or informally that you never actually made any contact with me, for most of the charge period? Explain;

4. What was the 'specific difference' between the Spring 2019 £650 fine for not attending the inquest and the charge that I went to prison for?

5. *Did you ever (even up to now) realise that you made a mistake or that you might have been 'played by' 'interested ex-charity stakeholders? If so, what did you do to reverse your actions against me?*

6. *You wrote about me in such a toxic manner to some of my professional stakeholders, the press, media etc., did you do this to any 'other charity stakeholder'? Explain...*

7. *Were you surprised that no 'government watch dog' was ever ready to take on board any of my complaints about you?*

8. *Do you feel that 'I got what I deserved'? And or was there others that you felt should have been imprisoned, decimated by the press and social media too? Explain:*

9. *Could you have empathised even a little about my father's passing and my mother being physically and mentally frail?*

10. *Do you have any thoughts about me trying to reverse my plea, submit evidence and submit witnesses?*

11. *Did you at any time personally and or professionally hinder my evidence 'coming to light'?*

Questions and thoughts like these were never once explained in writing and or brought out in any of the court hearings.

This is one of the chapters that I often give to potential employers when I am applying for jobs... the part of the memoir draft that is dirty and messy (at least to me), I do this for them to get some glimpse of what it was like during the period, say from my perspective.

Sometimes, maybe two out of ten times after reading this chapter some very learned people knock me off by saying something like "...hey Duncan something is very wrong here... how could one 'small guy' like you brought in to assist a small but problematic social care organisation, then be held with 'absolute responsibility', absolute accountability when sadly, a service user took her own life??? "...Where was the 'duty of care to him...to Duncan...".

'Social Care' used to have Trustees and Management Committees to keep them 'supported and out of trouble' in the areas of programme development, staffing, finance, management, service users, diversity and inclusion, etc.. In those days they were also 'legally responsible' for their social care project too. Where were they during any investigations?

The Trustee Chair, may he rest in peace, what about the founder/Advisor where were her written accounts...as my memoirs show, she seemed to seek out my assistance until she didn't.

What about the external HR that the organisations used, why weren't they key to any coroner inquiry and any related legal investigation.

What about the charities own solicitors...going on the 'Internet' and reading about the coroner's investigation lacks so many important stakeholder perspectives and there is no one person/organisation responsible enough or brave enough to insure that I do not take the heat for the organisations short comings...ironically I shared similar concerns to the assistant coroner but always tried to put them in writing...might be interesting our readers to re-read earlier chapters prior to reading this coroner chapter.

I went to the highest (at least I thought at the time) Coroner in the UK and it took several emails to get any action from his post but I can almost guarantee that even with my case and the intrenched chaos arising from West London Coroners Office, there have been no safeguarding improvements, especially those that stops one person from writing narratives that are unsafe and far from the truth, one that tried to regularly bully me and then weaponise coroner process into a legal charge.

Going back to my initial comments about applying for jobs, only two (of many) actually said something like " ...wait, didn't I just read a witness statement from you, dated before the coroner's inquiry? In his reports and leaks to the press he made it seem like you gave him nothing ...rest assured working for us, keep your paperwork 'fit for purpose' and like a collective we will always share the burden in the good times and especially during the bad time. Employers definitely are not doing their 'due diligence' using one 'unsafe source' before deciding whether or not to hire someone or not.

If I can create an ally within one or all of the UK institutions (health, education, welfare, law, press etc), to just be brave and curious to investigate any ' unsafe areas ' ... I promise to then give you any materials, interviews etc and then get out of your way.

There are so so many stakeholders that make me guilty and keep me in this difficult place by the lies and their lack of bravery . Some potential employer made me feel like I was on trial...I provide them my memoir draft and they think 'watching and reading the internet sources is easier', will give them what they need and never consider what they have 'missed' from not reading the memoirs and or what damage that inadvertently they might project onto me and to their job selection.

...would really like anything related to this coroner's case on the internet to be revised and have links to this book's contents, especially any letters received before and after, to add magistrate court summary from the social care charity and ex-CEO being found guilty and being fined. Without a more well-rounded and less Duncan centre narrative, the public and related professionals eg Law, public health, social care, police etc will not really realise how unsafe the initial coroners inquiry really was.

I think that was 'the strategy', e.g., cloudy the charge against me, push out an emotional narrative in court and in the social media and press...never let me present evidence ... I could then never win my case (if my factual evidence stayed hidden).

The court never questioned my 'first contacts' with the assistant coroner, the press and social media were not interested in looking at these facts either and my short lived legal team at the time were absolutely useless and seemed to be in 'awe' and 'overwhelmed' by the 'public interest' in the 'emotive narrative ' that says that I was regularly withholding information from the assistant coroner/family, where in reality, missing the inquest was where I withheld my time and presence.

They threw in a crazy story that I hired a white impersonator in Dec 2018 for a coroner video test...all key moves to keep the court and public away from the truth...Bamboozled in plain sight!

I felt so overwhelmed during this period, my mother not being well, losing long term clients once my name hit the press, charity not offering a legal support...a difficult time for me personally and I just began to await toxic emails from the assistant coroner and toxic news media stories rather than be surprised by them.

Begin forwarded message:

From: Julie Ford <Julie.Ford@hilldickinson.com>
Date: 31 August 2018 at 14:01:24 BST
To: "diversitymanagementlcl@btinternet.com"
    <diversitymanagementlcl@btinternet.com>
Cc: Kate Fawell-Comley
    <Kate.Fawell-Comley@hilldickinson.com>

Subject: Request for assistance concerning a coroner's inquiry. [HD-UKLive.12014150.1]

Dear Mr Lawrence

I am assisting a colleague, Kate Fawell-Cowley in a matter in which you have been asked to provide a statement for a Coroner's inquiry. Further details are set out in the letter attached which is password protected (password to follow).

I should be grateful if you would contact me to confirm receipt of the letter and your response the queries set out within it.

I look forward to hearing from you at your earliest convenience.

With kind regards

Your sincerely

Julie Ford
Legal Director
Healthcare
Hill Dickinson LLP
Julie.Ford@hilldickinson.com
The Broadgate Tower, 20 Primrose Street, London, EC2A 2EW
TEL: +44 (0)20 7280 9338
FAX: +44 (0)20 7283 1144

Hill Dickinson
www.hilldickinson.com

This email and its contents, together with any attachments, are confidential to the sender and the intended recipient(s) and may be covered by legal professional privilege. If you are not the intended recipient of this email and its attachments (if any), you must take no action based upon them, nor must you copy them or show them to anyone. Please contact the sender if you believe you have received this email in error. Hill Dickinson LLP is a firm of lawyers authorised and regulated by the Solicitors Regulation Authority under registration number 424853. It is a limited liability partnership registered in England and Wales No. OC314079. Its registered office is at No.1 St. Paul's Square, Liverpool L3 9SJ.

This e-mail and any attachments is intended only for the attention of the addressee(s). Its unauthorised use, disclosure, storage or copying is not permitted. If you are not the intended recipient, please destroy all copies and inform the sender by return e-mail. Internet e-mail is not a secure medium. Any reply to this message could be intercepted and read by someone else. Please bear that in mind when deciding whether to send material in response to this message by e-mail. This e-mail (whether you are the sender or the recipient) may be monitored, recorded and retained by the Ministry of Justice. Monitoring / blocking software may be used, and e-mail content may be read at any time. You have a responsibility to ensure laws are not broken when composing or forwarding e-mails and their contents.

diversitymanagementlcl@btinternet.com

Your Ref.
Our Ref. 12014150.1.JDF.JDF
Doc Ref: 1539414I9.1
Date: 31 August 2010

Direct Line +44(0)20 7260 9338
julio.ford@hilldickinson.com

Dear Mr Lawrence

The Inquest touching the death of Ms SB

I act on behalf of RPFI in relation to the inquest concerning the death of SB. As part of the Coroner's investigation he has asked RPFI to provide statements concerning the care provided to SB from April 2015 up to and including her death in May1 2016. The Coroner has indicated that he will be focusing on the period from December 2015 onwards and, in particular, he intends to investigate:

- The new management regime at Lancaster Lodge after April 2015;
- Details concerning the turnover in staff at Lancaster Lodge;
- the number of residents leaving Lancaster Lodge during the key period;
- Steps taken to arrange the transfer of SB to an alternative residential setting.

The coroner has specifically requested that you provide a statement as part of his investigation into the death of SB. You are just one of a number of individuals who has been asked to provide such evidence. As such, I should be very grateful if you would contact me upon receipt of this letter so that I may discuss the steps that need to be taken in order to provide the requested statement with you.

I do appreciate that this letter may have arrived 'somewhat out of the blue'. I wish to reassure you that a Coroner's inquiry is simply that. It is not a trial and it is not a court of blame. The Coroner, assisted by a Jury in this case, is required to answer four questions, namely: who, where when, how (and in what circumstances) SB came by her death.

It would be very helpful to understand what aspects of the queries raised by the Coroner that you can assist with in the form of a statement. In order to complete your statement, you will obviously need to review some RPFI documentation which I can assist you with.

Hill Dickinson LLP
No. 1 St. Paul's Square
Liverpool L3 9SJ
hilldickinson.com
Tel: +44 (0)151 600 8000
The Hill Dickinson Legal Services Group has offices in Liverpool, Leeds, Manchester, London, Piraeus, Singapore, Monaco and Hong Kong.
Fax: +44 (0)151 600 8001

Hill Dickinson LLP is a limited liability partnership registered in England and Wales with registered number OC314079. Its registered office is at No. 1 St. Paul's Square, Liverpool L3 9SJ.
Hill Dickinson LLP is authorised and regulated by the Solicitors Regulation Authority

D.Lawrence 'Chief Coroner' and 'Senior Coroner emails'

From: Duncan Lawrence
<duncan@considercelebratingdiversityandsport.com>
Date: 30 June 2020 at 08:35:33 BST
To: chiefcoronersoffice <chiefcoronersoffice@judiciary.uk>
Subject: Re: Coroner's Response

Good morning,

Thank you very much for coming back to me so promptly and also for your previous advice.

It seems so amazing that in our modern times, that the coroner process does not have transparent internal and external quality assurance processes that would keep everyone 'safe' and one that provided a 'reliable pathway ' to identify and rectify mistakes when they occur.

Either way, best wishes to you.

Respectfully submitted by:

Duncan Lawrence
London SE26 5LB
D.E.Lawrence:

Diversity, Equality, Inclusion and Sport Specialist/Management and Team Coach.

2020+ : Please only use diversitymanagementlcl@gmail.com and company emails relating to 'consider celebrating diversity and sport' to make contact in the future...thanks and be safe!

Please think of the environment – do you really need to print this email or its attachments?

On Jun 30, 2020, at 8:20 AM, chiefcoronersoffice <chiefcoronersoffice@judiciary.uk> wrote:

Dear Mr Lawrence,

Thank you for your e-mails.

I am afraid we are unable to assist with the restoration you seek. The Chief Coroner does not have the power to review or alter the decision of a coroner which the coroner has made in the exercise of his or her judicial position as a coroner. That includes matters of a judicial nature which are within the discretion of a coroner exercising his inquisitorial function in inquest proceedings, at inquest, before and afterwards. There is no independent or reviewing specialist coroner/ service that you can be referred to. Coroner proceedings are covered by the Coroners and Justice Act 2009 and like all legal proceedings follow specified routes of appeal dependant on the circumstances.

The right of appeal to the Chief Coroner under section 40 of the Coroners and Justice Act 2009 against a decision made by a coroner was repealed by the present Government before it came into force. In addition, the Chief Coroner, who under the 2009 Act must be a senior judge, may sit, on cases brought to the High Court by way of judicial review or with the Attorney General's fiat under section 13 of the Coroners Act 1988. It is for these reasons that he has no power to countermand the judicial decisions of coroners.

I regret to say that some of the matters of which you complain appear to fall within the judicial discretion of the assistant coroner within these proceedings and are directed to his conduct and handling of the inquest.

Complaints about personal misconduct as opposed to judicial error should be directed to the Judicial Conduct Investigations Office as the appropriate authority for such matters. In this instance you have written directly to the Senior Coroner at West London who has responded to you.

I am afraid that the office of the Chief Coroner cannot expand on or offer alternative remedy to the concerns you raise.

Yours sincerely,

A.M. Aherne
Deputy head of the Chief Coroner's Office
Chief Coroner's Office
Judicial Office for England and Wales
Royal Courts of Justice, London, WC2A 2LL
Telephone 020 7947 6642
www.judiciary.uk

From: Duncan Lawrence [mailto:duncan@
     considercelebratingdiversityandsport.com]
Sent: 20 June 2020 11:49
To: chiefcoronersoffice <chiefcoronersoffice@judiciary.uk>
Subject: Fwd: Coroner>s Response

Good morning,

I am taking the liberty to write one last time asking your advice.

Thanks for your past efforts, unfortunately after months of delay the Senior Coroner did not comment upon 99.9 % of the information that was presented to him.

Is there a such thing as an independent coroner/coroner specialist (or retired coroner)that you can refer me to? I really want someone that can objectively review information in it's totality and present comprehensive written feed that relates to the evidence presented?

I am able to pay for this service.

Thanks in advance for this service.

Duncan Lawrence
London SE26 5LB

D.E.Lawrence:

Diversity, Equality, Inclusion and Sport Specialist/Management and Team Coach.

2020+ : Please only use diversitymanagementlcl@gmail.com and company emails relating to 'consider celebrating diversity and sport' to make contact in the future...thanks and be safe!

Please think of the environment – do you really need to print this email or its attachments?

Sent from my iPhone

Begin forwarded message:

From: Duncan Lawrence
      <duncan@considercelebratingdiversityandsport.com>
Date: 19 June 2020 at 14:07:52 BST
To: chiefcoronersoffice <chiefcoronersoffice@judiciary.uk>
Cc: Ellie Reeves <ellie.reeves.mp@parliament.uk>
Subject: Fwd: Coroner's Response

FYI

Thanks in advance for your consideration.

Duncan E.Lawrence
London SE26 5LB

Begin forwarded message:

From: Duncan Lawrence
          <duncan@considercelebratingdiversityandsport.com>
Date: 19 June 2020 at 14:01:32 BST
To: «Bent Kathy: H&F» <Kathy.Bent@lbhf.gov.uk>
Subject: Re: Coroner's Response

Dear Senior Coroner,

Thank you for holding an 'internal inquiry ' into some of my concerns about my unfair treatment and the toxic bias that I received from the Assistant Coroner over the past few months.

You are the first senior person to give an opinion on the presented facts, the court did not allow me to present any witnesses or evidence, one counselling body panel unfairly treated me based upon 'trial by media/press'(and did not value the same exact evidence that I sent to you) and the Charities Commission had the same comprehensive evidence pack from me as you and they have not even acknowledged that I had sent it to them via recorded delivery ...again, my sincere thanks sir.

If you need me to resend my February 2020 email pack, please do ask...it's no problem. With all of the related protests around the world, the courageous and transparent uncovering of bias, white male privilege and lies are key to achieving any level of fairness within this complicated situation (at least on the surface).

Secondly, I respectfully suggest the following clarifications be added (if not too late).

They're about clarifying within your report the types of information/evidence that I presented to you last February 2020 (otherwise people might wrongly assume that I have given you hearsay / "...he said/she said information... ").

They are in red font and added at the bottom of your report. I hope you find them constructive and helpful to be able to finalise your work.

On Fri, 19 Jun 2020 at 13:23, Bent Kathy: H&F <Kathy.Bent@lbhf.gov.uk> wrote:

Good Afternoon Mr Lawrence.

Please find the response from the senior coroner, Mr Inyama, attached herewith.

Kind regards

Kathy Bent
Clerk to Senior Coroner
West London Coroners Court
Tel: 0208 753 4422
www.westlondoncoroner.org
www.lbhf.gov.uk

Sometimes I action emails outside of normal working hours; this doesn't mean I expect a response outside your normal working hours.

Correspondence:

During the current pandemic Officers are now working remotely and will not be able to receive any correspondence sent by post or courier. Please therefore email or scan any future correspondence. We will be unable to access any documents sent by post or courier from now on.

<~WRD000.jpg>

Visit h&f CAN for more information

Do it online at www.lbhf.gov.uk

To sign up for regular news updates, please go to www.lbhf.gov.uk/newsupdates

If you have received this email in error, please delete it and tell the sender as soon as possible. You should not disclose the contents to any other person or take copies.

All emails you send over the internet are not secure unless they have been encrypted. For further details, please see www.getsafeonline.org/protecting-yourself

This e-mail and any attachments is intended only for the attention of the addressee(s). Its unauthorised use, disclosure, storage or copying is not permitted. If you are not the intended recipient, please destroy all copies and inform the sender by return e-mail. Internet e-mail is not a secure medium. Any reply to this message could be intercepted and read by someone else. Please bear that in mind when deciding whether to send material in response to this message by e-mail. This e-mail (whether you are the sender or the recipient) may be monitored, recorded and retained by the Ministry of Justice. Monitoring / blocking software may be used, and e-mail content may be read at any time. You have a responsibility to ensure laws are not broken when composing or forwarding e-mails and their contents.

From: Duncan Lawrence
      <duncan@considercelebratingdiversityandsport.com>
Date: 22 June 2020 at 13:10:24 BST
To: «Bent Kathy: H&F» <Kathy.Bent@lbhf.gov.uk>
Subject: D.Lawrence:

Thanks for coming back to me sir.

I really saw you as an opportunity, I had to knock on several dozen doors over the past year before I got to you...totally my initiative ...an objective human being that could read the RPFI 2016 emails and beyond and realise that the Assistant Coroner was going after the wrong persons reputation since Jan 2019...

realise that there are many RPFI/Assistant Coroner secrets that are 'held in plain sight'. I am sure the public would like to know that public officials can recognise within themselves that they might have gotten something wrong, without having to do it kicking and screaming and or begrudgingly.

Unfortunately it did not happen like that this time, but it is important for me to document that you had all of the tools to do so(comprehensively supplied by me last February 2020) but for some reason only known to you, you refused to even go down that road a little .

I honestly hope that you change your mind sir, I honestly really do. I am very sure however if not you, that someone else at your level will stand up and say "...hey folks, the 2016 email evidence shows that we may have gotten it wrong in Jan 2019 and that there are those from Jan 2019 Coroner process that should now be asked to re-explain their statements in light of the 2016 and beyond senior staff RPFI emails.

Either way best wishes to you and yours sirs.

Duncan E. Lawrence
London SE26 5LB

On Mon, 22 Jun 2020 at 12:59, Bent Kathy: H&F <Kathy.Bent@lbhf.gov.uk> wrote:

Good Afternoon Mr Lawrence

I write further to your email below and confirm that I passed your response on to the senior coroner Mr Inyama.

Mr Inyama has asked me to say that he has noted the additional material but it doesn't add anything to his conclusions, which were based very strictly on if the Assistant Coroner Mr Taylor had shown bias, or meted out unfair treatment to or harassed you and he found that Mr Taylor did not and that remains his view.

Kind regards

Kathy Bent
Clerk to Senior Coroner
West London Coroners Court
Tel: 0208 753 4422
www.westlondoncoroner.org
www.lbhf.gov.uk

Sometimes I action emails outside of normal working hours; this doesn't mean I expect a response outside your normal working hours.

Correspondence:

During the current pandemic Officers are now working remotely and will not be able to receive any correspondence sent by post or courier. Please therefore email or scan any future correspondence. We will be unable to access any documents sent by post or courier from now on.

From: Duncan Lawrence
        <duncan@considercelebratingdiversityandsport.com>
Sent: 15 June 2020 14:50
To: Bent Kathy: H&F <Kathy.Bent@lbhf.gov.uk>
Subject: Re: D.Lawrence:

Thanks for coming back to me Mrs Bent!

Best wishes,

Duncan Lawrence

D.E.Lawrence:

Diversity, Equality, Inclusion and Sport Specialist/Management and Team Coach.

2020+ : Please only use diversitymanagementlcl@gmail.com and company emails relating to 'consider celebrating diversity and sport' to make contact in the future...thanks and be safe!

Please think of the environment – do you really need to print this email or its attachments?

Sent from my iPhone

On 15 Jun 2020, at 13:27, Bent Kathy: H&F <Kathy.Bent@lbhf. gov.uk> wrote:

Good Afternoon Mr Lawrence

Thank you for your patience.

The Coroner will have his response sent to you by the end of the week.

Regards

Kathy Bent
Clerk to Senior Coroner
West London Coroners Court
Tel: 0208 753 4422
www.westlondoncoroner.org
www.lbhf.gov.uk

Sometimes I action emails outside of normal working hours; this doesn't mean I expect a response outside your normal working hours.

Correspondence:

During the current pandemic Officers are now working remotely and will not be able to receive any correspondence sent by post or courier. Please therefore email or scan any future correspondence. We will be unable to access any documents sent by post or courier from now on.

From: Duncan Lawrence
  <duncan@considercelebratingdiversityandsport.com>
Sent: 13 June 2020 19:18
To: Bent Kathy: H&F <Kathy.Bent@lbhf.gov.uk>
Subject: Re: D.Lawrence:

Good afternoon sir,

When should I expect to receive a response?

Once I receive it, I can provide some constructive feedback within 24 hours(before you finalise the report) if this is ok.

Either way, best wishes and thanks in advance for your time, your courage and your consideration.

Duncan Lawrence
London SE26 5LB

D.E.Lawrence:

Diversity, Equality, Inclusion and Sport Specialist/Management and Team Coach.

2020+ : Please only use diversitymanagementlcl@gmail.com and company emails relating to 'consider celebrating diversity and sport' to make contact in the future...thanks and be safe!

Please think of the environment – do you really need to print this email or its attachments?

Sent from my iPhone

On 26 May 2020, at 14:16, Bent Kathy: H&F <Kathy.Bent@lbhf.gov.uk> wrote:

Good Afternoon Mr Lawrence

Thank you for your email below that has been passed to Mr Inyama.

He has asked me to say thank you again for your patience and he expects to have read all the documents by the end of this week and be in a position to inform you of his view on your complaint by the end of next week 5th June 2020.

Regards

Kathy Bent
Clerk to Senior Coroner
West London Coroners Court
Tel: 0208 753 4422
www.westlondoncoroner.org
www.lbhf.gov.uk

Sometimes I action emails outside of normal working hours; this doesn't mean I expect a response outside your normal working hours.

Correspondence:

During the current pandemic Officers are now working remotely and will not be able to receive any correspondence sent by post or courier. Please therefore email or scan any future correspondence. We will be unable to access any documents sent by post or courier from now on.

From: Duncan Lawrence
 <duncan@considercelebratingdiversityandsport.com>
Sent: 23 May 2020 09:02
To: Bent Kathy: H&F <Kathy.Bent@lbhf.gov.uk>
Subject: From D.Lawrence: Care Quality Commission

Good morning Sir,

Duncan Lawrence 2019 CQC correspondence for your review.

I am forwarding my correspondence to the CQC, it is another example of the 'fictional narrative' that I was not trying to be helping and did not supply information about the charity...I never actually stopped.

I never had a sense that the Assistant Coroner added this in any of his inquest reports, nor did he let the media/ press/ Court know the full extent of my contributions during this period.

I hope the information is useful.

Respectfully submitted by:

Duncan Lawrence
London SE26 5LB

D.E.Lawrence:

Diversity, Equality, Inclusion and Sport Specialist/Management and Team Coach.

2020+ : Please only use diversitymanagementlcl@gmail.com and company emails relating to 'consider celebrating diversity and sport' to make contact in the future...thanks and be safe!

Please think of the environment – do you really need to print this email or its attachments?

Sent from my iPhone

Begin forwarded message:

From: Duncan Lawrence
    <duncan@considercelebratingdiversityandsport.com>
Date: 19 February 2019 at 15:27:08 GMT
To: «Gourgaud, Natalie» <Natalie.Gourgaud@cqc.org.uk>
Subject: Re: Care Quality Commission

Dear Natalie Gourgaud- CQC

Re:Complaint

I feel that I am being harassed by Wynn Price-Rees Re: Section 91 PACE Invite dated 12.2.19.

I have happened to have worked for a charity called RPFI(Richmond Fellowship Foundation International, <u>91 Heathfield N, Twickenham, TW2 7QN</u>) in the first few months of 2016 as an temp clinical lead/advisor for its the three homes,while at the time and providing some temporary management support to the Lancaster unit(which the above was responsible for assessing at the time for CQC).

During my last several days, the CEO at the time had been coming into Lancaster unit and assuming management tasks eg closed door meetings/groups etc with residents, doing weekend shifts and attending hospital meetings and visits. Being a team player I did not attempt to hinder her work and made written comments to the Chair of the Trustees and the charity founder at the time.

Was a very busy time in the charity when I was there, with only truly positive aims of better integration of the 'therapeutic model ' across the charity . <u>I can honestly state that all of the senior staff, Trustees and the Founder/Lead Consultant only had positive intentions</u>(just we were poor in bringing stakeholders along with us at times mainly due to being so busy).

The work ended after approximately three months .Sadly 3-4 months later after that a young woman took her own life within the same unit. I had already ended my work with the charity and I know nothing about the circumstances. I had literally only days supporting the Lancaster Unit(in terms of actual minutes onsite)of RPFI before my role ended.

There was recently a coroner inquiry which I could not attend due to a gravely ill mother.

This appears where the recent problems seemed to have peaked(although his name popped up several times as having looked at my LinkedIn details in 2017 so I anticipated something nasty would follow related to the coroner process).

The founder and consultant to the charity is Ms Elly Jansen (our management and trustees meetings were held at her home office and she provided 90% of my work instructions).I supported her past therapeutic community work and her hopes and intentions for this particular charity. We had no deputy manager grades at that time, so most of us were away from our primary areas of work at least 1-3 days per week for multiple disciplinary hearings led by an external group, multiple staffing interviews and multiple new staff inductions and senior meetings with all charity management, Trustees,including CEO at that time and charity founder/lead consultant.

For some reason unknown to me, Ms Jansen was not invited to the Coroner Inquiry and most attendees made wrong assumptions that most of us, were acting as individuals rather than following advice/guidance from the charity consultant /founder .The misrepresentation connected to me and other ex-charity staff was appalling and very misleading to all present.They also assumed that my entire time at RPFI I was in management support of the Lancaster unit, this was entirely untrue, I had this role (along side my other roles) for literally less than about 30+ days if you take out my other charity duties.

I tried to get registered in 2016 with CQC online but I kept getting it wrong and was never registered (I have CQC emails confirming this).

Upon reflection, this 'pace' was never ideal and the senior staff and Trustees should have regularly explained (to staff, residents and other stakeholders) across the three charity units about our intentions.

This continued onto the national news and press last week.

I was shocked and thoroughly embarrassed at the personal and professional attacks for literally such a brief work engagement.

I only sat with him for a few hours when he came to inspect the house when I was there. My role ended literally the next day for the charity, I am not sure where this strange obsession with me comes from. I can almost guarantee that this complaint will somehow find its way the press, I hope not...it needs to be taken seriously.

When I received an email today from him demanding that I attend a meeting (see attached), I was again feeling harassed and bullied related to 'CQC' by the above.

I am attaching my Coroner statement that covers my entire time with the charity. I have also updated(19 Feb 2019) my original CQC complaint, to be more concise and better illustrate conditions across the charity at this time, while better clarifying the very 'limited management power and influence' that I had generally within the charity...almost none. Both documents are of equal importance.

Please read both of these together as my statement on my time with RPFI. **The password is hdnhs.**

I am aware that the charity and CQC had different views on how the Lancaster Unit was actually functioning over the years and people like myself simply 'got caught in the crossfire' between the two parties. The longer charity staff would know this 'history' while residents and newer staff would not.

I just wish someone with 'clean hands' (no history with the Unit, and or the with past Trustees and no negative/ questionable history with charity founder nor its past staff) was involved and that this above CQC representative doesn't not keep doing 'divide and conquer' routine with all of us, rather than talk directly with the RPFI charity and its founder/ consultant that directed all the senior staff in the first place.

I am not, nor was I ever RPFI. Just an optimistic temporary staff that sincerely believed in the aims of the charity.

Respectfully submitted by:

Duncan Lawrence
19 Feb 2019

On Tue, 19 Feb 2019 at 11:26, Duncan Lawrence <duncan@ considercelebratingdiversityandsport.com> wrote:

Dear Natalie,

Thanks for getting back to me.

I have no confidence in Mr Price-Rees, and anything connected to him.

I do 100% understand and appreciate your interview assumptions and expectations .

I will update my original CQC complaint only slightly and additionally send you my original statement to the coroner in this matter.

I will do this without delay and hope that it further clarifies my role in the company during that period.

I have no desire to cause or be part of a media sideshow, where there is trial by media.

You will hear in full from me very shortly.

Respectfully submitted by:

Duncan Lawrence

Sent from my iPhone

On 19 Feb 2019, at 11:05, Gourgaud, Natalie <Natalie.Gourgaud@cqc.org.uk> wrote:

Dear Mr Lawrence,

Thank you very much for your email. I'm afraid it was only forwarded to me this morning as Mr Price-Rees' manager – I'm sorry for the delay in responding to you.

The interview is your opportunity to tell us your account of what occurred at Lancaster Lodge in late 2015 and early 2016. If you fail to attend the interview, we will need to take this into account when we consider who was responsible for making the decisions that so profoundly affected the young women who lived at Lancaster Lodge. If you wish to rely on the account of the circumstances you have provided below, it would be better for you to do so under caution as this is your opportunity to tell us your side of the story.

I look forward to seeing you.

Many thanks

Natalie

Natalie Gourgaud
Inspection Manager, Adult Social Care
Team C – Kingston, Lambeth, Merton, Richmond and Wandsworth
CQC London

natalie.gourgaud@cqc.org.uk
Tel: 03000 616 161
Fax: 03000 616 171
Mob: 07789 875 662
Direct tel: 020 8579 3616

By post to:
CQC London, Citygate, Gallowgate, Newcastle upon Tyne NE1 4PA

The Care Quality Commission is the independent regulator of all health and adult social care in England. www.cqc.org.uk. For general enquiries, call the National Customer Service Centre (NCSC) on 03000 616161 or email enquiries@cqc.org.uk. Personal data is processed in accordance with the General Data Protection Regulation (GDPR) and relevant data protection law. Information on the processing of personal data by CQC can be found at: http://www.cqc.org.uk/about-us/our-policies/privacy-statement. Statutory requests for information made under access to information legislation such as the GDPR and the Freedom of Information Act 2000 should be sent to: information.access@cqc.org.uk.

From: Duncan Lawrence [mailto:duncan@ considercelebratingdiversityandsport.com]
Sent: 14 February 2019 02:32
To: enquiries@cqc.org.uk
Subject: CQC Complaint

Dear CQC Re:Complaint

I feel that I am being harassed and personal and professionally bullied by **Wynn Price-Rees Re:** Section 91 PACE Invite dated 12.2.19.

I have happened to have worked for a charity called RPFI (**Richmond Fellowship Foundation International, 91 Heathfield N, Twickenham, TW2 7QN**) in the first few months of 2016 as an temp clinical lead/advisor and several 'as required duties ' for its three homes,while at the same time providing some temporary management support to the Lancaster unit(which the above was responsible for assessing at the time).

The charity spoke to me daily/weekly about about Quality Assurance of all three homes daily, asked me to assist in the wider charity HR -disciplinary activities daily(including participating in daily/weekly charity staff interviews and staff CPD activities across the company).So, multiple tasks to attend to during a busy busy time for the charity my entire brief employment supporting three units directly and or indirectly. Even though, worked enough for three staff, I was paid on a consultant basis throughout, nothing more nothing less.

The work ended after approximately three months. Sadly 3-4 months later after that a young woman took her own life within the same unit.

I had already ended my work with the charity and I know nothing about the circumstances surrounding her passing . I had literally only days (not months) supporting the Lancaster Unit of RPFI before my role ended.

There was recently a coroner inquiry which I could not attend due to a gravely ill mother.

This appears where the recent problems seemed to have peaked(although his name popped up several times as having looked at my LinkedIn details in 2017 so I anticipated something nasty could follow related to the 'coroner process').

The founder and consultant to the charity is Ms Elly Jansen,she provided 90% of my work instructions and is still very sharp and robust enough to answer any questions about the charity and its motives for how they assigned my areas of work and additional improvement activities that kept us all very busy.

For some reason unknown to me, Ms Jansen was not invited to the Coroner Inquiry and most attendees made wrong assumptions that most of us, were acting as individuals rather than following advice/guidance from the charity consultant /founder. The misrepresentation connected to me and other ex-charity staff was appalling, humiliating and very misleading to all present. They also assumed that my entire time at RPFI I was in management support of the Lancaster unit, this was entirely untrue, I had this role along side my other charity roles (see described above) for literally less than two months.

This continued onto the national news and press last week.

I was shocked and thoroughly embarrassed at the personal and professional attacks for literally such a brief work engagement.

I only sat with him for a few hours when he came to CQC inspect the house when I was there. My role ended literally the next day for the charity, I am not sure where this strange fixation with me comes from. I can almost guarantee that this complaint will somehow find its way the press, I hope not...it needs to be taken seriously.

If CQC was serious about the truth, a responsible CQC professional might have added to the coroner process, the media etc that I and other RPFI staff were only working to the Charity and the Charity Founder and not off our own backs.

When I received an email yesterday from him demanding that I attend a meeting for various levels of responsibility (see attached), I was again feeling harassed and bullied related to 'CQC' by the above. <u>Totally a misuse of CQC power for less than professional reasons. He personally seems to want to strip me bare, stop me from working rather than confronting the charity head on.</u>

I am a modest human being and this 'trial by media' (led by the above) has impacted upon my health and my ability to earn is hindered.

I am aware that the above had some not so positive assumptions with the charity well before my arrival ...the charity, its past CEOs and CQC had quite different views on how the Lancaster Unit was actually functioning. I think myself along with others just got 'caught up in crossfire' between CQC and RPFI pre-existing history.

I just wish, someone with 'clean hands' (no history with the Unit, and or the with past Trustees and no negative/ questionable history with charity founder nor its past staff) **was involved and that this above CQC representative doesn't not keep doing 'divide and conquer ' routine with me,** rather than **talk directly with the RPFI charity and its founder/ consultant that directed all the senior staff in the first place**, including me as a temporary hire(in a resilient charity that has been around for several years).

I am thinking of getting the police involved for any future harassment.

I am not, nor was I ever RPFI.I only had a temporary contract with them plain and simple.

Respectfully submitted by:

Duncan Lawrence

13 Feb 2019

Attached: D.Lawrence recent CQC letter

The contents of this email and any attachments are confidential to the intended recipient. They may not be disclosed to or used by or copied in any way by anyone other than the intended recipient. If this email is received in error, please notify us immediately by clicking "Reply" and delete the email. Please note that neither the Care Quality Commission nor the sender accepts any responsibility for viruses and it is your responsibility to scan or otherwise check this email and any attachments. Any views expressed in this message are those of the individual sender, except where the sender specifically states them to be the views of the Care Quality Commission. Information on how the Care Quality Commission processes personal data is available here http://www.cqc.org.uk/about-us/our-policies/privacy-statement

Visit h&f CAN for more information

Do it online at www.lbhf.gov.uk

To sign up for regular news updates, please go to www.lbhf.gov.uk/newsupdates

If you have received this email in error, please delete it and tell the sender as soon as possible. You should not disclose the contents to any other person or take copies.

All emails you send over the internet are not secure unless they have been encrypted. For further details, please see www.getsafeonline.org/protecting-yourself

Visit h&f CAN for more information

Do it online at www.lbhf.gov.uk

To sign up for regular news updates, please go to www.lbhf.gov.uk/newsupdates

If you have received this email in error, please delete it and tell the sender as soon as possible. You should not disclose the contents to any other person or take copies.

All emails you send over the internet are not secure unless they have been encrypted. For further details, please see www.getsafeonline.org/protecting-yourself

Visit h&f CAN for more information

Do it online at www.lbhf.gov.uk

To sign up for regular news updates, please go to www.lbhf.gov.uk/newsupdates

If you have received this email in error, please delete it and tell the sender as soon as possible. You should not disclose the contents to any other person or take copies.

All emails you send over the internet are not secure unless they have been encrypted. For further details, please see www.getsafeonline.org/protecting-yourself

D.Lawrence Assistant Coroner emails

Duncan Lawrence: Evidence Part 2

*Duncan Lawrence's **Self Assessment:** Impact upon email Communication and Practice when stressed*

Email Evidence 2: Related to Spring /Early Summer 2019 communication between DL and Coroner17

Stress during this period:

A. Mother Gravely ill, Homeless and mentally ill

B. Grieving –Father Passed away in March 2018

C. Mother Passed away l May 2019

D. Press/media storms

E. Coroner harassment e.g. writing to my professional associations, fining me £650 for not attending hearings and then sending MET police to my home in July 2019, charging me again, not ever positively acknowledging to return emails to him

F. Losing work as a result of media storms and coroner letters

---

17   These are some email communications that I still have, they are not to be considered as a 'total body of communication', more examples of communications from periods of my life.

Evidence contents list

Discussion:

This time period confuses me more than any other for the following reasons:

1. **This is not in the charge dates/period** yet the coroner communicated with me often during this period (although never discussed once the quality of my submissions except to) :

2. say that I was 'rewriting history'(hence I was so glad to find old charity communications that backed up everything I ever said),

3. wrote to several of my professional associations

4. Leaks the nastiest, racist, outrages, and disrespectful claims to regularly emerge from his processes directly to irresponsible press/media.

5. chooses not to verify my statements even though I respectfully showed him several times how he could do this(contacting the charity founder, the Trustees, and the ex-CEO)

6. Even after I paid £650 fine for not attending the Coroner Hearing sent two Met Officers to my home to arrange an interview...note: to this day no one has ever explained to me what the charge/potential charge I was on at that time when they came to my home. Even the officers once I showed them evidence that I had

paid my fine were confused (hence I was not arrested nor escorted to the station). My hunch is that 'this period of time' was filled with potential illegalities and 'questionable poor standards' of coroner practices and he did not wish to have his actions scrutinised here

7. Never answers any of my questions

I hope this can be explained to me as part of the plea hearing.

Duncan Lawrence

25.9.19

Contents/Discussion:

Self Assessment Areas

1. Does this man come across as professional?

2. Does he seem to push his ideas onto others, especially service users?

3. Does it seem like people have to track him down (generally) for information?

4. Do his suggestions and recommendations seem reasonable?

5. Does he seem to have an axe to grind against any one?

6. How would you say he has responded generally in 2019 requests for information, especially with a parent in various states of illness or dying and or homelessness?

Obituary

Jacob Lawrence Jr. passed away on March 18, 2018, at Alaska Regional Hospital. A Graveside Service will be held at Fort Richardson National Cemetery on June 14, 2018, at 11:30 a.m. Those who wish to attend should meet at the Joint Base Elmendorf-Richardson gate by 11:15 a.m. Arrangements are by Witzleben Legacy Funeral Home.

Published in Anchorage Daily News from June 10 to June 12, 2018

Print |

Begin forwarded message:

From: «Smith Louise: H&F» <Louise.Smith@lbhf.gov.uk>
Date: 23 May 2019 at 15:06:26 BST
To: Eric Lawrence <diversitymanagementlcl@btinternet.com>
Subject: Fine Hearing Outcome

Dear Dr. Lawrence,

This is notice to you that, at the hearing this morning, the Coroner decided that the amount of the fine which you have to pay is £650.

No Statement of Means was received from you by the time of the hearing.

Responsibility for collection, enforcement and remission of the fine now passes to the Magistrates' Court which is local to this Court. That is believed to be Lavender Hill Magistrates' Court, at 176a Lavender Hill, London SW11 1JU.

Kindly acknowledge safe receipt of this notice.

Kind regards

Louise Smith
Coroner's Officer
West London Coroner's Court
25 Bagleys Lane, Fulham
SW6 2QA
Tel: 0208 753 2739

Begin forwarded message:

From: Eric Lawrence
        <diversitymanagementlcl@btinternet.com>
Date: 6 July 2019 at 10:34:16 BST
To: hameera.chaudhry-khan@judicialconduct.gov.uk
Subject: Fwd: Outcome Of Hearing This Morning 1 May 2019

D.E.Lawrence:

Diversity, Equality, Inclusion and Sport Specialist/Management and Team Coach.

Please think of the environment - do you really need to print this email or its attachments?

Sent from my iPhone

Begin forwarded message:

From: Eric Lawrence
       <diversitymanagementlcl@btinternet.com>
Date: 21 May 2019 at 16:35:20 BST
To: «Smith Louise: H&F» <Louise.Smith@lbhf.gov.uk>
Subject: Re: Outcome Of Hearing This Morning 1 May 2019

Good afternoon,

I have been 'off line', away from media and social media for several days now and took some important time for belated grieving my fathers passing.

I will fill your form and post straight away...apologies for the delay.

I have no energy or interests in contesting your findings and recommendations, you had a very difficult task.I have had some difficultly with the process at times but do not wish to make it an issue at this time. Again, I will fill in your form ASAP and return.

For several months now I have stepped away from social care consultancy and interim management work and see no reason to ever go back...to me that part of me is assertively over and truly a retired memory.

My mother is currently in intensive care and we have been told by her medical team to prepare for her passing. I too am experiencing my own personal bowel cancer scare and choose to continue to learn, live and love. If my mother does pass away in the coming days, I will immediately move to support my family with arrangements and begin the grieving process. Communications may be very delayed in that situation.

All I respectfully ask is reasonable time to pay (especially with another Lawrence family potential funeral expense coming), and time to tend to my own cancer work.

The Bennett family loss is a very sad one, one that I will never forget...bless her soul. I hope that all of the diverse and reasonable suggestions will go forward with full transparency.

Respectfully submitted,

Duncan Lawrence

21 May 2019

D.E.Lawrence:

Diversity, Equality, Inclusion and Sport Specialist/Management and Team Coach.

Please think of the environment – do you really need to print this email or its attachments?

Sent from my iPhone

On 2 May 2019, at 08:42, Smith Louise: H&F <Louise.Smith@ lbhf.gov.uk> wrote:

Dear Dr Lawrence,

Please confirm receipt of this email.

Kind regards

Louise Smith
Coroner's Officer
West London Coroner's Court
25 Bagleys Lane, Fulham
SW6 2QA
Tel: 0208 753 2739

From: Smith Louise: H&F
Sent: 02 May 2019 08:12
To: Eric Lawrence
   <diversitymanagementlcl@btinternet.com>
Subject: FW: Outcome Of Hearing This Morning 1 May 2019
Importance: High

Dear Dr Lawrence

Please see email below and attachment.

Kind regards

Louise Smith
Coroner's Officer
West London Coroner's Court
25 Bagleys Lane, Fulham
SW6 2QA
Tel: 0208 753 2739

From: Smith Louise: H&F
Sent: 01 May 2019 13:43
To: Eric Lawrence
   <diversitymanagementlcl@btinternet.com>
Subject: Outcome Of Hearing This Morning 1 May 2019
Importance: High

Dear Dr. Lawrence,

I am directed by the Coroner to notify you that, at the hearing this morning, the Coroner decided:

1. that it was without reasonable excuse that you failed to attend the inquest, to give evidence in person (or to

give evidence by video link), despite the requirement that you should do so, set out in the Notice dated 8 October 2018

2. that a fine for such failure should accordingly be imposed upon you

3. that, in order that the Coroner may take any such information into account when deciding the amount of the fine, you are to complete and return to the Court no later than 11 May 2019 the attached Statement of Means

4. that he would, at the earliest opportunity thereafter, decide the amount of the fine

5. that he would refer to the Police (and the Crown Prosecution Service and Director of Public Prosecutions), for investigation and decision by them, as may be appropriate, the possibility of your having committed an offence under Paragraph 7(1)(b) and/or Paragraph 7(2)(a) of Schedule 6 to the Coroners and Justice Act 2009

I look forward to hearing from you with the completed Statement of Means.

Yours sincerely,

Louise Smith
Coroner's Officer
West London Coroner's Court
25 Bagleys Lane, Fulham
SW6 2QA
Tel: 0208 753 2739

Do it online at www.lbhf.gov.uk

To sign up for regular news updates, please click on the link https://www.lbhf.gov.uk/newsupdates

\<Statement of Means.pdf\>

👤   ReplyForward

Begin forwarded message:

From: «Smith Louise: H&F» \<Louise.Smith@lbhf.gov.uk\>
Date: 1 May 2019 at 13:43:05 BST
To: Eric Lawrence \<diversitymanagementlcl@btinternet.com\>
Subject: Outcome Of Hearing This Morning 1 May 2019

Dear Dr. Lawrence,

I am directed by the Coroner to notify you that, at the hearing this morning, the Coroner decided:

1. that it was without reasonable excuse that you failed to attend the inquest, to give evidence in person (or to give evidence by video link), despite the requirement that you should do so, set out in the Notice dated 8 October 2018

2. that a fine for such failure should accordingly be imposed upon you

3. that, in order that the Coroner may take any such information into account when deciding the amount of the fine, you are to complete and return to the Court no later than 11 May 2019 the attached Statement of Means

4. that he would, at the earliest opportunity thereafter, decide the amount of the fine

5. that he would refer to the Police (and the Crown Prosecution Service and Director of Public Prosecutions), for investigation and decision by them, as may be appropriate, the possibility of your having committed an offence under Paragraph 7(1)(b) and/or Paragraph 7(2)(a) of Schedule 6 to the Coroners and Justice Act 2009

I look forward to hearing from you with the completed Statement of Means.

Yours sincerely,

Louise Smith
Coroner's Officer
West London Coroner's Court
25 Bagleys Lane, Fulham
SW6 2QA
Tel: 0208 753 2739

Do it online at www.lbhf.gov.uk

To sign up for regular news updates, please click on the link https://www.lbhf.gov.uk/newsupdates

---

Begin forwarded message:

From: Eric Lawrence
         <diversitymanagementlcl@btinternet.com>
Date: 6 July 2019 at 10:27:56 BST
To: hameera.chaudhry-khan@judicialconduct.gov.uk
Subject: Fwd: D.Lawrence Reply 4.4.19

D.E.Lawrence:

Diversity, Equality, Inclusion and Sport Specialist/Management and Team Coach.

Please think of the environment - do you really need to print this email or its attachments?

Sent from my iPhone

Begin forwarded message:

From: «Smith Louise: H&F» <Louise.Smith@lbhf.gov.uk>
Date: 23 April 2019 at 15:34:17 BST
To: Eric Lawrence <diversitymanagementlcl@btinternet.com>
Subject: RE: D.Lawrence R4eply 4.4.19

Dear Mr Lawrence,

I have forwarded your email to the Coroner.

In order to give you information regarding complaints procedures I need to know what the complaint is about and who or what it is regarding. I can then direct you to the correct department.

Kind regards

Louise Smith
Coroner's Officer
West London Coroner's Court
25 Bagleys Lane, Fulham
SW6 2QA
Tel: 0208 753 1427

From: Eric Lawrence
    [mailto:diversitymanagementlcl@btinternet.com]
Sent: 20 April 2019 05:18
To: Smith Louise: H&F <Louise.Smith@lbhf.gov.uk>
Subject: Re: D.Lawrence Reply 4.4.19

Dear Coroner,

Re:Your email that I received 16.4.19

-I have nothing else for you. I have approximately 50% (my best estimate) of my charity emails from that period saved and some for a period after that(the charity founder/ advisor and I have communicated on a 'friendly casual' but infrequent email basis up through earlier this year).

Generally speaking, going back decades, my emails with large attachments (from my various writings,reports etc) were usually deleted every year by me to make space on my web mail for new and future emails and their attachments.

Additionally , some of my communications between myself and the charity were also on my RPFI email address that I had(and that I lost complete access to that account soon after I left the charity). I can not remember which information relating to this process would've been on the RPFI systems.

Additionally, I often sent and received charity communications via my private mobile phone texts as well , I have upgraded two phones since my time ended with the charity and no longer have access to them, nor did I save them(eg any text or phone records from that period).

Please note, I generally use my own private phone and private emails for 90% of my work going back to the 90s and no company or charity has yet to have asked me to save my 'work emails' after I had left their employment. Although upon reflection from this experience, it would have been a prudent thing to do (eg saved all electronic communications).

I generally save all emails on my private email addresses and usually only delete anything over five years old and especially ones with any large attachments as previously described above.

I had previously and respectfully asked the Coroner to ask the charity/Board directly for their emails to/from me if it could help the process.

- their board and supervision minutes should also include my daily/weekly comments to/from them.

-Regarding my 'credential email' , I can safely say that what I sent you in my last email is exactly what I would have sent any of my potential employers/customers during that year-period , although educational clients would have additionally received 2-3 'education fellowship and assessor certifications' from me...nothing is missing to the best of my recollection from what I sent to the charity during my initial engagement period. As mentioned earlier, I am sure that I deleted the original Charity email in 2016 due to its size.

-Since I became aware of an upcoming Coroner Hearing last year, I have never deleted any old charity communications from either of my two main private email accounts.

-I am sure if you saw charity/Board notes, that refer to emails and texts that I originally sent/received to and from my time with them (and referred to in this process) , you would also see that they are consistent with my original Coroner submission and my recent email to you as well.

-In conclusion, I continue to be deeply concerned that for reasons unknown to me, that I was not asked any follow up questions from my original Coroner submission, nor from my last email to you,and that it specifically was not even acknowledged for its 'literal contents'.

It seems like both are 'not what was expected' from me and possibly(there is no way that I can be sure, just a 'feeling' for me at this point),a negative narrative ' had been created around me (with regard to my character ,my roles, my worth, my effort, my competency, etc) within this process thus far, so it appears easy to disregard my only two submissions as not being constructive and hence no point of even acknowledging that they exist, that both were respectfully and constructively submitted to you to assist with this process. I was only with the charity for a short time, but the learning from this unfortunate death is my learning too (as an individual and part of the team), none of us should be too proud to learn, but as as a person and as a professional I am 100% confident that I have added to the potential learning here in this process as well, regardless of any acknowledgement.

For decades I have been on enough UK and international panels reviewing critical events/incidents and some of the issues and ways forward from these past professional experiences are similar to some of things I have consistently been commenting about in my statements regarding my time within the charity.

My ego and reputation can handle being stomped on a bit more (as bad as it got a few months ago I expect similar 'unfair trial by media storms' to continue) , I am ready and cautiously optimistic for within this process if my truth can finally be verified by only limited stakeholders that had regular communications with me during this period (this was primarily the charity founder/advisor , the Chair the Trustees and those Trustees and RPFI mangers from the White House and the Adolescent unit present at our weekly management meetings and that also received their primary work instructions from the Charity founder/advisor, ex-CEO etc.) , and be added to the 'body of lessons learned ` for myself and for other charity related stakeholders regarding this sad and unfortunate death.

There are so many pertinent stakeholder viewpoints, Charity and relevant staff time frames that could and should be highlighted and personalities involved here, 'crucial gaps' of information that might be missed , hidden or purposely disregarded. Why not look at these 'wider root problems' and challenges too?

It is always very very sad and unfortunate when someone takes their own life, I have been trying critical and evidence based self reflection even when there is uneasy learning for and from myself and others that could easily get missed when deep and often conflicting human and professional feelings are around, such as within this process.

But, it would be a regrettable shame however if my previous feedback, statements and recommendations to the Coroner do not get a chance to see the 'light of day' within this process, due to some sort of unfortunate misinformed, misguided, biased and or otherwise incorrect view about the validity of me personally and my statements.

I continue to be very aware that I only have control over what I do and do not do or say so I can only continue to try to be honest as I can.

I can also accept that whether I am finally taken seriously or not within this process is totally out of my control.

-I assertively chose to not supply evidence about my recent/current unemployment history and wish to keep this information private and not be made public .

- I have always done my best in both submissions to comply with your requests , while also trying to provide additional constructive feedback and suggestions to this process(although only mainly the charity founder/advisor can easily confirm most of my statements, and the chair of Trustees somewhat). I know that being away supporting my family did not help (we lost my father and my mentally and physically fragile mother was made homeless all within approximately the past year).My mother's challenges are still on-going and and a focus of family attention .

Because you refuse to acknowledge these for whatever reason, I will not do this again(eg respectfully provide further feedback, observations and recommendations). I may have had charity titles such as Advisor, Clinical Lead, Interim Management Support etc these did not mean that I had a free rein to control my daily activities (my hunch is that this is ' the least believable' of my past submissions and the root of my misrepresentations within this process) and most of how my days and weeks were spent , these were 80%+ dictated by others above me and further complicated by chronic staff and management shortages).

Where I had any professional or ethical concerns about what was being asked of me I generally and assertively put it in writing usually within the same day (so my managers and founder/advisor could consider them in their own time).

It may not sound logical within this process , but without 'blaming others ' , I always did something constructive with my concerns rather than just sit on them(via emails primarily to the charity founder/advisor and Chair of the Trustees).

-my second respectful request for a complaints procedure : As per my last submission email to you, I would respectfully like to be directed to your complaints procedure ASAP(eg being to referred to the complaints procedure website, and or being sent a Word copy of the complaints policy/form)... thanks in advance for directing me to this information/ procedure , I am sure that you are very busy.

I will review my options once I receive a copy of the complaints procedure and complete it in full within a week of receiving it(if I see it as the best option for me).

Respectfully submitted by:

Duncan Lawrence
19.4.19

C.C: Solicitor file

Sent from my iPhone

On 16 Apr 2019, at 09:03, Smith Louise: H&F <Louise.Smith@ lbhf.gov.uk> wrote:

Dear Mr Lawrence

The Coroner has considered your e-mail, and the documents sent with it, but notes:

1. that you have not provided all the documents which the Coroner directed you to produce

2. that, where such documents are no longer available, you have failed to provide the explanation required for such non-availability

3. that you have failed to comply with the Coroner's direction that you provide evidence as to your means

I am directed by the Coroner to remind you that:

A. you are required to comply with the Coroner's directions - and you should do so without further delay

B. in addition to the risk of a fine being imposed for your non-attendance, it is open to the Coroner to refer the matter to the DPP and, if it were to be found that you had committed an offence (by distorting evidence, preventing it from being given, or intentionally suppressing or destroying a relevant document), you could be liable to a further fine and/or imprisonment for up to 51 weeks

Again, I ask you to confirm safe receipt of this e-mail.

Kind regards

Louise Smith
Coroner's Officer
West London Coroner's Court
25 Bagleys Lane, Fulham
SW6 2QA
Tel: 0208 753 1427

Do it online at www.lbhf.gov.uk

Help us keep your council tax bill down and protect spending on vital public services - use our website to find information, view your account, make payments, apply for services and report problems.

New - create an account - Want to manage your council tax, benefits claim or parking permits online? Create an account now at www.lbhf.gov.uk/myaccount

Begin forwarded message:

From: Eric Lawrence
                <diversitymanagementlcl@btinternet.com>
Date: 6 July 2019 at 10:27:56 BST
To: hameera.chaudhry-khan@judicialconduct.gov.uk
Subject: Fwd: D.Lawrence Reply 4.4.19

D.E.Lawrence:

Diversity, Equality, Inclusion and Sport Specialist/Management and Team Coach.

Please think of the environment - do you really need to print this email or its attachments? Sent from my iPhone

Begin forwarded message:

From: «Smith Louise: H&F» <Louise.Smith@lbhf.gov.uk>
Date: 23 April 2019 at 15:34:17 BST
To: Eric Lawrence <diversitymanagementlcl@btinternet.com>
Subject: RE: D.Lawrence Reply 4.4.19

Dear Mr Lawrence,

I have forwarded your email to the Coroner.

In order to give you information regarding complaints procedures I need to know what the complaint is about and who or what it is regarding. I can then direct you to the correct department.

Kind regards

Louise Smith
Coroner's Officer
West London Coroner's Court
25 Bagleys Lane, Fulham
SW6 2QA
Tel: 0208 753 1427

From: Eric Lawrence
           [mailto:diversitymanagementlcl@btinternet.com]
Sent: 20 April 2019 05:18
To: Smith Louise: H&F <Louise.Smith@lbhf.gov.uk>
Subject: Re: D.Lawrence Reply 4.4.19

Dear Coroner,

Re:Your email that I received 16.4.19

-I have nothing else for you. I have approximately 50%(my best estimate) of my charity emails from that period saved and some for a period after that(the charity founder/ advisor and I have communicated on a 'friendly casual' but infrequent email basis up through earlier this year).

Generally speaking, going back decades, my emails with large attachments (from my various writings,reports etc) were usually deleted every year by me to make space on my web mail for new and future emails and their attachments.

Additionally , some of my communications between myself and the charity were also on my RPFI email address that I had(and that I lost complete access to that account soon after I left the charity). I can not remember which information relating to this process would've been on the RPFI systems.

Additionally, I often sent and received charity communications via my private mobile phone texts as well , I have upgraded two phones since my time ended with the charity and no longer have access to them, nor did I save them(eg any text or phone records from that period).

Please note, I generally use my own private phone and private emails for 90% of my work going back to the 90s and no company or charity has yet to have asked me to save my 'work emails' after I had left their employment. Although upon reflection from this experience, it would have been a prudent thing to do(eg saved all electronic communications).

I generally save all emails on my private email addresses and usually only delete anything over five years old and especially ones with any large attachments as previously described above.

I had previously and respectfully asked the Coroner to ask the charity/Board directly for their emails to/from me if it could help the process.

- their board and supervision minutes should also include my daily/weekly comments to/from them.

-Regarding my 'credential email' , I can safely say that what I sent you in my last email is exactly what I would have sent any of my potential employers/customers during that year-period , although educational clients would have additionally received 2-3 'education fellowship and assessor certifications' from me...nothing is missing to the best of my recollection from what I sent to the charity during my initial engagement period. As mentioned earlier, I am sure that I deleted the original Charity email in 2016 due to its size.

-Since I became aware of an upcoming Coroner Hearing last year, I have never deleted any old charity communications from either of my two main private email accounts.

-I am sure if you saw charity/Board notes, that refer to emails and texts that I originally sent/received to and from my time with them (and referred to in this process) , you would also see that they are consistent with my original Coroner submission and my recent email to you as well.

-In conclusion, I continue to be deeply concerned that for reasons unknown to me, that I was not asked any follow up questions from my original Coroner submission, nor from my last email to you,and that it specifically was not even acknowledged for its 'literal contents'.

It seems like both are 'not what was expected' from me and possibly(there is no way that I can be sure, just a 'feeling' for me at this point),a negative narrative ' had been created around me (with regard to my character ,my roles, my worth, my effort, my competency, etc) within this process thus far, so it appears easy to disregard my only two submissions as not being constructive and hence no point of even acknowledging that they exist, that both were respectfully and constructively submitted to you to assist with this process. I was only with the charity for a short time, but the learning from this unfortunate death is my learning too (as an individual and part of the team), none of us should be too proud to learn, but as as a person and as a professional I am 100% confident that I have added to the potential learning here in this process as well, regardless of any acknowledgement.

For decades I have been on enough UK and international panels reviewing critical events/incidents and some of the issues and ways forward from these past professional experiences are similar to some of things I have consistently been commenting about in my statements regarding my time within the charity.

My ego and reputation can handle being stomped on a bit more(as bad as it got a few months ago I expect similar 'unfair trial by media storms' to continue) , I am ready and cautiously optimistic for within this process if my truth can finally be verified by only limited stakeholders that had regular communications with me during this period (this was primarily the charity founder/advisor , the Chair the Trustees and those Trustees and RPFI mangers from the White House and the Adolescent unit present at our weekly management meetings and that also received their primary work instructions from the Charity founder/advisor, ex-CEO etc.) , and be added to the 'body of lessons learned ' for myself and for other charity related stakeholders regarding this sad and unfortunate death.

There are so many pertinent stakeholder viewpoints, Charity and relevant staff time frames that could and should be highlighted and personalities involved here, 'crucial gaps' of information that might be missed , hidden or purposely disregarded. Why not look at these 'wider root problems' and challenges too?

It is always very very sad and unfortunate when someone takes their own life, I have been trying critical and evidence based self reflection even when there is uneasy learning for and from myself and others that could easily get missed when deep and often conflicting human and professional feelings are around, such as within this process.

But, it would be a regrettable shame however if my previous feedback, statements and recommendations to the Coroner do not get a chance to see the 'light of day' within this process, due to some sort of unfortunate misinformed, misguided , biased and or otherwise incorrect view about the validity of me personally and my statements.

I continue to be very aware that I only have control over what I do and do not do or say so I can only continue to try to be honest as I can.

I can also accept that whether I am finally taken seriously or not within this process is totally out of my control.

-I assertively chose to not supply evidence about my recent/current unemployment history and wish to keep this information private and not be made public .

- I have always done my best in both submissions to comply with your requests , while also trying to provide additional constructive feedback and suggestions to this process(although only mainly the charity founder/advisor can easily confirm most of my statements, and the chair of Trustees somewhat). I know that being away supporting my family did not help (we lost my father and my mentally and physically fragile mother was made homeless all within approximately the past year).My mother's challenges are still on-going and and a focus of family attention .

Because you refuse to acknowledge these for whatever reason, I will not do this again(eg respectfully provide further feedback, observations and recommendations). I may have had charity titles such as Advisor, Clinical Lead, Interim Management Support etc these did not mean that I had a free rein to control my daily activities (my hunch is that this is ' the least believable' of my past submissions and the root of my misrepresentations within this process) and most of how my days and weeks were spent , these were 80%+ dictated by others above me and further complicated by chronic staff and management shortages).

Where I had any professional or ethical concerns about what was being asked of me I generally and assertively put it in writing usually within the same day (so my managers and founder/advisor could consider them in their own time).

It may not sound logical within this process , but without 'blaming others ' , I always did something constructive with my concerns rather than just sit on them(via emails primarily to the charity founder/advisor and Chair of the Trustees).

-my second respectful request for a complaints procedure : As per my last submission email to you, I would respectfully like to be directed to your complaints procedure ASAP(eg being to referred to the complaints procedure website, and or being sent a Word copy of the complaints policy/form)... thanks in advance for directing me to this information/ procedure , I am sure that you are very busy.

I will review my options once I receive a copy of the complaints procedure and complete it in full within a week of receiving it(if I see it as the best option for me).

Respectfully submitted by:

Duncan Lawrence
19.4.19

C.C: Solicitor file

Sent from my iPhone

On 16 Apr 2019, at 09:03, Smith Louise: H&F <Louise.Smith@ lbhf.gov.uk> wrote:

Dear Mr Lawrence

The Coroner has considered your e-mail, and the documents sent with it, but notes:

1. that you have not provided all the documents which the Coroner directed you to produce

2. that, where such documents are no longer available, you have failed to provide the explanation required for such non-availability

3. that you have failed to comply with the Coroner's direction that you provide evidence as to your means

I am directed by the Coroner to remind you that:

A. you are required to comply with the Coroner's directions – and you should do so without further delay

B. in addition to the risk of a fine being imposed for your non-attendance, it is open to the Coroner to refer the matter to the DPP and, if it were to be found that you had committed an offence (by distorting evidence, preventing it from being given, or intentionally suppressing or destroying a relevant document), you could be liable to a further fine and/or imprisonment for up to 51 weeks

Again, I ask you to confirm safe receipt of this e-mail.

Kind regards

Louise Smith
Coroner's Officer
West London Coroner's Court
25 Bagleys Lane, Fulham
SW6 2QA
Tel: 0208 753 1427

Do it online at www.lbhf.gov.uk

Help us keep your council tax bill down and protect spending on vital public services - use our website to find information, view your account, make payments, apply for services and report problems.

New - create an account - Want to manage your council tax, benefits claim or parking permits online? Create an account now at www.lbhf.gov.uk/myaccount

Begin forwarded message:

From: «Smith Louise: H&F» <Louise.Smith@lbhf.gov.uk>
Date: 16 April 2019 at 09:03:24 BST
To: Eric Lawrence <diversitymanagementlcl@btinternet.com>
Subject: D.Lawrence Reply 4.4.19

Dear Mr Lawrence

The Coroner has considered your e-mail, and the documents sent with it, but notes:

1. that you have not provided all the documents which the Coroner directed you to produce

2. that, where such documents are no longer available, you have failed to provide the explanation required for such non-availability

3. that you have failed to comply with the Coroner's direction that you provide evidence as to your means

I am directed by the Coroner to remind you that:

A. you are required to comply with the Coroner's directions – and you should do so without further delay

B. in addition to the risk of a fine being imposed for your non-attendance, it is open to the Coroner to refer the matter to the DPP and, if it were to be found that you had committed an offence (by distorting evidence, preventing it from being given, or intentionally suppressing or destroying a relevant document), you could be liable to a further fine and/or imprisonment for up to 51 weeks

Again, I ask you to confirm safe receipt of this e-mail.

Kind regards

Louise Smith
Coroner's Officer
West London Coroner's Court
25 Bagleys Lane, Fulham
SW6 2QA
Tel: 0208 753 1427

Do it online at www.lbhf.gov.uk

Help us keep your council tax bill down and protect spending on vital public services – use our website to find information, view your account, make payments, apply for services and report problems.

New – create an account – Want to manage your council tax, benefits claim or parking permits online? Create an account now at www.lbhf.gov.uk/myaccount

---

Received, thank you.
Well done!
Interesting.

Begin forwarded message:

From: «Smith Louise: H&F» <Louise.Smith@lbhf.gov.uk>
Date: 18 April 2019 at 08:12:35 BST
To: Eric Lawrence <diversitymanagementlcl@btinternet.com>
Subject: Schedule 5 Notice

Dear Mr Lawrence,

Please see attached schedule 5.

Kind regards

Louise Smith
Coroner's Officer
West London Coroner's Court
25 Bagleys Lane, Fulham
SW6 2QA
Tel: 0208 753 1427

Attachments area

NOTICE REQUIRING EVIDENCE TO BE GIVEN OR PRODUCED
Paragraph 1 of Schedule 5 to the Coroners and Justice Act 2009

To: **DUNCAN LAWRENCE**

Inquest into the death of **SOPHIE BENNETT**

I hereby give notice that you are required, by 26 April 2019:

1. to provide the remaining documents in your custody or under your control (as listed in paragraphs A2 and A3 of the Court e-mail sent to you on 1 April 2019) which you have been called upon by the Court to produce

2. to provide the following evidence in the form of a written statement:

    a) full details of the times and dates on which you claim to have been unavailable to attend the inquest (and to give evidence)
    b) evidence as to your means, as called for in paragraph A4 of the Court e-mail sent to you on 1 April 2019
    c) (as may be appropriate, depending upon your ability to comply with paragraph 1 above) the explanation called for in paragraph B of that e-mail

and you are also required

3. to attend to give evidence at the hearing listed to commence at 10:00 on 1 May 2019

If you consider that you are unable to comply with the terms of this notice or consider that it would be unreasonable to require or compel you to do so, you must make representations to the Coroner by 4pm on 24 April 2019.

Any such submissions will be considered by the Coroner, who may revoke or vary this Notice.

If you fail to comply with the terms of this notice without reasonable excuse, you may be liable to a fine not exceeding £1,000 (Paragraph 6 of Schedule 6 to the Coroners and Justice Act 2009).

It is an offence for a person to do anything that is intended to have the effect of:

(a) distorting or otherwise altering any evidence, document or other thing that is given, produced or provided for the purposes of an investigation under Part 1 of the Coroners and Justice Act 2009, or

(b) preventing any evidence, document or other thing from being given, produced or provided for the purposes of such an investigation,

or to do anything that the person knows or believes is likely to have that effect.

It is also an offence for a person:

(c) intentionally to suppress or conceal a document that is, and that the person knows or believes to be, a relevant document, or

(d) intentionally to alter or destroy such a document.

A person guilty of such offences is liable on summary conviction to a fine not exceeding level 3 on the standard scale, or to imprisonment for a term not exceeding 51 weeks, or to both (Paragraph 7 of Schedule 6 to the Coroners and Justice Act 2009).

Date: 17 April 2019

Signature:

Assistant Coroner for West London

Begin forwarded message:

From: Eric Lawrence
<diversitymanagementlcl@btinternet.com>
Date: 6 July 2019 at 10:27:13 BST
To: hameera.chaudhry-khan@judicialconduct.gov.uk
Subject: Fwd: D.Lawrence Reply 4.4.19

D.E.Lawrence:

Diversity, Equality, Inclusion and Sport Specialist/Management and Team Coach.

Please think of the environment *– do you really need to print this email or its attachments?*

Sent from my iPhone

Begin forwarded message:

From: «Smith Louise: H&F» <Louise.Smith@lbhf.gov.uk>
Date: 16 April 2019 at 09:03:24 BST
To: Eric Lawrence <diversitymanagementlcl@btinternet.com>
Subject: D.Lawrence Reply 4.4.19

Dear Mr Lawrence

The Coroner has considered your e-mail, and the documents sent with it, but notes:

1. that you have not provided all the documents which the Coroner directed you to produce

2. that, where such documents are no longer available, you have failed to provide the explanation required for such non-availability

3. that you have failed to comply with the Coroner's direction that you provide evidence as to your means

I am directed by the Coroner to remind you that:

A. you are required to comply with the Coroner's directions - and you should do so without further delay

B. in addition to the risk of a fine being imposed for your non-attendance, it is open to the Coroner to refer the matter to the DPP and, if it were to be found that you had committed an offence (by distorting evidence, preventing it from being given, or intentionally suppressing or destroying a relevant document), you could be liable to a further fine and/or imprisonment for up to 51 weeks

Again, I ask you to confirm safe receipt of this e-mail.

Kind regards

Louise Smith
Coroner's Officer
West London Coroner's Court
25 Bagleys Lane, Fulham
SW6 2QA
Tel: 0208 753 1427

Received, thank you.
Well done!
Interesting.

Fwd: Sophie Bennett - Hearing of Duncan Lawrence

Inbox   x

Eric Lawrence
19:26 (7 minutes ago)
to Diversity

D.E.Lawrence:

Diversity, Equality, Inclusion and Sport Specialist/Management and Team Coach.

Please think of the environment – do you really need to print this email or its attachments? Sent from my iPhone

Begin forwarded message:

From: Eric Lawrence
        <diversitymanagementlcl@btinternet.com>
Date: 6 July 2019 at 10:26:35 BST
To: hameera.chaudhry-khan@judicialconduct.gov.uk
Subject: Fwd: Sophie Bennett - Hearing of Duncan Lawrence

D.E.Lawrence:

Diversity, Equality, Inclusion and Sport Specialist/Management and Team Coach.

Please think of the environment – do you really need to print this email or its attachments?

From: «Smith Louise: H&F» <<u>Louise.Smith@lbhf.gov.uk</u>>
Date: 1 April 2019 at 12:32:39 BST
To: Eric Lawrence <<u>diversitymanagementlcl@btinternet.com</u>>
Cc: Rachel Harger<<u>R.Harger@bindmans.com</u>>
Subject: Re: Sophie Bennett – Hearing of Duncan Lawrence

Dear Mr Lawrence,

With a view to having the relevant material to hand in good time before the hearing on 1 May, the Coroner directs that you take the following steps, no later than 15 April 2019:

A. You are to produce to the Court:

1. the credentials which you sent via e-mail on or around 22 December 2015 to Elly Jansen and to the RPFI Board (see paragraph 8 of your statement dated 13 December 2018)

2. the e-mails exchanged on or around 22 December 2015 relating to your role and credentials (see paragraph 13 of that statement)

3. all e-mails "flying around" between Peggy Jhugroo, the RPFI Board and you on or around 1 March 2016, particularly in relation to the CQC unannounced visit, and your e-mail of 1 March 2016 containing suggestions for responsive action, including your proposal to close down Lancaster Lodge (which were mentioned by Peggy Jhugroo in her oral evidence at the inquest)

The Coroner understands that RPFI's solicitors, Hill Dickinson, confirmed (on 18 January 2019) that they had asked you to produce the documents listed under 1 and 2.

4. evidence as to your means (as mentioned in the e-mail notifying you of the hearing on 1 May)

B. If you are unable to produce any of the documents itemised under 1 to 3 above, you are to provide a statement saying:

1. when you last had the documents in question

2. why you do not have them now

3. if you chose to dispose of them, what was/were your reason(s) for disposing of them

Kindly confirm safe receipt of this e-mail.

Kind regards

Louise Smith
Coroner's Officer
West London Coroner's Court
25 Bagleys Lane, Fulham
SW6 2QA
Tel: 0208 753 1427

Louise Smith
Coroner's Officer
West London Coroner's Court
25 Bagleys Lane, Fulham
SW6 2QA

Subject: Re: Sophie Bennett – Hearing of Duncan Lawrence

Dear Coroner,

As per my last email, I am not in dispute with your office nor any past-present RPFI Charity stakeholder, due to my mother's ill mental and physical health I did not attend the original inquiry, I expected to be fined (and because of being unemployed I asked could I pay in instalments and I am not asking for any special reductions) and would very much like to move on now.

I am voluntarily answering your questions because they seem reasonable, I would like to be helpful and I have additionally taken the liberty to add some voluntary feedback of my own that includes one suggestion. I hope that you find them constructive and no longer see a reason to make further contact.

Respectfully submitted,

Duncan Lawrence 4 April 2019

Points A:

1. **See below**
2. **See below**
3. **See below**

Point A-1

e-Learning | BYTSYZ

online training and assessment

www.bytsyz.co.uk

This is to certify that

DUNCAN LAWRENCE

has achieved

Award in Managing Equality and Diversity in an Organisation

having completed a TQUK endorsed course of learning.

Award Date: 04/03/2015

Certificate Number: 00008666

Equivalent CPD Hours: 20

BYTSYZ e-Learning Registration: KTG74QXXAKEESAW

QCF Level Equivalence: Level 4

Andrew Walker

STRICTLY PRIVATE AND CONFIDENTIAL

A copy of this Disclosure has been sent to

DUNCAN LAWRENCE
21 THORNSETT ROAD
LONDON

SE20 7XB

STEPHEN HALL
SOCIAL WORK MANAGER
LONDON BOROUGH OF CROYDON
SOCIAL SERVICES TABERNER HS
CROYDON
SURREY

02398801

Applicant copy

Enhanced Disclosure

Page 1 of 2

disclosure

Disclosure Number	001291791505
Date of Issue:	16 AUGUST 2010

Applicant Personal Details

Surname:	LAWRENCE
Forename(s):	DUNCAN ERIC
Other Names:	NONE DECLARED
Date of Birth:	16 FEBRUARY 1959
Place of Birth:	TOPEKA
Gender:	MALE

Employment Details

Position applied for:
BACK-UP FOSTER CARER

Name of Employer:
LONDON BOROUGH OF CROYDON

Countersignatory Details

Registered Person/Body:
LONDON BOROUGH OF CROYDON

Countersignatory:
STEPHEN HALL

Police Records of Convictions, Cautions, Reprimands and Warnings

NONE RECORDED

Information from the list held under Section 142 of the Education Act 2002

NONE RECORDED

ISA Children's Barred List information

NONE RECORDED

ISA Vulnerable Adults' Barred List information

Institute of Leadership & Management

Certificate of
Membership

This is to certify that

Duncan Lawrence

has fulfilled the criteria to join the
Institute of Leadership & Management

Grade	Fellow
Membership number	0010140325
Date of issue	28 April 2014

Charles Elvin
Chief Executive
ILM

John Jenkins
Chairman
ILM

ILM is part of the City & Guilds Group and is a company limited by guarantee no 601049, registered charity 241625.
The City and Guilds of London Institute, incorporated by Royal Charter, founded 1878.

e-Learning BYTSYZ
online training and assessment

www.bytsyz.co.uk

s is to certify that

UNCAN LAWRENCE

been awarded

ward in Equality and Diversity

ing satisfied the requirements for TQUK endorsed qualifications.

rd Date: 13/01/2015
rtificate Number: 00007898
valant CPD Hours: 10
3YZ e-Learning Registration: PNEQKWFBEMZZ23L
* Level Equivalence: Level 3

Exempt
Qualifications

Andrew Walker
Managing Director of TQUK

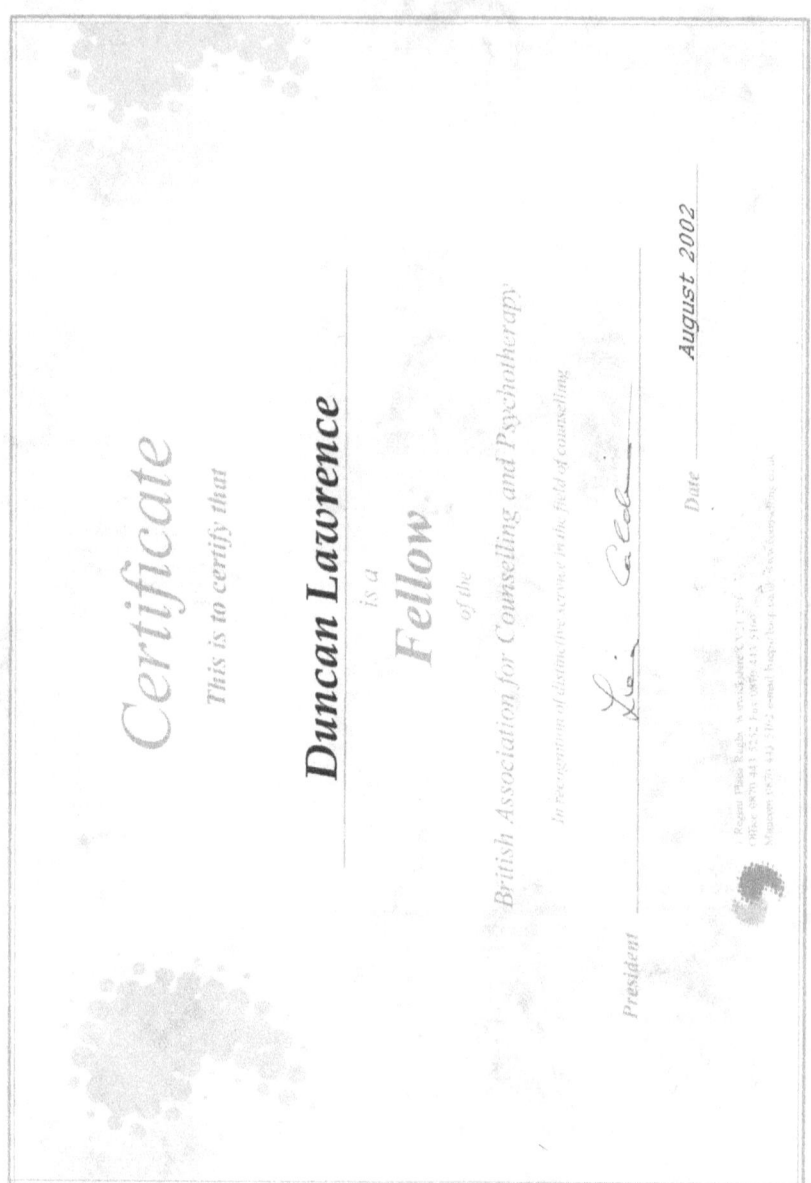

Certificate

This is to certify that

Duncan Lawrence

is a

Fellow.

of the

British Association for Counselling and Psychotherapy

In recognition of distinctive service in the field of counselling

President

Date _____ August 2002

Knightsbridge University

This is to certify that

Duncan Eric Lawrence

has been awarded the degree of

Doctor of Public Administration

having satisfied the requirements of the Admissions Committee and Executive Council of the University who by virtue of the authority vested in them, and upon recommendation of Faculty have granted this degree certificate as evidence thereof. Dated this twenty-third day of May 1996.

Registrar

President

Point A-2

From: Geoff Benton <<u>bentongeoff@gmail.com</u>>
Date: 24 December 2015 at 13:23:35 GMT
To: Duncan Lawrence <<u>diversitymanagementlcl@</u>
 <u>btinternet.com</u>>, Elly Jansen <<u>elly.jansen@rpfi.org</u>>,
 Elly Jansen <<u>ellywjansen@hotmail.com</u>>
Subject: Fwd: DRAFT LETTER FOR DUNCAN

Dear Duncan,

Having carefully weighed up the many factors surrounding the building up of both RPFI and RCI, We have concluded that you might make an important contribution to our work.

Therefore would like to offer you a consultancy for 3 months with a review in March which could lead to a more permanent role in our charities.

The new board and Peggy, our co-ordinator, have been in place less than 6 months and we are in the middle of reviewing and renewing many aspects of the work and the workers. So, this is a good time to come in and take part in this mission.

We have explained our financial difficulties and we would hope that you can accept the compromise we offered at £125 per day for a 50% working week, ie. 20 hour per week.

In order to avoid an impression that you have taken over half of Peggy's job, we would like to use the profesional term "Clinical and Operational Lead". Our job description is for a full -time person, which we are no longer looking for but the attached JD, will indicate the main areas of the post.With a healthy staff team, monitoring will be less nessasary than training and "feeding".

The supervision of Peggy is carried out by Elly Jansen on behalf of the board and, whilst you would be accountable to Peggy, it is likely that the three of you would need to meet regularly to discuss management issues.

I look forward to hearing from you and to a much enhanced senior team, which will bring fruition to our work with residents and harmony to the staff!

Please be kind enough to copy in Elly to your response .

Have a great break.

Geoff Benton

On Behalf Of The Boards

CLINICAL/OPERATIONAL LEAD

A) Definition: The COL is a member of the RPFI top management team, appointed by the CEO to direct, supervise and promote the proper functioning of specific projects through direct and concentrated involvement with them, and to undertake and train staff in clinical assessments of new applicants.

B) Task: The COL's primary task is to ensure that the staff of each of the projects under his or her control achieve and sustain the purposes for which the projects have been created and do so in accordance with the goals, principles, therapeutic policies and managerial structure of the Organisation as well as in keeping with all the relevant laws and regulations.

C) Accountability: The COL is directly accountable to the CEO. He or she is accountable for the *therapeutic and practical work* of the project managers and all staff under the project manager's control and supervision.

D) Time Distribution: The needs for supervision of different projects are bound to vary at different times, but the COL will need to spend around 70 % of his or her working time at the projects under their supervision. The demands of the work can be heavy and the COL must expect to work up to 48 hours per week at times, especially during the first 3 – 6 months, whilst later the average working week will be 40 hours. The remaining 30 % of time will be spent undertaking PR to ensure full occupancy, dealing with administrative tasks and specific problems, and attending meetings with the CEO and/or Consultant or undertaking other tasks which promote the work of RPFI.

E) Time in the projects: As a minimum the COL will spend the equivalent of two whole day (or four half days) in each of the projects during a two week period. During each visit a specific period of 1,5 hours is set aside for supervision with the manager and a further 1,5 hours for meeting with the whole staff group to participate in agenda discussions and to review systematically the specific tasks of the staff team - *especially where it concerns the therapeuticcontent-* and, where necessary, specific areas of difficulty.

At least 2,5 hours of every visit will be spent on reviewing, inspecting and training in: professional social work activities, administration and practical duties. Part of this time will be set aside for a staff dynamics meeting to ensure that problems do not foster and to create a healthy climate for team work. The COL needs to emphasise the need to remain aware of safety and health regulations and to streamline good administrative and home-making procedures so that a sound structure is created and *so that maximum time is available for understanding the residents and the best means of caring.*

F) Case load: The COL is expected to cope with a case load of at least 5 Projects, one of which may be a new project. During each three months' period each project needs a two-day "overhaul " visit during which all aspects of the project can be taken under the loupe – *especially the therapeutic issues* - and for the writing up of a three-monthly report for the CEO – hopefully demonstrating satisfactory progress.

H) Mode of Activity: The COL performs his or her tasks through both formal and informal meetings with the project manager (and, when necessary, with other staff individually), the staff team and residents. He or she needs to get familiarised with all aspects of life in the project e.g. the management of the staff team, including staff rotas, social work procedures (such as admissions and discharges, care plans and risk assessments, counselling and group meeting), administration, maintenance and home making, work and creative programmes, social activities, catering and meals procedures, PR, liaison with referral agencies, families and schools (and sometimes meetings with a house committee or with groups of family and friends of the residents). *He or she will particularly focus on the therapeutic quality and the functioning of the project as a TC* and the input of staff members individually and jointly..

The COL regularly, systematically and formally appraises the work of each staff member, provides clarification of policy and problems, gives formal and informal feedback and constructively reviews with those areas identified as in need of strengthening. He or she provides support, both by managerial action and by consultancy, training and guidance over planning, and ensures that management information is passed on and clarified and, if directives are not adhered to, disciplines staff, following RPFI procedures..

He or she also discusses and advises on new proposals and initiatives and puts these to the CEO and Consultant, whether it concerns re-organisation of rooms, new activities or new procedures or suggestions regarding the whole Organisation. The COL needs to ensure that each project manager produces a full report on all aspects of the operation of the project and passes this on to the CEO with appropriate commentary.

l)   Team work: As a member of the senior management team, the COL needs to remain in close contact to be aware of existing policies and the reasons why they exist, to participate in the development of new policies and to provide relevant feedback from and to the projects and liaise over action to be taken. He or she must avoid getting used as "complaints officer" and develop the ability to see issues clearly and assist staff in gaining real skill to use their scope and creativity ad therby derive satisfaction from their task.

The COL needs to be able to portray genuine warmth and reflection n what is conveyed to him or her. At the same time it is essential that the COL demonstrates independence and is seen to act without fear or vavour!

The displacement of occupational anxieties and disappointments to pre-occupation by the house staff with the task of senior staff (and accompanying neglect of attention to project problems) is a recurring issue. The COL needs to build up confidence in senior staff by sticking to his or her own brief and keeping the project staff to their own task.

Our work tends to encourage staff to deal with pressures and problems they experience by attempts to create a split between senior staff members or by splitting their "good" function (listening and support) from their bad" function (inspection, feedback, control and direction) in favour of the former. The COL, in representing both, models the choices as well as the constraints of our work which the managers in turn have to apply with both staff and residents, thereby enabling the manager to use choices and constraints responsibly, creatively and effectively.

From: diversitymanagementlcl<u>diversitymanagementlcl@btinternet.com</u>>
Date: 1 January 2016 at 17:45:03 GMT
To: «<u>peggwegg@hotmail.com</u>" <<u>peggwegg@hotmail.com</u>>, Elly Jansen <<u>elly.jansen@rpfi.org</u>>
Subject: Discussion Draft RPFI/RCI 7.1.16

Best wishes for joy and happiness in 2016!

Duncan

P.s: My initial 7.1.16 Company-wide Training Day Draft Programme Notes for your review.

See you both tomorrow...Duncan

Sent from my iPad

Better integration by the Sharing of Good Practice

Themes:

1. Clarity of our 'model of working'(as related to our Statement of Purpose)

2. Creating an environment for learning and development.

3. Roadblocks and Roadblock Removers

9am:Welcome to Lytton House/The day(Colin)

9:20am: Setting the stage for today(Duncan)
Audit and Results
Therapeutic Communities
Sharing good practice
Quality Assurance

10am: Lancaster House (sharing and open discussion)
Coffee/Tea

11:30am:White House(sharing and open discussion)
Pre-Lunch Thoughts ...what types of things might hinder better integration between the houses?

1-1:45:Lunch

1:45: Lytton House(Sharing and open discussion)

2:30: Measuring Outcomes/Evidence based Practice(and working Coffee/Tea Break)

4pm: Closing Session(One thing that I got from today's session and one thing that is still left for me to do as a result of today?) facilitated by Duncan

Some Suggestions from Duncan

Tuesdays
- **(7am) While House**
- **(11am)Lancaster House**
- **(3pm) Lytton**

Thursdays
- **(9-11am) Manager/ Sr. Staff Group Supervision** (monthly or fortnightly/ organisational)
- **(12noon-5pm) Staff Training** (Monthly/ organisational)
- **(12noon-5pm) Staff Training** (Monthly/ House)
- **(12noon-5pm) Staff Training** (Monthly/ HQ-Admin)
- **Unannounced visits** (TBA)

Clinical Supervision/ Quality Assurance Visits to include):

- Clinical Supervision with Manger (fortnightly)
- Team Supervision (fortnightly)
- review daily logs
- visit residents
- observations

½ Days TBA with Peggy and or Elly

- Ideally Tuesday or Thursday evenings (first preferences) evening or Monday or Wednesday Evening (second preferences) or Saturday (my least Favourite preference)
- **Regarding Fridays:** I teach and coach all day. I would need to give one term notice to give up these teaching/coaching commitments.

- **Note:** There is one Tuesday this winter/spring 2016 that I have previous commitments and the Feb 2016 half-term I have previous commitments (I am open to re-arrange my work week for these or take unpaid leave, whatever is best for the company). I will always give one at least month's notice of any pre-existing commitments

Duncan Lawrence 29.12.15

Point A-3

(and some respectfully submitted Feedback and Suggestion from Duncan Lawrence 4.4.19)

1. I could not find any 'stand alone' emails for this topic. This could be because it was mainly 'spoken about' by me within meetings with the Charity founder/advisor, and or Trustees and or the ex-CEO in **every month at least once during my time.** I stand by my multiple suggestions, advice and guidance to the Charity. I was not there long enough to see any initial ideas and initiatives through nor was I there long enough to support anyone within the Charity to follow them up and or further develop them either.

   However, once the charity founder/advisor told me about 'the history' of the Lancaster Unit (going back several years), from that exact same first week of coming to the charity I advised her that what she is wishing for is almost impossible to deliver (e.g. updating a programme with existing staff and residents in place) and most quality leadership training programs across the world would never advise going down this route either without extreme caution.

2. I seem to be used as a distraction by some at times (e.g. taking 1-2 of my charity suggestions out of context, misrepresentations of me and my actions within the

charity, over a short space of time etc) rather than considering my entire integrated body of work/advice within a short period of time within the charity. For example, early on I also suggested adding parents, ex-residents and current staff to the charity Trustees Board (even in my brief time in the charity, the atmosphere, Charity governance and practical stakeholder outcomes would have been vastly different had this single recommendation been taken up...still makes me sad for us all when considering this fact)...only the founder/advisor and Board of Trustees can answer why these regular recommendations were never taken up. I would respectfully suggest asking them.

3. No disrespect to the Coroner but <u>we were told </u>(in advance of preparing our written statements for the Coroner last Autumn 2018) <u>to not talk about Charity's past history </u>(because the Coroner is not interested) of animosity between some managers, staff, ex CEOs,CQC,etc... No 'super CEO', extra high quality staff and consultants could have done much in 2015/2016 without first addressing 'the Charity's history with Lancaster Lodge'. <u>I tried my best within the 'team/board/charity context' to get these issues out there and dealt with...I did not avoid them.</u>

4. I am 100% sure the founder/advisor would agree that I had asked her and the Trustees often about the above issues and many more developmental 'practice' and 'HR' related issues (and 'not just once' at the end of my time with the charity as it has been misrepresented).

5. **I did however find one 'related email'...see below.**

Date: 2 March 2016 at 16:55:39 GMT
To: Geoff Benton <<u>bentongeoff@gmail.com</u>>, "<u>peggwegg@</u> <u>hotmail.com</u>" <<u>peggwegg@hotmail.com</u>>, *Elly Jansen* <<u>ellywjansen@hotmail.com</u>>, *Elly Jansen* <<u>elly.jansen@rpfi.</u> <u>org</u>>, *Colin McDonald* <<u>colin_newatlantis@hotmail.com</u>>
Subject: LL

Good evening all,

I hope today was enlightening and not too stressful.

I think now it is imperative to take stock and think laterally in order to get a strategic LL plan.

I think all ideas should be put on the table and none discounted e.g...temporarily close LL down and rebuild decor, staff team and carefully develop a more suitable resident base, divide the house in two(with two separate lounges, etc) and have a side for current programme and half for adult semi-independent unit, etc. example of two LL ideas.

We need to continue to give confidence to staff that actually RPFI/RCI own and run the houses and not them...I think the last two days may have led some to think that we have either 'retreated' or have been made to do 'something different' by CQC.

Either way some of our past interventions have needed more time to be effective and or were only short term fixes and or were not well thought out ideas full stop.

I look forward to the transformation!

Duncan

P.S: I am in LL Thursday. Dom is still very very interested in being interviewed but can only do week day interviews.

We need to be prepared to be tested .

Duncan

D.E.Lawrence:

Diversity,Equality,Inclusion and Sport Specialist / Management and Team Coach.

Skype: diversitymanagementlcl

Sent from my iPhone

From: Diversity Management LCL <diversitymanagementlcl@btinternet.com>

Date: 9 February 2016 at 06:39:56 GMT

To: Elly Jansen <elly.jansen@rpfi.org>, Elly Jansen <ellywjansen@hotmail.com>, "peggwegg@hotmail.com" <peggwegg@hotmail.com>, Peggy Jhugroo<pjhugroo@wandsworth.gov.uk>

Cc: Geoff Benton <bentongeoff@gmail.com>

Subject: RPFI/RCI Board Composition

Good morning to us all,

Just a reminder of my ideas have a monthly or quarterly charity blog/news letter to alert staff and service users to the 'vision' and to consider expanding the board to include staff member rep and a service user/parent-carer rep...

<u>because we always have so much to do when we all meet I am aware that these ideas might have gotten lost.</u>

Every day when doing this charity's work, I am reminded that each month we may be stepping over a great opportunity to bring the charity together more efficiently.

Have a great day!

Duncan

D.E.Lawrence:

Diversity,Equality,and Inclusion Specialist / Management and Team Coach.

Skype: diversitymanagementlcl

Sent from my iPhone

6. This past valuable history 'knowledge' would have explained the various Lancaster Lodge residents(clearly not all of them) going back several years (before 2016) that were accepted into the unit that were not at times suitable because the 'at-risk nature' of their mental status. Self-harm and suicide gestures were rare but did actually occur each and every year and well before people like myself arrived at the charity, to assume otherwise would be very unfair and very untrue. <u>I would respectfully suggest asking founder/ advisor and past Board to confirm that what I am saying is indeed a fact (rather than me casting out any blame to any one person and or any one period of time)</u>. I do not have access to this information.

7. **Roots of animosity** between past Lancaster Unit Managers, past CEOs, Past Boards, ex staff and ex

resident: I respectfully ask the Coroner to speak with founder, ex CEOs, ex Chair of Trustees, ex Lancaster unit managers, ex-staff, ex-residents etc... even going back ten years from 2016 at least, the unit had dysfunctional internal and external relationships deeply embedded within it...so, looking for any 'roots of neglect' and potential for self-harm, suicide etc you'd have to look much much further than any stakeholders that were around in 2015/2016 (including residents, staff, board members,myself, etc.).<u>I have personally and professionally been disappointed that this route has not been travelled recently</u> and that the related 'trial by media frenzy' never uncovered the very long 'dysfunctional Charity/Lancaster Lodge history'.

8. <u>Important to note</u>, even with great intentions, great residents, great staff, great boards etc there are multiple reasons why 'dysfunctional interpersonal relationships ' can develop/continue to develop over the days...months...years, which can then lead to serious physical, emotional, psychological and professional consequences and implications for evidence based practices/ways of operating, where there are never any 'winners'(especially if problems are not identified and corrected along the way).

9. Related to this, I was concerned that the past/ present staff, CEO, past Lancaster Unit manager, past CEOs, Past Boards, etc. credentials were not a focus as well. The charity generally had a very positive history of developing its inexperienced workers along-side

experienced staff and I am confident, again going back ten years for example 'the staffing trends' would be similar up through 2015/2016 (e.g. some experienced staff working alongside staff that are 'brand new to the field' and or have limited experience).

The public and other interested stakeholders (after 2016) would have had more to reflect upon (when trying to consider any lessons learned from the tragic loss of Ms Bennett) if they had seen/reviewed/considered these more well-rounded although rarely spoken about/rarely documented historical accounts from 'the Charity and the Lancaster Unit relationship'.

I do not like thinking this but I am inclined to believe that some (not all) different past 'Lancaster Unit connections and some other related stakeholders' were never really actually looking for the truth and or carefully and responsibly considering what lessons could be learned so this never happens again, but some it seems were interested in only 'taking pot shots' at each other, protecting their own backs, playing to the media, getting revenge, blaming others to deflect attention away from actually considering the long history-internal/external dysfunctional relationship between the Charity and the Lancaster unit etc..

If I could, I respectfully and assertively make a suggestion to this process:

- Please consider recommending that a 'voluntary' focus group (not an adversarial environment) be setup, e.g. made up of Charity founder/advisor, ex Charity stakeholders from at least 2006(to present) to talk to each other about their experiences and **make recommendations** to the Coroner, to the Bennett family and to the Charity within 30 days of its first meeting. I would welcome being part of any such group too.

- Does the 'coroner process' have a complaints procedure that I can look at? Thanks in advance for this information.

D.Lawrence 4.4.19

c.c. Solicitor File.

Sent from my iPhone

Begin forwarded message:

From: «Smith Louise: H&F» <Louise.Smith@lbhf.gov.uk>
Date: 1 April 2019 at 12:32:39 BST
To: Eric Lawrence <diversitymanagementlcl@btinternet.com>
Cc: Rachel Harger <R.Harger@bindmans.com>
Subject: Re: Sophie Bennett – Hearing of Duncan Lawrence

Dear Mr Lawrence,

With a view to having the relevant material to hand in good time before the hearing on 1 May, the Coroner directs that you take the following steps, no later than 15 April 2019:

A. You are to produce to the Court:

1. the credentials which you sent via e-mail on or around 22 December 2015 to Elly Jansen and to the RPFI

Board (see paragraph 8 of your statement dated 13 December 2018)

2. the e-mails exchanged on or around 22 December 2015 relating to your role and credentials (see paragraph 13 of that statement)

3. all e-mails "flying around" between Peggy Jhugroo, the RPFI Board and you on or around 1 March 2016, particularly in relation to the CQC unannounced visit, and your e-mail of 1 March 2016 containing suggestions for responsive action, including your proposal to close down Lancaster Lodge (which were mentioned by Peggy Jhugroo in her oral evidence at the inquest)

The Coroner understands that RPFI's solicitors, Hill Dickinson, confirmed (on 18 January 2019) that they had asked you to produce the documents listed under 1 and 2.

4. evidence as to your means (as mentioned in the e-mail notifying you of the hearing on 1 May)

B. If you are unable to produce any of the documents itemised under 1 to 3 above, you are to provide a statement saying:

1. when you last had the documents in question

2. why you do not have them now

3. if you chose to dispose of them, what was/were your reason(s) for disposing of them

Kindly confirm safe receipt of this e-mail.

Kind regards

Louise Smith
Coroner's Officer
West London Coroner's Court
25 Bagleys Lane, Fulham
SW6 2QA
Tel: 0208 753 1427

Do it online at www.lbhf.gov.uk

Help us keep your council tax bill down and protect spending on vital public services - use our website to find information, view your account, make payments, apply for services and report problems.

New - create an account - Want to manage your council tax, benefits claim or parking permits online? Create an account now at www.lbhf.gov.uk/myaccount

---

Received, thank you.
Thanks for the update.
Thank you.

Begin forwarded message:

From: diversitymanagementlcl <<u>diversitymanagementlcl@</u>
    <u>btinternet.com</u>>
Date: 15 March 2019 at 14:52:26 GMT
To: «Smith Louise: H&F» <<u>Louise.Smith@lbhf.gov.uk</u>>
Subject: Re: Duncan Lawrence Hearing Date

Good afternoon,

With meaning no disrespect what so ever to the Coroner
or to the family, I respectfully would not like to attend any
future hearing.

I have no new or additional evidence and do not wish to
add to anything other than my several emails that I sent
attempting to update the coroner/coroner staff on my
efforts here and abroad with my family, the last one being
a copy of an email from a senior police officer in the states
that was assisting me with moving my frail and elderly
mother from a homelessness and medical crisis situation
to care home situation . This was my choice to support my
family and believe me it was never an easy one that I took
lightly.

I know the last few months have been very stressful all
around and I am not looking for sympathy and the 'trial by
media' at times has been very hurtful and distressing for my
family and I would respectfully and humbly ask for a chance
to move on.

I am just recently trying to pick up the pieces, emotionally and financially for myself and for my family in the states. With my modest lifestyle,I have nothing literally and hope that I can have additional time to settle any fine.

Thanks very much for considering this email and it's contents.

Respectfully submitted,

Duncan E.Lawrence

Sent from my iPad

On 15 Mar 2019, at 13:50, Smith Louise: H&F <Louise.Smith@ lbhf.gov.uk> wrote:

Dear Mr Lawrence

Please see email below and attachment.

The Coroner needs a response as a matter of urgency.

Kind regards

Louise Smith
Coroner's Officer
West London Coroner's Court
25 Bagleys Lane, Fulham
SW6 2QA
Tel: 0208 753 1427

From: Smith Louise: H&F
Sent: 21 February 2019 11:02
To: Eric Lawrence <<u>diversitymanagementlcl@btinternet.com</u>>
Subject: FW: Duncan Lawrence Hearing Date
Importance: High

Dear Mr Lawrence,

Please confirm receipt of this email and confirm that you will be attending.

Kind regards

Louise Smith
Coroner's Officer
West London Coroner's Court
25 Bagleys Lane, Fulham
SW6 2QA
Tel: 0208 753 1596

From: Smith Louise: H&F
Sent: 18 February 2019 13:20
To: Eric Lawrence <<u>diversitymanagementlcl@btinternet.com</u>>;
   Rachel Harger <<u>R.Harger@bindmans.com</u>>; Kate Fawell-
   Comley <<u>Kate.Fawell-Comley@hilldickinson.com</u>>
Subject: Duncan Lawrence Hearing Date

Dear All

Please see attachment.

Kind regards

Louise Smith
Coroner's Officer
West London Coroner's Court
25 Bagleys Lane, Fulham
SW6 2QA
Tel: 0208 753 1596

Do it online at www.lbhf.gov.uk

Help us keep your council tax bill down and protect spending on vital public services – use our website to find information, view your account, make payments, apply for services and report problems.

New – create an account – Want to manage your council tax, benefits claim or parking permits online? Create an account now at www.lbhf.gov.uk/myaccount

---

If you have received this email in error, please delete it and tell the sender as soon as possible. You should not disclose the contents to any other person or take copies.

All emails you send over the internet are not secure unless they have been encrypted. For further details, please see: www.getsafeonline.org/protecting-yourself

---

<Sophie Bennett - Duncan Lawrence hearing.docx>

👤   ReplyForward

.ıl Vodafone WiFiCall 🛜 02:38   ☾ ⌁ ◔ ▬

❮ All Inboxes   ∧ ∨

From: **APD world...** ❯

To: ⭐ DuncanLa... ❯ Hide

RE: Update on Mrs Lawrence

Today at 00:58

Hi Duncan ~

I am so happy to hear that your mom has gotten into a safe place. This is wonderful news, and you put so much hard work into making it happen. Thank you for sharing!

Respectfully,

Lieutenant Nancy Reeder
Internal Affairs Commander
Anchorage Police Department
4501 Elmore Road
Anchorage, Alaska 99507-1599
907.786.2634

From: Eric Lawrence <<u>diversitymanagementlcl@btinternet.com</u>>
Date: 11 February 2019 at 16:26:39 GMT
To: <u>Louise.Smith@lbhf.gov.uk</u>
Subject: Duncan Lawrence
Re: Bennett Family Coroner Inquiry

Dear Ms Smith,

I have severe family problems, the main one being that my mother is and will continue to be gravely physically and mentally ill and I have had to put her first in this instance . I have never hidden this from the charity legal team nor the coroner from the beginning of this process.

The charity legal team supported my compiling my rather large statement to the coroner (with emails to back up everything that I wrote). I have have tried to be as helpful as I could.

There is learning for us all and hope this is never repeated... very very sad situation.

I am so so sorry for the family's loss and I have never ever meant any disrespect to them or to the coroner.We are broke and do the best we can to get by.

I know taking this route that I potentially with be open to slander or libel but that is nothing compared to the Bennett family's loss, while knowing that I can also be part of my mothers last days.

There has been recent moments, where as of Wednesday she is in a care home(see attached brief video) If was not easy it involved the police and several agencies because the main carers(one of my brothers) was drug infested and we had to remove her from staying with him.

She still needs a new pacemaker and an additional heart operation and we struggle to find the funds but we will succeed.

Mr Bennett reached out to me as a father a few days ago and I responded back to him as a father and eldest son(with lead responsibilities for my mom).

I have nothing else to add and hope you will see that I have tried to be helpful in my Coroner submission, while also trying to deal with the dynamic situation with my mom(some days situation changed hourly).

Respectful submitted by:

Duncan Lawrence

Peace to us all,

SEARCH

- Obituaries and Guest Books

BROWSE

- Most Recent
- By Location
- Notable Deaths

SUBMIT

- <u>Submit an Obituary</u>

-

-

Jacob Lawrence Jr.

Service Information

Legacy Funeral Homes & Cremation Services - Witzleben Chapel
1707 S. Bragaw St.
Anchorage, AK
99508
(800)-820-1682
WebsiteView Map

Obituary

Jacob Lawrence Jr. passed away on March 18, 2018, at Alaska Regional Hospital. A Graveside Service will be held at Fort Richardson National Cemetery on June 14, 2018, at 11:30 a.m. Those who wish to attend should meet at the Joint Base Elmendorf-Richardson gate by 11:15 a.m. Arrangements are by Witzleben Legacy Funeral Home.
Published in Anchorage Daily News from June 10 to June 12, 2018

Print |

Myth: Charity Solicitor was 'objective'

Begin forwarded message:

From: Eric Lawrence <<u>diversitymanagementlcl@btinternet.com</u>>
Date: 31 August 2018 at 15:49:11 BST
To: Julie Ford <<u>Julie.Ford@hilldickinson.com</u>>
Cc: Kate Fawell-Comley
       <<u>Kate.Fawell-Comley@hilldickinson.com</u>>
Subject: Re: Request for assistance concerning a coroner's inquiry. [HD-UKLive.12014150.1]

Good afternoon again,

Elly Jansen, has been in contact with me for several months via email asking for my 'recollection of history '.

I have tried my best to advise her honestly and professionally as I could. I have not yet seen how those several pages of emails have been used by the charity...if my comments have been incorporated into their draft statement for this matter, I am 100% ok with seeing their draft statement(and no need for the Board Meeting minutes)...this may be enough to help me to decide whether I would write a statement with the support of the charity.

I have a lot of respect for Elly's past work but I need evidence that it has not been wasted or missed used(re my various past detailed emails to Mrs Jansen).

I am not trying to be awkward, I just do not wish to be taken for granted.

I still have most of my emails and can forward these to you if they would be helpful.

Duncan

D.E.Lawrence:

Diversity, Equality, Inclusion and Sport Specialist/Management and Team Coach.

Please think of the environment – do you really need to print this email or its attachments?

Sent from my iPhone

On 31 Aug 2018, at 14:42, Julie Ford <Julie.Ford@hilldickinson.com> wrote:

Dear Mr Lawrence

Thank you for getting back to me so quickly. Would it be possible to speak to you briefly this afternoon or on Monday.

I appreciate your involvement was very limited but the coroner has requested a statement from you and so even if you were not supported by RPFI, you would still need to provide the coroner with a statement in due course.

I have requested a copy of the board meetings relevant to the period of time in question. I am not really sure however, why you would need to the board minutes 12 month prior to your employment and 12 months after your employment? Would you be able to explain the reason for me?

As mentioned, the coroner's inquiry is a fact finding inquiry to ascertain the circumstances leading to the death only. It is for that reason I am querying why you need so may board papers to provide such a statement.

Perhaps we could speak?

My office number is set out below or you can contact me on my mobile number – 07985588438.

I look forward to hearing from you.

With kind regards

Your sincerely

<image006.jpg>

Julie Ford

Legal Director
Healthcare
Hill Dickinson LLP
Julie.Ford@hilldickinson.com
The Broadgate Tower, 20 Primrose Street, London, EC2A 2EW
TEL: +44 (0)20 7280 9338
FAX: +44 (0)20 7283 1144

<image003.jpg> <image004.jpg>
<image005.jpg>

From: Eric Lawrence [mailto:diversitymanagementlcl@btinternet.com]
Sent: 31 August 2018 14:28
To: Julie Ford
Cc: Kate Fawell-Comley
Subject: Re: Request for assistance concerning a coroner>s inquiry. [HD-UKLive.12014150.1]

CAUTION EXTERNAL EMAIL: This message originated outside the organisation. Do not click links or open attachments unless you recognise the sender and know the content is safe.

Good afternoon,

Re: the above mentioned email.

I was literally only involved with the Charity for a few weeks and was removed from my work by non mutual consent so am unsure how I can be of assistance in this matter.

With the charity's assistance I could consider writing a statement.

I would need to review documents such as:

1. Board Meeting minutes for period of 12 months before I was taken on.

   1.1   Board Meeting minutes for the period that I was engaged by the charity.

   1.2   Board Meeting minutes for the period of 12 months after I was let go by the charity.

Without these documents I will not even consider making a statement.

Respectfully submitted by,

Duncan Lawrence

D.E.Lawrence:

Diversity, Equality, Inclusion and Sport Specialist/Management and Team Coach.

Please think of the environment – do you really need to print this email or its attachments?

Sent from my iPhone

On 31 Aug 2018, at 15:01, Julie Ford <u>Julie.Ford@hilldickinson.com</u>> wrote:

Dear Mr Lawrence

I am assisting a colleague, Kate Fawell-Cowley in a matter in which you have been asked to provide a statement for a Coroner's inquiry. Further details are set out in the letter attached which is password protected (password to follow).

I should be grateful if you would contact me to confirm receipt of the letter and your response the queries set out within it.

I look forward to hearing from you at your earliest convenience.

With kind regards

Your sincerely

<image006.jpg>

Julie Ford
Legal Director
Healthcare
Hill Dickinson LLP
Julie.Ford@hilldickinson.com

The Broadgate Tower, 20 Primrose Street, London, EC2A 2EW
TEL: +44 (0)20 7280 9338
FAX: +44 (0)20 7283 1144

<u>image003.jpg</u> <u>image004.jpg</u>

Hill Dickinson
www.hilldickinson.com

This email and its contents, together with any attachments, are confidential to the sender and the intended recipient(s) and may be covered by legal professional privilege. If you are not the intended recipient of this email and its attachments (if any), you must take no action based upon them, nor must you copy them or show them to anyone. Please contact the sender if you believe you have received this email in error.

Hill Dickinson LLP is a firm of lawyers authorised and regulated by the Solicitors Regulation Authority under registration number 424853. It is a limited liability partnership registered in England and Wales No. OC314079. Its registered office is at No.1 St. Paul's Square, Liverpool L3 9SJ.

<Letter to duncan Lawrence.doc>

Hill Dickinson
www.hilldickinson.com

This email and its contents, together with any attachments, are confidential to the sender and the intended recipient(s) and may be covered by legal professional privilege. If you are not the intended recipient of this email and its attachments (if any), you must take no action based upon them, nor must you copy them or show them to anyone. Please contact the sender if you believe you have received this email in error.

Hill Dickinson LLP is a firm of lawyers authorised and regulated by the Solicitors Regulation Authority under registration number 424853. It is a limited liability partnership registered in England and Wales No. OC314079. Its registered office is at No.1 St. Paul's Square, Liverpool L3 9SJ.

Myth: Founder /Leader had no animosity towards the Lancaster unit manager: A collections of emails to- from the founder/lead advisor

Fact: The founder/lead advisor was really unhappy about the Lancaster unit going back several years.

MANAGEMENT OF LANCASTER LODGE

Inbox

Elly Jansen <elly.jansen@rpfi.org>
26 Apr 2017, 22:01
to Duncan

I WONDER WHETHER YOU CAN HELP. YOU ROTE A SHORT REPORT ABOUT THE FAILINGS OF L.L. - PAPERS MISSING, LACK OF PROGRAMME, RISKS WITH RESIDENTS ETC. I HAVE LOOKED EVERYWHERE BUT CANNOT FIND IT. WOULD YOU STILL HAVE IT AND CAN YOU SEND IT?

ALSO, WHEN YOU SAID V.H. WOULD RESIGN, I COULD NOT BELIEVE IT. CAN YOU LET ME KNOW WHAT WAS SAID BETWEEN THE TWO OF YOU AND WHY YOU THOUGHT VH WOULD RESIGN?

THE TOXIDITY OF THAT MAN IS WITH US STILL!

I HOPE YOU HAVE FOUND YOUR NICHE. YOU MAY KNOW THAT PEGGY LEFT AN THAT WE HAVE A NEW CEO.

Diversity Management LCL
<diversitymanagementlcl@gmail.com>

27 Apr 2017, 06:15
to Elly,

Dear Elly,

You folks seem to forget that I was a victim of Peggy too and you and the board in those days seem to have a naive co-dependent relationship with her. Most tasks that I can do in my sleep were hindered by her and the board's poor management and poor assessment of the level of dysfunction at the Lancaster Unit...without completely gutting out the place and starting over, even superman could not have saved the place with staff and residents still in place.

I will find what you need in the next day or two and send it to you Elly.

Just remember I believe in your work but you and the board were guilty for keeping Peggy around so long and allowing here get away with treating clients and staff/consultants like crap.

Again, give me a day or two to get you the information.

Also...if you wished to do a paid review, I still have texts, emails etc warning you, board, Peggy of potential threats to company, residents, etc..

Duncan

D.E.Lawrence:

Diversity,Equality,and Inclusion Specialist / Management and Team Coach.

Skype: diversitymanagementlcl

Sent from my iPhone

Duncan Lawrence <diversitymanagementlcl@gmail.com>
27 Apr 2017, 10:12
to Elly, ellywjansen,

ALSO, WHEN YOU SAID V.H. WOULD RESIGN, I COULD NOT BELIEVE IT. CAN YOU LET ME KNOW WHAT WAS SAID

BETWEEN THE TWO OF YOU AND WHY YOU THOUGHT VH WOULD RESIGN?

He stated that he realised that he was very very bitter about the company, felt that various boards did not know of his achievements and often rather chose to try to degrade and or control him rather that provide him CPD, more pay, more chance to develop within the company(although he admitted at the time, that he did not know the company's current vision and had not pushed it within his staff [hence their resistance, protectiveness and negativity...Vincent openly admitted this]). **He was not rude or closed within our discussions. I always found him polite and open.**

Duncan

From: Elly Jansen <elly.jansen@rpfi.org>
Date: 27 April 2017 at 21:13:12 BST
To: Duncan Lawrence <diversitymanagementlcl@gmail.com>
Subject: Re: MANAGEMENT OF LANCASTER LODGE

DEAR DUNCAN,

THANK YOU FOR YOUR RESPONSE AND INFORMATION, SOME OF WHICH FEELS NEW TO ME. IT WILL BE VERY DIFFICULT EVER TO KNOW FULLY WHO DID WHAT WHEN. THERE WAS LACK OF THOUGHT AND TRANSPARENCY IN THE SITUATION WHICH WAS INHERITED. THE BOARD WERE NEW AND RELIED ON INFORMATION FROM THE COORDINATOR.

I HAVE SEEN A SHORT REPORT FROM YOU WHICH IDENTIFIED THE OMISSION OF ESSENTIAL PAPERWORK AND THE LACK

OF COHESION AND BOUNDARIES AT L.L. EARLY JANUARY. AT THE TIME YOU INFORMED ME THAT YOUR CHALLENGING THE MANAGER WOULD LEAD TO HIS RESIGNATION WHICH I FOUND HARD TO BELIEVE. IT IS THAT REPORT I WAS LOOKING FOR SINCE IT SHOWED CLEARLY THE ISSUES THAT HAD OBVIOUSLY FAILED TO BE CHECKED BY CQC.

I DO NOT THINK YOU WERE AWARE OF THE LONGER-TERM ISSUES THAT WERE BEING PLAYED OUT AND THE WAY THE NEW BOARD AND PEGGY WERE SET UP BY THE PREVIOUS BOARD, INCLUDING GIVING STAFF NEW CONTRACTS 3 DAYS BEFORE HANDING OVER TO THE NEW BOARD. THAT WAS A TIME BOMB BECAUSE THE MONEY WAS NOT THERE TO IMPLEMENT CRAZY INCREASES. THE BOARD WAS NOT UNAWARE OF THE COMPLEXITY OF THE SITUATION AND HAD FEW CHOICES. CERTAINLY I AGREE THAT IT WAS NECESSARY TO FIND A COMPLETELY NEW STAFF TEAM FOR THE LODGE

THERE IS EVEN LESS MONEY NOW THAN WE HAD AT THAT TIME DUE TO THE COST OF TEMPORARY CLOSURE, SO WE CANNOT TAKE ON NEW STAFF. WE HAVE A GOOD AND TRUSTWORTHY TEAM NOW BUT STILL HAVE NOT RECEIVED THE MONEY FROM DORSET BECAUSE IT APPEARS THAT VINCENT HAD NOT ACQUIRED A WRITTEN AGREEMENT FOR THE CARE OF THEIR REFERRAL WHICH LASTED 8 MONTHS.

I DO NOT UNDERSTAND HOW THAT COULD HAVE HAPPENED.

AM I RIGHT IN THINKING THAT YOU HAD AMONGST YOUR PAPERS AN EMAIL I SENT TO DAVID? IN THAT CASE PLEASE KEEP IT AS CONFIDENTIAL.

THANKS AGAIN FOR SENDING INFORMATION WHICH IS VERY HELPFUL.

ELLY

On 27 April 2017 at 14:08, Duncan Lawrence <diversitymanagementlcl@gmail.com> wrote:

Elly,

Sorry for rushed emails, a very busy period here. Please let me know if you need anything else....I have dozens of RPFI related emails and text.

Duncan

From: Diversity Management LCL <diversitymanagementlcl@btinternet.com>
Date: 2 May 2017 at 20:00:37 BST
To: Elly Jansen <elly.jansen@rpfi.org>
Subject: Re: Supportive Strategy add ons from Duncan

Still looking Elly

D.E.Lawrence:

Diversity,Equality,and Inclusion Specialist / Management and Team Coach.

Skype: diversitymanagementlcl

Sent from my iPhone

On 2 May 2017, at 19:50, Elly Jansen <elly.jansen@rpfi.org> wrote:

THANKS A LOT!

CAN YOU NOT FIND THE SHORT REPORT YOU SENT LISTING FAILURES NOT RECOGNISED BY CQC?

ELLY

Sent from my iPhone

On 30 Apr 2017, at 12:15, Elly Jansen <elly.jansen@rpfi.org> wrote:

Dear Duncan,

Thank you for letting m have these emails,some of which I cannot remember having ever had sight of.

The hostility Peggy received and had to cope with from Lancaster set the scene and she never overcame it.

My role was to advice - not rule - and it is hard to know what happens at the coal front, even when basic principles are agreed..

I know you entered a complex scene and rivalry would have been hard to avoid. And there were no winners.

I wish I could find the document in which you list all the failings which were overlooked by CQC. IT PUT OUR CASE WELL!

We still have not received the report of the CPS. This is holding us back.

Also Dorset are still refusing to pay a bill of £ 48,000 because they say there is no written evidence that they ever accepted to pay.

I cannot believe that Vincent would have allowed Hailey to stay with us without getting that agreement and for there being minimally

SOME EMAILS TO THAT EFFECT, BUT NO ONE HAS BEEN ABLE TO LOCATE ANY. It may come to a Court Case where all parties will have to give a statement on oath. Do you have an Email address for Vincent? Dave, our present CEO, who is a very humble person, would be very glad to be able to communicate with him - partly to get a clearer picture of what actually occurred. i will share your emails with him.

I hope you are happy with the situation you are now in.

Elly

On 28 April 2017 at 09:40, Diversity Management LCL <diversitymanagementlcl@btinternet.com> wrote:

D.E.Lawrence:

Diversity,Equality,and Inclusion Specialist / Management and Team Coach.

Skype: diversitymanagementlcl

Sent from my iPhone

From: Diversity Management LCL
<u>diversitymanagementlcl@btinternet.com</u>>
Date: 30 April 2017 at 13:28:09 BST
To: Elly Jansen <<u>elly.jansen@rpfi.org</u>>, Elly Jansen
<<u>ellywjansen@hotmail.com</u>>
Subject: Fwd: Lancaster Lodge Investigation 12.1.16(final draft)

D.E.Lawrence:

Diversity,Equality,and Inclusion Specialist / Management and Team Coach.

Skype: diversitymanagementlcl

Sent from my iPhone

Begin forwarded message:

From: diversitymanagementlcl <<u>diversitymanagementlcl@btinternet.com</u>>
Date: 14 January 2016 at 15:08:10 GMT
To: «<u>peggwegg@hotmail.com</u>" <<u>peggwegg@hotmail.com</u>>,
Peggy Jhugroo <<u>pjhugroo@wandsworth.gov.uk</u>>
Subject: Lancaster Lodge Investigation 12.1.16(final draft)

Lancaster Lodge House:Jan 2016 Investigation Notes

Incident: A member of staff supported a service user through a suicide gesture/attempt and was concerned that he was left alone for two hours with an 'at risk' service user and that he received no 'after incident support' from LL Management.

Interviewed:Vincent-LL Manager, Angella-LL Support Staff(in charge of Rota), Paul-Long time LL bank staff, Danny-LH Support Staff and Colin-LH Manager

Interview Summary(original statements attached):

Vincent:

States he was on holiday leave during the incident

He said that he first heard of the incident when he received a belated handover

States that it is his policy to support all staff immediately and on an on-going basis (with regard to critical incidents).

Related to above, he states that he was instructed to not discuss the incident(due to the investigation) but told Danny that he would speak to him after the investigation.

Angella:

States that she had a bad chest infection but felt that she did not wish to call in sick(due to LL being short staff), before her shift she called LL to ask could she come in two hours late to have more time to recover

She admits that it is 'LL policy' that staff involved in critical incidents are meant to contact manager/on-Call support. Although upon reflection she admitted that there had been several 'at risk' LL staff incidents involving lone staff and was confused why RPFI was only investigating now.

She states that her only calls that shift were to Paul explaining her medical situation and checking in.

She assumed that Danny knew to contact manager on call

Paul:

Felt comfortable leaving 'C' with Danny because she seemed happy and well for the previous 48 hours

He states that he worked his full hours and that there is no staff sign in/out book.

He assumed that Danny knew to call on-call manager

Danny:

Felt comfortable beginning his work shift

Felt uneasy once 'C' returned to LL because she seemed " ...not in her ordinary mood..."

He stated that he asked Paul what to do the support the above mentioned service user and mentioned that he was "...a bit anxious..." about the situation

He called Angella during the incident and he never considered calling a manager

Felt numb and emotional afterwards and was left wanting Vincent to debrief him and to get clinical supervision to review how he handled the situation

Colin:

When he was alerted to the situation he immediately provided 'post-incident support' to Danny. Danny was insistent that he did not wish to get anyone at LL in trouble and was "... generally ok...".

Because of the above (and pending investigation)Colin did not speak to Vincent directly about the incident.

Belatedly he found out that Danny contacted Angella about LL shifts without his knowledge. LL is now clear that all staffing requests/assignments come via him only.

Initial Impressions:

This is clearly a 'system problem/dysfunction', one that had been going on for a long time, with all staff involved not using best practice/good teamwork and are very lucky staff, volunteers and residents were not hurt in the past Related to the above,It is not clear that the LL rota is currently designed to be accurate

The manager (and senior staff) could have been more insistent about providing Danny support but in seems 'desensitisation' has infected all levels at LL(so all see these situations as 'normal' and just part of the LL work).

Recommendations:

1. Deal with LL 'systems of dysfunction' as a matter of urgency. All involved did not show examples of good practice/good teamwork.

2. Provide critical incident support to Danny and any other LL staff that feel that they need it(but within a supportive atmosphere and not a 'blame' setting).

3. With all the related challenges within LL, it is felt that for the sake of the service users, the staff and the wider credibility of RPFI, the house need an urgent shake up(e.g the manager and senior staff should work at different houses, all manager leave time should be used immediately and an on-the-job 'training/ mentoring manager' should step in asap to shadow Vincent and ensure best practice/quality assurance. I recommend that should be carried out for at least 60 days. Since change is never easily accepted for some adults, service users and staff will need maximum support and consistency during this transition period.

4. Ultimately the manager is responsible for what goes on within their units, however this situation is not a straight forward one. All LL staff interviewed mentioned the impact of regular RPFI SMT/CEO coming and going as a major factor in their personal and profession self esteem.

Submitted by: Duncan Lawrence 12.1.16

From: Diversity Management LCL
    <diversitymanagementlcl@btinternet.com>
To: Elly Jansen <elly.jansen@rpfi.org>; Elly Jansen
    <ellywjansen@hotmail.com>
Sent: Friday, 28 April 2017, 9:25
Subject: Fwd: Supportive Strategy add ons from Duncan II

D.E.Lawrence:

Diversity,Equality,and Inclusion Specialist / Management and Team Coach.

Skype: diversitymanagementlcl

Sent from my iPhone

Begin forwarded message:

From: diversitymanagementlcl <diversitymanagementlcl@
    btinternet.com>
Date: 3 March 2016 at 21:04:58 GMT
To: Geoff Benton <bentongeoff@gmail.com>
Subject: Re: Supportive Strategy add ons from Duncan II

Hi Geoff,

You work too hard...take some time to rest your body.

I stand by my suggestion for Peggy to temporarily stand down
and come into LL as a 'team member'...'a TC member' to do
specific and transparent pieces of work(see below) and not
boss anyone around.

This would help staff and residents to see her/SMT in a new
light and leave me to get on with my tasks(see below).

I will respectfully step away from day one if she comes in as a 'boss'...we have a image that needs to be repaired in a timely manner.

Giving up the CEO role temporarily means a break for her too...Colin would do well.

This isn't an interpersonal thing, just a good and clear headed judgement thing.

Best wishes and please get some rest,

Duncan

Sent from my iPad

On 3 Mar 2016, at 10:41, Diversity Management LCL <diversitymanagementlcl@btinternet.com> wrote:

Fyi

D.E.Lawrence:

Diversity,Equality,Inclusion and Sport Specialist / Management and Team Coach.

Skype: diversitymanagementlcl

Sent from my iPhone

Begin forwarded message:

From: diversitymanagementlcl <<u>diversitymanagementlcl@</u>
   <u>btinternet.com</u>>
Date: 3 March 2016 at 06:41:33 GMT
To: Peggy Jhugroo <<u>pjhugroo@wandsworth.gov.uk</u>>, "<u>peggwegg@</u>
   <u>hotmail.com</u>" <<u>peggwegg@hotmail.com</u>>, Colin McDonald
   <<u>colin_newatlantis@hotmail.com</u>>, Elly Jansen <<u>elly.jansen@</u>
   <u>rpfi.org</u>>, Elly Jansen <<u>ellywjansen@hotmail.com</u>>
Subject: Supportive Strategy add ons from Duncan

Hi Peggy,

Some add on ideas that might help with your Strategy
Development.

Called: Transformation phase II (Phase I is 1 March Enhanced TC)

Could include:

— You temp giving up your CEO role(say to Colin)for 2-3
   weeks
— You coming to LL as an Well being Specialist to model/
   lead practitioner championing the enhanced TC for at
   least 2-3 weeks
— You being coordinator of LL decor upgrade
— Getting skip for Monday for a two week stint...to do a
   whole house and office clear up.
— DL then has time to supervise staff and give each
   a rating competency/capacity and support them
   accordingly (see attached examples...there are two

on one page) and sort out LL case management system(paperwork) and begin 1-1 and group therapy.
— We interview like crazy and get a team leader or deputy to replace your LL role when you resume CEO
— 1 April I resume my clinical Lead and Operational Role and we continue with a nationwide LL service manager search.

With these types of things in place I could just support any reasonable strategy...without them I can't.

I have cancer tests Friday,that will need to be urgently rearranged, please confirm if 2pm today or Friday at WH.

Sorry for rushing, I wanted to contribute to your ideas, even on a busy day.

Duncan

<IMG_0663.JPG>

Sent from my iPad

RPFI/RCI Quality Assurance Checks carried out by Duncan Lawrence Week commencing 4.1.16:

Summary Notes

White House:

- Staff spent almost two hours + in the office 'counting money' (e.g they made coffees, teas, breakfast, etc for residents but made no effort to sit with them, have teas together,etc.).

- Handover read more like a 'compliant judgement' of service users rather than reflecting on a service users comments(verbally and non verbally) about their own experiences of 'their day'

- Acting Lead detailed a long list of support staff negative communications, refusals to 'work the house floor' along side/with the residents, lack of interest or enthusiasm to work to care plans and limited demonstration of good teamwork.

Conclusion:

1. Recommend the entire permanent staff team receive a verbal warning for a 'POOR QUALITY ASSURANCE CHECK', one that could be revoked if they quickly improve this situation within 30 days.

2. Regarding the above,if HR is not able to 'action' this, I would like my original visit notes(that were given to the Acting Lead) typed (say in size 18 font) and posted in the staff office for the next month.

Lancaster House:

- General demonstration of practice with service users to a SATISFACTORY + at this Quality Assurance Check.

- The main challenge this visit related to House Manager coming to terms that the home can't easily afford so many external service providers(and responding to giving notice to external service providers to cease services).

- After a rather lengthy consideration, a 'counter proposal' was put forward...''...what if we kept an 80% occupancy rate, could we then ask for things on a case by case basis(e.g keep our current level of external providers)?...''

- Was suggested by this writer to explore how to develop staff in a timely way(as a way of creating in-house career development opportunities).

Conclusion:

1. I Recommend that the RPFI/RCI CEO/Board consider the 'counter proposal' and to consider what is possible/practical in terms of staff development plan(to reduce reliance on external service providers).

2. Related to the above, this writer respectfully asks that the CEO/Board turn around a clear and concise written response within a week if possible. Additionally, consider a 'company wide' policy of staff development that encourages 'trainee professional' development in the areas of art therapy, music therapy, counselling, group facilitation, staff supervision, etc.. Would be great to announce this as 'an ideal',say at this weeks company training day.

Lytton House:

- Preparations for children's home occupancy and or semi-independent unit occupancy appears on track(but this writer recommends one day staff training asap on 'Dealing with Stress and Aggressive situations' and to consider diverse provisions, ones that include the use of trained volunteers).

Conclusion:

1. Continue to prepare a 'fit for purpose' staff compliment, one that meets the organisation's short-medium term needs. Important that the 'service user group' is 100% at the front of all planning and development .

2. If the semi-independent unit is pursued, the company should consider how they use the current Lytton House management resource(Colin). Most Semi-Independent Units do not have full-time management provision. Could prove useful to allow Colin to manage White House and Lytton House together. He would need at least 20-30 CPD Hours in the area of 'adult social care' covering mental health, age related provision,etc.. A good link for a 'Social Care' CPD Certificate is http://www.skillsforcare.org.uk/Standards/Care-Certificate/Care-Certificate.aspx Duncan Lawrence(BA-Ed,MA-Counselling,DPA-Public Admin, FiLM,Reg. MBACP and FBACP)

RPFI/RCI DISCUSSION NOTES FROM D.LAWRENCE 14.1.16

After considering the recent company audit that I completed, my consultancy experiences thus far and my recent initial investigation of Lancaster Lodge Jan 2016,I suggest the organisation take an urgent strategy such as outlined below.

1. Send a company wide letter/email to all staff such as:

Memo to: All RPFI/RCI Personnel

Date:15.1.16

RE:Company Integrated Strategy Jan/Feb/March 2016 for Lancaster Lodge,Lytton House and the White House

Statement of Purpose: Lytton House has updated its Statement of Purpose in December 2015, and the White House is in the early stages of reviewing and updated its Statement of Purpose. Lancaster Lodge in consultation with Duncan Lawrence and Greetha will need to start its review and update process as soon as possible.

The aim is to have a Statement of Purpose that best reflects the wider company values, reflects the 'added value' that the home could/actually bring(s) and is readable by multiple stakeholders(e.g referral sources,staff, volunteers, service users, family members,etc.).

Staffing Developments: the review and development work that began in June 2015 with the Company Coordinator continues to highlight some great areas of practice and some very poor areas of practice,practice that often puts service users, staff and the company's credibility at risk.

To that end we are making considered staffing changes to take advantage our current strengths, our attempts to quickly shore up areas needing immediate improvement and finally create regular staff development opportunities, while providing others the opportunity to 'recharge their personal energy'.

2. Vincent will use up all of his accrued leave starting 1 Feb 2016.

3. Rohit will deputise in Vincent's absence.

4. Duncan Lawrence will shadow Rohit and provide 24/7 on-the-job management mentoring support for at least 60 days beginning 25 Jan 2016(hours TBC). This will include evening and weekend support/guidance.

5. Note: To limit the 'amount of change' at one time, the previous instruction from the Company Coordinator for Lancaster Lodge to wind down their use of external practitioners, the time to wind down will now be extended to 1 March 2016. We expect this time to be used wisely and for the benefit of the residents.

6. There will be an Acting Manager the White House by 1 Feb 2016.

7. Manager supervision and Staff supervision will need to begin by 1 Feb 2016. All house managers will need

to arrange this around Duncan Lawrence's time schedule.

8. Lancaster Lodge will host the next company wide sharing good practice day(tbc).

9. Finally, it is the company's aim to improve the atmosphere within the homes. Any negative gossiping, bad mouthing the RPFI/RCI, etc. is considered a bad health and safety risk because it interferes with individuals and their teams ability to work unhindered.

If any current staff member feels that they can not assertively foster good practice, positive teamwork and emotional competency, please firstly make good use of your supervision and your personal therapist.

If this does not work, the board will put aside two days(tbc) for these staff to meet with them and 'get anything off their chest'. Staff will be paid for these sessions.

The Board of the RPFI/RCI honestly wishes to give the best possible care to our service users,while also providing opportunity for our personnel to professionally develop if they choose to do so.

RPFI/RCI BOARD

1.1 Expand Duncan Lawrence role to four days per week to additionally include him providing on-the-job Management Mentoring to Lancaster Lodge.

I could do if for a temporary employee contract of £40k pro rata(four days per week role) or £200 per day as a freelance consultancy basis.

Respectfully submitted by,

DuncanLawrence
15.1.16

Re: Please disregard earlier email...I changed one word Elly

Inbox

From: Elly Jansen <elly.jansen@rpfi.org>
Date: 3 May 2017 at 17:23:00 BST
To: diversitymanagementlcl <diversitymanagementlcl@btinternet.com>
Subject: Re: Did you see this Elly...copy of my suggestion to Geoff, with regard to writing to CQC(following their surprise visit)...it speaks of LL

WAS THIS A DRAFT OR WAS THIS SENT TO CQC? I DO NOT REMEMBER SEEING IT, AND IT IS NOT THE SHORT AND CONCISE MEMO FROM YOU I REMEMBER.

THANKS FOR SENDING IT.

E

On 3 May 2017 at 15:49, diversitymanagementlcl <diversitymanagementlcl@btinternet.com> wrote:

Dear

Re:Lancaster Lodge

3rd March 2016

Firstly, apologies for no senior staff being available to you today...Duncan is really gutted because he found you 'brutally constructive'.

Duncan has a pre-existing professional meeting that he can't get out of and Peggy is attending a hospital panel meeting for C J. (Lancaster Lodge resident). Both are available anytime Thursday.

Duncan describes that you saw "...a mess..." today with vital evidence based practice opportunities missing throughout the house's paperwork systems.

As a board, over the years this house kept us out and as such we could not reliably vouch for the quality of service.

It was not until our December 2015 Audit(see attach) and from speaking with exiting Lancaster Lodge staff, that we were made aware of the true scope of multi-layered problems within Lancaster Lodge.

It perplexed us even further when you gave the house a glowing CQC inspection report...quite a confusing situation.

To make a long story even shorter, the board takes full responsibility for the state of the house and the current ability and current motivation of staff to carry out their duties to a high standard. By the end of this week with will have part-time admin support within all of our homes.

We admit that we thought that our December 2015 notification of our charity's intent to improve our service delivery was not enough 'notice' (six months would have been better), but we felt that it was important to move forward at that time.

The past Lancaster Lodge manager did not warm to the strategy nor did he cascade this information down to his staff or the house residents...hence further complicating the scene even further.

Duncan and Peggy have worked very hard to improve the situation and seemed to find more and more problems literally each day!

We anticipated that it would take until the end of April 2016 to make things better for the residents while training old and new staff on-the-job.

Rumours were rife that somehow the charity SMT sacked the last manager and made Peggy and Duncan 'the bad guys' to staff and residents. Their commitment to residents and belief in standards kept them coming back each week.

We started charity wide emails(see attached Feb-March 2016) to make communication better, having learned from our recent mistakes.

Finally, we learned that no one at Lancaster Lodge had a practitioner registration(eg with the BACP, UKCP,BPs,etc) and the senior staff acting as clinical lead for past five years, has yet to provide evidence of his psychology degree...even with multiple requests.

Yes there has been recent strides but there is still needing for everyone at RPFI/RCI to work even harder to satisfactorily evidence its practice.

We hope you will give us time to make things right, 'with our eyes wide open'.

Respectfully submitted by:

Geoff Benton-RPFI chair.

D.E.Lawrence:

Diversity,Equality,Inclusion and Sport Specialist / Management and Team Coach.

Skype: diversitymanagementlcl

Thought Questions:

? =How does this chapter's emails/ information relate to what you read in the news and or social media, and or that you saw on television about D.Eric Lawrence?

?=Any thoughts about the 'three levels of Coroners(Chief, Senior and the Assistant) treatment of D.Eric Lawrence? Y/N Explain

3. Witness Statement and Exhibits

Some Reflective thoughts from D.Eric Lawrence

> **Bamboozled Wisdom:**(Number 3) Even if everyone tells 'their story', the rule makers still go forward with 'a story' and 'the story' gets buried far from the prying eyes.

"...how can you only tell 'part of the story' and still get to the truth...?"

I was initially suspicious when asked by the charity's solicitor to write a witness statement after so many months of limited and no contact with the charity. They never once actually even informed me when the young woman took her life!

I have always sensed that the Senior Charity Members(founder, Trustee Chair, ex-CEO,etc.) only used 'headline statements' rather than actual factual documentation and that most will be surprised if and when they read my memoirs.

I have always been a 'documentation person, "...if it is not there it did not happen..." and can grow impatient in situations where people are 'just recalling from memory' rather that showing us 'documentation. At the same time, was not always surprised when the 'talkers' could convince others to their side...quite scary and unfortunate.

I told the charity solicitor, that I would like the Board of Trustees meeting minutes for my time with charity to aid in developing my witness statements and they were hesitant (to this day I never saw any minutes). I really wanted to have my witness statement to be accurate and reflect the Trustees Meeting and Trustee Chair notes. I wonder how forgiving the court and the press/media would have been if the charity solicitors had been a black law firm? Would the case have been presented differently, would I still have been scapegoated, presented as a 'whistle blower' and or competent long experienced consultant that I was. I also wonder what the assistant coroner, judiciary and press would have done if they had had access to actual Trustee minutes, senior staff and general staff daily logs...those integrated with the external HR and my own presentation would have presented a 'different RPFI', one without me at the centre of the assistant coroner's universe.

I was hesitant too because I had history of the charity founder/ advisor regularly using me to 'jog her memory' during this period, especially about rather important 2015-16 issues (e.g. history of long running charity interpersonal issues, details on past HR related grievances and sackings, the types of training and written charity content that I had provided, 'rewriting my views' and reports on those that she had any mutual animosity with and about, etc.).

I tried to be as thorough in my witness statement as possible, although in my eyes it was very weak and let the charity founder/advisor/Chair of the Trustees (RIP) 'off the hook' and downplayed my suggestions, warnings, and advice to them. Upon reflection I should have been more assertive with the charity and its solicitors and should have realised much earlier that my old emails, reports and diagrams would have proved useful within my witness statements. Had they been available in court (rather than being withheld and hidden in plain sight), even with human rights violations(especially my article 6 rights), racism and white male privilege and the like, etc. assistant coroner, and the judiciary would have found it difficult to come after me so hard as they did.

The other senior ex-charity staff and Trustees were very secretive and never once allowed me to review their witness statements, yet it was always ok for them to see my notes (via simply asking the charity solicitor for them). I would love to get my hands on a full copy of these.

In the spring and early summer of 2019 when the Assistant Coroner was still chasing me up, I knew since the rest of the ex-senior stakeholders were not telling the entire truth about 2015-16 with email back up, the assistant coroner thought that I was telling lies and withholding information, where in fact, it was the opposite.

Even now, I am confident that if an independent person looked at my 2015-16 work emails, my witness statement and exhibitions and my spring/summer 2019 comments to the Assistant coroner, they would then say that I was consistent, furthermore they would say that the assistant coroner should further review the other stakeholders 'statements' against my 'factual evidence' (in terms of 'comparing and contrasting' the types and range of evidence possibilities).

The Assistant Coroner was never really clear about if he ever actually received my 13 Dec 2018 witness statement and exhibits and in court the prosecutor never actually showed what they had received from me, nor did they allow me to show what I had summitted to the charity solicitor,or what I had submitted to the Assistant Coroner during Spring/Summer 2019... Bamboozled again and a continuation of systematic violation of my Article 6 Human Rights, from my coroner experience up to now, nothing has been clear and transparent...decisions and discussions were all made away from me and I always had a hunch that Judge and the prosecutor knew more about my written submissions and contributions than they ever let on.

Myth: Charity Solicitor was 'objective'

Begin forwarded message:

From: Eric Lawrence
<u>diversitymanagementlcl@btinternet.com</u>>
Date: 31 August 2018 at 15:49:11 BST
To: Julie Ford <<u>Julie.Ford@hilldickinson.com</u>>
Cc: Kate Fawell-Comley
<<u>Kate.Fawell-Comley@hilldickinson.com</u>>
Subject: Re: Request for assistance concerning a coroner's inquiry. [HD-UKLive.12014150.1]

Good afternoon again,

Elly Jansen, has been in contact with me for several months via email asking for my 'recollection of history'.

I have tried my best to advise her honestly and professionally as I could. I have not yet seen how those several pages of emails have been used by the charity...if my comments have been incorporated into their draft statement for this matter, I am 100% ok with seeing their draft statement(and no need for the Board Meeting minutes)...this may be enough to help me to decide whether I would write a statement with the support of the charity.

I have a lot of respect for Elly's past work but I need evidence that it has not been wasted or missed used(re my various past detailed emails to Mrs Jansen).

I am not trying to be awkward, I just do not wish to be taken for granted.

I still have most of my emails and can forward these to you if they would be helpful.

Duncan

D.E.Lawrence:

Diversity, Equality, Inclusion and Sport Specialist/Management and Team Coach.

Please think of the environment – do you really need to print this email or its attachments?

Sent from my iPhone

On 31 Aug 2018, at 14:42, Julie Ford <Julie.Ford@hilldickinson.com> wrote:

Dear Mr Lawrence

Thank you for getting back to me so quickly. Would it be possible to speak to you briefly this afternoon or on Monday.

I appreciate your involvement was very limited but the coroner has requested a statement from you and so even if you were not supported by RPFI, you would still need to provide the coroner with a statement in due course.

I have requested a copy of the board meetings relevant to the period of time in question. I am not really sure however, why you would need to the board minutes 12 month prior to your employment and 12 months after your employment? Would you be able to explain the reason for me?

As mentioned, the coroner's inquiry is a fact finding inquiry to ascertain the circumstances leading to the death only. It is for that reason I am querying why you need so may board papers to provide such a statement.

Perhaps we could speak?

My office number is set out below or you can contact me on my mobile number – 07985588438.

I look forward to hearing from you.

With kind regards

Your sincerely

<image006.jpg>

Julie Ford
Legal Director
Healthcare
Hill Dickinson LLP
Julie.Ford@hilldickinson.com
The Broadgate Tower, 20 Primrose Street, London, EC2A 2EW
TEL: +44 (0)20 7280 9338
FAX: +44 (0)20 7283 1144

<image003.jpg> <image004.jpg>
<image005.jpg>

From: Eric Lawrence [mailto:diversitymanagementlcl@
btinternet.com]
Sent: 31 August 2018 14:28
To: Julie Ford
Cc: Kate Fawell-Comley
Subject: Re: Request for assistance concerning a coroner›s
inquiry. [HD-UKLive.12014150.1]

CAUTION EXTERNAL EMAIL:This message originated outside the organisation. Do not click links or open attachments unless you recognise the sender and know the content is safe.

Good afternoon,

Re: the above mentioned email.

I was literally only involved with the Charity for a few weeks and was removed from my work by non mutual consent so am unsure how I can be of assistance in this matter.

With the charity's assistance I could consider writing a statement.

I would need to review documents such as:

1. Board Meeting minutes for period of 12 months before I was taken on.

1.1 Board Meeting minutes for the period that I was engaged by the charity.

1.2 Board Meeting minutes for the period of 12 months after I was let go by the charity.

Without these documents I will not even consider making a statement.

Respectfully submitted by,

Duncan Lawrence

D.E.Lawrence:

Diversity, Equality, Inclusion and Sport Specialist/Management and Team Coach.

<u>Please think of the environment</u> – do you really need to print this email or its attachments?

Sent from my iPhone

On 31 Aug 2018, at 15:01, Julie Ford <<u>Julie.Ford@hilldickinson.com</u>> wrote:

Dear Mr Lawrence

I am assisting a colleague, Kate Fawell-Cowley in a matter in which you have been asked to provide a statement for a Coroner's inquiry. Further details are set out in the letter attached which is password protected (password to follow).

I should be grateful if you would contact me to confirm receipt of the letter and your response the queries set out within it.

I look forward to hearing from you at your earliest convenience.

With kind regards

Your sincerely

Julie Ford
Legal Director
Healthcare
Hill Dickinson LLP
Julie.Ford@hilldickinson.com
The Broadgate Tower, 20 Primrose Street, London, EC2A 2EW
TEL: +44 (0)20 7280 9338
FAX: +44 (0)20 7283 1144

<image003.jpg> <image004.jpg>
<image005.jpg>

Hill Dickinson
www.hilldickinson.com

This email and its contents, together with any attachments, are confidential to the sender and the intended recipient(s) and may be covered by legal professional privilege. If you are not the intended recipient of this email and its attachments (if any), you must take no action based upon them, nor must you copy them or show them to anyone. Please contact the sender if you believe you have received this email in error.

Hill Dickinson LLP is a firm of lawyers authorised and regulated by the Solicitors Regulation Authority under registration number 424853. It is a limited liability partnership registered in England and Wales No. OC314079. Its registered office is at No.1 St. Paul's Square, Liverpool L3 9SJ.

<Letter to duncan Lawrence.doc>

Hill Dickinson
www.hilldickinson.com

This email and its contents, together with any attachments, are confidential to the sender and the intended recipient(s) and may be covered by legal professional privilege. If you are not the intended recipient of this email and its attachments (if any), you must take no action based upon them, nor must you copy them or show them to anyone. Please contact the sender if you believe you have received this email in error.

Hill Dickinson LLP is a firm of lawyers authorised and regulated by the Solicitors Regulation Authority under registration number 424853. It is a limited liability partnership registered in England and Wales No. OC314079. Its registered office is at No.1 St. Paul's Square, Liverpool L3 9SJ.

BEFORE HM CORONER FOR WEST LONDON

**INQUEST TOUCHING THE DEATH OF
SOPHIE BENNETT**

**WITNESS STATEMENT OF
DUNCAN LAWRENCE**

1

INQUEST TOUCHING THE DEATH OF

SOPHIE BENNETT

WITNESS STATEMENT OF

DUNCAN LAWRENCE

---

1. My name is Duncan Lawrence. I make this statement in connection with the inquest into the death of Miss Sophie Bennett, who died on 4th May 2016 at Kingston Hospital. Sophie Bennett was a resident of Lancaster Lodge at the time of her death.

2. This statement covers the period of time I was employed or engaged by RPFI between December 2015 and March 2016.

3. This statement reflects my personal recollection and my review of documents including the initial audit I undertook on behalf of RPFI in December 2015 and other documents created during my tenure at RPFI.

Introduction

4. My formal background qualifications are a BA in Education, a Masters in Counselling and a Doctorate in Public Administrator. Since 1981, I have undertaken the following roles of an Educator. This includes being a teacher and lecturer at all levels of education up through teaching doctoral students, as a

2

trainer in health and social care, mental health, education, working with vulnerable young people and their parents/carers, counselling, management and leadership, music therapy, criminal justice and sport.

5.   I have also worked as a consultant in health and social care, mental health, education, working with vulnerable young people and their parents/carers, counselling, management and leadership, music therapy, criminal justice ,sport and as a writer in the field of managing stress and aggressive situations, counselling, management and leadership, diversity and inclusion, childcare. I am currently engaged as a Special Education Needs Lecturer, counselling tutor, in counselling, I am a sports coach and a social care consultant.

6.   I was first engaged as a Consultant in December 2015 by the Board of RPFI to undertake an audit of RPFI concentrating on all three of the Charity's homes (see further comments below). Following completion of the Audit, I was offered the post of clinical lead by Geoff Benton on 24 December 2015 which I took up in January 2016 on a part time basis Following the resignation of Vincent Hill, I also took on the role of Interim Manager at Lancaster Lodge from the week commencing 18 Jan 2016.

7.   A copy of my Audit report can be found at **Exhibit 1.**

Audit of RPFI in December 2015

8.   When I was first approached to undertake the audit, the overall aims of the audit were to assess the 'strengths and weaknesses' of the three operating charity units and make practical recommendations to the Board. I then was asked to present my findings, first to Elly on 23 December 2015 and then to the Board also on 23 December 2015. Elly was very interested as to my views on 'how close'

3

and or 'how far away' each unit was to be able to maintain itself financially, the ability to meet the aims of the charity and the ability to attract appropriate service users. I gave her my opinion, which was that with charity wide integration of training, clinical supervision and Board support that it would take between six-twelve months to meet her aim of a 'healthy and functional 'set of residential units. I said the same thing to the Board and they offered me the post of Clinical Lead on 24 December 2015. I sent copy of credentials (via email) approximately on 22 December 2015 to Elly and the Board. I was initially offered a three-month consultancy contract via email on 24 December 2015. A copy of the emails referred to above can be found at **Exhibit 2.**

9. I met regularly with both Peggy Jhugroo and Elly Jansen (at least 1-2 days per week). Most of my assignments came through Elly and about ¼ came through Peggy.

10. Regarding the Audit, I primarily looked at four areas: the programmes, the atmosphere, the admin/ paperwork systems and I made comments on other areas. With specific regard to Lancaster House, the programme's strengths related to the fact that I saw that The Statement of Purpose has been integrated somewhat into all areas of the programme (although it could be revised to better reflect the full range of this home's actual work while also considering it's 'readability' with service users, staff, volunteers, parents/ carers and referral sources. I also noted at the time that it currently read at that time vastly different than the RPFI (Richmond Psychosocial Foundation International) Philosophy.

11. The charity's philosophy was based upon Elly's 'therapeutic community' approach, where all staff and residents took responsibility for the development of the unit (including cooking, shopping, and gardening) within the ethos of the

4

charity and to assist each other to develop mental and emotional resiliency together while also developing ways to be an active and useful citizen prior to moving onto a more independent living opportunity. Upon my visit in January 2016, there was no apparent evidence that the unit reflected Elly's ethos. In fairness to the unit management at the time, he did not dispute this (and explained his ideas).

12.   Based on my visit to Lancaster Lodge and my discussions with staff only (at that time I had not yet seen any copies of any of the unit staff credentials) I thought the Home manager was a very qualified practitioner as was his clinical lead. From my discussions with Rohit (Clinical Team Lead), Paul (long term bank staff member), and a 'home resident' all appeared to be clear on the 'Therapeutic Community' approach and felt very secure and contained within it.

13.   Vincent, the Home Manager, joined us after finishing a professional meeting with a resident. He clearly detailed his vision for the home's staff and residents and seemed to be consistent with what the staff and resident stated to me earlier.

14.   They had a very positive CQC report (from earlier in the year), one that carefully detailed a happy and productive home. To me, the unit had very much a positive 'home' feel although it has a slightly messy and dated appearance too. Stairways were full of wonderful resident artwork (apparently the house had an open house celebrating resident artwork) and common room was full of music instruments, games and art materials. The 'Resident friendly' garden that provided regular fresh vegetables and opportunities to work with nature was clearly a strength to the unit at that time.

15.   Areas needing improvement from my audit at that time included that the current senior staff morale level was poor, and was very very unsafe for a home that works so hard, especially with diverse service users' needs, hopes and

5

challenges. Staff within the unit felt that they had been 'a victim' of ever changing (charity) organisation CEO and Board Members (this is their words and not the report author's views) and were often short staffed, and were unsure at times 'if they are getting it right'.

16. I noted that when discussing the work of the unit, all of the units' staff faces positively lit up, even the young adult resident that was present (for my audit). Unfortunately most discussions eventually led to feeling that 'external Board events' made work much more harder and impacted morale generally and that staff and Volunteer CPD opportunities regularly passed them by. The staff at my audit visit voiced that several staff had left recently and that they were currently working without a full complement of 'Lancaster trained' staff.

17. I recorded the unit atmosphere during my audit as one where most of the residents were out of the house during my visit and those present seemed happy and relaxed getting on with things in the house. I was left satisfied with the young adult residents that felt confident enough to come into the living room area and join our discussions and engage the staff in discussions of their own. The house structure was very lovely from the outside but the inside décor needed some urgent attention and the common areas such as the lounge, kitchen and dining room were very messy.

18. I assessed the unit's 'admin and paperwork systems' as satisfactory, but commented that they could easily be reviewed to make sure that the current system works well for the benefit of the service users while ensuring that 'best practice' / evidence based practice is evident (in all areas of written work e.g. daily logs, key work reports, linking all activities to resident care plans [including any external practitioners]). Care plans viewed were a bit dated. I also noted that

6

some residents (two) seemed to have stayed much longer that the house target of 18 months to two years before moving onto independent living.

19.   My recommendations from this audit mainly focused on the following areas; I felt that the Lancaster house appeared to be in need of a 'morale boost' (primarily within the senior staff) and that it needed better and more transparent integration into the wider RFPC/ RPFI organisation. I commented that to keep the current situation (at my audit period) as it is would make the home's work more difficult and keep the staff team 'at risk' of gossip, mistakes (including being 'secretive', etc.). It would also maintain a practice of 'working inwards' and not looking to the CEO/Board as a 'resource' and an important Quality Assurance function. I also recommended that the unit consider monthly or fortnightly non-managerial supervision/ coaching for the senior staff. I strongly felt that it was important to keep an 'outside' professional trusted quality assurance and professional development resource in place. I also noted that Lytton House Therapeutic Community and Lancaster House's model of working 'seem very similar'.

20.   Because of this, I felt that they should have regular joint training and monthly 'large team' meetings. Even though Lancaster House has MA level counselling and psychotherapy staff, any 'potential joint work' does not have to include the use of 'jargon' (the Lancaster House Senior staff seemed to used 'jargon' as a way of separating themselves from the charity generally and the charity's wider staff specifically), something that would potentially cause 'a split' and add a potential 'resistance' between those two homes (rather than enhancing the 'shared' ways of working and the measuring of outcomes).

21.   I strongly urged that senior staff took all of their holiday leave entitlement. They all appeared to work very hard, but I noted that a good 'work/life' balance would potentially lead to a more productive staff member. I also suggested that time

7

needed to be given to 'team building/resource valuing' between the current Board and the senior home staff.

22.   Lancaster Lodge staff and residents did not view the Board (during my audit period) as helpful and readily admitted to "...only telling them enough to keep them away...". Finally, I recommended that the latter suggestion could also work across the wider organisation too and could include a Board Member spending a ½ day in each home per month. I additionally recommended to, have a Board Member at any future home/company Teambuilding Sessions (recommend at least one per year).

Lancaster Lodge

23.   The original purpose of Lancaster Lodge was to provide residential accommodation to support young adults with mental distress using a therapeutic community approach, where resident stayed for 1-2 years to build emotional and vocational stability and then move on to more semi-independent accommodation

January 2016

24.   I facilitated all staff (entire charity) in a training/team building event on 7 January 2016. The event was meant to be a fun day for all staff to get to know people from the charity that they would not normally see, an opportunity for all units to share something about their current unit work and for all staff to consider and share their ideas on how the charity could be better integrated and better communicate across the charity. This seemed very well received and a positive day.

8

25.   I was asked by Elly and Peggy to be involved in an investigation at Lancaster Lodge on approx. 15 January 2016 relating to an incident not connected to Sophie that had occurred during the Christmas period. Following this investigation I clarified the protocol (and existing challenges) for handling emergencies such as self-harm across the charity and developed better recording systems (for recording all incidents within the unit).

26.   Vincent Hill met with me as part of the January 2015 Investigation, shared that he had not felt supported by the charity for quite a few years and decided to resign. The unit seemed to be always shorted staffed so the charity was regularly interviewing for residential staff.

27.   The Manager at Lancaster Lodge (Vincent Hill) resigned on 16 January 2018 and on the same day, I was offered the Interim Manager role, alongside my other charity work. As I progressed in my Lancaster Lodge role, the 'cross charity' brief seemed to 'take a back seat. This was partly due to having general staffing shortages, some staff were off with flu and one senior staff with pregnancy-related challenges. At times I was more of an 'on-shift' staff that an interim manager that was trying to facilitate change and development on-the-job. No one within the charity took up the 'charity wide' development brief as I put it down. We asked all senior staff to apply for senior staff post such as team leaders.

28.   At the beginning of January, Lancaster Lodge was staffed by a combination of permanent staff, bank staff and some staff from other part of the charity. Residents had weekly therapy with external counsellors and art students from Roehampton University. They also have some 1-1 and groups facilitated by Rohit as a solo facilitator.

29.   Notice was given to external therapists that their therapy sessions were going to be discontinued before I arrived at Lancaster Lodge but my role was to take over

9

supervision for the various therapists and help the resource to wind down (hence I sent follow up emails to all therapists, arranged to communicate with the university, look at past therapy notes and consider how the work could be integrated/carried on with in the 're-emerging therapeutic community'.

30.   I used to meet regularly with Peggy Jhugroo to discuss various staff dynamics within each unit and develop improvement strategies. We also considered ways to improve the re-occurring charity wide staffing shortages.

31.   During January 2016, the charity asked me to do a charity wide training event and develop a 'company-wide' email/newsletter. As part of informing the staff of the 'developments that were coming', in advance of this charity wide training even we sent out a charity-wide email introducing some of the new thinking (please refer to the charity newsletter attached to this statement at **Exhibit 3).**

32.   When I took over as interim manager of the house, in addition to my audit findings I also (once I was actually in post) initially observed the unit as not having many observable connections to the original 'therapeutic community' ethos (nor could I find any written evidence to this) created by the founder of the charity, Elly Jansen. She regularly admitted to this at our regular weekly meetings and additionally within our numerous email communications post March 2016.

33.   Some residents during this period would sit around the unit all day watching television and those enrolled in college seemed to only attend intermittently. Evidence of healthy eating and fitness were missing throughout the unit, and 'employability development' was not strongly integrated into the unit residents' care plans.

34.   In consultation with Elly and Peggy, I actively attempted to re-write The Statement of Purpose for Lancaster House that focused on improving resident health and

10

well-being generally and this included adding exercise, yoga and dancing to the unit weekly activities. Please refer to **Exhibit 4** in which I have marked in green where the suggested amendments were made to the Statement of Purpose.

35. 'Employability' was not part of the unit programme before (in terms of a high priority of getting the residents to be more independent and learn how to develop skills for employment). After I re wrote the Statement of Purpose, 'Employability' had a higher profile. All of the staff were meant to be involved in taking responsibility for 'Employability'.

36. The use of 'outside counsellors/practitioners' was put on hold. This latter idea was initially suggested by Elly and Peggy, but I too thought that the unit 'would heal quicker' with an internal staff/volunteer focus for a while.

37. The 'new program' attempted to encouraged a better use of therapeutic community house meetings (more in line with the 'Elly Jansen Model', one with resident and staff members that actively planned and evaluated the running of the unit). Residents would be encouraged to take more responsibility for the running of the house

38. Finally, the aim was that the Lancaster Unit staff would be more integrated into the 'wider charity' via monthly charity training/ CPD events and some charity staff (including the Lancaster Unit staff) would be trained/supported to work across the charity.

39. 'Change' is often difficult to most people, even with positive intentions and up through my departure, the new program was rejected and not allowed to even reach one quarter of its potential. Long term staff primarily rejected it (mainly led by 'the deputy manager') and two-three key residents, all who were not making good use of the unit and all who stayed past the time originally allowed/program

11

design. Often new staff saw Rohit as a sort of a 'guru' and refused to give the programme developments a fair chance and seemed in an 'alliance' with him.

40. We assertively sent Rohit, the most senior charity staff member at the time onto an internal 'management training and development programme'. The intention was to re-induct him into the wider charity, to encourage him to make practical recommendations to the wider charity while also giving himself and the Lancaster unit a break from each other. His only instructions were to attend the full programme and to not contact the residents, unfortunately he did not attend the sessions fully and he still made unhelpful and unauthorized contact with the Lancaster unit residents (in person and over the telephone) He called in sick 1-2 days and had some transport problems along the way too If I remember correctly The management initiative with Rohit was completed but he did not get the full benefit (see above). I was not involved, but I later heard that Rohit and the Chaity agreed to part ways, although this was well after I had already left the charity myself.

41. Simultaneously, the charity CEO was getting more involved with the daily work of the unit, something that must have been confusing to the staff, the residents and stakeholders. I recommended in writing that if the CEO was going to continue with her Lancaster Unit involvement, that she temporarily step aside as the charity CEO and to allow another very competent charity senior manager to take over. This idea was also rejected.

February 2016

42. The weeks leading up to the CQC visit were busy and often a period of 'knee jerk' senior management decisions, these did not add to the staff, residents and other stakeholders such as parents/carers, students, social workers etc. gaining

12

confidence in my management initiatives, nor in the CEO, not 'the wider charity' in general and not with the 'Elly Jansen therapeutic community ethos' specifically. We seemed to always be playing 'catch up' with regard to interviewing and training new charity staff, we never (initially during my interim management period) fully apologised to the residents, staff and other stake holders to challenges associated with 'the good intentioned' but poorly rolled out 'new programmes'. No residents left the programme during this period.

43.   We had wrongly assumed that by informing the entire charity staff at the 'charity-wide' training event about the wider charity developments (which included explaining specific initiatives and intentions for the Lancaster unit), that this would be enough for them to explain and 'sell' to the residents of the charity's three units. This never happened and we really misjudged the Lancaster unit reaction.

44.   From my experience, experienced Lancaster House staff were regularly calling in sick, unit documents that could have 'evidenced' Lancaster unit's good work and areas for further development had gone missing, staff did not always take the time to speak to each other properly.

March 2016

45.   We tried to launch the well-being programme, primarily using existing charity staff to role model how the charity could develop and run its own programmes, in line with the therapeutic community ethos. These were poorly attended.

46.   When the CQC inspector arrived unannounced , I felt that their initial observations on that day were 'somewhat accurate'. At the time of the inspection, I was asked questions about the updated Mission Statement and the lack of evidence of the work of the unit for Jan-March 2016. Most of it had 'suddenly' gone missing.

13

47. After the first CQC inspection day, I was not able to attend the next day due to an existing prior arrangement that I could not attend.

48. I sent my apologies via email to Elly and the Board Chair with my suggestions on how the CQC inspection could potentially work in the charity's benefit. I recommended to Elly and the Trustees via email, that we 'should come clean' as a charity and detail the long history (and the implication of) poor communication and lack of trust between the Charity and the Lancaster Lodge Unit. I felt had we done this (or something similar) in a timely way, that perhaps the CQC would have made positive moves toward the charity and given us more time to implement our changes. My ideas were rejected and I received an email the same week stating that due to financial constraints that my service were no longer needed. Please see **Exhibit 5**.

49. I am sure that the 'negativity/new program resistance' atmosphere did not help any of the staff or residents to make best possible use of the new program initiatives, especially without the support of the deputy manager and external counsellors and art therapist/art therapist students.

50. There were two residents in particular that often engaged in 'suicide gestures' while in the unit during this time period but were still allowed to stay on in the unit. This was another example of the unit acting in a manner that was vastly different from the charity's ethos generally and Elly Jansen's 'therapeutic community model' generally.

Account of contacts with deceased

51. Although I met with Sophie on an almost daily basis it was more on the basis of 'getting to know you basis' and as a wellness check. I was not involved in her day-to-day care or therapies.

14

52.   Whilst working at Lancaster Lodge between January to March 2016, I had witnessed personally that Sophie seemed to be making progress by coming out of her room more and engaging more with staff and limited other residents than she previously did prior to January 2016.

53.   I had left Lancaster Lodge prior to any decisions being made about transferring Sophie to a different residential unit.

STATEMENT OF TRUTH

The contents of this statement are true to the best of my knowledge and belief.

Signed

Dated   13.12.18

IN THE WEST LONDON CORONER'S COURT

THE INQUEST TOUCHING THE DEATH OF

MISS SOPHIE BENNETT

EXHIBIT

This is the exhibit marked "DL1" referred to in the witness statement of Duncan Lawrence.

Signed ....

Dated 13.12.18

155292984.1

D.E.Lawrence *(BA-Ed, MA-Counselling, DPA-Public Admin, FinstLM, Registered MBACP and FBACP)*
18-C,Kenthouse Road. London SE26 5LB diversitymanagementicl@btinternet.com/07733130306

Audit Report: Carried out over w/c 14.12.15

Presented by: D. E. Lawrence 18.12.15

The Audit looked the following projects:

1. White House
2. RPFI HQ
3. Lytton House Therapeutic Community
4. Lancaster House

The Main Review and Evaluation areas:

☐ Programme

☐ Atmosphere

☐ Admin/Paperwork Systems

☐ Other Comments

Some Limits to this Audit:

✓ Was not able to personally visit any evening and overnight staffing patterns

✓ Only spent a day with each project.

✓ Have not interviewed Board Members

Discussion Draft Only!

D.E.Lawrence (BA-Ed, MA-Counselling, DPA-Public Admin, FInstLM, Registered MBACP and FBACP)
18-C,Konthouse Road. London SE26 5LB diversitymanagementlcl@btinternet.com/07733130306

White House

Main Review and Evaluation areas:

Programme:

Strengths: The weekend programme has wide and varied 1-1 and group activities for all residents. Programmes were designed to stimulate them personally, and as 'a community'.

Weekend meal preparations, etc. are inclusive celebrations of human diversity and seem to be highlighted during the weekend more and encourage all residents to be involved, regardless of their disability/level of functioning. Weekend staff should be commended.

-Ope, a 'borrowed' Lytton House TC Clinical Team Leader has done very well in her 'acting up' leadership role. She is very competent, hardworking and has clear ideas for staff and programme development (e.g. to remove current roadblocks, while bringing residents and staff along with her).

-All staff appears very nice and friendly.

Areas needing improvement:

-front and back gardens are very untidy and it is clear this area is not a house priority and does not involve 'resident' ownership. It is important to keep positive relationships with the home's local neighbours, while developing a sustainable resident centred garden and nature space.

-Statement of Purpose/Programme description does not actually relate to what the staff and residents are engaging in daily/weekly/monthly (including meal prep/menu selection, expenditures that relate to the programme aims/missions, etc.).

-there is no ethos/ethos areas that this house can say is 'their selling point' and or their area of innovation and or is their area of 'good'- 'great' practices

-Not clear what staff are actually doing with the residents. This is especially concerning since several staff have been in post for 5+ years.

Atmosphere:

-Very respectful atmosphere, but related to my comments above, there was not a 'buzz' from staff being pleased with being great with their work and or joy with working as a team and to the same 'programme page'. I am left confused how they get 'good' CQC reports. This place is very 'sluggish' and appears to be in a 'deep rut'.

Discussion Draft Only!

D.E.Lawrence (BA-Ed, MA-Counselling, DPA-Public Admin, FinstLM, Registered MBACP and FBACP)
18-C,Kenthouse Road. London SE26 5LB diversitymanagementicl@btinternet.com/07733130306

-Does not feel like 'anyone's home' overall... a clear 'institutional tinge' in the air. I know there was recently a fire but there still could be evidence of an 'established home' environment.

Admin/Paperwork Systems:

-No evidence of regular Care Plan reviews

-No evidence of any staff working to Care Plans

-Daily Log entries are not standardized and range from 'poor' to just 'satisfactory'

-No current risk assessments

Other Comments:

-Does not seem to be a sense of urgency to 'get it right' e.g. treating the residents as important, diverse and interesting human beings in their own right.

D.E.Lawrence (BA-Ed, MA-Counselling, DPA-Public Admin, FInstLM, Registered MBACP and FBACP) 18-C,Kenthouse Road London SE26 5LB diversitymanagementlcl@btinternet.com/07733130306

RPFI HQ/HR

Main Review and Evaluation areas:

Programme:

-No apparent 'ethos' or 'way of working' (e.g. that could relate to the company's overall values of teamwork, 'service user centred focus', etc.).

-It appears not much understanding of the work within the homes that they are supposed to serve, nor their service users.

Atmosphere:

-Friendly staff during this audit

-'Total disconnect' from the Homes and their staff and volunteers

Admin/Paperwork Systems:

-See above and no clear evidence of HQ/HR Team being efficient with their time and or being a useful resource to the 'wider company' and or being a resource to staff and volunteers.

Other Comments: Appears that the 'HR Role' has not been developed for a few years.

Discussion Draft Only!

D.E.Lawrence (BA-Ed, MA-Counselling, DPA-Public Admin, FinstLM, Registered MBACP and FBACP) 18-C,Kenthouse Road. London SE26 5LB diversitymanagementlcl@btinternet.com/07733130306

RPFI HQ/HR

Main Review and Evaluation areas:

Programme:

-No apparent 'ethos' or 'way of working' (e.g. that could relate to the company's overall values of teamwork, 'service user centred focus', etc.).

-It appears not much understanding of the work within the homes that they are supposed to serve, nor their service users.

Atmosphere:

-Friendly staff during this audit

-'Total disconnect' from the Homes and their staff and volunteers

Admin/Paperwork Systems:

-See above and no clear evidence of HQ/HR Team being efficient with their time and or being a useful resource to the 'wider company' and or being a resource to staff and volunteers.

Other Comments: Appears that the 'HR Role' has not been developed for a few years.

Discussion Draft Only!

D.E.Lawrence (BA-Ed, MA-Counselling, DPA-Public Admin, FinstLM, Registered MBACP and FBACP)
18-C,Kenthouse Road. London SE26 5LB diversitymanagementld@btinternet.com/07733130306

Lytton House Therapeutic Community

Main Review and Evaluation areas.

Programme:

Strengths: The Statement of Purpose has been integrated into all areas of the 're-imagined' house programme.

-Home manager is very talented and committed to working hard, while delegating opportunities and responsibilities to his staff team (including volunteers). He has several tangible achievements after only six weeks in post.

-Collection of staff and volunteers are exceptional group of people (most with advanced qualifications and great attitudes).

Areas needing improvement:

-Level of 'uncertainty' for the past six months + regarding the home's Ofsted status. The situation has hindered the unit's focus at times (e.g. in terms of setting realistic time scales, setting staff training plan, liaising with social services and developing positive and practical relationships has been held up, etc.).

-Statement of Purpose is only about 90% completed and staff readiness currently at about 70-75% readiness.

Atmosphere:

-Generally a healthy workplace, where all that enter genuinely appear to want to do the best for their future service users.

It is important to note that this progress comes within the backdrop of several home staff being loaned out each week to two other RFPI homes.

In saying this, the staff seems to be gaining invaluable experiences in 'social care' from working within the other homes.

Admin/Paperwork Systems:

-Still very much a work-in-progress area

Discussion Draft Only!

D.E.Lawrence (BA-Ed, MA-Counselling, DPA-Public Admin, FinstLM, Registered MBACP and FBACP)
18-C,Kenthouse Road. London SE26 5LB diversitymanagementlcl@btinternet.com/07733130306

Lancaster House

Main Review and Evaluation areas:

Programme:

<u>Strengths:</u> The Statement of Purpose has been integrated somewhat into all areas of the programme (although it could be revised to better reflect the full range of this home's actual work, while also considering it's 'readability' with service users, staff, volunteers, parents/carers, referral sources, etc. It currently reads vastly different than the RPFI/RCI Philosophy).

-Home manager is a very qualified practitioner as is his clinical lead. From my discussions with Rohit (Clinical Team Lead), Paul (long term bank staff member), and a home resident' all appear to be clear on the TC approach and feel very secure and contained within it.

-Vincent, the Home Manager joined us after finishing a professional meeting with a resident. He clearly detailed (similar to above) his vision for the home's staff and residents and seemed to be consistent with what the staff and resident stated to me earlier.

-Very positive CQC report, one that carefully detailed a happy and productive home.

-Very much as positive 'home' feel although slightly messy and dated appearance. Stairways full of wonderful resident artwork (apparently the house had an open house celebrating resident artwork) and common room full of music instruments, games and art materials.

-'Resident friendly' garden that provides regular fresh vegetables and opportunities to work with nature.

<u>Areas needing improvement:</u>

-The current senior staff morale level is poor, very very unsafe for a home that works so hard, especially with diverse service users needs, hopes and challenges. Staff feels that they have been 'a victim' of ever changing organisation CEO and Board Members (<u>this is their words and not the report author's views</u>) and often are short staffed, are unsure at times 'if they are getting it right', etc..

-When discussing the work, all faces positively light up, even the young adult resident that was present but unfortunately most discussions eventually led to feeling that 'external Board events' make work much more harder and impacts morale generally and that staff and Volunteer CPD opportunities regularly pass them by.

-It was voiced that they have had several staff leave recently and that they are currently working without a full complement of 'Lancaster trained' staff.

Discussion Draft Only!

D.E.Lawrence (BA-Ed, MA-Counselling, DPA-Public Admin, FinstLM, Registered MBACP and FBACP)
18-C,Kenthouse Road. London SE26 5LB diversitymanagementlcl@btinternet.com/07733130306

Atmosphere:

-Most residents were out of the house during my visit and those present seem happy and relaxed getting on with things in the house. I was left satisfied with the young adult residents that felt confident enough to come into the living room area and join our discussions and engage the staff in discussions of their own. The house structure was very lovely from the outside but the inside décor needed some urgent attention and the common areas such as the lounge, kitchen and dining room were very messy.

Admin/Paperwork Systems:

-Satisfactory, but could easily be reviewed to make sure that current system works well for the benefit of the service users while ensuring that 'best practice'/evidence based practice is evident(in all areas of written work e.g. daily logs, key work reports, linking all activities to resident care plans[including any external practitioners] etc.). Care plans viewed were a bit dated.

Other Comments:

-some residents (two) seemed to have stayed much longer that the house target of 18 months to two years before moving onto independent living.

Discussion Draft Only!

D.E.Lawrence *(BA-Ed, MA-Counselling, DPA-Public Admin, FinstLM, Registered MBACP and FBACP)*
18-C,Kenthouse Road. London SE26 5LB diversitymanagementlcl@btinternet.com/07733130306

Recommendations:

1. <u>White House</u> needs a major programme overhaul because the residents are not getting the best that they could get at present.

✓ Need a House Manager prepared to work very hard to make things work in a very timely manager (and a suitable staff team to help the house become an example of great and happy practice).

✓ Statement of Purpose needs a total re-write to be 'fit for purpose'.

✓ Statement of Purpose should be reflected in all areas of the programme delivery.

✓ Should treat residents as if their happiness and consideration really mattered.

✓ Home would be well suited as 'a Therapeutic Community' Model.

Discussion Draft Only!

D.E.Lawrence (BA-Ed, MA-Counselling, DPA-Public Admin, FinstLM, Registered MBACP and FBACP)
18-C,Kenthouse Road. London SE26 5LB diversitymanagementlcl@btinternet.com/07733130306

✓ (related to the above) 'Whole company' staff training/CPD should begin as a matter of urgency.

✓ Develop staff led 'resident health and well-being pampering sessions' (monthly or fortnightly).

✓ Development of volunteer resource potential.

✓ Re-direct returning manager to other useful RFPI work/role. (related to the above) Begin 'company-wide' staff training asap (standardising etc.).

✓ In some cases any 'stuck staff' should be offered 're-induction' and or be assisted to secure new work opportunities outside of RPFI/RFCI.

Discussion Draft Only!

D.E.Lawrence (BA-Ed, MA-Counselling, DPA-Public Admin, FInstLM, Registered MBACP and FBACP)
18-C,Kenthouse Road. London SE26 5LB diversitymanagementlcl@btinternet.com/07733130306

2. <u>HQ/HR</u> activities need to be better linked to the current and future development needs of the homes, future homes, etc..

✓ HQ Staff need to attend an induction at each of the homes (and collect suggestions on how the HQ role could be a better resource).

✓ HQ role might need to become 'virtual' and embedded into each home.

✓ HQ could have a weekly visit schedule to each home in order to carry out their work (staff need not visit HQ) and to have practical linkage with all admin staff within the homes.

✓ This role could benefit from 30 hours of 'in house' company CPD (per year). This would also aid in overall company team building efforts as well.

✓ Does not appear currently to be enough work for full time 'HQ/HR' role, the company should consider redeveloping the role, and

Discussion Draft Only!

D.E.Lawrence (BA-Ed, MA-Counselling, DPA-Public Admin, FinstLM, Registered MBACP and FBACP)
18-C.Kenthouse Road. London SE26 5LB diversitymanagementlcl@btinternet.com/07733130306

to make it say a three-day a week
'integrated' post (in total).

✓ Related to the above, maybe all of the
HQ/HR Team (say next week for example)
can sit together (after visiting the homes and
gathering staff feedback) and review and
revise the HQ/HR role, function, activities,
etc.. *This would however potentially include
making some of their current roles
redundant.*

Discussion Draft Only!

D.E.Lawrence (BA-Ed, MA-Counselling, DPA-Public Admin, FinstLM, Registered MBACP and FBACP)
18-C,Kenthouse Road. London SE26 5LB diversitymanagementlcl@btinternet.com/07733130306

3. <u>Lytton House Therapeutic Community</u> needs to remove any preventable 'areas of uncertainty'.

✓ Consider CQC registration as alternative to Ofsted registration. From speaking with some of the house staff and the home manager, the majority of the current team have their main experiences from working with adults and or young adults. Note: <u>Authors of any new registration application would need at least one full week of 'protected time' to complete the application to a good standard.</u>

✓ (related to the above) Begin 'company-wide' staff training asap (standardising etc.). In some cases any 'stuck staff' should be offered 're-induction' and or be assisted to secure new work opportunities outside of RPFI/RFCI.

D.E.Lawrence (BA-Ed, MA-Counselling, DPA-Public Admin, FinstLM, Registered MBACP and FBACP)
18-C,Kenthouse Road. London SE26 5LB diversitymanagementlcl@btinternet.com/07733130306

4. <u>**Lancaster House**</u> appear to be in need of a 'morale boost' (primarily within the senior staff) and better , more transparent integration into the wider RFPC/RFCI organisation.

   ✓ Keeping the current situation as it is will make home's work more difficult and keep the staff team 'at risk' of gossip, mistakes(including being 'secretive',etc), staff 'working inwards' and not looking to the CEO/Board as a 'resource' and an important Quality Assurance function.

   ✓ Consider monthly or fortnightly non managerial supervision/coaching for the senior staff. Important to keep an 'outside' professional trusted quality assurance and professional development resource in place.

   ✓ Lytton House TC and Lancaster House's model of working seem very similar. They should have regular joint training and monthly 'large team' meeting. Note: even though Lancaster House has MA level

Discussion Draft Only!

D.E.Lawrence (BA-Ed, MA-Counselling, DPA-Public Admin, FinstLM, Registered MBACP and FBACP)
18-C,Kenthouse Road. London SE26 5LB diversitymanagementlcl@btinternet.com/07733130306

counselling and psychotherapy staff, the
joint work does not have to include the use
of 'jargon', something that would potentially
cause 'a split' and a potential 'resistance'
between those two homes (rather than
enhancing the 'shared' ways of working and
the measuring of outcomes).

✓ Ensure that senior staff takes all of their
holiday leave entitlement. They all appear to
work very hard, but a good 'work/life'
balance potentially leads to a more
productive staff member.

✓ Time needs to be given to 'team
building/resource valuing' between the
current board and the senior home staff.
Lancaster Lodge staff and residents do not
view the board as helpful and readily admit
to "…only telling them enough to keep them
away…"

This suggestion would work across the
wider organization too and could include a
Board Member spending a ½ day in each

D.E.Lawrence (BA-Ed, MA-Counselling, DPA-Public Admin, FinstLM, Registered MBACP and FBACP)
18-C,Kenthouse Road. London SE26 5LB diversitymanagementicl@btinternet.com/07733130306

home per month. Additionally, have a Board
Member at any future home/company
Teambuilding Sessions (recommend at least
one per year).

Discussion Draft Only!

IN THE WEST LONDON CORONER'S COURT

THE INQUEST TOUCHING THE DEATH OF

MISS SOPHIE BENNETT

EXHIBIT

This is the exhibit marked "DL3" referred to in the witness statement of Duncan Lawrence.

Signed ... *N.E.Y*

Dated ... 13.12.18

Kate Fawell-Comley

From:	Eric Lawrence <diversitymanagementlcl@btinternet.com>
Sent:	01 September 2018 05:53
To:	Kate Fawell-Comley; Julie Ford
Subject:	Fwd: DRAFT LETTER FOR DUNCAN
Attachments:	COL job desriptoion June 2013 EJ.doc; ATT00001.htm

CAUTION EXTERNAL EMAIL: This message originated outside the organisation. Do not click links or open attachments unless you recognise the sender and know the content is safe.

D.E.Lawrence:
Diversity, Equality, Inclusion and Sport
Specialist/Management and Team Coach.

Please think of the environment - do you really need to print this email or its attachments?

Sent from my iPhone

Begin forwarded message:

From: Geoff Benton <bentongeoff@gmail.com>
Date: 24 December 2015 at 13:23:35 GMT
To: Duncan Lawrence <diversitymanagementlcl@btinternet.com>, Elly Jansen <elly.jansen@rpfi.org>, Elly Jansen <ellywjansen@hotmail.com>
Subject: Fwd: DRAFT LETTER FOR DUNCAN

Dear Duncan,

Having carefully weighed up the many factors surrounding the building up of both RPFI and RCI,
We have concluded that you might make an important contribution to our work.

Therefore would like to offer you a consultancy for 3 months with a review in March which could

1

lead to a more permanent role in our charities.

The new board and Peggy, our co-ordinator, have been in place less than 6 months
and we are in the middle of reviewing and renewing many aspects of the work and
the workers. So, this is a good time to come in and take part in this mission.

We have explained our financial difficulties and we would hope that you can accept the compromise we offered at £125 per day for a 50% working week, ie. 20
hour per week. .

In order to avoid an impression that you have taken over half of Peggy's job, we would like to use the profesional term "Clinical and Operational Lead". Our job description is for a full -time person, which we are no longer looking for but the attached JD, will indicate the main areas of the post.With a healthy staff team, monitoring will be less nessasary than training and "feeding".

The supervision of Peggy is carried out by Elly Jansen on behalf of the board and,
whilst you would be accountable to Peggy, it is likely that the three of you would need to meet regularly to discuss management issues.

I look forward to hearing from you and to a much enhanced senior team, which will bring fruition to our work with residents and harmony to the staff!

Please be kind enough to copy in Elly to your response .

Have a great break.

Geoff Benton

On Behalf Of The Boards

IN THE WEST LONDON CORONER'S COURT

THE INQUEST TOUCHING THE DEATH OF

MISS SOPHIE BENNETT

E X H I B I T

This is the exhibit marked "DL2" referred to in the witness statement of Duncan Lawrence.

Signed ....

Dated ....

185202084.1

Richmond Psychosocial Foundation International
"Quality support to transform lives"

February 2016

Greetings to us all,

RPFI/RCI as a Charity has on-going continuing commitment to all residents and staff *Health and Well-Being* (within all of its Therapeutic Communities).

The RPFI/RCI Theme for this coming Spring 2016 is 'Transformation'

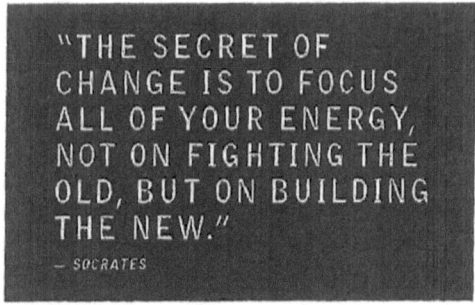

"THE SECRET OF CHANGE IS TO FOCUS ALL OF YOUR ENERGY, NOT ON FIGHTING THE OLD, BUT ON BUILDING THE NEW."
— SOCRATES

As part of this Spring 2016 theme, could all staff and residents consider the following:

1. We encourage the staff and residents to participate and enjoy the Well-Being Sessions that begin next week (as part of the Enhanced TC programmes).
2. No smoking of any kind on RPFI/RCI property from 15.3.16
3. Try to purchase non toxic cleaning products and please also consider 'side effects' of any sprays, etc used within the houses.
4. Staff and volunteers should aim to be engaging in TC related activities 90% of their shifts (minimal staff office time). Please refer to your manager or supervisor if you need support in doing so.
5. Incident Reports to be filed no later than 8 hours from any incidents.
6. All incidents of self harm to be recorded on incident report forms and reported to service managers.
7. The next charity wide training event will be Thursday 24th March (Location TBC). *The theme*

<u>will be 'Transforming our 'TC'; Improving our Health and Well-Being!</u>

8. All key work sessions to be written up within the same shift that they occur.

IN THE WEST LONDON CORONER'S COURT

THE INQUEST TOUCHING THE DEATH OF

MISS SOPHIE BENNETT

EXHIBIT

This is the exhibit marked "DL4" referred to in the witness statement of Duncan Lawrence.

Signed ...D.4.V...

Dated ...13.12.18...

155292984.1

Richmond Psychosocial Foundation International

"Maximising Recovery and Potential within a Therapeutic Community Setting"
STATEMENT OF PURPOSE

Lancaster Lodge
21 Lancaster Park,
Richmond
London
TW10 6AB
Telephone: 020 8940 1052
E-mail: lancaster.lodge@rpfi.org

The main factors for enhanced self management and resiliency are the service users initial, continued ability and willingness take 'good enough' responsibility for their individual contract and demonstrate 'good enough' motivation to try to benefit from and to contribute to a therapeutic group-living experience(alongside their other 'partnership' relationships).

ISSUED IN ACCORDANCE WITH THE NATIONAL MINIMUM STANDARDS FOR
CARE HOMES REGULATIONS (18 – 65) 2003, SCHEDULE 1, REGULATION 4

Statement of Purpose - NMS Standard 1 (Regulations 4 and 5)

1

D.Eric Lawrence

CONTENTS

Section number	TITLE	
1	Introduction	
2	Service model and Lancaster Lodge Aims	
3	Facilities and Services	
4	Diverse Therapeutic Activities & Supervision	
5	Admission Criteria	
6	Background of RFPI	
7	Registered Provider	
8	Qualifications and Experience of Senior Management	
9	Qualifications and Experience of Staff Team	
10	Equal Opportunities, Diversity and Inclusion	
11	Supervision, Training and Development	
12	Organisational Structure	
13	Health Care	
14	Medication	
15	Social contact	
16	Review of Placement Plan (Service User Plan)	
17	Education and training	
18	Transition to adulthood	
19	Safeguarding	
20	Unauthorised absences	
21	Privacy & Dignity	
22	Complaints	
23	Fire Precautions	
24	Further Information	

2

1. Introduction

Growing and changing within today's society can be challenging and confusing at times to most of us. A community resource looking to be useful must be holistic and deal with whole person (mind, body and spirit), support better active community citizenship, create employability, and set the stage for better self management, resilience and fulfillment. Lancaster Lodge is such a community resource.

It is within this premise that Lancaster Lodge, a 'charity-within-the community', develops important and diverse partnerships with potential residents and significant other stakeholders such family, friends, referral sources and the valuable 'therapeutic community ' framework.

One of the important and central relationships is the partnership between the potential service user, the referral source and the Lancaster Lodge Therapeutic Community. Lancaster Lodge would never wish to see itself as more important than the service users.

These Lancaster Lodge key partnerships are able to support and encourage significant service user changes while keeping the service user as the central stakeholder, working alongside a dedicated and committed staff team, community residents, professionals from within and outside of the organisation and local community opportunities.

Range of needs and personal challenges catered for at Lancaster Lodge Community

Low self esteem and self image, identity challenges, limited emotional competency and limited self management(usually the 'situations' that cause 'vulnerability '[self described by potential service users and significant others]) that can be related to and complicated by Personality Disorders, Psychosis, Mood disorders, Clinical depression, PTSD, Eating disorders, OCD, Phobias, Anxiety disorders, Dual Diagnosis, Forensic clients etc.

2. Service model

Lancaster Lodge's service model for therapeutic services is a modern integrated therapeutic community.

The Richmond Psychosocial Foundation International (RPFI), a Charity founded by Ms Elly Jansen, OBE, is dedicated to the development of soundly run therapeutic and enabling residential services and outreach support facilities for individuals and families faced with a variety of mental health challenges.

Within this therapeutic community, one that celebrates diversity and inclusion aims to be a place of healing, personal and professional growth/development, opportunity to develop better self management, develop resiliency , become more employable and able to consider, explore and engage in positive and practical relationships.

The integrative therapeutic community is underpinned by using person centred approaches, psycho-dynamic and analytical theories(TA, CBT, etc.), modern feminist thinking, modern advances in health and well being(nutritional awareness, exercise/stretch, yoga, mindfulness, massage, pedicures, manicures, etc), art ,drama and music programmes, men and women's groups, etc..

We use a wide range of interventions and opportunities such as one-to-one key working, counselling, coaching ,mentoring and individualised personal workshops, etc..

Small and large group sessions are used within the range of well-being activities, art/music/drama, group therapy and the very important range of the 'therapeutic community' daily living small and large group relations and activities.

We offer placements to suit the needs of each individual but on average the length of stay is between 15-18 months; self-funders on a recovery programme may stay up to 6 months.

3. Overall Aim of Lancaster Lodge

To provide residential services for service users where

- recovery and rehabilitation leading to enhanced self management 'in-the-community' is optimised (length of stay will depend on service users' needs and continued willingness to their own programme)
- A holistic experience is created within an accepting and inclusive environment which enables service users to achieve their potential by means of recovery planning, social inclusion, education, health promotion and preparation for employment and independent-living skills
- diverse and inclusive day services are provided with service users who are able to engage and support their recovery journey.
- Support healthy lifestyle which will include avoiding foods with 'E' numbers, encouraging five-a-day plates, morning exercise and stretching sessions, attending reiki sessions, meditation, mindfulness session, walks, etc..

We will achieve this by:

- Expecting and supporting the service users to make the best use of Lancaster Lodge Therapeutic Community
- Providing a practical residential 'community' environment which is suited to healing, learning, growth and development.
- Developing and deliver high quality and inclusive programmes that reflect the needs of service users which are regularly reviewed and evaluated (by service users and the significant stakeholders). Service users design their own care plan in conjunction with the Service Manager as they begin to transition into Lancaster Lodge (and then relocate into the community).
- Ensuring, through the provision of a safe and secure environment, that service users are afforded the opportunity to build or rebuild their sense of worth and confidence in their own coping and problem solving skills.
- Promoting service users' rights and ensuring that their views are represented.
- Providing regular inclusive stimulation and opportunity through both internal and external programmes which are tailored to meet individual and therapeutic community needs.
- Carrying out effective care planning and reviews and promoting partnerships and increased employability with clinical commissioning groups, local authorities and other local community focused relationships.
- Having an outcome focused approach which sets achievable and practical goals with the individual service users.

3. Facilities and Services

Lancaster Lodge is a large detached property set in an attractive residential area. Service users are encouraged to integrate with the wider community; local, recreational and cultural facilities are actively utilised.

The house is spacious with pleasant communal rooms and comfortably furnished bedrooms. The sizeable kitchen is well-equipped and the dining area provides a homely atmosphere and has ample space for service users and staff to eat together.

The well-established rear garden provides for outdoor recreation, al fresco dining and includes a small kitchen garden. We grow as much fresh produce as possible to promote health and well-being as well as providing opportunities to enjoy gardening.

There are ten single bedrooms on three floors. Each room has its own washbasin and is well-furnished to make residents feel welcome as well as meeting Care Standards. One ground floor en suite room is designed to meet the needs of a resident with mobility needs.

4

In summary, the house is comfortable, spacious and offers non-institutional facilities for shared and personal space. It is decorated and furnished to a high standard and reflects a homely and welcoming environment.

4. Diverse Therapeutic Community Activities and Personal Support / Supervision

Service users' specific therapeutic community needs are identified and catered for within their overall care package. They are invited to express their own interests and preferences whilst being also encouraged - but not forced - to participate in interest groups, in social activities and in leisure interests both within and outside the house.

Lancaster Lodge offers a range of services and group activities that include:

- Weekly groups with social, psychological and educational focus(tba)
- Weekly community meetings (chaired by residents)
- Daily check in's/out's (chaired by residents)
- Walking
- Well-Being Activities (massage, pedicures, manicures, exercise, stretch, relaxation sessions, etc.)
- Employability activities
- Gardening (Community Project / Capitol Garden Project)
- Alternative Therapies including Music, Art, Sand tray, Drama
- Catering and Cooking
- Leisure Activities (Current Affairs/Music Appreciation groups / Jewellery Making)
- Volunteering in the Community
- Preparation for Employment
- Individual therapies
- Fortnightly Men's / Women's groups
- Weekly key working sessions
- Mindfulness
- Other community interventions and opportunities designed with the service user as central.

Personal Therapy Opportunities

Residents can use RPFI/RCI qualified 'in-house' therapist for 1-1 and group support.
Additionally if service users need and or wish to have outside therapist, LL staff will assist them along with their referral source to secure such an outside therapist.

Please note, the Lancaster Lodge does not pay for this cost.

Typical Week at Lancaster Lodge looks something like:

Monday-Friday
6:30* Well Being Activities (meditation, exercise, yoga, etc)
*7am wake ups/community breakfast prep/Light House Clean
*8am Community Breakfast
*Breakfast Check in

*10am-4pm Community Positive Employability and Personal Development Space (outside of the house)

This would include attending training, college, university, volunteering, attending church, temple, mosque ,museum trips, job interviews, gp visits, visiting therapist, part-time job,etc..

*4-6pm Keywork session(tba)/Community Dinner shop-Prep/House Light Clean

*6pm Community Dinner
*Community Dinner Check in
*7pm Evening Meeting e.g. Community Meeting(tba),Well Being Sessions, walks, pub visit,cinema,etc..

*8-10pm Unit Clean up

Additional Highlights:
- Annual house holiday
- House Open House to showcase resident art and music.
- TC led competitions

Participation by service users:

Our ethos at Lancaster Lodge is that all service users will be encouraged and empowered to participate fully and have their say in the community and in its meetings. Service users are therefore involved and consulted on all areas involved with the running of Lancaster Lodge.

A clear structure of community meetings provides a forum where service users can share their ideas and thoughts (including any complaints or concerns) about the day to day running of the service. This commitment to inclusiveness and participation and engaging in the social dialogue of the group/expectations of the local community (where Lancaster Lodge is and the community that the service users will relocate to upon discharge), which is both supportive and challenging, and which occurs 'informally', with in 'groups' and within 'key stakeholder relationships', all key elements in the recovery and therapeutic process.

Self Medication: it is our aim to get all service users on a 'self-medicated basis' as soon as they are able. Some are able to 'self medicate' straight away because they have been successfully doing this prior to their Lancaster Lodge admission. Positive risk assessments occur on a 24/7 basis to ensure safe dispensing of medication and that support is given to promote medication independence at the earliest point possible.

5. Admission Criteria

Serious consideration is given, during the initial process of exchanging information, to our ability to meet the needs of a particular service user. RPFI offers a unique level of commitment to the service user and we believe that, if we make an informed decision to work with a particular service user, we have a responsibility to honour our commitment, as long as it is deemed by all involved to be in the individual's best interests.

6

All admissions are determined by a pre-admission interview, risk assessment and planning process, which includes taking into account the composition of the existing group of service users. The initial referral is followed by several interviews and visits, which include an individual assessment of needs and a corresponding care plan. Referrals from prospective clients or concerned family members are welcome but will need to be supported subsequently by an appropriate professional.

The pre-admission programme may include the Service Manager, or Senior Clinical Support Worker, or Clinical Lead visiting the prospective client and/or a day visit is arranged for the person to meet the staff and others at Lancaster Lodge. Family and friends are also encouraged to visit the House. A copy of the Residents Handbook is given to the person or relatives, and staff can respond to any further queries.

Once the decision to come to Lancaster Lodge is agreed and the service user arrives, there is a six-week trial period, after which a review takes place with all involved in the placement. If confirmed, an initial agreement is reached as to probable length of stay.

We do not discriminate on the grounds of race, culture ethnic origin, sexual orientation, cultural, or religious beliefs.

Careful consideration is given especially concerning any service user whose history includes the following areas of concern:

- History of non compliance in their own previous Care Plans, etc.
- History of Racism, sexism, islamaphobia, intolerance and bullying/harassment
- History of fire raising,
- Sexually harmful behaviour,
- Self-Harm/Injury
- Active suicidal ideation,
- Dual diagnosis with active substance misuse and no motivation for rehabilitation,
- Severe learning disabilities,
- High levels of need for nursing or physical care.
- Significant history of physical violence

Period of Notice:

RPFI and service users (or their funders) need to give 4 weeks' notice of their decision to terminate their stay at Lancaster Lodge or pay in lieu of notice. Should a service user be hospitalised, his or her place will be kept for 4 weeks but if it is clear that a return is not possible, the 4 weeks' notice will apply nevertheless.

6. Background of RPFI

The Richmond Psychosocial Foundation International (RPFI), a Charity founded by Ms Elly Jansen, OBE, is dedicated to the development of soundly run therapeutic and enabling residential services and outreach support facilities for individuals and families faced with a variety of mental health challenges.

RPFI currently operates The White House, a home in Twickenham for adults with learning disabilities; 89 Heathfield North which offers supported living for those with mild learning disabilities; Lytton House in Wandsworth, as a Registered Care Home with Ofsted for young people aged 13-17 (18th birthday) who have complex needs; Lancaster Lodge in Richmond, as a therapeutic community for adults aged 17-65 with mental health issues and which can provide a move-on placement for those at Lytton House when they reach the age of 18 and have a diagnosed mental health condition and Lexham House in Kensington and Chelsea for adults aged 18-65 with substance misuse/dual diagnosis and/or mild learning disabilities. RPFI has extensive links with its international associates, which have developed through the work of Elly Jansen based on the model she initiated within the Richmond Fellowship which she founded in 1959. There is an International Development Officer who is co-ordinating RPFI's work abroad.

7. Registered Provider

RPFI registered on 25th April 2006 as a Charitable Company Limited by Guarantee (Company number: 579508, Charity number: 116206). The address is:

Clyde House, 109 Strawberry Vale, Twickenham, TW1 4SJ.

is the CQC registered manager at Lancaster Lodge

8. Qualifications and Experience of the Lancaster Lodge

9.   Qualities and Experience of the Staff Team

Overview:

The responsibility for the management of the Care Home lies with the Registered Service Manager, who ensures that sufficient staff with appropriate experience are scheduled so that 24-hour cover is provided. The needs of the service users at the home are paramount and RPFI allocates staff to a particular home to enable those needs to be met effectively and consistently. Normal staffing levels may be enhanced by the individual needs of the service users, based on assessment of risk.

Staff are recruited to ensure a broad range of age, experience, skills and background within the overall staff team. Some of the staff are graduates from a range of relevant fields (Psychology, psychotherapy, social care, sociology, counselling, social work) and some are, in addition, pursuing study at undergraduate and post graduate levels.

All members of the support worker team are currently enrolled in relevant training courses. The minimum staffing ratio is two at any time during the day, regardless of the level of occupancy. This will be continuously risk assessed and will be increased according to need. There will be additional staffing ratios provided for periods of time to cover critical incidents as they occur, as deemed necessary to provide safe care.

One staff member will be in the home each night between 10pm and 8 am.

RPFI provides an on-call system to which staff has access 24 hours 7 days a week.

RPFI promotes diversity and fully supports staff applications from all ethnic and minority groups. We endeavour to have a staff team from differing ethnic and cultural backgrounds in order to provide positive role models for all clients.

Our therapeutic community input is carried out by:-

· Support staff , those with diverse skills, interest and 'Champion' roles within Lancaster Lodge

* Duncan Lawrence leads on a clinical interventions and clinical supervision. Additionally he provides management support and leadership mentoring to all senior staff.

* There are a variety of Volunteers that support the community in the areas of art, music,drama,sport,community support work,befriending,etc.

* Lancaster Lodge has built up close liaisons with Roehampton University to take 2nd/3rd year students on placement from their Art Therapy MA programme, their Psychology and Psychotherapy MA programmes as well as taking students who are in their 3rd and final year of their doctorate Counselling Psychology course as well as the Institute of Arts in Therapy programmes. They attend Roehampton's supervisor placement days and CPD programmes.

8

The students are supervised by the registered manager on a fortnightly basis and monthly by the university supervisor. As of October 2013 there are a 2nd and 3rd year students on their MA Art Therapy course and two students in the 3rd year of their doctorate Counselling Psychologists course who are on placement at Lancaster Lodge. Students on this programme are supervised fortnightly by the Service Manager and by the Clinical Lead on a 5-7 weekly basis.

10. Equal Opportunities,Diversity and Inclusion

RPFI recognises that by encouraging and managing diversity and inclusiveness in our work force, we can more effectively meet the objectives of the organisation and therefore meet the needs of our service users.

RPFI promotes employment practices designed to eliminate discrimination and to ensure adherence to legislations and appropriate Codes of Practice.

The aim of RPFI's Equal Opportunities Policy is:-

- To ensure that no job application or employee receives less favourable treatment on the grounds of sex, race, colour, religion, disability, ethnic or national origins, sexual orientation or social class.
- To ensure that no job applicant or employee is disadvantaged by setting conditions or requirements which cannot be justified.

The Policy itself is contained within the RPFI Staff handbook that is available in each house; copies are available upon request.

Service users are encouraged and supported in attending appropriate services and celebrating any festivals,events, which relate to their individual religious and cultural beliefs. At RPFI we aim to ensure that positive arrangements are made to help the client observe and preserve their racial, religious, cultural, as well as their linguistic identity and heritage.

11. Supervision, Training and Development

Training Overview

All staff undertake an intensive induction programme which prepares staff to meet the needs of the home and the changing needs of each individual service user. This is signed off on satisfactory completion. Only then is a staff member placed on the rota.

The training and development needs of staff are reviewed monthly in supervision, and annually in appraisals. It is an expectation of all staff and their respective line manager that they will, in preparation for supervision and appraisal, actively seek to identify training and development needs.

Training to be undertaken by support workers is highlighted on each worker's individual supervision notes which are kept at the house. Within this, RPFI provides, and requires all support staff to attend training on Safeguarding Vulnerable Adults, Safeguarding Children and Young People, Equality and Diversity, basic first aid, health and safety, fire safety awareness, infection control, control and dispensing of medication, moving and handling, food hygiene. Staff at Lancaster Lodge also attend an in-house service culture training developed by the Service Manager. New training on areas such as breakaway & de-escalation took place in July 2013.

RPFI has, and is further developing, its on-going in-house training which includes confidentiality, data protection, Disability Discrimination Act, Crisis Prevention, stress management, HIV/Aids, substance abuse, report writing and record keeping, working in teams, Human Rights Act which addresses privacy and dignity and other areas of good practice as relevant.

Supervision and Appraisal

Staff are supervised at least once per month. However, there is opportunity for additional supervision as and when requested by staff. Team meetings, which also serve as an additional form of group supervision, are held once a week. Staff also have access to regular 'staff sensitivity peer supervision' and external group supervision.

All staff complete a 6 month probationary period during which they are assessed as to their suitability and capability. Each staff member has an individual training and development plan and is supported to develop the necessary expertise in working within a therapeutic ethos.

12.Organisation Structure

RPFI has a Board of Trustees who between them possess the expertise and skills relevant to its task. It has a small H.O. team who work in close proximity professionally and geographically to the Staff of the Care Homes.

13. Health Care

Our in-house assessment and care plan frameworks are underpinned by the National Minimum Care Standards of which the service user is the central focus

Each service user is registered with a local General Practitioner, a dentist, and an optician. RPFI's view of health care extends well beyond these very basic needs and service users are encouraged to think seriously about their health in a holistic way, paying attention to the quality of their diet, their daily routine and their physical and emotional well-being.

Psychological and physical well-being are seen as complementary to one another. Therefore the service user will also be advised and educated/challenged in respect of areas identified in their individual care plan, as well as being encouraged to assess their own behaviours and risks if relevant, such as substance and alcohol abuse, smoking, anti-social offending or interpersonally harmful behaviours.

14. Medication

Service users at Lancaster Lodge are encouraged and helped to manage their own medication following a risk assessment undertaken with their care team. Service users who are able to self-administer their own medication are empowered to do so by the community. We provide a lockable cabinet in every room so that service users who are assessed as able to self-administer are also assured that their medication is not accessible to others.

For service users who are not able to manage their own medication, staff will follow a clear process. We provide training for all staff in the control and the administering of medication, which entails following a clear policy and procedure.

15. Social contact

Family and social contacts are promoted by the home as social support structures are recognised as part of recovery planning. We encourage planning of family and social contacts as appropriate, having regard to the individual's therapeutic programme and the boundaries and structure of the house.

All visiting arrangements will be considered and are made with due attention to Safeguarding.

Family members may meet with the service user in their own personal living space (bedroom) provided this accords with the individual's wishes.

Service users may choose to meet non-family visitors either in a communal area of the house, in the garden or at a suitable venue outside Lancaster Lodge.

The restrictions on visiting include the need for visits to end visiting finishes by 10 pm and to note that the house is unable to provide overnight accommodation for visitors.

16. Review of Placement Plans

RPFI abides by the statutory review process and actively encourages each individual to participate in their review and contribute to the information gathering process. In addition to the statutory review, we also review informally through, our supervision, consultation and management and team meetings.

RPFI has developed Assessment, Care Plan and Review Report formats which are consistent with national documentation.

Specifically, during the initial six-week trial period following admission, the team will identify any changes to the support plan that are needed. Once a period of placement has been determined and agreed, a more comprehensive care plan is produced in agreement with the service user. This is then reviewed by support staff at least monthly to ensure that the plan is up to date and any necessary amendments are made. A six monthly professional review is held and a report produced and agreed by all parties attending. If circumstances should change and/or the service user requires an urgent review this will take place.

17. Education and training

Although all of the service users in Lancaster Lodge are beyond the age of compulsory education, we encourage participation in further learning and educational activities. We will support our service users in attending suitable local college programmes, relevant training, work experience or paid work. We will provide a designated work space within each bedroom for reading, home study etc. Our staff have a diverse range of skills and qualifications and will support and engage with the service user's learning as much as possible.

18. Transition to adulthood

We are aware that such areas as legislation, individual rights, access to services, safeguarding issues etc. straddle both Children's and Adult services. RPFI will ensure that all statutory requirements are met in relation to this transitional period and will support and help these young adults to understand and negotiate these issues in this potentially confusing time.

19. Safeguarding

The age range (17-55) and vulnerability of our client group necessitates that staff understand policy and procedures across Children's and Adult services. Staff are trained in both areas, embedded in practice through supervision and continuous professional development. RPFI operates within the relevant safeguarding guidelines of the particular local authority and complies with London's safeguarding policy and procedures.

20. Unauthorised absence

RPFI always takes its responsibilities seriously and will not readily call upon others to take over these responsibilities or to 'sort things out' on its behalf. For these reasons the involvement of the Police in any incidents requiring serious intervention are always to be seen as a 'last resort'. However, if incidents do occur where the Police need to be involved they will be called. We will always comply with statutory and good practice guidelines.

In the instance of unauthorised absence, action will be taken as per our policies and procedures. These will reflect the different levels of police involvement determined by the age of the service users as well as the particular details of the absence.

Unacceptability of bullying and harassment (previously anti-bullying)

RPFI recognises that bullying or harassment can occur but sees it as unacceptable and not tolerated in any form. To reduce the occurrence and impact on both residents and staff, training is provided within its equality and diversity training. RPFI has a policy and procedure which is applied as required.

21. Privacy and Dignity

The privacy and dignity of service users is considered to be of paramount importance. We recognise that moving into residential care can be unsettling and a period of adjustment to group living is needed. Staff are expected to abide by these guidelines which form part of their induction and on-going training and are discussed during supervision and appraisals.

It is essential that staff treat all service users as individuals and that they respect their needs, choices and wishes – which must be recorded in their care plan. Staff are expected to follow the care plan at all times.

- All staff undertake training relevant to privacy and dignity (see section 11 above)

- Service users can see their doctor in private at Lancaster Lodge (if unable to attend their Health Care Practise), or at the GP surgery.

- All service users are allocated a key worker.

- All service users have their own key to their room.

- All rooms are fully furnished, but in order to make the surroundings more personal service users participate in the selection of colour schemes of their bedroom and communal areas and are encouraged to bring some favourite items or to select or obtain them on arrival at the Lodge.

22. Complaints

The staff team ensures that service users can enjoy their time at Lancaster Lodge and receive the highest standards of care. Should a service user feel unhappy about any aspect of the services we want to hear about it as soon as possible so we can remedy the situation to the service user's satisfaction in the shortest possible time in accordance with our Complaints Policy. For every complaint we will endeavour to:

- provide a simple, clear and accessible Complaints Policy and corresponding procedures to be followed;
- deal sympathetically and sensitively with the concerns voiced, whilst maintaining the service user's dignity and the sense that they have a right to complain;
- take seriously and respond promptly to any service user complaints
- try to resolve the complaint as quickly as possible
- treat all complaints confidentially, fairly and equally.
- ensure that all service users have information with our appeals procedure
- General complaints can be raised and resolved in the community meetings. All complaints are reviewed regularly by the team and the manager as appropriate and corrective actions are taken where possible and communicated back to residents. A record is kept of all complaints and is available to inspectors.

23. Fire Precautions

The Registered Manager has full responsibility for the implementation of all necessary health and safety legislation at Lancaster Lodge. All staff are trained and undertake regular statutory fire drills e.g. six times per year (minimum); at least one of these will be during night time hours. On arrival, as part of their welcome and all round introductions, service users are made aware of the fire safety procedures.

In terms of fire safety the following procedures are in place:-

- All staff, as part of their induction in the house, acquaint themselves with the fire escape routes and the location of fire safety equipment.
- All staff are subject to mandatory fire training where they learn to operate extinguishers and on which fires they should be used.

If a fire occurs the following procedures are both taught and are on display in the property:-

12

Call the Fire Brigade.

- Instruct staff and service users to proceed to the assembly point. Do not run and do not stop to collect personal belongings etc. Close doors as you leave the rooms.

- If any of our staff or service users are disabled, able-bodied colleagues will assist their exit from the building.

- If an injured or disabled person cannot be evacuated, he/she should be placed in a safe area, e.g. stair head beyond fire safety door and a volunteer should stay with him/her. More detailed instructions are provided for staff.

- Proceed to the assembly point.

- Await instruction to return to the building from the assembly area.

- This instruction may come from either:

      a) The Fire Service Officer in charge of the incident
      b) The Senior staff member on duty
      c) The Fire Precautions Officer

Our Health and Safety Policy, Procedure and Guidance document is available upon request.

24. Further Information

This Statement of Purpose gives an outline of our work. Those who are considering placing an individual with us are welcome to make an appointment to visit. Further written information is available by mail or on our website (www.rpfi.org).. For re ⌐Directly opposite Lancaster Lodge, ⌐ eferred to in the body of the text please contact us at: at safe distance away from the house at No 31 Lancaster Park

Registered Provider

RPFI   Head Office

Clyde House,   Lancaster Lodge,

109 Strawberry Vale,   21 Lancaster Park,

Twickenham, TW1 4SJ   Richmond, TW10 6AB

Tel: 020 8744-1330   Tel: 020 8940-1052

Email: info@rpfi.org   Email:

IN THE WEST LONDON CORONER'S COURT

THE INQUEST TOUCHING THE DEATH OF

MISS SOPHIE BENNETT

EXHIBIT

This is the exhibit marked "DL5" referred to in the witness statement of Duncan Lawrence.

Signed ....

Dated ....

Kate Fawell-Comley

From:	Eric Lawrence <diversitymanagementlcl@btinternet.com>
Sent:	01 September 2018 05:56
To:	Julie Ford; Kate Fawell-Comley
Subject:	Fwd: RPFI

CAUTION EXTERNAL EMAIL:This message originated outside the organisation. Do not click links or open attachments unless you recognise the sender and know the content is safe.

D.E.Lawrence:
Diversity, Equality, Inclusion and Sport
Specialist/Management and Team Coach.

Please think of the environment - do you really need to print this email or its attachments?

Sent from my iPhone

Begin forwarded message:

From: Geoff Benton <bentongeoff@gmail.com>
Date: 13 March 2016 at 15:15:55 GMT
To: Duncan Lawrence <diversitymanagementlcl@btinternet.com>
Cc: Elly Jansen <ellywjansen@hotmail.com>, Elly Jansen <elly.jansen@rpfi.org>, Jonathan Manson <jonathan.manson@btinternet.com>, Catherine Keevil <catherine.keevil@yahoo.co.uk>, Peggy J <peggwegg@hotmail.com>
Subject: RPFI

Dear Duncan,

As you are aware we had a board meeting on Friday , the board has had to look very seriously at the end of year financial situation which is very disappointing , and immediate cuts are required.

I regret to inform you that we are unable to continue with your role at RPFI and will have to give you one weeks notice with immediate effect.

Thought Questions:

?= Do you think D.Eric Lawrence's expectations of the charity solicitors were reasonable?

?=Why do you think that they were reluctant to provide him with any Trustee Board Meeting Minutes?

?= Were D.Eric Lawrence's written submissions and statements consistent throughout? Yes/No

4. Police: Charmed by the jailers/ Being Charged

Some Reflective thoughts from D.Eric Lawrence

> **Bamboozled Wisdom:**(Number 4) Saying that someone 'is guilty' of being somewhere that they were not, 'humn'... being blamed for doing something that they did not do, this only usually works when no one is looking too closely to 'the details' and or when they do not have the will or the heart to even care if finding the truth no longer seems to matter.

Being 'charged' was such a very surreal experience...sent via email...felt like an unbelievably bad dream, one that I would soon wake up from and simply go about my business. The first step to being charged was having two policemen come to my home...I really thought that I was going to be arrested right there and then. The two policemen had a seat in my flat, they were very reasonable, we talked about my American accent, my musical equipment, and my art collection. After I showed them that I had actually paid my 'coroner fine', they called their boss and he asked them for my email details, and they left. Very civilised and respectful exchange.

After very politely being asked,again via email to voluntarily attend an interview at a local MET police station, where I was mainly and politely asked about my Spring/Early Summer 2019 correspondence with the Assistant Coroner. I admitted that I was 'low energy' and worn down for a variety for reasons such

mother's recent passing, losing work and having financial problems, being slated in the press/media, and I was in no mood for dealing with an Assistant Coroner that had regularly showed bias to me and was trying to decimate me within my professional associations and within the press/media etc) but then extraordinarily enough, I was then charged with a period from a year earlier...not even the period that I was being interviewed for...bamboozled!...I did not even see it coming... wow Duncan wow!

I was very foolish and naive to even think that the Met would agree with me, that the Assistant Coroner actually was treating me in a very cruel and unreasonable manner.

The black solicitor that attended the interview told me after the interview that it was clear to her that I am being scapegoated by either the charity, the Assistant Coroner or both. This led me to being supported by her boss and not her in my initial court preparations. I wonder at times how this case would have been had this original black solicitor taken my case, she showed insight and called things as they really were.

I sought clarity about this charge from the courts directly, from the Met Police directly and from the CPS directly etc all to no avail. I have dozens and dozens of emails that illustrate me trying to chase this up...it was like they were purposely giving me 'the run around' while they collectively got their own stories together... some of them (my communications with them) are located within this book and in Volume II, where I will explore our communications in more details.

The CPS (the Crown Prosecution Service) clearly did not care about the charge being appropriate to me and my actions, nor did they seem to care about the charge dates being accurate (these were drawn up by one of their lawyers they stated, she was very elusive, and she never answered my emails and 'snail mail letters' that were addressed to her...I wondered what was their 'motivation' for going after me?

Were they simply honouring the Assistant Coroner's request to 'teach me a lesson' for missing his hearings and for coming off so cocky with him...I did not have a clue. One CPS staff regularly mentioned in writing that I was trying to clear myself via emails...of course I was you foolish man but with the truth ...if only it was that easy.

The court case and the press/media were only interested in my 'low energy period comments' given to the London Met, although my comments where I admitted to having low energy(Spring/ Summer of 2019), these were all outside of the actual MET charge period dates of 10 June 2018 through to 4 Feb 2019... yes, all very surreal since 'my assistant coroner battles' did not even occur during the charge period...his trying to decimate me and my credentials, were still outside the charge period!

I bet 99% of the press and social media users that were paying attention to the court hearings, that they probably never actually knew what the actual charge was and what the 'charge periods' were and or even meant...some probably did not even care or think that it even mattered in my case and that 'I must be guilty of something' and probably assumed that I would never question my charges in such a persistent manner.

Because I was not allowed to give evidence and my four court letters were withheld by the judge and prosecutor, the case proceeded as if I was withholding information during the spring/summer of 2019 although the charge was going back to the summer of 2018...the press and the media even they wrote about 'the events' as if they had occurred over the spring/summer of 2019 too...very surreal!

People would ask me "...what is the difference between the Assistant Coroners May 2019 Fine and the Met Charges against you...", all I can say is that I did not know...if you looked at the fine sheet from the Assistant Coroner, you tell me...no legal professionals seemed confident enough to ever challenge the prosecutor about this. I am confident that the CCRC will seek clarification about this area18.

Hopefully once readers see the facts for themselves, they will see that 'the charge' was based upon a series of lies, assumptions, collusion, and false narratives.

Only one of my friends 'caught on' though... she always said that the 'charge and I' were on one page and, on the other pages were the Bennett family and the court/press/media... where 'the other page' was clearly an emotional narrative ... another page, somewhere far away from the factual period and the page where I was, where there was no one seemingly interested in drawing us all in together, especially with my four court letters being hidden in plain sight...bamboozled!

---

18   Unfortunately, this organisation did not take up the exploration of areas such as this!

Email Evidence-6 Met/Police

Discussion:

- Generally positive, although the police have not willing to take any responsibility for their inappropriate charge period dates.
- Eventually after initially saying that dates came from the Assistant Coroner, they then say the dates came from the CPS lawyer.
- I made complaints about the Met Police to the Police Authority, the Mayor's office and the Met's own complaints policy.

Conclusion

I think 'law' doesn't necessarily aim for truth and justice...at times it could be 'boys supporting other boys'.

Film makers like Spike Lee use to use the phrase ' Just us', with regard to illustrating the impact that race plays in criminal justice sentencing...I think my memoirs discusses this area significantly too.

I think my experiences and memories at times also reflect a range of issues such as racism, white male privilege and in some cases related to some levels of 'twisted male envy and jealousy'. Also in recent years there have been some rather loud suggestions that the London Metropolitan Police are institutionally corrupt, racism, misogynistic, inept, unethical, etc and should be disbanded . I think my experience gets lost somewhere here, between public apathy (my case does not light anyone's 'current fire')and I know powerful celebrities do not know enough about my case facts to be interesting and in this consideration I would also add potentially useful publishers, politicians, human rights groups, barristers and solicitors, who see no money in supporting my truth to come out...and so I plod on the best that I could. Friends and family are not the ones I have regularly confided in the last few years about the police generally and or the police charge specifically, believe when I tried I get a range of sadness, through to a range of naivety ('ignoring it' and just get on with Duncan being Duncan, "...he got good jobs in the past and will do so in the future, he is not really needing 'a break', he can create his own, etc)...I think we mirror each other at times, myself and others not really comprehending the level of '##8! that the London Met helped to put in, so me reaching out seems self-centred and I want people to enjoy their family and friends and not get bogged down with protecting and supporting me against the police, it's hasn't been 'like a cold' where it will get better in time...I think in some ways it's like a cancer that at times it is in remission and then comes roaring back with a vengeance...so I plod on wishing I was anywhere but here.

The police and the Assistant Coroner dragged me into this...I will keep chipping away until they help to directly and or indirectly get out...I never expected them to apologise, only realistically hoped that 'some honourable professional' around them would 'do them in'.

I think the legal system has damaged us all and had taken us prisoner too, to places where we never that we could venture.

One of my focus groups thinks this chapter reads more like poetry at times...

Police Correspondence

Re: Your complaint - COM-9095-19-0100-000

Met x

Mon, 13 Jan, 21:50

Eric Lawrence <diversitymanagementlcl@btinternet.com>

to Richard.Scott, Cps, London, !enquiries

Mr Scott,

Thanks for getting in touch, although I am not sure why I could not have had today's clarification several weeks ago...could not have hurt as information for use in the past court sessions either.

I still have not had my main questions answered, can you or your line manager answer them in a timely manner?

Left over questions to Mr Ward/Yourself:

In the 'spirit of transparency' and knowledge of what happened to my dates, who did you send my concerns onto and what was their response?

3.1 Did you take any additional steps Mr. Ward? Please be concise.

4 I was sentenced to prison based upon your charge sheet Mr.Ward, yet the prosecutor never actually referred to it nor the 'charge period dates listed upon it and ignored the fact that I sent my'original plea' directly to you before my actual first court date.

4.1 I tried very hard to get them to look at the dates on your charge sheet and the initial plea' sent to you, all to no avail.

4.2 Were you aware of this?

4.3 Did your charge sheet period dates (or charge period dates 'in general')and the receipt of my original plea hold any legal weight what so ever(is that why to this day they have easily been ignored by the magistrates, Judge, prosecutor, Assistant Coroner etc)? Please urgently clarify this point.

Going to prison based upon time frames when I either had no knowledge of any coroner and or was directly communicating with my old charity solicitor(related to the coroner), the situation leading me to prison was never actually fact checked and I can't let it go.

4.4. I am not sure the Assistant Coroner lied on purpose(or colluded with the 'non factual' dates that your colleague presented, eg he was not trying to keep me out of prison), but several of you within this 'criminal justice system' allowed him to perpetuate a serious miscarriage of justice without these ever being checked out and simply let them stand(the dates) and had those in the court and press thinking that they were factually accurate...disgusting ....I can not simply move on and let it go.

4.5 Is there another independent CPS body or related organisation that you could refer me to that might look into

my claims(and my experience of CPS thus far)? Thanks in advance for this information.

I eagerly await your reply Mr.Ward.

Duncan Lawrence

London SE26 5LB

D.E.Lawrence:

Diversity, Equality, Inclusion and Sport Specialist/Management and Team Coach.

Please think of the environment – do you really need to print this email or its attachments?

Sent from my iPhone

On 13 Jan 2020, at 12:39, Richard.Scott@met.police.uk wrote:

Dear Mr. Lawrence,

I have tried to call you on 07733 130 306 a few times this morning but could not get through. I have been asked to look into a complaint you made against Detective Constable Tyrone Ward. I have discussed the matter with him and reviewed his correspondence with the Crown Prosecution Service.

I can confirm that it was the CPS who set the dates on your indictment. DC Ward proposed a relatively narrow time frame over which the offence was said to have been committed, incorporating the dates of the inquest itself. This time frame was then widened by the CPS following their review of the evidence in your case. It is entirely proper for the CPS to make decisions on the particulars of a charge, and it is not within the gift of the police to amend them.

The reviewing lawyer at the CPS was Katie Sinnett- Jones. May I suggest you redirect your enquiry to her for an answer as to why this particular date range was chosen. I'm afraid I do not have her contact details, but the CPS website is www.cps.gov.uk.

Kind regards,

DS Richard Scott | Safeguarding Team =203 | Southwest BCU

Email richard.scott@met.pnn.police.uk

Address 2nd Floor, Eagle House, Ram Passage, High Street, Kingston-upon-Thames, Surrey, KT1 1HH

Wed, 15 Jan, 10:31

Richard.Scott@met.police.uk

to diversitymanagementlcl

Dear Mr. Lawrence,

As I have explained, the dates on your "charge sheet" were set by the CPS, not the police. I would suggest you take legal advice. If you believe there has been a miscarriage of justice, the Criminal Cases Review Commission may be able to offer advice on how to proceed.

Kind regards,

DS Richard Scott | Safeguarding Team 3 | Southwest BCU
Email richard.scott@met.pnn.police.uk
Address 2nd Floor, Eagle House, Ram Passage, High Street, Kingston-upon-Thames, Surrey, KT1 1HH
(Not protectively marked)

NOTICE – This email and any attachments are solely for the intended recipient and may be confidential. If you have received this email in error, please notify the sender and delete it from your system. Do not use, copy or disclose the information contained in this email or in any attachment without the permission of the sender. Metropolitan Police Service (MPS) communication systems are monitored to the extent permitted by law and any email and/or attachments may be read by monitoring staff. Only specified personnel are authorised to conclude binding agreements on behalf of the MPS by email and no responsibility is accepted for unauthorised agreements reached with other personnel. While reasonable precautions have been taken to ensure no viruses are present in this email, its security and that of any attachments cannot be guaranteed.

Tue, 21 Jan, 15:55

Eric Lawrence

to Diversity

D.E.Lawrence:

Diversity, Equality, Inclusion and Sport Specialist/Management and Team Coach.

<u>Please think of the environment</u> – do you really need to print this email or its attachments?

Sent from my iPhone

Begin forwarded message:

From: <u>Richard.Scott@met.police.uk</u>
Date: 15 January 2020 at 10:31:39 GMT
To: <u>diversitymanagementlcl@btinternet.com</u>
Subject: Your complaint – COM-9095-19-0100-000

Dear Mr. Lawrence,

As I have explained, the dates on your "charge sheet" were set by the CPS, not the police. I would suggest you take legal advice. If you believe there has been a miscarriage of justice, the Criminal Cases Review Commission may be able to offer advice on how to proceed.

Kind regards,

DS Richard Scott | Safeguarding Team 3 | Southwest BCU
Email <u>richard.scott@met.pnn.police.uk</u>
Address 2nd Floor, Eagle House, Ram Passage, High Street, Kingston-upon-Thames, Surrey, KT1 1HH
(Not protectively marked)

From: Eric Lawrence <diversitymanagementlcl@btinternet.com>
Sent: 13 January 2020 21:51
To: Scott Richard - SW-CU <Richard.Scott@met.police.uk>
Cc: Cps <info@cps.gov.uk>; London Magistrates Cps <London.Magistrates@cps.gov.uk>; !enquiries <enquiries@policeconduct.gov.uk>
Subject: Re: Your complaint - COM-9095-19-0100-000

Mr Scott,

Thanks for getting in touch, although I am not sure why I could not have had today's clarification several weeks ago... could not have hurt as information for use in the past court sessions either.

I still have not had my main questions answered, can you or your line manager answer them in a timely manner?

Left over questions to Mr Ward/Yourself:

In the 'spirit of transparency' and knowledge of what happened to my dates, who did you send my concerns onto and what was their response?

3.1 Did you take any additional steps Mr. Ward? Please be concise.

4 I was sentenced to prison based upon your charge sheet Mr.Ward, yet the prosecutor never actually referred to it nor the 'charge period dates listed upon it and ignored the fact that I sent my'original plea' directly to you before my actual first court date.

4.1 I tried very hard to get them to look at the dates on your charge sheet and the initial plea' sent to you, all to no avail.

4.2 Were you aware of this?

4.3 Did your charge sheet period dates (or charge period dates 'in general')and the receipt of my original plea hold any legal weight what so ever(is that why to this day they have easily been ignored by the magistrates, Judge, prosecutor, Assistant Coroner etc)? Please urgently clarify this point.

Going to prison based upon time frames when I either had no knowledge of any coroner and or was directly communicating with my old charity solicitor(related to the coroner), the situation leading me to prison was never actually fact checked and I can't let it go.

4.4. I am not sure the Assistant Coroner lied on purpose(or colluded with the 'non-factual' dates that your colleague presented, eg he was not trying to keep me out of prison), but several of you within this 'criminal justice system' allowed him to perpetuate a serious miscarriage of justice without these ever being checked out and simply let them stand(the dates) and had those in the court and press thinking that they were factually accurate...disgusting ....I can not simply move on and let it go.

4.5 Is there another independent CPS body or related organisation that you could refer me to that might look into my claims(and my experience of CPS thus far)? Thanks in advance for this information.

I eagerly await your reply Mr.Ward.

Duncan Lawrence

London SE26 5LB

D.E.Lawrence:

Diversity, Equality, Inclusion and Sport Specialist/Management and Team Coach.

<u>Please think of the environment</u> - do you really need to print this email or its attachments?

Sent from my iPhone

On 13 Jan 2020, at 12:39, <u>Richard.Scott@met.police.uk</u> wrote:

=

Dear Mr. Lawrence,

I have tried to call you on 07733 130 306 a few times this morning but could not get through. I have been asked to look into a complaint you made against Detective Constable Tyrone Ward. I have discussed the matter with him and reviewed his correspondence with the Crown Prosecution Service.

I can confirm that it was the CPS who set the dates on your indictment. DC Ward proposed a relatively narrow time frame over which the offence was said to have been committed, incorporating the dates of the inquest itself. This time frame was then widened by the CPS following their review of the evidence in = your case. It is entirely proper for the CPS to make decisions on the particulars of a charge, and it is not within the gift of the police to amen= d them.

The reviewing lawyer at the CPS was Katie Sinnett-Jones. May I suggest you redirect your enquiry to her for an answer as to why this particular date range was chosen. I'm afraid I do not have her contact details, but the CPS website is <u>www. cps.gov.uk.</u>

Kind regards,

DS Richard Scott | Safeguarding Team =203 | Southwest BCU

Email <u>richard.scott@met.pnn.police.uk</u>
Address 2nd Floor, Eagle House, Ram Passage, High Street, Kingston-upon-Thames, Surrey, KT1 1HH
(Not protectively marked)

 ReplyForward

RE: Urgent: Duncan Lawrence's coroner's'first contact' letter/evidence in full IIII

Met x

Sat, 26 Oct 2019, 13:54

Tyrone.Ward@met.police.uk

to diversitymanagementlcl

Dear Mr Lawrence,

I'm afraid you have been incorrectly advised – I am absolutely powerless to amend the date range of the charge, only the CPS can make such an amendment, and as it was them that set the date range in the first place, I do not see how they will be prepared to do so. As mentioned previously, the Assistant Coroner has submitted an evidential statement in which he states he first requested documents on 11/06/18. Given the inquest concluded on 03/02/19, this is the reason why the CPS have chosen the specified date range of 10/06/18 – 04/02/19.

I have submitted to the CPS your protestations at the selection of dates, but I'm afraid I cannot do any more than relay your concerns. It will be a matter for your defence team (or yourself, if you will be unrepresented) to make representations to the court around your issue with the date range.

As for the possibility of an adjournment, I'm afraid this is entirely a decision for the court.

I'm sorry I cannot be of further help. If there is anything further you need from me, do not hesitate to contact me.

Kind regards,

Tyrone

DC Tyrone Ward
Safeguarding – SW BCU – Team 3B
Mobile 07741702833
Email tyrone.ward@met.police.uk
Address Eagle House, Ram Passage, Kingston upon Thames, KT1 1HL

From: Eric Lawrence [mailto:diversitymanagementlcl@ btinternet.com]
Sent: 26 October 2019 11:47
To: Ward Tyrone - SW-CU <Tyrone.Ward@met.police.uk>
Cc: Cps <info@cps.gov.uk>
Subject: Re: Urgent: Duncan Lawrence's coroner's'first contact' letter/evidence in full IIII

Good morning Mr Ward,

Can my 30.10.19 sentencing be suspended until the 'the charge dates' can be sorted out?

Duncan Lawrence

D.E.Lawrence:

Diversity, Equality, Inclusion and Sport Specialist/Management and Team Coach.

Please think of the environment – do you really need to print this email or its attachments?

Sent from my iPhone

On 25 Oct 2019, at 09:23, Eric Lawrence <diversitymanagementlcl@btinternet.com> wrote:

Dear Mr Ward,

Earlier this week I met with the Probation Service to get my pre-sentence report drafted.

It was very surreal because they had already seen proof via myself that I was only introduced to the idea of a coroner three months into the 'six month charge period date'. They too are looking for clarification that the CPS/MET takes this seriously now and will take immediate steps to correct this significant charge period date error, one that could criminalise a 60 year old man, one with no criminal record and one that has spent his entire adult life supporting individuals, families and communities.

I have written so many emails recently and no results except for one person called and informally told me that only you can correct the error quickly, this week and well before my sentencing date(where it is then more difficult to correct the implications of a incorrect charge period).

I desperately urge you to correct this problem and not let me bring this needless stress into the weekend.

Respectfully submitted by,

Duncan Lawrence
London
SE26 5LB

D.E.Lawrence:

Diversity, Equality, Inclusion and Sport Specialist/Management and Team Coach.

Please think of the environment - do you really need to print this email or its attachments?

Sent from my iPhone

Begin forwarded message:

From: Eric Lawrence <diversitymanagementlcl@btinternet.com>

Date: 21 October 2019 at 06:09:40 BST

To: Mr Tyrone Ward <tyrone.ward@met.police.uk>

Subject: Duncan Lawrence's coroner's'first contact' letter/ evidence in full

Mr.Ward,

I am resending my first RPFI Charity Solicitors letter with its attachment(I previously did not send the letter's attachment (...the password is hdnhs .

I hope any CPS 'review' decisions about if my charge should stand or be dropped(or 'something else') happens quite quickly.

We are talking about *half* the charge period being inappropriately given to me sir.

The charge dates have been very stressful and confusing throughout my legal journey and the prosecutor at one time was talking about 'custodial sentence' because of them.I want my life back, ideally today sir.

I pray for a timely and full reply Mr.Ward.

Duncan Lawrence
London SE26 5LB

D.E.Lawrence:

Diversity, Equality, Inclusion and Sport Specialist/Management and Team Coach.

Please think of the environment – do you really need to print this email or its attachments?

Sent from my iPhone

Begin forwarded message:

From: Julie Ford <Julie.Ford@hilldickinson.com>
Date: 31 August 2018 at 14:01:24 BST
To: «diversitymanagementlcl@btinternet.com"
<diversitymanagementlcl@btinternet.com>
Cc: Kate Fawell-Comley
     <Kate.Fawell-Comley@hilldickinson.com>
Subject: Request for assistance concerning a coroner's inquiry. [HD-UKLive.12014150.1]

Dear Mr Lawrence

I am assisting a colleague, Kate Fawell-Cowley in a matter in which you have been asked to provide a statement for a Coroner's inquiry. Further details are set out in the letter attached which is password protected (password to follow).

I should be grateful if you would contact me to confirm receipt of the letter and your response the queries set out within it.

I look forward to hearing from you at your earliest convenience.

With kind regards

Your sincerely

Julie Ford
Legal Director
Healthcare
Hill Dickinson LLP
Julie.Ford@hilldickinson.com

The Broadgate Tower, 20 Primrose Street, London, EC2A 2EW
TEL: +44 (0)20 7280 9338
FAX: +44 (0)20 7283 1144

<Letter to duncan Lawrence.doc>

 ReplyReply to allForward

2023 Updates:

When the Senior Coroner from the West London Coroners Court got sacked recently (refer to earlier newspaper report), I wrongly it seems assumed that there might be 'less resistance' to the 'truth' coming out as why this office allowed the Assistant coroner to have the London Metropolitan Police put into their charge sheet that for a large period of time that the Assistant Coroner knew me and I was withholding information from him over that time period!

The Mets own 2019 Statement that the dates were not accurate, the Charity own solicitors 2019/2023 statement verifying when they first informed me of the Assistant Coroners existence, these areas seemed to want to remain hidden in plain sight...you decide.

Was I wrong to alert the Wimbledon magistrates Court judiciary during my case in 2019?(this would have included the judge, the prosecutor, the court clerk and my various limited court legal teams)...**what is it about these ' charge dates' that the London Metropolitan Police find it easier to violate my Article 6 Human Rights regularly rather than publicly share/discuss that their charge dates were a miscarriage of justice** that has been further 'hidden in plain sight' by all of the UK criminal justice actors...institutions... bamboozled in plain sight!

I decided to try one more time to complain...I tried several times to get the police to look at itself ...several forms and over several years...all to no avail, the police will always cover up for its members where it can...each and every time I tried to lay out a logical and factual complaint, the person tasked with assessing my submission, they used the police's own words as if they were 'gospel' and no reason to even be questioned, even in a minor way.

I will explore this in volume II and ideally compare and contrast my case to modern cases where police actually went to prison and or were otherwise sentenced.

Thought Questions:

?= Should charges be based upon accurate charge periods? Yes/No Explain

?= Should all of the actors that conspired to get D.Eric Lawrence Sentenced and charged be themselves charged and or at least fined themselves? Y/N Explain

Why you?

5. **Media/Press...** a study on bias and false narratives

Some Reflective thoughts from D.Eric Lawrence

> **Bamboozled Wisdom:**(Number 5) How can 'eyewitnesses' only record 'a story' rather than 'the story' and 'the public' then goes on to still buying more newspapers, then throws away those newspapers and then goes to sleep eagerly dreaming about the next day's 'story'. An example of 'willing empty-headed privilege'!

Seeing the truth but saying and doing nothing is extremely wicked and karma catches up to us all.

Do you want 'to believe' what you read in the paper or what you may watch on a television platform...why? ...does 'believing what you are digesting' help you to make sense of your world?, .does the same logic(or illogic) apply if the 'news content' does not work for you and is not easily digestible. Does that mean that it might be untrue? I wonder.

I watch a lot of CNN and Aljazeera News...they are as 'different' as night and day. CNN is primarily 'US Centric', 'EU Centric', loads of white presenters and rarely is there any in-depth news about Africa, Middle East, South Asia, etc.. Aljazeera on the other hand has news from all over the world and usually in-depth stories and interviews from areas of the world that are 'anti-Western', so stories always have non-western perspective. My point is 'my story' arising from the young woman that took her own life in 2016 three months after I had left, was never ' Duncan Centric' and more about the person being interviewed e.g. the family, the ex-unit manager, the ' lead' reporter, etc. . I was threatened several times by mainly weekly and evening newscasters that if I did not give them an interview, that they would publish 'a story' a few hours from then regardless.

Press and Social Media 'Free Speech Rights' versus the Article 6 of the Human Rights Act...which is more important?

"...D.Eric Lawrence, why do you keep mentioning Article 6 of the Human Rights Act...we all know that papers and social media do what it takes to 'sell', papers, advertisement, etc.. When was the last time, or ever for that fact have you seen or heard someone present 'news' comparing what was coming out of a 'court session' with the expectations of Article 6 ?..."

"...You are right brother but I can only hope!..."

Brief Reminder:

Article 6 protects your right to a fair trial

You have the right to a fair and public trial or hearing if:

- you are charged with a criminal offence and have to go to court, or
- a public authority is making a decision that has an impact upon your civil rights or obligations.

What rights do you have at a criminal trial?

You have the right to:

- be presumed innocent until you are proven guilty
- be told as early as possible what you are accused of
- remain silent
- have enough time to prepare your case
- legal aid (funding) for a lawyer if you cannot afford one and this is needed for justice to be served
- attend your trial
- access all the relevant information
- put forward your side of the case at trial
- question the main witness against you and call other witnesses, and
- have an interpreter, if you need one.

A false narrative is one in which a complete narrative pattern is perceived in a given situation, but it is not an actual narrative at work in the situation. The perception of a false narrative can be due to insufficient or inaccurate information or to insufficient or inaccurate assessment.

The False Narrative | Dramaticapedia

dramaticapedia.com/2013/07/05/the-false-narrative/

2019:

I did not even recognise myself the first time someone told me that I was on a late-night news program...they used a picture from the early 2000s... the image was quite scary and unflattering, but I guess that was the point...launch crazy tearjerker stories and the big and unfair black man casted as 'the villain'...me!

I got use to (after the initial inquest media storm) that every time that I did not attend any Spring/Summer coroner 'follow up' hearings(I soon come to see them as opportunities to add to the 'emotional narratives' and or add to the 'non-factual narratives'...without these 'follow up' coroner hearings, these toxic narrative circuses would have potentially shrinking audiences and then soon move onto another foolish story, another press and social media piece of flesh...)that always included some kind of media and or other press scramble, or that after I sent him my credentials (that)...I would first be spoken about by an ex-charity unit manager, then the parents would go for their pound of flesh...then I finally would be in the press/media with their 'no fact checking journalism' and it was like 'clockwork'... from a 'very predictable toxic clock'.

I stopped watching the news for several months and still feel quite disturbed at times now about some of the continued patterns of bias, racism, white privilege, white male privilege etc that are regularly integrated into the modern press and social media 'stories' behind the banner of 'free speech'...say anything, write anything, decimate anyone, and call it 'free speech'...crazy! Those that fight back are labelled as "...having a chip on their shoulder...", "...they do not have a sense of humour...", "why come on tv or go on twitter and then expect people to play nice, what do you expect...", "... the 'public' are interested and have a right to know...", I can guarantee that the victims of the press and social media do not talk like this.

The press and the media did not really ask me anything(although I had a few notes through my door telling me to give them what they wanted to hear and usually threatening that a story was going out with or without my help), although they regularly found the time to tell me and their readers 'who I was'...usually in quite an unflattering and biased manner and with a regular use of racist imagery and a rewrite of my professional history...there were some that even thought that I owned the charity(some of these images were purposely done, 'images' that helped to perpetuate the non-factual narratives and 'myths and stereotypes' often unfairly associated with black and Asian charities), that I was 'a social worker', that I peddled myself as 'a medical doctor' and they regularly rubbished my 90s educational background. My CPD record was and still is always about me being a 'lifetime student', not about what doctorate programme that I went to in the 90s...a racist character assassination big time!

The 'privilege group' allowed this to happen unchallenged. Some of the toxic actors soon realized that whatever they said about me, that there was someone with a mike, a phone, pen and a pad,etc. all ready to take down sensational, often 'non fact checked' lies, bias and misrepresentations

When I left each court hearing I was chased with cameras... being an introvert I did not enjoy the attention one bit (even *though some say that I should have spoken to the media every chance that I could have).*

I always hoped that there would be this one journalist, maybe someone trying to make a name for themselves, that this person would be interested enough to try to seek out the truth behind these sensational headlines...unfortunately not one came to me...I am still waiting.

My daughters and some of my close friends haven't said it directly to me, but they are somewhat concerned that these memoirs will attract negative press and trolls...I wonder what types of people would 'blow back'(if at all)...would it be race related, 'social care related'...groups and individuals that that have had their emails illustrated up and down these memoirs...I wonder.

Some organisations, especially those with weak leadership worry that my memoirs could potentially attract more attention than their actual organisations deserve and they are not sure if this could be good for the organisation(e.g. whether I am seen as a hero or a villain) . Ironically enough there are still others, a small minority of social and social care organisations that see me as a 'symbol of bravery and righteousness'...go figure.

2020+

I am still hoping and would very much welcome doing an 'Op Ed' piece, one going through the criminal justice system while being a competent and an innocent black man.

When the Black Lives Matter movement had a positive revival all over the world last spring 2020, I really wanted to be involved too.

But seeing all the good work younger people were doing (which made me very proud), I thought let me just keep a back seat until my name is cleared. Did not wish to be a toxic distraction for any forces still trying to keep me quiet and decimated.

If I am honest, I secretly hoped one of the activists would have sought me out too, either to help with BLM movement and or help me get myself cleared.

I think the media and press, more so than going to prison, it was them that really really really disappointed me about being a citizen of Britain.

When I knew something was coming on the evening news and or within evening papers, I would literally keep my head down in a pub or hide in my flat with the lights out.

I understand trash and sensational stories sell but it was not nice not being able to influence what was being put out about me.

Three people go to court, only the short service black man goes to jail while everyone else gets a relatively low fine! The press seems to see nothing wrong with this reality.

Unless I get compensation, I will never be able to afford to 'scrub the internet' and its negative stories connected to 'my name'.

2023:

When the problematic Senior Coroner from the Chaotic West London Coroners Court was sacked, there was no press scrum to explore the impact upon all of his past coroner cases,nor any consideration of the cases that he supervised, including mine and the Assistant Coroner in 2019...no, the press and social media have moved onto other stories, other 'news cycle feeding frenzy'...the damage to me and so many others in their toxic haze will not get a second look!

Thought Questions:

?= Have you ever been publicly accused of something that you did not do? What did it feel like and what was the impact upon you, your friends and family and professionally?

?=Did you believe what you read or saw on television about D.Eric Lawrence ?

2020+ Thought Questions:

Please read the links below and consider;

Spring 2021 News Clips:

https://eminetra.co.uk/the-chaotic-care-home-fined-40000-for-the-judges-failure-to-protect-the-patient-who-hung-his-neck/332261/

https://www.thirdsector.co.uk/charity-fined-40000-death-teenager-its-care/management/article/1709412

?= Was his 'situation' a 'race thing', victim of others trying to hide the truth, 'greedy' individuals looking for a pay out, individuals seeking revenge on the charity and or charity founder, etc.???

?= why was the media/social media drastically less interested in D.Eric Lawrence in their spring 2021 discussions (compared to their 2019 discussions) about the social care charity?

Where was the truth?

6. Getting to the Truth: Myths and Facts about DL, RPFI and Elly Jansen

Some Reflective thoughts from D.Eric Lawrence

> **Bamboozled Wisdom** (Number 5) highlighting the truth will never work when you are only taking the time for 're-painting a local landscape' from a perspective of a re-imagined and different universe that's very full of lies, bias and hate![19]

The 'Evidence' Speaks for itself

I knew after the poor quality CQC surprise visit (Spring 2016), that I was going to be blamed for any unsatisfactory report that followed even though key staff were sabotaging my efforts big time on a daily basis. 'Social Care' would not be social care without 'blame being prominently being paraded somewhere'. Leading up to my contract not being renewed there were staff quitting and new staff being hired across the organisation at a blistering pace, very much like a revolving door...not a good time to shout "...success... "at any level(as an organisation, as team members, as a therapeutic community, as Trustees, as Senior Management Team, etc.).

---

[19]

I was even pulling overnight shifts across the charity in addition to my regular day work just to cover the shortage of staff, very crazy days for a very dysfunctional organisation where no one was really being honest with each other about their genuine grievances... with each other and with the wider organisation. A tired looking Duncan, not a good look either.

There were several rumours going around Lancaster Lodge Unit about the various things that I might have said and might have done from day one of my consultancy. On one side was the senior unit staff, and the art students on placements within the Lancaster Lodge Unit and on the other side, the founder/advisor that was supported by the CEO of the day. I had to walk a very balanced path,one that could genuinely allow me to help to generate various compromises, ones that were practical and 'tension easing'. It was always a very paranoid situation for me during this work assignment, I never really knew who was being genuine when they are speaking to me(with regards to long term staff and their team leaders) because it seemed as if one day we'd progress a few steps and then the next day, it would seem like any progress made was a 'figment of my imagination'. Although what 'news' filtered down to the assistant coroner, It was like in less than three months of my consultancy, that I had actually rebuilt the entire charity in my own image. It reminded me of childhood, when children might have 'historical' childhood enemies, ones that their friends had to hate too in order to keep their friendships, their parents had to hate them too to be seen as being supportive parents, etc.. In this instance you had art students, long term staff, some long term service users and their parents/carers against everyone else. On the 'other perspective' you had the founder/advisor and CEO against everyone else. In reality, they were all intelligent people that should have been talking to each other rather than adding negativity to the Lancaster Lodge community, when it already had toxic long term relationship angst thriving and infecting all of those within it and around it.

I think the Lancaster staff and their senior staff took the 'pre-Duncan arrival narrative' and added onto it with my name, my professional standards and my reputation, these were dragged right squarely into the middle of the mess... 'the comprehensive truth' had no place with all of these feuding parties.

This 'free speech' thing that seems to be very strong in the UK, it often does not usually have 'ethical filters' to keep people from hurting others (personally and or professionally)...the myths, the fantasy and the downright lies originating from this charity generally and within the Lancaster Lodge specifically spreads like wildfire with no 'gatekeeper' to keep it in check. I never once heard "...stop..., let's look at the facts...", not from the assistant coroner, not from the prosecutors, not from the CPS, not from the Met, not from the Judge, not from some of my past and present employers and definitely not from the press and social media.

I think because of 'fear' there were several key senior staff, trustees, etc. ones that were 'in a position to know', had their feet under the table, a lot more than support workers, temporary staff,etc. and knew about actual 'RPFI practice atmosphere' three months after I had already left the organization...they kept quiet about their own roles and insights leading up through the young woman's taking her own life and kept quiet with the assistant coroner and some even have the audacity to rewrite their own 'Duncan stories' rather than only comment about what they themselves saw, heard, were involved in with leading up to this very sad incident. Some even offered me 'post RPFI work' which sometimes I took for financial survival reasons but would have preferred them to have shown 'courage and bravery-in-the moment', to have made official witness statements, led some protests, spoken to the press, etc.. **I was not there for at least three months**, they were and they should and still could start speaking up...start stepping up. Tokens and expressions of 'minor assistance' way way way after the fact really meant little to me then and now, especially with regard to the 'talkers' that focused upon me rather than their own acts, actions and patterns during and after their RPFI careers ended. A shame really, personal friendships, professional respect, it was these things that sadly died for me too and a past pattern reemerged recently ... of the 'rewriting of history' right in front of me, this made me sadly and regrettably realise how hard it is to this very day to be honest, truthful and simply quiet around me about 2015-16 and beyond, especially within 'important past relationship(s) desperately trying to make a comeback'(but will never have a chance without individual self-reflection, bravery and courage for positive energy to help them grow, thrive and win!).

Below are examples of some of the myths, the fantasy and the outright lies, ones that impacted upon the charity, ones that made their way to the press and ones that led an innocent man to prison...ironically I have always had the facts, but was not allowed to present them up until these readers being able to read my memoirs.

'Unfiltered Free speech' and white privilege is a very scary combination!

I was never officially told about the young woman that took her life in May 2016, they must have assumed that I had already known.

After I had left the charity, ironically it was primarily the charity founder kept in touch just for me to help her to compile a case for her legal team to build against Lancaster Lodge Unit.

I was busy doing freelancing work across the UK, but from time to time I felt 'the spectre' of the toxic side of the charity primarily via LinkedIn, for example the CQC inspector that the charity founder and ex-CEO that seemed to have mutual dislike for (with me caught in between), he would shadow me on the LinkedIn platform.

My guess upon reflection, this was part of the reason I kept supporting Elly with answers to her continuing questions even though I no longer worked for her. I had built up no respect for either organisation, the CQC or Elly's charity... she was just the 'Devil that I knew'.

Myth 1: DL Pushed 'Unrealistic Change' onto the service users: Illustrating the differences between RPFI (Lancaster Lodge weekly programme in this example from 2016) before DL draft well-being weekly ideas from DL in 2016. Note: There is no edit on any document (these are from 2016).

Myth 2: DL Pushed Unrealistic Change onto the service users: DL asking the ex-CEO to delay the well-being rollout across the charity

Myth 3: RPFI took DL suggestions: Examples of DL suggestions that would have eased the tension between the Lancaster Lodge and the charity

Myth 4: DL Pushed External Therapists out

Myth 5: RPFI took DL suggestions: DL Views about progress at Lancaster Lodge

Myth 6: RPFI took DL suggestions: Some relevant 'Post CQC Lancaster Lodge Inspection' discussions between DL and Elly Jansen Founder/CEO was up to the task-Suggestions for CEO to step down

Myth 8: DL was not up to the task: Letter to all RPFI Staff

Myth 9: DL was not up to the task: DL update CEO about RPFI generally

Myth 10: DL was not up to the task: Lancaster Lodge Training Programme for the Acting Deputy Manager

Myth 11: Staff were happy and content-Example of time consuming RPFI HR disciplinary related issues

Myth 12: DL Wanted to be Lancaster Unit Service Manager

Myth 13: DL Pushed out the Lancaster Unit Service Manager

Myths 14: DL pushed Service Manager: Emails related to ex-Lancaster Lodge Manager departure

Myths 15: LD pushed Service Manager: HR Related to Lancaster Lodge II

Myths 16: LD pushed Service Manager: HR Related to Lancaster Lodge III

Myths 17: LD pushed Service Manager: Ex-Manager LL Handover notes

Myth 18: DL Staff did not Sabotage DL work

Myth 19: DL Did not provided Assistant Coroner Information in advance of initial inquest: DL Dec 2018 Coroner Witness Statement

Myth 20: DL Did not provided Assistant Coroner Information in advance of initial inquest: DL Dec 2018 Exhibits:

- ☐ Audit
- ☐ DL Job Offer
- ☐ First DL Charity Wide news letter
- ☐ DL Draft Mission Statement(never completed)
- ☐ DL Dismissal Letter.

Myth 21: Charity Solicitor was objective

Myth 22: Founder /Leader had no animosity towards the Lancaster unit manager: A collection of email to- from the founder/lead advisor

Myth: 1 DL Pushed Unrealistic Change onto the service users: Illustrating the differences between RPFI (Lancaster Lodge weekly programme in this example from 2016) before DL draft well-being weekly ideas from DL in 2016. **Note:** There is no edit on any document (these are from 2016).

Fact: The average senior management /founder/Chair/CEO has 25+ years experience in mental health and or well-being and or youth work etc. Doing the cross charity audit was the work that the charity hired me afterwards doing a few initial training tasks for them.. If there was a problem you'd see it reflected in the company emails and they would not have hired me after my initial few days because of it. The charity founder/advisor was openly encouraging me to come down harder on the Lancaster unit.

Fact: If you' compare and contrast 'the existing Lancaster unit programme when I arrived in Feb 2015 to my draft charity wide integrated well-being programme, even in its draft form[20] it greatly offered so much more to the charity's service users and helped them to become more employable (on paid or volunteering basis).

Lancaster Lodge weekly programme when DL arrived Jan 2016:

---

[20] I was not able to 'finalise' my updated Lancaster Lodge programme prior to leaving the charity.

Draft Well-Being Programme as devised by DL Jan/Feb 2016 (for the entire RPFI Charity):

Typical Week at Lancaster Lodge looks something like:

Monday-Friday
6:30* Well Being Activities (meditation, exercise, yoga, etc)
*7am wake ups/community breakfast prep/Light House Clean
*8am Community Breakfast
*Breakfast Check in

*10am-4pm Community Positive Employability and Personal Development Space (outside of the house)

This would include attending training, college, university, volunteering, attending church, temple, mosque ,museum trips, job interviews, gp visits, visiting therapist, part-time job,etc..

*4-6pm Keywork session(tba)/Community Dinner shop-Prep/House Light Clean

*6pm Community Dinner
*Community Dinner Check in
*7pm Evening Meeting e.g. Community Meeting(tba),Well Being Sessions, walks, pub visit,cinema,etc..

*8-10pm Unit Clean up

Additional Highlights:
- Annual house holiday
- House Open House to showcase resident art and music.
- TC led competitions

Participation by service users:

Our ethos at Lancaster Lodge is that all service users will be encouraged and empowered to participate ful and have their say in the community and in its meetings. Service users are therefore involved and consulte on all areas involved with the running of Lancaster Lodge.

A clear structure of community meetings provides a forum where service users can share their ideas and thoughts (including any complaints or concerns) about the day to day running of the service. This commitment to inclusiveness and participation and engaging in the social dialogue of the group/expectation of the local community (where Lancaster Lodge is and the community that the service users will relocate to upon discharge), which is both supportive and challenging, and which occurs 'informally', with in 'groups' an within 'key stakeholder relationships', all key elements in the recovery and therapeutic process.

Self Medication: it is our aim to get all service users on a 'self-medicated basis' as soon as they are able. Some are able to 'self medicate' straight away because they have been successfully doing this prior to their Lancaster Lodge admission. Positive risk assessments occur on a 24/7 basis to ensure safe dispensing of medication and that support is given to promote medication independence at the earliest point possible.

Myth 2: DL Pushed Unrealistic Change onto the service users: DL asking the ex-CEO to delay the well-being rollout across the charity

Fact: I felt with all of the HR disciplinary actions we had going on, alongside disgruntled staff, Lancaster staff and residents sabotage etc I suggested we hold off on the launch of the cross charity well-being programme, it was the CEO that pushed the launch forward.

From: Peggy J <peggwegg@hotmail.com>
Date: 29 February 2016 at 07:13:22 GMT
To: <diversitymanagementlcl@btinternet.com>
Subject: RE: M and Rohit LL Launch Brief

Hi Duncan,

I hope today is the start of a new enhanced TC at LL.

As I worked last night I feel I need to feed back on my observations and conversations with residents.

I observed that the living room curtains are filthy and not hanging correctly. please can you arrange for these to be cleaned and hung correctly. Office is dirty and needs cleaning.

Residents

W was up and down and feeling confused. She informed me that her mother is going to pay for 2 more sessions with Y. I asked how she would feel after the 2 more. She said she would be alright. I would like to discuss this with you. please call me. She also said she'd like to start working on moving on to her own flat. B and I tested her by saying she would have to start with self meds and demonstrate more independency. She got slightky upset but said she would work towards this. B believes she may be upset as Joanne removed cut glass from her room earlier and she probably noticed it missing when she went up to get ready for bed. she has a care leaver's review meeting tomorrow, it is important that you attend along with Joanne. I think the 2 of you need to agree what is presented to Care leaver PA. She agreed to try to get up early and try Exercise and Pilates.

K is doing great, W2 is going to look into BSL course for her and she said she will try and do all activities, starting with Exercise and Pilates. D is also going to buy a Chess set as she plays that. They will teach the house to play.

G spent at least 4 hours in bathroom so I didn't get to speak to her. I think her key worker should work with to get her to on reducing her rituals by 30 mins per day.

P was in a good mood, we agreed to have a chat but she got involved with a TV programme and did not come back down.

I spoke to Z on the phone, she is doing okay but says her mother does not want the section lifted. She will remain in hospital for next few days. She needs her clothes, I hope Colin can drop them to me and I can go and see her around 3pm or someone from the team can visit. Let me know either way.

I haven't spoken to W, she is supposed to be coming home today. the ward said they would call me if this is the case. I will keep you informed.

The residents would like the revised programme displayed, they don't know what is going on. please can they have this up on the wall this morning and old ones taken down. Also can we have fresh flowers in hall way.

Good luck with referrals, I hope you are able to get some new ones in soon, the atmosphere needs diluting!

Peggy

Subject: M and Rohit LL Launch Brief
From: diversitymanagementlcl@btinternet.com
Date: Sun, 28 Feb 2016 13:40:46 +0100
CC: colin_newatlantis@hotmail.com; @hotmail.co.uk
To: rohit.sharma@rpfi.org; @rpfi.org; peggwegg@hotmail.com

Sent from my iPad

From: Peggy J <peggwegg@hotmail.com>
Date: 29 February 2016 at 07:26:46 GMT
To: diversitymanagementlcl@btinternet.com, elly.jansen@ rpfi.org, colin_newatlantis@hotmail.com, pjhugroo@ wandsworth.gov.uk, opeoyinsan@hotmail.com, heathergrant@elliswhittam.com, bentongeoff@gmail. com, ellywjansen@hotmail.com
Subject: RE: This week

Hi Duncan,

I understand your frustrations about HR issues but u hope you are not proposing to further delay your new programme at LL as it is a new initiative. **I have spoken to Resudents and they are looking forward to new activities and sessions are booked.**

Peggy

Subject: This week
From: <u>diversitymanagementlcl@btinternet.com</u>
Date: Mon, 29 Feb 2016 07:14:13 +0000

To: <u>elly.jansen@rpfi.org</u>; <u>peggwegg@hotmail.com</u>; <u>colin_ newatlantis@hotmail.com</u>; <u>pjhugroo@wandsworth.gov.uk</u>; <u>opeoyinsan@hotmail.com</u>; <u>heathergrant@elliswhittam. com</u>; <u>bentongeoff@gmail.com</u>; <u>ellywjansen@hotmail.com</u>

Good morning to us all,

Busy week all around. Thanks in advance for lending me your staff and your managers.

I respectfully suggest that we do not start any new initiatives before our existing ones are well underway or completed eg opening plans, disciplinary hearings, probation staff reviews, Rohit, new staff interviews,etc..

Enjoy our RPFI/RCI week!

Duncan

D.E.Lawrence: Diversity,Equality,Inclusion and Sport Specialist / Management and Team Coach.

Skype: diversitymanagementlcl

Sent from my iPhone

Myth 3: RPFI took DL suggestions: DL example 'suggested' responses to parents/carers, CQC, service users, etc.

Fact: Most suggestions that I made that would have helped to develop better communication between the wider charity and its stakeholders was often held up by the charity founder/ advisor, CEO and Chair....they often did not even let me know the outcome of my suggestions.

EXAMPLE:

From: Diversity Management LCL <<u>diversitymanagementlcl@btinternet.com</u>>
Date: 12 February 2016 at 17:20:03 GMT
To: Geoff Benton <<u>bentongeoff@gmail.com</u>>
Cc: Elly Jansen<<u>elly.jansen@rpfi.org</u>>, Elly Jansen<<u>ellywjansen@hotmail.com</u>>, Peggy J <<u>peggwegg@hotmail.com</u>>
Subject: Re: Lancaster Lodge

Hi Geoff,

There is no way to directly defend RPFI /RCI because had we contacted residents, parents carers, commissioner in late Dec 2015 (when we first consulted all staff)we would have less pr challenges right now.

With good intentions we thought all teams including LL would cascade info to residents, parents and carers.

WH residents took to the changes easier and have better staff-resident relationships and 24/7 activities because of the changes.

LL lodge did not take to new energy that new staff brought in, they had been so used to a 'closed house' that did not have 'well being' and ' all staff are important ' culture.

This parent is right but had LL cascaded info to residents, etc we would be in a different position today.

We can't blame LL to parents, residents etc but need a 'mid road' where we apologise for limited consultation but get key staff ready for an attractive 1 March LL lift off(rather than a wimper).

Hope this makes some sense Geoff(am coaching bball and writing to you).

Good evening!

Duncan

D.E.Lawrence: Diversity,Equality,and Inclusion Specialist / Management and Team Coach.

Skype: diversitymanagementlcl

Sent from my iPhone

On 12 Feb 2016, at 16:47, Geoff Benton <<u>bentongeoff@gmail.com</u>> wrote:

FYI

I would appreciate your comments for me to respond.

Thank you

Geoff

---------- Forwarded message ----------

From: >
Date: Friday, February 12, 2016
Subject: Lancaster Lodge
To: "bentongeoff@gmail.com" <bentongeoff@gmail.com>

Dear Mr Benton,

It is with regret that I am contacting you about the implementation of changes occurring at Lancaster Lodge.

I am absolutely flabbergasted at the level of neglect that they have caused. My daughter has been a resident at Lancaster Lodge for the past year during which she has made some excellent progress.

I went to see H for a routine visit on Tuesday. When I arrived, I was told that the house was in the midst of a meeting. I decided to wait until it finished but I was invited to sit in. I was expecting a routine meeting but as time progressed, it revealed itself to be a very important stage in the lives of the residents.

As time progressed during the meeting, I became concerned for my daughter and the other residents who were expressing their concerns:

The removal of one to one therapies
Lack of staff and trained staff on duty
Residents providing for their basic needs at the expense of educational commitments because there was no staff member at hand to do it

The implementation of and adherence to a new timetable for which they have had no input

The new staff not listening to the needs of residents and how the new strategy and lack of a crisis plan have impacted on their recovery management

Change is not a bad thing but the current situation has been badly negotiated. The changes were sudden, there was no prior warning, no transitional period, no crisis plan and implemented without any consultation or true understanding of the Lodge residents. I should not have to tell you that the Community at LL is vulnerable and can be volatile at times, given that each resident presents with different psychological and emotional challenges. A thorough understanding of how the Community functions, the needs of its residents and the provision of adequate care are central to the entire operation, your duty and legal responsibility. Since the new management came in with an ill-prepared agenda, this has had serious consequences and the palpable cost of this has changed the house dynamic creating an "us and them" divided mentality. This does not seem to uphold in anyway the ethos of the Richmond Fellowship.

For the past year and a half while I have been liaising with Lancaster Lodge, it has always upheld transparency and been a place where the residents were involved in their life choices and were encouraged to do so by staff. At the meeting, Peggy stated that responsibility for this transition should have been provided by the previous Service Manager, Vincent, who left abruptly. However, I cannot accept this point because, in conjunction with his departure, there have been major staff changes, the cancellation of therapies and the introduction of a new itinerary. All of this implies that there was already a strategy to be implemented regardless of whether he stayed or not. That strategy could have prepared staff, residents and carers but was not only withheld but unrealistic and badly implemented.

Unfortunately, the residents have been blindsided by the changes that have, consequently, left them even more vulnerable than they already are. On Monday, my daughter had to restrain another service user for three hours to help the only staff member staying over. This situation put all the residents at risk, not to mention my daughter who had to resist her own triggers during the incident. This is just unacceptable and constitutes a highly neglectful situation.

I would sincerely like to know:

a) why there was no communication or meeting about the new strategy for service users, their families/ carers and staff?
b) why the cancellation of one to one therapies?
c) why there is no realistic transitional period for service users to get used to the changes?
d) why the staff shortages?
e) why the staff are unfamiliar with the needs of each service user?
f) who is legally responsible if there is serious harm to the residents or fatalities?

I really would have appreciated a letter or some other such communication detailing the changes so that I could understand and gage their impact on my daughter's care.

Yours sincerely,

TN

From: Elly Jansen <elly.jansen@rpfi.org>
Date: 13 February 2016 at 16:45:51 GMT
To: Geoff Benton <bentongeoff@gmail.com>, Peggy J <peggwegg@hotmail.com>, Duncan Lawrence <diversitymanagementlcl@btinternet.com>
Subject: Re: RESPONSE TO LETTER

the draft letter does not say that we are consulting; we intended to inform relatives of the facts that changes that we consider to be important are occurring!

However, may be we could say INSTEAD OF: THE FACT that a letter of information was sent to commissioners and social workers, which was intended to go to families also, but through a misunderstanding failed to be sent to relatives.

(I was not informed that it had not gone to families till just now!)

new reading forthis 1st par. After the decision was reached that the therapy and therapeutic programme which had been wrongly outsourced, should again be provided in-house, rather than be brought in by a number of outsiders, a meeting with residents led to the agreement that the outside therapists would continue for two months, which is a reasonable period to adjust to such a change. THE manager was duty-bound to communicate this information the the families, an we apologise for the fact that he did not do so.

THE STAFF ARE TRAINED AND EXPERIENCED PEOPLE ; THEY SHOULD NOT BE

USED AS SECURITY STAFF AND HAVE THEIR PSYCOLOGICAL AND THERAPEUTIC ABILITIES BYPASSED. the HOUSE ITSELF WITH ALL ITS STAFF ARE PROVIDED TO ENABLE THE STAFF AND RESIDENTS TO WORK TOGETHER TO MAXIMISE THE OPPORTUNITIES FOR RESIDENTS TO MATURE AND LEARN THE REWARDS OF HELPING EACH OTHER.

maybe we should not be so ready to admit any failings, and just tell the mother that her queries are welcome and are responded to as per letter

i provided with alterations provided by peggy and commented on.

Elly

Myth 4: DL Pushed External Therapists out

Fact: It was CEO and Founder/lead advisor that initiated reduction of outside practitioners. I professionally agreed with it. I was one of the few staff that experienced the original Richmond Fellowship in the 1980s(that Elly founded), they developed staff from within via a world class training programme and internships, it worked extremely well.

On 12 February 2016 at 21:17, Peggy J <<u>peggwegg@hotmail.com</u>> wrote:

Hi All,

I have made further comments in red in the below email.

Peggy

Date: Fri, 12 Feb 2016 19:50:30 +0000
Subject: RESPONSE TO LETTER
From: <u>elly.jansen@rpfi.org</u>
To: <u>bentongeoff@gmail.com</u>; <u>peggwegg@hotmail.com</u>;
   <u>diversitymanagementlcl@btinternet.com</u>

Difficult to respond without getting further criticisms.

To start with, if this lady came at the same time each week, she should have been advised to come later. The meeting was very important and admitting a parent was a very risky act. It will have been hard to know what to do, but that was an obvious mistake. Anyhow it may help our claim on transparency, but not all that happens or the decisions made are the business of all paRTIES.

1. remember drafting a letter that included families to keep them informed. What happened with that letter. Can i have a copy of what was sent? it may give a response to question 1; we did communicate.

   The letter has gone out to all commissioners and social workers however we have not been able to find addresses for any of our residents' carers/families as we only have mobile numbers for them. Goethe has left messages on their voicemail and we are hoping to hear back from them. I will send the letter in another email.

   I don't think we can use the letter as keeping carers informed as the letter was post decision and not consultation.

2. one to ones have not been cancelled. With a therapist in charge, residents will receive more rather than less therapeutic input, not only in individual sessions but also in other activities in the day which had over time fizzled out. Whilst the rehabilitation programme should be enjoyable, it will have elements that differ from a holiday, like getting up in the morning and learning to make your own breakfast and to make your own room a nice place to be in.

3. Where the change of the therapeutic programme is concerned, after consulting with the residents, a two

months transition period was agreed which is a quite a long time for such a change.

This is not true. After meeting with Duncan and you over the Christmas, **we agreed that I should email Vincent instructing him to give notice to therapists.** There wasn>t any prior consultation, there was agreement to extend the therapy following Vincent>s resignation.

4. Lancaster Lodge is fully staffed with responsible and appropriately trained staff, although I should perhaps mention that, on one occasion, a staff member did not come on duty for two hours. This meant that there was only one staff member on duty - which would not necessarily matter, but it happened to co-incide with a disturbed episode of one of the residents.

   I do not feel we should be airing this incident as it will only demonstrate our weakness. I believe we limit the response to that mention in Thea's complaint as mentioned in my previous email.

5. During the last year a number of longer-serving staff had left and rather than continuing to call in agency staff, we have made it a point to recruit and train our own staff. They have been carefully chosen but it naturally takes time for them to develop a deep understanding of what makes each resident feel and act in a specific way.

6. Both the Charity's Chief Executive and the Board of Trustees carry and exercise the responsibility for the quality of care provided. They take this task very seriously and support the staff, especially during a period of change as is the case with Lancaster lodge. An internal audit was undertaken and the opportunity was used to correct gaps and to clear the decks for a partly new programme in which the residents will be much more involved than was the case in the past.

I hope this draft which should be commented on by Peggy and Duncan for accuracy etc will be of use.

I should add that I believe that there has been crisis management at Lancaster Lodge - some unavoidable - but also because not enough considered thought was given. However I am not sure that it would help to share this opinion or fact with the concerned mother.

Elly

EXAMPLE II:

From: Duncan Lawrence <<u>karmicrecycling@icloud.com</u>>
Date: 1 February 2016 at 06:05:05 GMT
To: Peggy J <<u>peggwegg@hotmail.com</u>>
Subject: Good morning Peggy....draft LL letter ideas

Dear Commissioner,

Re:RPFI-Lancaster Lodge

Over December 2015 we completed an audit of the company. As a result we realised that our charity's core philosophy was not fully integrated within some of our houses.

To that end, Lancaster Lodge programme has been updated to better create a holistic service user experience, one that will lead to our service users developing increased self motivation,resiliency and more practical development and support leading up to the 'moving on phase' to independent living environment.

You will also see evidence of this development at our case reviews, where we are more in keeping the service user central to evaluating e.g. 'what works well and or less well' and the forging creative partnerships for their 'post' Lancaster Lodge moving on.

Some service users have adjusted to the programme's development more easily than others. Hopefully all will settled into the Therapeutic Community developments very soon.

We will have an open house this Spring 2016, we will keep you posted as to the dates and genuinely hope that you will attend.

Feel free to get in touch with Duncan Lawrence, the Lancaster Lodge Service Manager Support and Clinical Lead for RPFI.

Best wishes for 2016,

Dear Family, Carers and Supportive others.

The Lancaster Lodge Therapeutic Community has been improved over the past few weeks as a result of a winter 2015 Audit Report that recommended various initiatives to help your loved one develop enhanced self management skills, confidence and the belief that they can grow and change within the Therapeutic Community....ultimately leading to a positive independent living setting upon their Lancaster Lodge graduation.

Some of the residents initially found the initial changes and development very difficult to adjust to, but we are very confident that all will embrace the changes and development soon.

Feel free to contact Duncan Lawrence(Lancaster Lodge's Service Manager Support and RPFI's Clinical Lead if you would further information about our programme.

We will have a Spring 2016 Open House, once we send out our invitations, we hope to see you here!

Thanks for your continuing support to your son or daughter during their time at Lancaster Lodge.

Duncan

EXAMPLE III

From: Diversity Management LCL <<u>diversitymanagementlcl@</u> <u>btinternet.com</u>>

Date: 2 March 2016 at 16:55:39 GMT

To: Geoff Benton <<u>bentongeoff@gmail.com</u>>, "<u>peggwegg@</u> <u>hotmail.com</u>" <<u>peggwegg@hotmail.com</u>>, Elly Jansen <<u>ellywjansen@hotmail.com</u>>, Elly Jansen <<u>elly.jansen@</u> <u>rpfi.org</u>>, Colin McDonald <<u>colin_newatlantis@hotmail.</u> <u>com</u>>

Subject: LL

Good evening all,

I hope today was enlightening and not too stressful.

I think now it is imperative to take stock and think laterally in order to get a strategic LL plan.

I think all ideas should be put on the table and none discounted eg...temporarily close LL down and rebuilt decor, staff team and carefully develop a more suitable resident base, divide the house in two (with two separate lounges, etc) and have a side for current programme and half for adult semi independent unit, etc..example of two LL ideas.

We need to continue to give confidence to staff that actually RPFI/RCI own and run the houses and not them...I think the last two days may have led some to think that we have either 'retreated' or have been made to do 'something different' by CQC.

Either way some of our past interventions have needed more time to be effective and or were only short term fixes and or were not well thought out ideas full stop.

I look forward to the transformation!

Duncan

P.S: I am in LL Thursday. Dom is still very very interested in being interviewed but can only do week day interviews.

We need to be prepared to be tested and I am 100% sure Joanne told her peers about her situation and I expect several tough questions like there were for Vincent and Rohit absences...all ideas greatly appreciated.

Duncan

Myth 5.1: RPFI took DL suggestions: Examples of DL suggestions that would have eased the tension between the Lancaster Lodge and the charity

EXAMPLE:

From: Diversity Management LCL
Date: 9 February 2016at 06:39:56 GMT
To: EllyJansen,Elly Jansen, «peggwegg@hotmail.com", Peggy Jhugroo
Cc: Geoff Benton
Subject: RPFI/RCI Board Composition

Good morning to us all,

Just a reminder of my ideas have a monthly or quarterly charity blog/news letter to alert staff and service users to the 'vision' and to consider expanding the board to include staff member rep and a service user/parent-carer rep... because we always have so much to do when we all meet I am aware that these ideas might gotten lost.

Every day when doing this charity's work, I am reminded that each month we may be stepping over a great opportunity to bring the charity together more efficiently.

Have a great day!

Duncan

D.E.Lawrence: Diversity,Equality,and Inclusion Specialist / Management and Team Coach.
Skype: diversitymanagementlcl
Sent from my iPhone

From: Elly Jansen <elly.jansen@rpfi.org>

Date: 9 February 2016 at 15:40:15 GMT

To: Diversity Management LCL <diversitymanagementlcl@btinternet.com>, Peggy J <peggwegg@hotmail.com>

Subject: Re: Apologies....problem with phone.

I believe we need to have greater stability before inviting a person with mental health problems.

WE JUST LOST TWO PEOPLE IN THAt category - one a long-term excellent boardmember and one who nearly banrupted us and we are still suffering the after-effect. WE NEED TO START AN APPEAL AS WELL AS A TIGHTER ORGANISATION.

ELLY

On 9 February 2016 at 08:08, Diversity Management LCL <diversitymanagementlcl@btinternet.com> wrote:

Please disregard last two messages...my phone seems to push 'send' on its own recently!

Good morning to us all,

Just a reminder of my ideas to have a monthly charity blog/news letter to alert staff and service users to the 'vision' and to expand the board to include staff member rep and a service user/parent-carer rep...because we always have so much to do when we all meet that these ideas might 'get lost in the crowd'.

Every day when doing this charity's work, I am reminded that each month we may be stepping over a great opportunity for the charity to get its ideas across more effectively.

Have a great day!

Duncan

D.E.Lawrence: Diversity,Equality,and Inclusion Specialist / Management and Team Coach.

Skype: diversitymanagementlcl

Sent from my iPhone

Myth 5.2:RPFI took DL suggestions: DL Views about progress at Lancaster Lodge

Fact: The founder/lead advisor was unhappy about the Lancaster unit going back several years.

From: diversitymanagementlcl<<u>diversitymanagementlcl@btinternet.com</u>>

Date: 6 January 2016at 06:56:06 GMT

To: Peggy Jhugroo<<u>pjhugroo@wandsworth.gov.uk</u>>, "<u>peggwegg@hotmail.com</u>" <<u>peggwegg@hotmail.com</u>>, Elly Jansen <<u>elly.jansen@rpfi.org</u>>, Elly Jansen <<u>ellywjansen@hotmail.com</u>>

Subject: DL-Quality Assurance Check Wc 4.1.16

Sent from my iPad

RPFI/RCI Quality Assurance Checks carried out by Duncan Lawrence Week commencing 4.1.16: **Summary Notes**

White House: · Staff spent almost two hours + in the office 'counting money' (e.g they made coffees,teas,breakfast,etc for residents but made no effort to sit with them, have teas together,etc.). · Handover read more like a 'compliant judgement' of service users rather than reflecting on a service users comments(verbally and non verbally) about their own experiences of 'their day' · Acting Lead detailed a long list of support staff negative communications, refusals to 'work the house floor' along side/with the residents, lack of interest or enthusiasm to work to care plans and limited demonstration of good teamwork.

Conclusion: 1. Recommend the entire permanent staff team receive a verbal warning for a 'POOR QUALITY ASSURANCE CHECK', one that could be revoked if they quickly improve this situation within 30 days. 2. Regarding the above,if HR is not able to 'action' this, I would like my original visit notes(that were given to the Acting Lead) typed (say in size 18 font) and posted in the staff office for the next month.

Lancaster House: · General demonstration of practice with service users to a SATISFACTORY + at this Quality Assurance Check. · The main challenge this visit related to House Manager coming to terms that the home can't easily afford so many external service providers(and responding to giving notice to external service providers to cease services). · After a rather lengthy consideration, a 'counter proposal' was put forward..."...what if we kept an 80% occupancy rate, could we then ask for things on a case by case basis(e.g keep our current level of external providers)?..." · Was suggested by this writer to explore how to develop staff in a timely way(as a way of creating in-house career development opportunities).

Conclusion: 1.I Recommend that the RPFI/RCI CEO/Board consider the 'counter proposal' and to consider what is possible/practical in terms of staff development plan(to reduce reliance on external service providers).

2. Related to the above, this writer respectfully asks that the CEO/Board turn around a clear and concise written response within a week if possible.

Additionally, consider a 'company wide' policy of staff development that encourages 'trainee professional' development in the areas of art therapy, music therapy, counselling, group facilitation, staff supervision, etc..

Would be great to announce this as 'an ideal',say at this weeks company training day.

Lytton House: · Preparations for children's home occupancy and or semi-independent unit occupancy appears on track(but this writer recommends one day staff training asap on 'Dealing with Stress and Aggressive situations' and to consider diverse provisions, ones that include the use of trained volunteers).

Conclusion:

1. Continue to prepare a 'fit for purpose' staff compliment, one that meets the organisation's short-medium term needs. Important that the 'service user group' is 100% at the front of all planning and development .

2. If the semi-independent unit is pursued, the company should consider how they use the current Lytton House management resource(Colin). Most Semi-Independent Units do not have full-time management provision. Could prove useful to allow Colin to manage White House and Lytton House together. He would need at least 20-30 CPD Hours in the area of 'adult social care' covering mental health, age related provision,etc.. A good link for a 'Social Care'

CPD Certificate is http://www.skillsforcare.org.uk/ Standards/Care-Certificate/Care-Certificate.aspx

Duncan Lawrence(BA-Ed,MA-Counselling,DPA-Public Admin, FiLM,Reg. MBACP and FBACP[21]

---

[21] **Note to Editor:** Often emails are repeated in this section, but because they were part of the 'email chain', I thought that it is important to kept them, to show that I was not editing emails for the readers and could be accused of misleading/ misrepresentations.

Myth 6: RPFI took DL suggestions: Some relevant 'Post CQC Lancaster Lodge Inspection' discussions between DL and Elly Jansen Founder/Myth 7: CEO was up to the task-DL Suggestion for CEO to step down

From: Diversity Management LCL <diversitymanagementlcl@btinternet.com>
Date: 3 March 2016 at 10:40:40 GMT
To: Elly Jansen <elly.jansen@rpfi.org>
Cc: Peggy Jhugroo<pjhugroo@wandsworth.gov.uk>, "peggwegg@hotmail.com" <peggwegg@hotmail.com>, Colin McDonald <colin_newatlantis@hotmail.com>, Elly Jansen <ellywjansen@hotmail.com>
Subject: Re: Supportive Strategy add ons from Duncan

Sounds good!

Duncan

D.E.Lawrence: Diversity,Equality,Inclusion and Sport Specialist / Management and Team Coach.

Skype: diversitymanagementlcl

Sent from my iPhone

On 3 Mar 2016, at 10:21, Elly Jansen <elly.jansen@rpfi.org> wrote:

geoff proposes to come here at 5,15 to join thg senior staff meeting..

elly

On 3 March 2016 at 06:41, diversitymanagementlcl <diversitymanagementlcl@btinternet.com> wrote:

Hi Peggy,

Some add on ideas that might help with your Strategy Development.

Called:Transformation phase II(Phase I is 1 March Enhanced TC)

Could include:

- You temp giving up your CEO role(say to Colin)for 2-3 weeks
- You coming to LL as an Well being Specialist to model/ lead practitioner championing the enhanced TC for at least 2-3 weeks
- You being coordinator of LL decor upgrade
- Getting skip for Monday for a two week stint...to do a whole house and office clear up.
- DL then has time to supervise staff and give each a rating competency/capacity and support them accordingly (see attached examples...there are two on one page) and sort out LL case management system(paperwork) and begin 1-1 and group therapy.
- We interview like crazy and get a team leader or deputy to replace your LL role when you resume CEO
- 1 April I resume my clinical Lead and Operational Role and we continue with a nationwide LL service manager search.

With these types of things in place I could just support any reasonable strategy...without them I can't.

I have cancer tests Friday,that will need to be urgently rearranged, please confirm if 2pm today or Friday at WH.

Sorry for rushing, I wanted to contribute to your ideas, even on a busy day.

Duncan

From: diversitymanagementlcl<u>diversitymanagementlcl@btinternet.com</u>>
Date: 6 January 2016at 06:56:06 GMT
To: Peggy Jhugroo<<u>pjhugroo@wandsworth.gov.uk</u>>, "<u>peggwegg@hotmail.com</u>" <<u>peggwegg@hotmail.com</u>>, Elly Jansen <<u>elly.jansen@rpfi.org</u>>, Elly Jansen <<u>ellywjansen@hotmail.com</u>>
Subject: DL–Quality Assurance Check Wc 4.1.16

Sent from my iPad

☐ RPFI/RCI Quality Assurance Checks carried out by Duncan Lawrence Week commencing 4.1.16:**Summary Notes**

☐ **White House:** · Staff spent almost two hours + in the office 'counting money' (e.g they made coffees,teas,breakfast,etc for residents but made no effort to sit with them, have teas together,etc.). · Handover read more like a 'compliant judgement' of service users rather than reflecting on a service users comments(verbally and non verbally) about their own experiences of 'their day' · Acting Lead detailed a long list of support staff negative communications, refusals to 'work the house floor' along side/with the residents, lack of interest or enthusiasm to work to care plans and limited demonstration of good teamwork.

☐ **Conclusion:** 1. Recommend the entire permanent staff team receive a verbal warning for a 'POOR QUALITY ASSURANCE CHECK', one that could be revoked if they quickly improve this situation within 30 days. 2. Regarding the above,if HR is not able to 'action' this, I would like my original visit notes(that were given to the Acting Lead) typed (say in size 18 font) and posted in the staff office for the next month.

☐ **Lancaster House:** · General demonstration of practice with service users to a SATISFACTORY + at this Quality Assurance Check. · The main challenge this visit related to House Manager coming to terms that the home can't easily afford so many external service providers(and responding to giving notice to external service providers to cease services). · After a rather lengthy consideration, a 'counter proposal' was put forward..."...what if we kept an 80% occupancy rate, could we then ask for things on a case by case basis(e.g keep our current level of external providers)?..." · Was suggested by this writer to explore how to develop staff in a timely way(as a way of creating in-house career development opportunities).

☐ Conclusion: 1. I Recommend that the RPFI/RCI CEO/Board consider the 'counter proposal' and to consider what is possible/practical in terms of staff development plan(to reduce reliance on external service providers).

☐ 2. Related to the above, this writer respectfully asks that the CEO/Board turn around a clear and concise written response within a week if possible.

☐ Additionally, consider a 'company wide' policy of staff development that encourages 'trainee professional' development in the areas of art therapy, music therapy, counselling, group facilitation, staff supervision, etc..

☐ Would be great to announce this as 'an ideal',say at this weeks company training day.

☐ Lytton House: · Preparations for children's home occupancy and or semi-independent unit occupancy appears on track(but this writer recommends one day staff training asap on 'Dealing with Stress and Aggressive situations' and to consider diverse provisions, ones that include the use of trained volunteers).

☐ Conclusion:

☐ 1. Continue to prepare a 'fit for purpose' staff compliment, one that meets the organisation's short-medium term needs. Important that the 'service user group' is 100% at the front of all planning and development .

☐ 2. If the semi-independent unit is pursued, the company should consider how they use the current Lytton House management resource(Colin). Most Semi-Independent Units do not have full-time management provision. Could prove useful to allow Colin to manage White House and Lytton House together. He would need at least 20-30 CPD Hours in the area of 'adult social care' covering mental health, age related provision,etc.. A good link for a 'Social Care' CPD Certificate is http://www.skillsforcare.org. uk/Standards/Care-Certificate/Care-Certificate.aspx

☐ Duncan Lawrence(BA-Ed,MA-Counselling,DPA-Public Admin, FiLM,Reg. MBACP and FBACP

From: Diversity Management LCL <diversitymanagementlcl@ btinternet.com>

Date: 3 March 2016 at 10:40:40 GMT

To: Elly Jansen <elly.jansen@rpfi.org>

Cc: Peggy Jhugroo<pjhugroo@wandsworth.gov.uk>, "peggwegg@hotmail.com" <peggwegg@hotmail.com>, Colin McDonald <colin_newatlantis@hotmail.com>, Elly Jansen <ellywjansen@hotmail.com>

Subject: Re: Supportive Strategy add ons from Duncan

Sounds good!

Duncan

D.E.Lawrence: Diversity,Equality,Inclusion and Sport Specialist / Management and Team Coach.

Skype: diversitymanagementlcl

Sent from my iPhone

On 3 Mar 2016, at 10:21, Elly Jansen <<u>elly.jansen@rpfi.org</u>> wrote:

geoff proposes to come here at 5,15 to join thg senior staff meeting..

elly

On 3 March 2016 at 06:41, diversitymanagementlcl <<u>diversitymanagementlcl@btinternet.com</u>> wrote:

Hi Peggy,

Some add on ideas that might help with your Strategy Development.

Called: Transformation phase II (Phase I is 1 March Enhanced TC)

Could include:

— You temp giving up your CEO role(say to Colin)for 2-3 weeks
— You coming to LL as an Well being Specialist to model/ lead practitioner championing the enhanced TC for at least 2-3 weeks
— You being coordinator of LL decor upgrade
— Getting skip for Monday for a two week stint...to do a whole house and office clear up.

- DL then has time to supervise staff and give each a rating competency/capacity and support them accordingly (see attached examples...there are two on one page) and sort out LL case management system(paperwork) and begin 1-1 and group therapy.
- We interview like crazy and get a team leader or deputy to replace your LL role when you resume CEO
- 1 April I resume my clinical Lead and Operational Role and we continue with a nationwide LL service manager search.

With these types of things in place I could just support any reasonable strategy...without them I can't.

I have cancer tests Friday,that will need to be urgently rearranged, please confirm if 2pm today or Friday at WH.

Sorry for rushing, I wanted to contribute to your ideas, even on a busy day.

Duncan

Myth 7.1: CEO was up to the task–Suggestions for CEO to step down

From: Diversity Management LCL <diversitymanagementlcl@btinternet.com>

Date: 3 March 2016 at 10:40:40 GMT

To: Elly Jansen <elly.jansen@rpfi.org>

Cc: Peggy Jhugroo<pjhugroo@wandsworth.gov.uk>, "peggwegg@hotmail.com" <peggwegg@hotmail.com>, Colin McDonald <colin_newatlantis@hotmail.com>, Elly Jansen <ellywjansen@hotmail.com>

Subject: Re: Supportive Strategy add ons from Duncan

Sounds good!

Duncan

D.E.Lawrence: Diversity,Equality,Inclusion and Sport Specialist / Management and Team Coach.

Skype: diversitymanagementlcl

Sent from my iPhone

On 3 Mar 2016, at 10:21, Elly Jansen <elly.jansen@rpfi.org> wrote:

geoff proposes to come here at 5,15 to join thg senior staff meeting..

elly

On 3 March 2016 at 06:41, diversitymanagementlcl <diversitymanagementlcl@btinternet.com> wrote:

Hi Peggy,

Some add on ideas that might help with your Strategy Development.

Called: Transformation phase II (Phase I is 1 March Enhanced TC)

Could include:

- You temp giving up your CEO role(say to Colin)for 2-3 weeks
- You coming to LL as an Well being Specialist to model/ lead practitioner championing the enhanced TC for at least 2-3 weeks
- You being coordinator of LL decor upgrade
- Getting skip for Monday for a two week stint...to do a whole house and office clear up.
- DL then has time to supervise staff and give each a rating competency/capacity and support them accordingly (see attached examples...there are two on one page) and sort out LL case management system(paperwork) and begin 1-1 and group therapy.
- We interview like crazy and get a team leader or deputy to replace your LL role when you resume CEO
- 1 April I resume my clinical Lead and Operational Role and we continue with a nationwide LL service manager search.

With these types of things in place I could just support any reasonable strategy...without them I can't.

I have cancer tests Friday,that will need to be urgently rearranged, please confirm if 2pm today or Friday at WH.

Sorry for rushing, I wanted to contribute to your ideas, even on a busy day.

Duncan

From: Diversity Management LCL <<u>diversitymanagementlcl@ gmail.com</u>>
Date: 7 March 2016 at 03:55:39 GMT
Subject: Good morning Peggy,

Good morning Peggy,

Regarding your early am instructions today for LL, until I see a written strategic plan that I can buy into I am not stepping into LL.

I have always provided a steady flow of verbal and written RPFI/RPI strategic ideas(for at least short and medium term progression opportunities)...these contributions were before and after recent CQC inspections.

As recent as the second day of CQC being around and they did not get 'my letter idea',I put in writing to the entire RPFI/ RCI SMT and its Board Chair that I would not support any plan that involved you coming into LL as the CEO/Anyone's Boss.

I came in this past weekend only because I genuinely wanted you to have a few hours of rest to enjoy Mother's Day.

It is now Monday. I have David's WH complaint hearing this am. I am 100% open and ready to support you even without a written LL plan, but from outside the LL house only.

I am sure Colin has told you several times that an RPFI/RCI SM has never yet been given the power and authority to actually strategically lead and manage their own houses(and you recently heard from some LL residents that they were told to not comply with me...as were the staff...Martyna,Banu and Richard were the only fit for purpose LL staff that were ready to engage the residents and to give the Enhanced TC a chance,etc.)...not a good and secure position ever to be for an organisation that is trying to be strategic in its thinking (rather than as it is now day-to-day assessing, day-to-day planing and hourly and day-to-day instructions from the CEO).

I am not currently willing to be 'LL on-paper SM', or 'your LL Deputy' waiting to receive your hourly and or daily instructions and or a LL Bank Staff...a total waste of my talents,plus LL's current situation crosses so many of my 'ethical and leadership red lines'(on hourly and weekly basis).

I am not trying to be obstructive Peggy and I did give advance written notice last week of my intentions...e.g that to not assume that I would cooperate without a plan.

Without a plan(at least this week...I will assess my RPFI/ RCI options each week until the end of my March 2016 contract), I will however be open to assist the wider charity and LL indirectly (without ever entering the LL building) with interviews, staff and leadership training, assisting with inductions,developing paperwork systems,do HR hearings for LL and beyond, attend professional external meetings,doing 1-1 and group therapy, staff supervision, etc...but no 'LL SM',no LL Deputy to you, no more on-call and definitely no LL bank worker role.

I am willing and able to revise my current stance once I have seen and considered a written LL strategy.

Without this I think the charity continues to be very very very vulnerable and open CQC issues, local government issues, local resident issues and potential for growth in LL resident and staff non compliance movement, residents being unwell,staff shortages,etc..

Duncan

☐ **Emails related to DL credentials**

From: Geoff Benton <bentongeoff@gmail.com>
Date: 22 December 2015 at 18:53:05 GMT
To: diversitymanagementlcl<diversitymanagementlcl@btinternet.com>
Subject: Re: D.Lawrence Credentials

Hi Duncan

Received with thanks,

Regards

Geoff

On 21 Dec 2015 22:15, "diversitymanagementlcl" <diversitymanagementlcl@btinternet.com> wrote:

Dear Mr Benton,

Can you please,confirm that you have received my credentials by email,earlier this evening?

Thanks in advance,

Duncan Lawrence

Sent from my iPad

From: Diversity Management LCL <diversitymanagementlcl@btinternet.com>
Date: 24 December 2015 at 10:10:38 GMT
To: Chair Of Board <bentongeoff@gmail.com>
Subject: D.Lawrence DBS

D.E.Lawrence: Diversity,Equality,and Inclusion Specialist / Management and Team Coach.

Skype: diversitymanagementlcl

Sent from my iPhone

From: Diversity Management LCL <<u>diversitymanagementlcl@</u>
<u>btinternet.com</u>>
Date: 24 December 2015 at 10:10:38 GMT
To: Chair Of Board <<u>bentongeoff@gmail.com</u>>
Subject: D.Lawrence DBS

D.E.Lawrence: Diversity,Equality,and Inclusion Specialist / Management and Team Coach.

Skype: diversitymanagementlcl

Sent from my iPhone

☐ **DL Job description**

From: Elly Jansen <<u>elly.jansen@rpfi.org</u>>
Date: 17 January 2016 at 11:20:41 GMT
To: Duncan Lawrence <<u>diversitymanagementlcl@btinternet.</u>
<u>com</u>>
Subject: your response

I am very relieved and know that Peggy will be, that your consultancy days will be increased. i see you as training whatever you are doing by way of clinical operational work you are engaged in. This has been so necessary for so long.

I WELCOME YOU WHOLEHEARTEDLY.

ELLY

[22]**Where does it say you need a doctorate for any of my roles at RPFI?**

CLINICAL/OPERATIONAL LEAD

A) Definition: The COL is a member of the RPFI top management team, appointed by the CEO to direct, supervise and promote the proper functioning of specific projects through direct and concentrated involvement with them, and to undertake and train staff in clinical assessments of new applicants.

B) Task: The COL's primary task is to ensure that the staff of each of the projects under his or her control achieve and sustain the purposes for which the projects have been created and do so in accordance with the goals, principles, therapeutic policies and managerial structure of the Organisation as well as in keeping with all the relevant laws and regulations.

C) Accountability: The COL is directly accountable to the CEO. He or she is accountable for the *therapeutic and practical work* of the project managers and all staff under the project manager's control and supervision.

D) Time Distribution: The needs for supervision of different projects are bound to vary at different times, but the COL will need to spend around 70 % of his or her working time at the projects under their

---

[22] **Editor Note:** This was not part of the original emails, but the press made a big deal about me not having a medical degree (without ever seeing my contract) so in my memoir prep I wrote this comment and it seemed appropriate to keep it in.

supervision. The demands of the work can be heavy and the COL must expect to work up to 48 hours per week at times, especially during the first 3 – 6 months, whilst later the average working week will be 40 hours. The remaining 30 % of time will be spent undertaking PR to ensure full occupancy, dealing with administrative tasks and specific problems, and attending meetings with the CEO and/or Consultant or undertaking other tasks which promote the work of RPFI.

E) Time in the projects: As a minimum the COL will spend the equivalent of two whole day (or four half days) in each of the projects during a two week period. During each visit a specific period of 1,5 hours is set aside for supervision with the manager and a further 1,5 hours for meeting with the whole staff group to participate in agenda discussions and to review systematically the specific tasks of the staff team - *especially where it concerns the therapeutic content-* and, where necessary, specific areas of difficulty.

At least 2,5 hours of every visit will be spent on reviewing, inspecting and training in: professional social work activities, administration and practical duties. Part of this time will be set aside for a staff dynamics meeting to ensure that problems do not foster and to create a healthy climate for team work. The COL needs to emphasise the need to remain aware of safety and health regulations and to streamline good administrative and home-making procedures so that a sound structure is created and *so that maximum time is available for understanding the residents and the best means of caring.*

F) Case load: The COL is expected to cope with a case load of at least 5 Projects, one of which may be a new project. During each three months' period each project needs a two-day "overhaul " visit during which all aspects of the project can be taken under the loupe – *especially the therapeutic issues* – and for the writing up of a three-monthly report for the CEO – hopefully demonstrating satisfactory progress.

G) Mode of Activity: The COL performs his or her tasks through both formal and informal meetings with the project manager (and, when necessary, with other staff individually), the staff team and residents. He or she needs to get familiarised with all aspects of life in the project e.g. the management of the staff team, including staff rotas, social work procedures (such as admissions and discharges, care plans and risk assessments, counselling and group meeting), administration, maintenance and home making, work and creative programmes, social activities, catering and meals procedures, PR, liaison with referral agencies, families and schools (and sometimes meetings with a house committee or with groups of family and friends of the residents). *He or she will particularly focus on the therapeutic quality and the functioning of the project as a TC* and the input of staff members individually and jointly..

The COL regularly, systematically and formally appraises the work of each staff member, provides clarification of policy and problems, gives formal and informal feedback and constructively reviews with those areas identified as in need of strengthening. He or she provides support, both by managerial action and by consultancy, training and guidance over planning, and ensures that management information is passed on and clarified and, if directives are not adhered to, disciplines staff, following RPFI procedures..

He or she also discusses and advises on new proposals and initiatives and puts these to the CEO and Consultant, whether it concerns re-organisation of rooms, new activities or new procedures or suggestions regarding the whole Organisation. The COL needs to ensure that each project manager produces a full report on all aspects of the operation of the project and passes this on to the CEO with appropriate commentary.

H) Team work: As a member of the senior management team, the COL needs to remain in close contact to be aware of existing policies and the reasons why they exist, to participate in the development of new policies and to provide relevant feedback from and to the projects and liaise over action to be taken. He or she must avoid getting used as "complaints officer" and develop the ability to see issues clearly and assist staff in gaining real skill to use their scope and creativity ad therby derive satisfaction from their task.

The COL needs to be able to portray genuine warmth and reflection n what is conveyed to him or her. At the same time it is essential that the COL demonstrates independence and is seen to act without fear or vavour! The displacement of occupational anxieties and disappointments to pre-occupation by the house staff with the task of senior staff (and accompanying neglect of attention to project problems) is a recurring issue. The COL needs to build up confidence in senior staff by sticking to his or her own brief and keeping the project staff to their own task.

Our work tends to encourage staff to deal with pressures and problems they experience by attempts to create a split between senior staff members or by splitting their "good" function (listening and support) from their bad" function (inspection, feedback, control and direction) in favour of the former. The COL,in representing both, models the choices as well as the constraints of our work which the managers in turn have to apply with both staff and residents, thereby enabling the manager to use choices and constraints responsibly, creatively and effectively.

CLINICAL/OPERATIONAL LEAD

A) Definition: The COL is a member of the RPFI top management team, appointed by the CEO to direct, supervise and promote the proper functioning of specific projects through direct and concentrated involvement with them, and to undertake and train staff in clinical assessments of new applicants.

B) Task: The COL's primary task is to ensure that the staff of each of the projects under his or her control achieve and sustain the purposes for which the projects have been created and do so in accordance with the goals, principles, therapeutic policies and managerial structure of the Organisation as well as in keeping with all the relevant laws and regulations.

C) Accountability: The COL is directly accountable to the CEO. He or she is accountable for the *therapeutic and practical work* of the project managers and all staff under the project manager's control and supervision.

D) Time Distribution: The needs for supervision of different projects are bound to vary at different times, but the COL will need to spend around 70 % of his or her working time at the projects under their supervision. The demands of the work can be heavy and the COL must expect to work up to 48 hours per week at times, especially during the first 3 – 6 months, whilst later the average working week will be 40 hours. The remaining 30 % of time will be spent undertaking PR to ensure full occupancy, dealing with administrative tasks and specific problems, and attending meetings with the CEO and/or Consultant or undertaking other tasks which promote the work of RPFI.

E) Time in the projects: As a minimum the COL will spend the equivalent of two whole day (or four half days) in each of the projects during a two week period. During each visit a specific period of 1,5 hours is set aside for supervision with the manager and a further 1,5 hours for meeting with the whole staff group to participate in agenda discussions and to review systematically the specific tasks of the staff team - *especially where it concerns the therapeutic content-* and, where necessary, specific areas of difficulty.

At least 2,5 hours of every visit will be spent on reviewing, inspecting and training in: professional social work activities, administration and practical duties. Part of this time will be set aside for a staff dynamics meeting to ensure that problems do not foster and to create a healthy climate for team work. The COL needs to emphasise the need to remain aware of safety and health regulations and to streamline good administrative and home-making procedures so that a sound structure is created and *so that maximum time is available for understanding the residents and the best means of caring.*

F) Case load: The COL is expected to cope with a case load of at least 5 Projects, one of which may be a new project. During each three months' period each project needs a two-day "overhaul " visit during which all aspects of the project can be taken under the loupe – *especially the therapeutic issues* - and for the writing up of a three-monthly report for the CEO – hopefully demonstrating satisfactory progress.

G) Mode of Activity: The COL performs his or her tasks through both formal and informal meetings with the project manager (and, when necessary, with other staff individually), the staff team and residents. He or she needs to get familiarised with all aspects of life in the project e.g. the management of the staff team, including staff rotas, social work procedures (such as admissions and discharges, care plans and risk assessments, counselling and group meeting), administration, maintenance and home making, work and creative programmes, social activities, catering and meals procedures, PR, liaison with referral agencies, families and schools (and sometimes meetings with a house committee or with groups of family and friends of the residents). *He or she will particularly focus on the therapeutic quality and the functioning of the project as a TC* and the input of staff members individually and jointly..

The COL regularly, systematically and formally appraises the work of each staff member, provides clarification of policy and problems, gives formal and informal feedback and constructively reviews with those areas identified as in need of strengthening. He or she provides support, both by managerial action and by consultancy, training and guidance over planning, and ensures that management information is passed on and clarified and, if directives are not adhered to, disciplines staff, following RPFI procedures..

He or she also discusses and advises on new proposals and initiatives and puts these to the CEO and Consultant, whether it concerns re-organisation of rooms, new activities or new procedures or suggestions regarding the whole Organisation. The COL needs to ensure that each project manager produces a full report on all aspects of the operation of the project and passes this on to the CEO with appropriate commentary.

H) Team work: As a member of the senior management team, the COL needs to remain in close contact to be aware of existing policies and the reasons why they exist, to participate in the development of new policies and to provide relevant feedback from and to the projects and liaise over action to be taken. He or she must avoid getting used as "complaints officer" and develop the ability to see issues clearly and assist staff in gaining real skill to use their scope and creativity ad therby derive satisfaction from their task.

The COL needs to be able to portray genuine warmth and reflection n what is conveyed to him or her. At the same time it is essential that the COL demonstrates independence and is seen to act without fear or vavour!The displacement of occupational anxieties and disappointments to pre-occupation by the house staff with the task of senior staff (and accompanying neglect of attention to project problems) is a recurring issue. The COL needs to build up confidence in senior staff by sticking to his or her own brief and keeping the project staff to their own task.

Our work tends to encourage staff to deal with pressures and problems they experience by attempts to create a split between senior staff members or by splitting their "good" function (listening and support) from their bad" function (inspection, feedback, control and direction) in favour of the former. The COL,in representing both, models the choices as well as the constraints of our work which the managers in turn have to apply with both staff and residents, thereby enabling the manager to use choices and constraints responsibly, creatively and effectively.

Letter from the RPFI Board to all Its Staff – January 2016

As you know we have recently carried out an audit on RPFI. Whilst we are proud of our services it is of course always essential to be on the alert how to improve the quality and effectiveness of work we jointly undertake.

We are drawing up a strategy for ensuring that all RPFI staff get as much training and clinical supervision as possible, and that the 1 to 1 sessions, the community and staff meetings are used as tools to enhance our work for both our individual residents and the community as a whole, including staff. We highly value the unselfish work of staff whilst also needing to ensure that our safeguarding and our intensive work with residents remains under review.

To that end we are making considerable staffing changes to take advantage of our current strength to shore up areas needing improvement and to create regular staff development opportunities.

This is particularly important as, now that ... daughter is leaving the UK, ...has decided to leave also. Vincent has also informed us of his resignation which means that both projects will need timely cover. We will miss their dedicated service and need to ensure that the White House and Lancaster Lodge will have sufficient support for staff and residents.

Duncan Lawrence, who most of you will have met during his audit visits and his training sessions, is willing to provide

clinical and operational guidance and supervision for both projects. He will provide the necessary therapy for residents and operational supervision for the senior staff of both houses. Those of you who have been in his training session will realise the value of his input.

Peggy and Duncan will shortly inform you of the company wide 'sharing good practice' date.

Senior Management will put aside one day for appointment for any staff who wish to discuss any issues personally.

With appreciation for your work with RPFI.

Good wishes,

Geoff Benton

On behalf of the R

Myth 11: Staff were happy and content-Example of time consuming RPFI HR disciplinary related issues

Fact: the charity, for its small size had a large amount of ongoing disciplinary actions going on at the same time. Myself and other senior managers had at least 1-2 days per week taken from our normal duties to deal with these hr disciplinary tasks (which included interviews for new staff, exit interviews etc).

From: Peggy J
Date: 3 February 2016 at 21:53:21 GMT
To: "diversitymanagementlcl@btinternet.com"
Cc: "heathergrant@elliswhittam.com",Elly Jansen
Subject: Disciplinary/Investigations

Hi Duncan,

Please see attached update on staffing issues. I would like to get dates set for investigations/hearings.

Peggy

Staffing Issues

Staff	Issues	Action so far	Outstanding Action	Update from HR
Vincent Hill	Resigned but may bring constructive dismissal case. He is also in touch with residents and may be encouraging them to act against RPFI.	Resignation received and offers to deal with his issue through grievance procedures rather than resignation – declined. VH met with residents last week and may help fuel them complaints.	PJ to establish facts around VH's meeting with residents and email HR.	
	Investigation into leaving staff member alone despite concerns about residents.	Conclusion from hearing is to draw a line as insufficient evidence to cast blame.	HR to draft a post-hearing letter.	
	Refusing to follow a reasonable instruction on more than one occasion and also going off sick following hearing.	Hearing carried out and notes sent to HR .	DL to investigate BC's claims by interviewing PJ and FA this week. DL to forward report to HR who will draft outcome letter.	

| DF | Falsifying signing book and going sick. | Hearing postponed due to DF going sick. He sent in a response and a lodged discrimination complaint abut is off work until 11/2. | DL to oversee a Grievance Hearing into discrimination complaints.

PJ to facilitate a new hearing. | |
|---|---|---|---|---|
| WA | Refusing to follow return to work following a problem with her thumb even though she was informed that she could go on light duties. | Inconsistencies in statement and request for medical information. | DL to interview FA re: inconsistency with PJ' accounts of facts. | |
| Ja C | Sickness levels, latest sickness possibly due to non-payment of salary. | PJ lodged a request to payroll to reassess Jas's sick pay entitlement, as she believed she had exceeded sick pay allowance. Payroll failed to do calculations and di did not pay her but also failed to inform RPFI. | PJ to ascertain if there is any outstanding or overpayment. To inform HR who will advise on this matter. | |
| Rohit Sharma | Issue with terms of interim team leader post, despite at least 3 separate requests from managers, not being able to provide copies of degree certs or offer to do PHD. | RS is currently doing leadership training; this may be for his current post of Senior Support Worker or temp. Upgrade of Team Leader Post. | To be advised by HR | |

J	On probation and possibly colluding with residents and not understanding the RPFI Vision.			
General Issues	Contracts have slightly changed in terms of sick leave.		PJ to email latest contract to HR.	

From: Diversity Management LCL <diversitymanagementlcl@gmail.com>

Date: 23 February 2016 at 19:56:59 GMT

To: Martyna Karbowiak <martyna.karbowiak@rpfi.org>, Rohit Sharma <rohit.sharma@rpfi.org>

Subject: "plan b" for this Thursday and Friday

Hello to you both,

I would like Rohit to lead the staff that are on duty in a house clean up Thursday.

Example leadership facilitation Opening Statements Rohit might look like:

"...good morning, today we are doing an experiment on working together as a TC.

We have three jobs;

1. Clean up the sitting room

2. Prepare resident two rooms that are near each other that we can show to visitors next week.

3. Involve residents where possible, work around the art students and make lunch for and both other staff on duty and for residents.

If you are around Friday I would like you to run an induction until noon ?Martyna.

Thanks,Duncan

Sent from my iPad

From: Diversity Management LCL <<u>diversitymanagementlcl@ gmail.com</u>>
Date: 12 February 2016 at 06:15:25 GMT
Subject: Good morning,

Good morning,

Your statement is still not clear enough and it does not illustrate what you have actually learned from this experience.

Firstly, please number your statement as I originally asked you to, I have started the process for you.

Secondly, you need to add a reflective statement at the end of your statement (see my example below).

And finally, you need to start coming to staff meeting on Tuesdays from next week. There are so many things for you to learn. You specifically need to quickly learn from your actions,there are phone records for myself and others so please make sure to not record any future untrue details that can be checked and verified (we will not use you at LL any more if any lies are found out...being fully truthful now helps us to learn).

This incident caused so many problems simply because of poor communication and poor choices...but you can learn from this as well the entire staff team.

On Tuesday you will present this incident to the staff team meeting so that everyone can learn from it. Please sign, date and add this entire statement to the LL incident book within 24 hours. Please make sure up update it first and make sure to tell the entire truth before adding it to LL incident book.

Duncan

Example:

My 'post incident reflections':

1. After working through this incident with Duncan, I realised that I made a stressful work situation for me much worse simply by my poor choices on that evening.

2. I really should have sought Duncan's advice early in the evening and especially not let residents do my job for me(I have since found out that they were distraught having to support Hannah with her self harming that evening and myself and the staff on duty should have looked after their welfare too.). I will unconditionally apologise to the residents within 24 hours and let them know that I will do better in the future(without blaming them what so ever).

3. Once an ex-staff member was called by the residents and offered her advice, I could have simply said "... thanks but no thanks..." I am working through the incident with Duncan.

3.1 By not actually doing the above I complicated the situation because I violated the residents confidentiality by discussing them with an ex-staff member and did not make good use of other staff on duty earlier in the evening. I unfairly used Rohit's name and motives and since learned that Duncan has apologised to him on my behalf(in this situation, Rohit did nothing wrong).

3.2 My communication challenges got Paul involved and my slow written communication of this incident could lead others to think that I was hiding from this...all my fault and would be fair assumptions.

I have learned from my actions and am very very grateful to Paul and his leadership moments when I was clearly stressed and overwhelmed. I will apologise for taking him away from his home to assist me and humbly thank Paul for his excellent teamwork assistance, he clearly made a positive outcome for Hannah.

3.3 I will share this incident without ego within the next staff meeting and collect peer feedback and support others to learn from this.

3.4 Thanks to Duncan for his support and guidance.

Myth 12: DL Wanted to be Lancaster Unit Service Manager

Fact: I was very initially interested in managing the Lancaster unit (alongside my other cross charity role), but with continued dysfunctional senior leadership, it was easier to step away from this idea.

EXAMPLE I: **From:** Geoff Benton <bentongeoff@gmail.com>
Date: 12 February 2016 at 11:18:55 GMT
To: Diversity Management LCL <diversitymanagementlcl@btinternet.com>, Elly Jansen <elly.jansen@rpfi.org>, Elly Jansen <ellywjansen@hotmail.com>, Jonathan Manson <jonathan.manson@btinternet.com>, Catherine Keevil <catherine.keevil@yahoo.co.uk>
Subject: Re: Duncan Lawrence and RPFI/RCI

Hi Duncan

Many thanks for this, I will ask the board for their views and comments and get back to you next week.

Kind regards

Geoff

On Friday, February 12, 2016, Diversity Management LCL <diversitymanagementlcl@btinternet.com> wrote:

Dear Geoff,

Re: My continuing role within RPFI/RCI

While I have enjoyed working with the charity very much,now that I have been firmly working within the Lancaster Lodge I can see the full range of work needed (to get it to a good standard of care and administration).

From current LL staff(and recently departed staff) and LL residents I have found a 'pattern of neglect':

— Neglect of adherence to care plans(including residents having sporatickeyworkingsessions,some residents being allowed to 'vegetate' on the settee 24/7, residents with eating disorders and no dedicated plans,etc.).

— neglect of case management systems(files are missing attention going back several months)

— Neglect of staff training, especially relating to understanding RPFI Policy, Procedures, teambuilding, leadership,etc).

— Neglect of any transparent programme.

Although we have made great strides, we still have a long way to go and I feel that I have neglected my work within the WH and the LH.

Finally, LL staff,residents, parents,CFC,etc are expecting a medium/long term commitment from me.

What I need from RPFI/RCI?

1. Have all disciplinary actions sorted next week(I can 100% do more toil time to make this happen).

2. Have all 'non value' staff removed asap...they sap so much of my time and energy. They also potentially get in the way of new referral visits/planning.

3. £40k to work flexible 40 hours from 1 March 2016.

3.1 Three-10 hour days at LL

3.2 10 hour day at WH

* = The above includes integrating my Clinical Lead/ Operational Role.

4. I would do medication training,etc in order to play a more practical role at LL andWH.

5. If you get a deputy manager at LL then I could do 1 day at WH,1 day at LH and 2days at LL.

Without an increased commitment, I would like to return to my non service manager role from 1 March 2016.

Geoff, thanks in advance for considering this letter.

Duncan

D.E.Lawrence: Diversity,Equality,and Inclusion Specialist / Management and Team Coach.

Skype: diversitymanagementlcl

Sent from my iPhone

From: Diversity Management LCL <<u>diversitymanagementlcl@gmail.com</u>>

Date: 27 February 2016 at 11:56:27 GMT

Subject: Hi Geoff,

Hi Geoff,

I hope that you are starting to feel better, colds seem to last longer these days.

Thanks for this offer letter.

I can consider it but I would need written assurances such as:

1. That my original role will always be part of my contract...service manager(on site)

EXAMPLE II:

From: diversitymanagementlcl

Date: 7 March 2016at 04:21:38 GMT

To: Peggy J, Peggy Jhugroo, Elly Jansen, Elly Jansen,

Subject: Fwd: Peggy Support

Good morning Peggy,

Regarding your early am text instructions today (to me for LL), until I see a written strategic plan that I can buy into I am not stepping into LL.

I have always provided a steady flow of verbal and written RPFI/RPI strategic ideas(for at least short and medium term progression opportunities)...these contributions were before and after recent LL CQC inspections.

As recent as the second day of CQC being around and they did not get 'my letter idea',I put in writing to the entire RPFI/ RCI SMT and its Board Chair that I would not support any plan that involved you coming into LL as the CEO/Anyone's Boss.

I came in this past weekend only because I genuinely wanted you to have a few hours of rest to enjoy Mother's Day.

It is now Monday. I have to do David's WH complaint hearing this am. I am 100% open and ready to support you today even without a written LL plan, but from outside the LL house only.

I am sure Colin has told you several times that an RPFI/RCI SM has never yet been given the power and authority to actually strategically lead and manage their own houses(and you recently heard from some LL residents that they were told to not comply with me...as were the staff...M,B and R were the only fit for purpose LL staff that were ready to engage the residents and to give the Enhanced TC a chance,etc.)... not a good and secure position ever to be for an organisation that is trying to be strategic in its thinking (rather than as it is now e.g. day-to-day assessing, day-to-day planning and hourly and day-to-day instructions from the CEO).

I am not currently willing to be 'LL on-paper SM', or 'your LL Deputy' waiting to receive your hourly and or daily instructions and or a LL short notice Bank Staff...a total waste of my talents,plus LL's current situation crosses so many of my 'ethical and leadership red lines'(on an hourly and weekly basis).

I am not trying to be obstructive Peggy and I did give advance written notice last week of my intentions...e.g that to not assume that I would cooperate without a plan.

Without a plan(at least this week...I will assess my RPFI/RCI options each week until the end of my current March 2016 contract), I will however be open to assist the wider charity and LL indirectly (without ever entering the LL building) with interviews, staff and leadership training, assisting with inductions,developing paperwork systems,do HR hearings for LL and beyond, attend professional external meetings,doing 1-1 and group therapy, staff supervision, etc...but no 'LL SM' role, no LL Deputy to you, no more on-call and definitely no LL bank worker role.

I am willing and able to revise my current stance once I have seen and considered a written LL strategy.

Without this I think the charity continues to be very veryvery vulnerable and open to CQC issues, local government issues, local resident issues and potential for growth in LL resident and staff non compliance movement, residents being unwell,staffshortages,etc..

Duncan

Sent from my iPad

From: Diversity Management LCL <<u>diversitymanagementlcl@</u>
<u>btinternet.com</u>>
Date: 5 March 2016 at 19:05:36 GMT
To: Geoff Benton <<u>bentongeoff@gmail.com</u>>
Subject: Peggy Support

Good evening Geoff,

Peggy is really investing a lot of herself into Transforming LL but I worry that she is leaving herself vulnerable to staff spite and criticism, and residents accusations of her putting too much upon them(and potentially use RPFI as an excuse to stay unwell).

I am not sure of what her short and medium term vision is, my preference is still to restructure LL. Is there a 'plan b'?

Staff and residents in a community meeting yesterday abused Peggy something terrible.

I have to chair a grievance hearing at 9am Monday at WH,but will leave and work away from there soon afterwards.

Have difficulty being with staff that do not even check to see that Peggy was ok .

Duncan

D.E.Lawrence: Diversity,Equality,Inclusion and Sport Specialist / Management and Team Coach.

Sent from my iPhone

Myth 13: DL Pushed out the Lancaster Unit Service Manager

From: Diversity Management LCL <<u>diversitymanagementlcl@</u>
<u>btinternet.com</u>>
Date: 17 January 2016 at 09:28:10 GMT
To: Vincent Hill <<u>vincent.hill@rpfi.org</u>>
Cc: Peggy J <<u>peggwegg@hotmail.com</u>>
Subject: Re: Response to Resignation Letter

Hi Vincent,

I am trying to quickly get up to speed so I hope emailing you at weekend is ok.

I have been tasked with supporting you and your senior staff Monday.

I am hoping to be able to collect any written hand over details/instructions from you, keys, laptops,passwordsetc in order to pass them on.

Would 10am be ok time to arrive?

I genuinely would like to not rush you and I have the day allocated for this task.

Duncan

D.E.Lawrence: Diversity,Equality,and Inclusion Specialist / Management and Team Coach.

Skype: diversitymanagementlcl

Sent from my iPhone

On 17 Jan 2016, at 08:59, Vincent Hill <vincent.hill@rpfi.org> wrote:

Dear Duncan

Further to Peggy's e-mails below, please advise when you would wish to meet with me?

Best wishes

Vincent

From: Peggy J [mailto:peggwegg@hotmail.com]
Sent: 16 January, 2016 20:27
To: Vincent Hill <vincent.hill@rpfi.org>
Subject: RE: Response to Resignation Letter

Hi Vincent,

I suggest you meet with Duncan and discuss how and when you say goodbye to the residents.

Peggy

From: vincent.hill@rpfi.org
Subject: Re: Response to Resignation Letter
Date: Sat, 16 Jan 2016 18:15:42 +0000
To: peggwegg@hotmail.com

Dear Peggy

Community meeting's are on Wednesday's at 3pm.

Vincent

Sent from my iPhone

On 16 Jan 2016, at 17:07, <peggwegg@hotmail.com><peggwegg@hotmail.com> wrote:

Dear Vincent,

Following your letter of resignation, I have asked Duncan to act as change manager and to meet you at Lancaster to discuss the operational aspects.

I also think it is particularly important that you meet with the residents at their community meeting to say goodbye so there is a proper ending. Am I right in thinking this is Monday afternoon? If so, I suggest meeting with Duncan at 12.30pm and residents after.

Regards,

Peggy Jhugroo
RPFI Coordinator

Sent from my BlackBerry® wireless device

From: "Vincent Hill" <vincent.hill@rpfi.org>
Date: Sat, 16 Jan 2016 16:04:08 +0000
To: 'Peggy J'<peggwegg@hotmail.com>
Subject: RE: Response to Resignation Letter

Dear Peggy

Many thanks for your e-mail.

I just need to clarify the bit about Monday's shift as I find it a bit ambiguous. You say 'this will be effective from your next shift', it's not clear whether this means that I don't need to return for my next shift, or that Monday's shift should be my last?

Irrespective of whether I am required to do the Monday shift or not, I shall always be available if you or the staff team require any support in effecting the handover.

Should I not hear from you by Sunday pm I will assume that I am not required to come in to Lancaster Lodge on Monday morning.

Best wishes

Vincent

From: Peggy J [mailto:peggwegg@hotmail.com]
Sent: 16 January, 2016 10:39
To: vincent.hill@rpfi.org
Subject: Response to Resignation Letter

Hi Vincent,

Please see my response to your letter of resignation, you will also receive a hard copy in the post.

Peggy

From: diversitymanagementlcl<diversitymanagementlcl@
btinternet.com>
Date: 17 January 2016 at 13:02:29 GMT
To: Vincent Hill <vincent.hill@rpfi.org>
Cc: Peggy J <peggwegg@hotmail.com>
Subject: Re: Response to Resignation Letter

Thanks Vincent...see you then.

Duncan

Sent from my iPad

On 17 Jan 2016, at 11:29, Vincent Hill <vincent.hill@rpfi.org> wrote:

Dear Duncan

10am tomorrow at Lancaster Lodge will be fine with me.

Best Wishes

Vincent

From: Diversity Management LCL
[mailto:diversitymanagementlcl@btinternet.com]
Sent: 17 January, 2016 09:28
To: Vincent Hill <vincent.hill@rpfi.org>
Cc: Peggy J <peggwegg@hotmail.com>
Subject: Re: Response to Resignation Letter

Hi Vincent,

I am trying to quickly get up to speed so I hope emailing you
at weekend is ok.

I have been tasked with supporting you and your senior staff Monday.

I am hoping to be able to collect any written hand over details/instructions from you, keys, laptops,passwordsetc in order to pass them on.

Would 10am be ok time to arrive?

I genuinely would like to not rush you and I have the day allocated for this task.

Duncan

D.E.Lawrence: Diversity,Equality,and Inclusion Specialist / Management and Team Coach.

Skype: diversitymanagementlcl

Sent from my iPhone

On 17 Jan 2016, at 08:59, Vincent Hill <vincent.hill@rpfi.org> wrote:

Dear Duncan

Further to Peggy's e-mails below, please advise when you would wish to meet with me?

Best wishes

Vincent

From: Peggy J [mailto:peggwegg@hotmail.com]
Sent: 16 January, 2016 20:27
To: Vincent Hill <vincent.hill@rpfi.org>
Subject: RE: Response to Resignation Letter

Hi Vincent,

I suggest you meet with Duncan and discuss how and when you say goodbye to the residents.

Peggy

From: vincent.hill@rpfi.org
Subject: Re: Response to Resignation Letter
Date: Sat, 16 Jan 2016 18:15:42 +0000
To: peggwegg@hotmail.com

Dear Peggy

Community meeting's are on Wednesday's at 3pm.

Vincent

Sent from my iPhone

On 16 Jan 2016, at 17:07, <peggwegg@hotmail.com><peggwegg@hotmail.com> wrote:

Dear Vincent,

Following your letter of resignation, I have asked Duncan to act as change manager and to meet you at Lancaster to discuss the operational aspects.

I also think it is particularly important that you meet with the residents at their community meeting to say goodbye so there is a proper ending. Am I right in thinking this is Monday afternoon? If so, I suggest meeting with Duncan at 12.30pm and residents after.

Regards,

Peggy Jhugroo
RPFI Coordinator
Sent from my BlackBerry® wireless device

From: "Vincent Hill" <vincent.hill@rpfi.org>
Date: Sat, 16 Jan 2016 16:04:08 +0000
To: 'Peggy J'<peggwegg@hotmail.com>
Subject: RE: Response to Resignation Letter

Dear Peggy

Many thanks for your e-mail.

I just need to clarify the bit about Monday's shift as I find it a bit ambiguous. You say 'this will be effective from your next shift', it's not clear whether this means that I don't need to return for my next shift, or that Monday's shift should be my last?

Irrespective of whether I am required to do the Monday shift or not, I shall always be available if you or the staff team require any support in effecting the handover.

Should I not hear from you by Sunday pm I will assume that I am not required to come in to Lancaster Lodge on Monday morning.

Best wishes

Vincent

From: Peggy J [mailto:peggwegg@hotmail.com]
Sent: 16 January, 2016 10:39
To: vincent.hill@rpfi.org
Subject: Response to Resignation Letter

Hi Vincent,

Please see my response to your letter of resignation, you will also receive a hard copy in the post.

Peggy

From: Peggy J <peggwegg@hotmail.com>
Date: 17 January 2016 at 20:53:48 GMT
To: «diversitymanagementlcl@btinternet.com"
   <diversitymanagementlcl@btinternet.com>
Subject: hand-over

Hi Duncan,

Please call Heather (HR Officer) on 08452268393, she gets into work around 9am and she is familiar with the case. Heather wanted us to steer clear of meeting with Vincent until he decided if he is bringing a grievance or resigning.

Once Vincent emailed me, Elly was insistent that I ask him to come in for a hand-over. Im not sure if we have compromised things.

If Heather advises that you can go ahead with hand over then please get as much information as possible and I'm sure you will have it covered but it doesn't hurt to have a list of things that we definitely need from him:

1. Care Plans
2. Contact details and (Contracts if possible) for each resident inc. families, providers...
3. Information on residents agreed exists in the near future
4. Correspondence re: new referrals and their providers, review meetings manager's diary
5. Residents monies, action plans...
6. Staff sickness records, annual leave cards.
7. Staff supervision notes, appraisals and verbal/written warnings
8. Maternity leave
9. Rotas
10. Therapists, art therapists agreements contact details
11. Agency Staff details
12. Stationery suppliers
13. Compliance paper work
14. Financial records...
15. C of C peer reviews
16. Health and Safety
17. Online Staff Training

18. Set up at LL - Community meetings, Check in/out, Reflective Space...
19. New Commissioners, contacts at Queen Mary's...
20. Business plan

From: Diversity Management LCL <diversitymanagementlcl@btinternet.com>
Date: 18 January 2016 at 09:18:12 GMT
To: Peggy J <peggwegg@hotmail.com>
Subject: Re: hand-over

Hi Peggy,

Just spoke to Heather. She said ok to meet with Vincent regarding handover today but to not engage him or other staff today as to his reasons/circumstances of his leaving(and to refer him or other staff directly to you).

Take care,

Duncan

D.E.Lawrence: Diversity,Equality,and Inclusion Specialist / Management and Team Coach.

Skype: diversitymanagementlcl

Sent from my iPhone

Handover details for Lancaster Unit Manager(Additional)

From: Elly Jansen <elly.jansen@rpfi.org>
Date: 3 May 2017 at 00:29:50 BST
To: Diversity Management LCL <diversitymanagementlcl@btinternet.com>
Subject: Re: Lancaster Lodge

reply to...?

On 2 May 2017 at 20:26, Diversity Management LCL <diversitymanagementlcl@btinternet.com> wrote:

D.E.Lawrence: Diversity,Equality,and Inclusion Specialist / Management and Team Coach.

Skype: diversitymanagementlcl

Sent from my iPhone

From: Diversity Management LCL <diversitymanagementlcl@btinternet.com>
Date: 18 January 2016 at 16:28:36 GMT
To: Peggy J <peggwegg@hotmail.com>, Elly Jansen <elly.jansen@rpfi.org>, Elly Jansen <ellywjansen@hotmail.com>, Peggy Jhugroo<pjhugroo@wandsworth.gov.uk>
Subject: Re: Lancaster Lodge

Hi Peggy and Elly,

Relatively easy handover at LH with Vincent. I helped him carry his belonging to the station a while ago.

What I did not anticipate was that all staff on duty found their way to speak to me(away from Vincent) and let me know they were open to LH opportunities.

Things were not as Vincent explained, for example A says she has been acting as a senior for quite a long time but was told there were no posts.

I also spoke to the Art Therapist, ...she is especially an 'all around' young talent, being trained in Holland she is used to working in multidisciplinary teams, supervises art therapy students elsewhere and works three days per week with young people in schools. She will send her cv later. I could easily see her as a 1-2 day per week (or more) Senior Support Worker across the company developing art/activity staff and supervising them too.

Back to A, to limit change for LH staff/residents...even though she is early stage of pregnancy, she'd make good senior/ team Leader with Rohit acting up as Deputy to myself as his /staff supervisor -mentor. She would need a back up(in title only, would suit an ambitious staff)to learn the role and cover(with pay) during A maternity leave(for example).

Tuesday will meet with A and Rohit to explore what can be done 'in house' and what that only I can do.

Speaking of Rohit, he has no counselling or psychology degrees...I respectfully suggest if you offer him temp Deputy Post at LH, that he be required to enrol on a counselling or psychology course by Easter(even if he starts in Sept/Oct 2016).

Additionally, as suggested before,we really should become Organisational Members of the British Association of Counselling and Psychotherapy...we were very very vulnerable with Vincent and Rohit not registered as practitioners.

Will keep you posted Tuesday.

Duncan Lawrence

D.E.Lawrence: Diversity,Equality,and Inclusion Specialist / Management and Team Coach.

Skype: diversitymanagementlcl

Sent from my iPhone

Myth 18: DL Staff did not Sabotage DL work

Fact: the founder/ lead advisor often mentioned the level of staff sabotage with regard to DL work

From: Elly Jansen <elly.jansen@rpfi.org>
Date: 15 April 2016 at 19:51:00 BST
To: diversitymanagementlcl<diversitymanagementlcl@btinternet.com>
Subject: Re: ROHIT

THANK YOU OR YOUR RESPONSE, WHICH CONFIRMS WHAT I HAVE GLEANED ELSEWHERE.

IT IS TRUE THAT RPFI DID NOT MANAGE L.L. DUE TO THE CHAIR FAILING TO INTEREST HERSELF AND FAILING TO SUPPORT THE CEO.

I WAS NOT ACTING AS CONSULTANT FOR A YEAR UNTIL JULY 2016. THE PROBLEMS HAVE DRAINED ME.

BEST REGARDS,

ELLY

On 15 April 2016 at 18:03, diversitymanagementlcl <diversitymanagementlcl@btinternet.com> wrote:

From: Elly Jansen <elly.jansen@rpfi.org>
To: Duncan Lawrence <diversitymanagementlcl@btinternet.com>
Sent: Friday, 15 April 2016, 16:09
Subject: ROHIT

DEAR DUNCAN, *Good afternoon Elly,*

I WAS INFORMED TODAY THAT ROHIT, WHO IGNORED DIRECTIONS FROM MOST OF HIS SENIORS, DID THE SAME TO YOU.

I can not give dates Elly,but;

- his performance (to my instruction, to RPFI aims,etc) was 100% linked to whether or not he believed in them(their worth, their validity and if they did not devalue his self important role with LL staff or residents).
- I did not experience him to be 'new' to the attitude described above(clearly learned behaviour developed over several years before and during LL).
- often I thought he did not check his emails and hence him always being late to complete tasks I gave him and or not complete tasks at all(upon refection I think this directly relates to my first point)
- he was very influential upon new and older staff members ...some residents as well (primarily Hosannah, Clarissa,and the other older resident[her name escapes me at present])...they saw him as a 'guru' that was persecuted by myself,Peggy and the Board...this led to their regular 'non compliance' and 'mischief'(e.g. not following tasks/instructions,hiding key papers/work, **unfairly disrupting residents mental health for their own benefits[I felt as times additionally that Peggy disregarded residents mental state for her own benefit]. NOTE: All LL staff, students**

etc. need to take responsibility for their actions too, they were very vulnerable to a 'Rohit' or something similar. Martina did not collude however

- related to the above, none of the staff,students,residents and external professional professionals would have ever believed that he was unqualified for LL and most would have thought the SMT/Board would have 'made it up' because of his 'rebel' status.
- he is a very talented but dysfunctional professional and 'a walking contradiction' e.g. simple things and common sense things he found very very difficult
- he only cared about,showed understanding of, controlling LL(what comes in, what goes out, what happens inside,etc.)
- He is not 'modern' and does not wish to be e.g. does not know approaches to holistic health and well being, policies and procedures, safeguarding,etc....in urgent need of quality CPD and a transfer to another charity home
- RPFI did not supervise him for years(I am sure that he was hard to pin down and took pride in this fact) and should take some responsibility for Rohit that we see today

WE HAVE TO COMPLETE A STATEMENT OF HIS PERFORMANCE AND ATTITUDE, AND I WOULD BE VERY GRATEFUL IF YOU COULD SEND ME YOUR EXPERIENCE WITH HIM - HOPEFULLY WITH DATES AND - WHERE OTHERS WERE PRESENT - WHO WAS PRESENT TO WITNESS WHAT WAS SAID OR DONE.

IT HAS BEEN LEFT TO ME TO GATHER WHATEVER RELIABLE INFORMATION IS AVAILABLE, SO IT WOULD HELP ME IF YOU HAVE ANYTHING TO CONTRIBUTE.

I HOPE THAT YOU HAVE FOUND A SUITABLE AND ENJOYABLE PLACE TO WORK. WE ARE SLOWLY RECOVERING FROM THE PROBLEMS BUT STILL NEED TO CATCH UP FINANCIALLY. I hope that the charity will consider my services one day in the future...I still believe in the charity. Be well Elly,Duncan

BEST REGARDS,

ELLY

From: Diversity Management LCL <<u>diversitymanagementlcl@gmail.com</u>>
Date: 12 February 2016 at 00:15:56 GMT
Subject: Dear Art Students,

Dear Art Students,

Yesterday I was made aware that you pulled up Peggy(our company CEO) in front of the LL residents for accidentally coming into your Art Group space.

1. It is very important that this never ever happens again.

1.1 Ideally, there would be signs on the doors('group in progress',etc.) and ;

1.2 additionally, any one stepping through the door would most likely verbally and or non verbally quickly apologise for stepping into your group space and exit.

In a 'thriving' TC the above is an excellent example of adult behaviours to occur and to 'model', there is never a logical reason to 'tell off/pull up' anyone in front of the residents for mistakenly entering your group space.

2. Your professionalism needs to be under-pinned weekly by humility and a genuine gratitude(for the opportunity that the RPFI's Lancaster Lodge provides to you).

3. If there is a repeat of this action at any RPFI/RCI homes, your placement will be over for good without any further notice.

3.1 We are trying to promote self motivated positive attitudes and actions from within all that enter the Lancaster Lodge TC.

Duncan Lawrence

From: Diversity Management LCL <diversitymanagementlcl@ gmail.com>
Date: 10 February 2016 at 07:01:52 GMT
Subject: Hi Peggy,

Hi Peggy,

This was a very good letter, hopefully it will keep Angela from telling anyone else.

Fiza has 'a weak' streak running through her.

Even though her shift unknown to her was complicated by the residents calling Angela,she was not strong enough to put a stop to it once Angela called the LL...instead she shared/verbalised her vulnerabilities rather than share them with me.

Angela is part of the group of staff who along with Rohit, Alison, Martyna,etc that just got on at LL and kept Vince out of the loop...the secrets finally killed LL and I would hate for it to get around the we buried the Fiza story(because we are still vulnerable with the WH resident falling down and Fiza connection to her).

I really need her to start coming to staff meetings and begin to build a backbone for her, while publicly dissecting(within the staff meeting) how she made loads of bad choices Monday night, especially once she let Angela 'back into LL'.

Additionally,I am concerned that she did not understand that she was also violating the residents confidentiality by sharing with Angella, initiating unauthorised staffing via Paul(all Fiza had to tell Angela, thanks for calling but I have this LL situation in hand, but she did not...the only other person that I think would have done similar would have been Joanna).

As we were speaking about yesterday, Elly would have to give me more now(a new contract say 1 March 2016) to get more from me eg. say one 10 hour day at WH and three 10 hour days at LL(being flexible as I need to be).

With medication training myself(will not do this on a consultancy contract),etc.. along side having the psych nurse at night, could reduce the need and dependency on so many rookie staff in the short/medium term at both WH and LL and close several vulnerability gaps.

Paul(and potentially Joanna and Rohit at the least) know the 'new LL secrets'...If Fiza can not come to the staff meeting next week and see me this Thursday or Friday am for supervision, then I am sure that her 'WH pattern' will infect LL without not really ever sitting her down and reading her the riot act.

She seems to have great potential and great vulnerability in equal measure.

Either way Peggy, please enjoy your non RPFI day too...I will!

Duncan

Hi Martyna,

1. I hope that you are well. Last night the residents shared quite a lot and all generally admitted that they wanted regular key work contact(some saying that they have not had one for months and Clarissa voiced the 'most neglect' from LL going back over three years.

   Can you please put in the communication book for all key working to begin asap(for all staff to make sure that they see me anytime Thursday or Friday-I leave by 1pm to share their experience.

2. Can we possibly limited our end of the month training to two days, Thursday/Friday (25th and 26th of Feb

2016)? We tried to give everyone a weekend off, but sadly not possible this time.

3. In the short term we will have a Psych Nurse on the night shift at least for a week to support Hannah and inexperienced new staff.

3.1 Can someone liaise with Hannah and any other regular 'house bound' LL residents and get them out of the house at least 2-4 daytime hours eg. River walks with pack lunch, walk within Richmond park,etc.... any walk is 'progress' and staff need to be persistent and consistent....we can't let neglect become the new normal.

Have a great day Martyna and apologies for a long email.

Duncan.

Myth 19: DL Did not provided Assistant Coroner Information in advance of initial inquest: DL Dec 2018 Coroner Witness Statement

Fact: Refer to Witness Statement Provided by the charity solicitor

Myth 19.1: DL Did not provided Assistant Coroner Information in advance of initial inquest: DL Dec 2018 Exhibits: Refer to the following documents that were submitted as part of the Witness Statement

- Audit

- DL Job Offer

- First DL Charity Wide news letter

- DL Draft Mission Statement(never completed)

- DL Dismissal Letter.

Myth 22: Founder /Leader had no animosity towards the Lancaster unit manager: A collections of emails to- from the founder/lead advisor

Fact: The founder/lead advisor was really unhappy about the Lancaster unit going back several years.

MANAGEMENT OF LANCASTER LODGE

Inbox x

26 Apr 2017, 22:01

Elly Jansen <elly.jansen@rpfi.org>

to Duncan

I WONDER WHETHER YOU CAN HELP. YOU ROTE A SHORT REPORT ABOUT THE FAILINGS OF L.L. - PAPERS MISSING, LACK OF PROGRAMME, RISKS WITH RESIDENTS ETC. I HAVE LOOKED EVERYWHERE BUT CANNOT FIND IT. WOULD YOU STILL HAVE IT AND CAN YOU SEND IT?

ALSO, WHEN YOU SAID V.H. WOULD RESIGN, I COULD NOT BELIEVE IT. CAN YOU LET ME KNOW WHAT WAS SAID BETWEEN THE TWO OF YOU AND WHY YOU THOUGHT VH WOULD RESIGN?

THE TOXIDITY OF THAT MAN IS WITH US STILL!

I HOPE YOU HAVE FOUND YOUR NICHE. YOU MAY KNOW THAT PEGGY LEFT AN THAT WE HAVE A NEW CEO.

27 Apr 2017, 06:15

Diversity Management LCL <diversitymanagementlcl@gmail. com>

to Elly,

Dear Elly,

You folks seem to forget that I was a victim of Peggy too and you and the board in those days seem to have a naive co-dependent relationship with her. Most tasks that I can do in my sleep were hindered by her and the board's poor management and poor assessment of the level of dysfunction at the Lancaster Unit...without completely gutting out the place and starting over, even superman could not have saved the place with staff and residents still in place.

I will find what you need in the next day or two and send it to you Elly.

Just remember I believe in your work but you and the board were guilty for keeping Peggy around so long and allowing here get away with treating clients and staff/consultants like crap.

Again, give me a day or two to get you the information.

Also...if you wished to do a paid review, I still have texts, emails etc warning you, board, Peggy of potential threats to company, residents, etc..

Duncan

D.E.Lawrence: Diversity,Equality,and Inclusion Specialist / Management and Team Coach.

Skype: diversitymanagementlcl

Sent from my iPhone

27 Apr 2017, 10:12

Duncan Lawrence <diversitymanagementlcl@gmail.com>

to Elly, ellywjansen,

ALSO, WHEN YOU SAID V.H. WOULD RESIGN, I COULD NOT BELIEVE IT. CAN YOU LET ME KNOW WHAT WAS SAID BETWEEN THE TWO OF YOU AND WHY YOU THOUGHT VH WOULD RESIGN?

He stated that he realised that he was very very bitter about the company, felt that various boards did not know of his achievements and often rather chose to try to degrade and or control him rather that provide him CPD, more pay, more chance to develop within the company(although he admitted at the time, that he did not know the company's current vision and had not pushed it within his staff [hence their resistance, protectiveness and negativity...Vincent openly admitted this]). **He was not rude or closed within our discussions. I always found him polite and open**.

Duncan

From: Elly Jansen <elly.jansen@rpfi.org>
Date: 27 April 2017 at 21:13:12 BST
To: Duncan Lawrence <diversitymanagementlcl@gmail.com>
Subject: Re: MANAGEMENT OF LANCASTER LODGE

DEAR DUNCAN,

THANK YOU FOR YOUR RESPONSE AND INFORMATION, SOME OF WHICH FEELS NEW TO ME. IT WILL BE VERY DIFFICULT EVER TO KNOW FULLY WHO DID WHAT WHEN. THERE WAS LACK OF THOUGHT AND TRANSPARENCY IN THE SITUATION WHICH WAS INHERITED. THE BOARD WERE NEW AND RELIED ON INFORMATION FROM THE COORDINATOR.

I HAVE SEEN A SHORT REPORT FROM YOU WHICH IDENTIFIED THE OMISSION OF ESSENTIAL PAPERWORK AND THE LACK OF COHESION AND BOUNDARIES AT L.L. EARLY JANUARY. AT THE TIME YOU INFORMED ME THAT YOUR CHALLENGING THE MANAGER WOULD LEAD TO HIS RESIGNATION WHICH I FOUND HARD TO BELIEVE. IT IS THAT REPORT I WAS LOOKING FOR SINCE IT SHOWED CLEARLY THE ISSUES THAT HAD OBVIOUSLY FAILED TO BE CHECKED BY CQC.

I DO NOT THINK YOU WERE AWARE OF THE LONGER-TERM ISSUES THAT WERE BEING PLAYED OUT AND THE WAY THE NEW BOARD AND PEGGY WERE SET UP BY THE PREVIOUS BOARD, INCLUDING GIVING STAFF NEW CONTRACTS 3 DAYS BEFORE HANDING OVER TO THE NEW BOARD. THAT WAS A TIME BOMB BECAUSE THE MONEY WAS NOT THERE TO IMPLEMENT CRAZY INCREASES. THE BOARD WAS NOT UNAWARE OF THE COMPLEXITY OF THE SITUATION AND HAD

FEW CHOICES. CERTAINLY I AGREE THAT IT WAS NECESSARY TO FIND A COMPLETELY NEW STAFF TEAM FOR THE LODGE

THERE IS EVEN LESS MONEY NOW THAN WE HAD AT THAT TIME DUE TO THE COST OF TEMPORARY CLOSURE, SO WE CANNOT TAKE ON NEW STAFF. WE HAVE A GOOD AND TRUSTWORTHY TEAM NOW BUT STILL HAVE NOT RECEIVED THE MONEY FROM DORSET BECAUSE IT APPEARS THAT VINCENT HAD NOT ACQUIRED A WRITTEN AGREEMENT FOR THE CARE OF THEIR REFERRAL WHICH LASTED 8 MONTHS.

I DO NOT UNDERSTAND HOW THAT COULD HAVE HAPPENED.

AM I RIGHT IN THINKING THAT YOU HAD AMONGST YOUR PAPERS AN EMAIL I SENT TO DAVID? IN THAT CASE PLEASE KEEP IT AS CONFIDENTIAL.

THANKS AGAIN FOR SENDING INFORMATION WHICH IS VERY HELPFUL.

ELLY

On 27 April 2017 at 14:08, Duncan Lawrence <diversitymanagementlcl@gmail.com> wrote:

Elly,

Sorry for rushed emails, a very busy period here. Please let me know if you need anything else....I have dozens of RPFI related emails and text.

Duncan

From: Diversity Management LCL <<u>diversitymanagementlcl@</u>
        <u>btinternet.com</u>>
Date: 2 May 2017 at 20:00:37 BST
To: Elly Jansen <<u>elly.jansen@rpfi.org</u>>
Subject: Re: Supportive Strategy add ons from Duncan

Still looking Elly

D.E.Lawrence: Diversity,Equality,and Inclusion Specialist / Management and Team Coach.

Skype: diversitymanagementlcl

Sent from my iPhone

On 2 May 2017, at 19:50, Elly Jansen <<u>elly.jansen@rpfi.org</u>> wrote:

THANKS A LOT!

CAN YOU NOT FIND THE SHORT REPORT YOU SENT LISTING FAILURES NOT RECOGNISED BY CQC?

ELLY

Sent from my iPhone

On 30 Apr 2017, at 12:15, Elly Jansen <<u>elly.jansen@rpfi.org</u>> wrote:

Dear Duncan,

Thank you for letting m have these emails,some of which I cannot remember having ever had sight of.

The hostility Peggy received and had to cope with from Lancaster set the scene and she never overcame it.

My role was to advice - not rule - and it is hard to know what happens at the coal front, even when basic principles are agreed..

I know you entered a complex scene and rivalry would have been hard to avoid. And there were no winners.

I wish I could find the document in which you list all the failings which were overlooked by CQC. IT PUT OUR CASE WELL!

We still have not received the report of the CPS. This is holding us back.

Also Dorset are still refusing to pay a bill of £ 48,000 because they say there is no written evidence that they ever accepted to pay.

I cannot believe that Vincent would have allowed Hailey to stay with us without getting that agreement and for there being minimally

SOME EMAILS TO THAT EFFECT, BUT NO ONE HAS BEEN ABLE TO LOCATE ANY. It may come to a Court Case where all parties will have to give a statement on oath. Do you have an Email address for Vincent? Dave, our present CEO, who is a very humble person, would be very glad to be able to communicate with him - partly to get a clearer picture of what actually occurred. i will share your emails with him.

I hope you are happy with the situation you are now in.

Elly

On 28 April 2017 at 09:40, Diversity Management LCL <<u>diversitymanagementlcl@btinternet.com</u>> wrote:

D.E.Lawrence: Diversity,Equality,and Inclusion Specialist / Management and Team Coach.

Skype: diversitymanagementlcl

Sent from my iPhone

From: Diversity Management LCL <<u>diversitymanagementlcl@ btinternet.com</u>>
Date: 30 April 2017 at 13:28:09 BST
To: Elly Jansen <<u>elly.jansen@rpfi.org</u>>, Elly Jansen <<u>ellywjansen@hotmail.com</u>>
Subject: Fwd: Lancaster Lodge Investigation 12.1.16 (final draft)

D.E.Lawrence: Diversity,Equality,and Inclusion Specialist / Management and Team Coach.

Skype: diversitymanagementlcl

Sent from my iPhone

Begin forwarded message:

From: diversitymanagementlcl<<u>diversitymanagementlcl@ btinternet.com</u>>
Date: 14 January 2016 at 15:08:10 GMT
To: «<u>peggwegg@hotmail.com</u>" <<u>peggwegg@hotmail.com</u>>, Peggy Jhugroo<<u>pjhugroo@wandsworth.gov.uk</u>>
Subject: Lancaster Lodge Investigation 12.1.16(final draft)

Lancaster Lodge House: Jan 2016 Investigation Notes

Incident: A member of staff supported a service user through a suicide gesture/attempt and was concerned that he was left alone for two hours with an 'at risk' service user and that he received no 'after incident support' from LL Management.

Interviewed:Vincent-LL Manager, Angella-LL Support Staff(in charge of Rota), Paul-Long time LL bank staff, Danny-LH Support Staff and Colin-LH Manager

Interview Summary(original statements attached):

Vincent:

States he was on holiday leave during the incident

He said that he first heard of the incident when he received a belated handover

States that it is his policy to support all staff immediately and on an on-going basis (with regard to critical incidents).

Related to above, he states that he was instructed to not discuss the incident(due to the investigation) but told Danny that he would speak to him after the investigation.

Angella:

States that she had a bad chest infection but felt that she did not wish to call in sick(due to LL being short staff), before her shift she called LL to ask could she come in two hours late to have more time to recover

She admits that it is 'LL policy' that staff involved in critical incidents are meant to contact manager/on-Call support.

Although upon reflection she admitted that there had been several 'at risk' LL staff incidents involving lone staff and was confused why RPFI was only investigating now.

She states that her only calls that shift were to Paul explaining her medical situation and checking in.

She assumed that Danny knew to contact manager on call

Paul:

Felt comfortable leaving 'C' with Danny because she seemed happy and well for the previous 48 hours

He states that he worked his full hours and that there is no staff sign in/out book.

He assumed that Danny knew to call on-call manager

Danny:

Felt comfortable beginning his work shift

Felt uneasy once 'C' returned to LL because she seemed " ...not in her ordinary mood..."

He stated that he asked Paul what to do the support the above mentioned service user and mentioned that he was "...a bit anxious..." about the situation

He called Angella during the incident and he never considered calling a manager

Felt numb and emotional afterwards and was left wanting Vincent to debrief him and to get clinical supervision to review how he handled the situation

Colin:

When he was alerted to the situation he immediately provided 'post-incident support' to Danny. Danny was insistent that he did not wish to get anyone at LL in trouble and was "... generally ok...".

Because of the above (and pending investigation)Colin did not speak to Vincent directly about the incident.

Belatedly he found out that Danny contacted Angella about LL shifts without his knowledge. LL is now clear that all staffing requests/assignments come via him only.

Initial Impressions:

This is clearly a 'system problem/dysfunction', one that had been going on for a long time, with all staff involved not using best practice/good teamwork and are very lucky staff,volunteers and residents were not hurt in the past

Related to the above,It is not clear that the LL rota is currently designed to be accurate

The manager (and senior staff) could have been more insistent about providing Danny support but in seems 'desensitisation' has infected all levels at LL(so all see these situations as 'normal' and just part of the LL work).

Recommendations:

1. Deal with LL 'systems of dysfunction' as a matter of urgency. All involved did not show examples of good practice/good teamwork.

2. Provide critical incident support to Danny and any other LL staff that feel that they need it(but within a supportive atmosphere and not a 'blame' setting).

3. With all the related challenges within LL, it is felt that for the sake of the service users, the staff and the wider credibility of RPFI, the house need an urgent shake up(e.g the manager and senior staff should work at different houses, all manager leave time should be used immediately and an on-the-job 'training/ mentoring manager' should step in asap to shadow Vincent and ensure best practice/quality assurance. I recommend that should be carried out for at least 60 days. Since change is never easily accepted for some adults, service users and staff will need maximum support and consistency during this transition period.

4. Ultimately the manager is responsible for what goes on within their units, however this situation is not a straight forward one. All LL staff interviewed mentioned the impact of regular RPFI SMT/CEO coming and going as a major factor in their personal and profession self esteem.

Submitted by: Duncan Lawrence 12.1.16

From: Diversity Management LCL <<u>diversitymanagementlcl@</u><u>btinternet.com</u>>

To: Elly Jansen <<u>elly.jansen@rpfi.org</u>>; Elly Jansen <<u>ellywjansen@hotmail.com</u>>

Sent: Friday, 28 April 2017, 9:25

Subject: Fwd: Supportive Strategy add ons from Duncan II

D.E.Lawrence: Diversity,Equality,and Inclusion Specialist / Management and Team Coach.

Skype: diversitymanagementlcl

Sent from my iPhone

Begin forwarded message:

From: diversitymanagementlcl<<u>diversitymanagementlcl@</u><u>btinternet.com</u>>

Date: 3 March 2016 at 21:04:58 GMT

To: Geoff Benton <<u>bentongeoff@gmail.com</u>>

Subject: Re: Supportive Strategy add ons from Duncan II

Hi Geoff,

You work too hard...take some time to rest your body.

I stand by my suggestion for Peggy to temporarily stand down and come into LL as a 'team member'...'a TC member' to do specific and transparent pieces of work(see below) and not boss anyone around.

This would help staff and residents to see her/SMT in a new light and leave me to get on with my tasks(see below).

I will respectfully step away from day one if she comes in as a 'boss'...we have a image that needs to be repaired in a timely manner.

Giving up the CEO role temporarily means a break for her too...Colin would do well.

This isn't an interpersonal thing, just a good and clear headed judgement thing.

Best wishes and please get some rest,

Duncan

Sent from my iPad

On 3 Mar 2016, at 10:41, Diversity Management LCL <diversitymanagementlcl@btinternet.com> wrote:

Fyi

D.E.Lawrence: Diversity,Equality,Inclusion and Sport Specialist / Management and Team Coach.

Skype: diversitymanagementlcl

Sent from my iPhone

Begin forwarded message:

From: diversitymanagementlcl<diversitymanagementlcl@btinternet.com>
Date: 3 March 2016 at 06:41:33 GMT
To: Peggy Jhugroo<pjhugroo@wandsworth.gov.uk>, "peggwegg@hotmail.com" <peggwegg@hotmail.com>, Colin McDonald <colin_newatlantis@hotmail.com>, Elly

Jansen <elly.jansen@rpfi.org>, Elly Jansen <ellywjansen@hotmail.com>

Subject: Supportive Strategy add ons from Duncan

Hi Peggy,

Some add on ideas that might help with your Strategy Development.

Called: Transformation phase II(Phase I is 1 March Enhanced TC)

Could include:

— You temp giving up your CEO role(say to Colin)for 2-3 weeks
— You coming to LL as an Well being Specialist to model/lead practitioner championing the enhanced TC for at least 2-3 weeks
— You being coordinator of LL decor upgrade
— Getting skip for Monday for a two week stint...to do a whole house and office clear up.
— DL then has time to supervise staff and give each a rating competency/capacity and support them accordingly (see attached examples...there are two on one page) and sort out LL case management system(paperwork) and begin 1-1 and group therapy.
— We interview like crazy and get a team leader or deputy to replace your LL role when you resume CEO
— 1 April I resume my clinical Lead and Operational Role and we continue with a nationwide LL service manager search.

With these types of things in place I could just support any reasonable strategy...without them I can't.

I have cancer tests Friday,that will need to be urgently rearranged, please confirm if 2pm today or Friday at WH.

Sorry for rushing, I wanted to contribute to your ideas, even on a busy day.

Duncan

Sent from my iPad

RPFI/RCI Quality Assurance Checks carried out by Duncan Lawrence Week commencing 4.1.16:

Summary Notes

White House:

- Staff spent almost two hours + in the office 'counting money' (e.g they made coffees,teas,breakfast,etc for residents but made no effort to sit with them, have teas together,etc.).

- Handover read more like a 'compliant judgement' of service users rather than reflecting on a service users comments(verbally and non verbally) about their own experiences of 'their day'

- Acting Lead detailed a long list of support staff negative communications, refusals to 'work the house floor' along side/with the residents, lack of interest or enthusiasm to work to care plans and limited demonstration of good teamwork.

Conclusion:

1. Recommend the entire permanent staff team receive a verbal warning for a 'POOR QUALITY ASSURANCE CHECK', one that could be revoked if they quickly improve this situation within 30 days.

2. Regarding the above,if HR is not able to 'action' this, I would like my original visit notes(that were given to the Acting Lead) typed (say in size 18 font) and posted in the staff office for the next month.

Lancaster House:

- General demonstration of practice with service users to a SATISFACTORY + at this Quality Assurance Check.

  - ☐ The main challenge this visit related to House Manager coming to terms that the home can't easily afford so many external service providers(and responding to giving notice to external service providers to cease services).

- After a rather lengthy consideration, a 'counter proposal' was put forward..."...what if we kept an 80% occupancy rate, could we then ask for things on a case by case basis(e.g keep our current level of external providers)?..."

- Was suggested by this writer to explore how to develop staff in a timely way(as a way of creating in-house career development opportunities).

Conclusion:

1. I Recommend that the RPFI/RCI CEO/Board consider the 'counter proposal' and to consider what is possible/practical in terms of staff development plan(to reduce reliance on external service providers).

2. Related to the above, this writer respectfully asks that the CEO/Board turn around a clear and concise written response within a week if possible. Additionally, consider a 'company wide' policy of staff development that encourages 'trainee professional' development in the areas of art therapy, music therapy, counselling, group facilitation, staff supervision, etc.. Would be great to announce this as 'an ideal',say at this weeks company training day.

Lytton House:

*   Preparations for children's home occupancy and or semi-independent unit occupancy appears on track(but this writer recommends one day staff training asap on 'Dealing with Stress and Aggressive situations' and to consider diverse provisions, ones that include the use of trained volunteers).

Conclusion:

1. Continue to prepare a 'fit for purpose' staff compliment, one that meets the organisation's short-medium term needs. Important that the 'service

user group' is 100% at the front of all planning and development .

2. If the semi-independent unit is pursued, the company should consider how they use the current Lytton House management resource(Colin). Most Semi-Independent Units do not have full-time management provision. Could prove useful to allow Colin to manage White House and Lytton House together. He would need at least 20-30 CPD Hours in the area of 'adult social care' covering mental health, age related provision,etc.. A good link for a 'Social Care' CPD Certificate is http://www.skillsforcare.org.uk/Standards/Care-Certificate/Care-Certificate.aspx Duncan Lawrence(BA-Ed,MA-Counselling,DPA-Public Admin, FiLM,Reg. MBACP and FBACP)

RPFI/RCI DISCUSSION NOTES FROM D.LAWRENCE 14.1.16

After considering the recent company audit that I completed, my consultancy experiences thus far and my recent initial investigation of Lancaster Lodge Jan 2016,I suggest the organisation take an urgent strategy such as outlined below.

1. Send a company wide letter/email to all staff such as:

Memo to: All RPFI/RCI Personnel

Date:15.1.16

RE:Company Integrated Strategy Jan/Feb/March 2016 for Lancaster Lodge,Lytton House and the White House

Statement of Purpose: Lytton House has updated its Statement of Purpose in December 2015, and the White House is in the early stages of reviewing and updated its Statement of Purpose. Lancaster Lodge in consultation with Duncan Lawrence and Greetha will need to start its review and update process as soon as possible.

The aim is to have a Statement of Purpose that best reflects the wider company values, reflects the 'added value' that the home could/actually bring(s) and is readable by multiple stakeholders(e.g referral sources,staff, volunteers, service users, family members,etc.).

Staffing Developments: the review and development work that began in June 2015 with the Company Coordinator continues to highlight some great areas of practice and some very poor areas of practice,practice that often puts service users, staff and the company's credibility at risk.

To that end we are making considered staffing changes to take advantage our current strengths, our attempts to quickly shore up areas needing immediate improvement and finally create regular staff development opportunities, while providing others the opportunity to 'recharge their personal energy'.

1. Vincent will use up all of his accrued leave starting 1 Feb 2016.

2. Rohit will deputise in Vincent's absence.

3. Duncan Lawrence will shadow Rohit and provide 24/7 on-the-job management mentoring support for at least 60 days beginning 25 Jan 2016(hours TBC). This will include evening and weekend support/guidance.

4. Note: To limit the 'amount of change' at one time, the previous instruction from the Company Coordinator for Lancaster Lodge to wind down their use of external practitioners, the time to wind down will now be extended to 1 March 2016. We expect this time to be used wisely and for the benefit of the residents.

5. There will be an Acting Manager the White House by 1 Feb 2016.

6. Manager supervision and Staff supervision will need to begin by 1 Feb 2016. All house managers will need to arrange this around Duncan Lawrence's time schedule.

7. Lancaster Lodge will host the next company wide sharing good practice day(tbc).

8. Finally, it is the company's aim to improve the atmosphere within the homes. Any negative gossiping,bad mouthing the RPFI/RCI,etc. is considered a bad health and safety risk because it interferes with individuals and their teams ability to work unhindered.

If any current staff member feels that they can not assertively foster good practice, positive teamwork and emotional competency, please firstly make good use of your supervision and your personal therapist.

If this does not work, the board will put aside two days(tbc) for these staff to meet with them and 'get anything off their chest'.Staff will be paid for these sessions.

The Board of the RPFI/RCI honestly wishes to give the best possible care to our service users,while also providing opportunity for our personnel to professionally develop if they choose to do so.

RPFI/RCI BOARD

1.1 Expand Duncan Lawrence role to four days per week to additionally include him providing on-the-job Management Mentoring to Lancaster Lodge.

I could do if for a temporary employee contract of £40k pro rata(four days per week role) or £200 per day as a freelance consultancy basis.

Respectfully submitted by,

DuncanLawrence

15.1.16

Re: Please disregard earlier email...I changed one word Elly

Inbox

From: Elly Jansen <<u>elly.jansen@rpfi.org</u>>

Date: 3 May 2017 at 17:23:00 BST

To: diversitymanagementlcl<<u>diversitymanagementlcl@btinternet.com</u>>

Subject: Re: Did you see this Elly...copy of my suggestion to Geoff, with regard to writing to CQC(following their surprise visit)...it speaks of LL

WAS THIS A DRAFT OR WAS THIS SENT TO CQC? I DO NOT REMEMBER SEEING IT, AND IT IS NOT THE SHORT AND CONCISE MEMO FROM YOU I REMEMBER.

THANKS FOR SENDING IT.

E

On 3 May 2017 at 15:49, diversitymanagementlcl <<u>diversitymanagementlcl@btinternet.com</u>> wrote:

Dear

Re:Lancaster Lodge

3rd March 2016

Firstly, apologies for no senior staff being available to you today...Duncan is really gutted because he found you 'brutally constructive'.

Duncan has a pre-existing professional meeting that he can't get out of and Peggy is attending a hospital panel meeting for C J.(Lancaster Lodge resident).Both are available anytime Thursday.

Duncan describes that you saw "...a mess..." today with vital evidence based practice opportunities missing throughout the house's paperwork systems.

As a board, over the years this house kept us out and as such we could not reliably vouch for the quality of service.

It was not until our December 2015 Audit(see attach) and from speaking with exiting Lancaster Lodge staff, that we were made aware of the true scope of multi-layered problems within Lancaster Lodge.

It perplexed us even further when you gave the house a glowing CQC inspection report...quite a confusing situation.

To make a long story even shorter, the board takes full responsibility for the state of the house and the current ability and current motivation of staff to carry out their duties to a high standard. By the end of this week with will have part-time admin support within all of our homes.

We admit that we thought that our December 2015 notification of our charity's intent to improve our service delivery was not enough 'notice' (six months would have been better), but we felt that it was important to move forward at that time.

The past Lancaster Lodge manager did not warm to the strategy nor did he cascade this information down to his staff or the house residents...hence further complicating the scene even further.

Duncan and Peggy have worked very hard to improve the situation and seemed to find more and more problems literally each day!

We anticipated that it would take until the end of April 2016 to make things better for the residents while training old and new staff on-the-job.

Rumours were rife that somehow the charity SMT sacked the last manager and made Peggy and Duncan 'the bad guys' to staff and residents. Their commitment to residents and belief in standards kept them coming back each week.

We started charity wide emails(see attached Feb-March 2016) to make communication better, having learned from our recent mistakes.

Finally, we learned that no one at Lancaster Lodge had a practitioner registration(eg with the BACP, UKCP,BPs,etc) and the senior staff acting as clinical lead for past five years, has yet to provide evidence of his psychology degree...even with multiple requests.

Yes there has been recent strides but there is still needing for everyone at RPFI/RCI to work even harder to satisfactorily evidence its practice.

We hope you will give us time to make things right, 'with our eyes wide open'.

Respectfully submitted by:

Geoff Benton-RPFI chair.

D.E.Lawrence: Diversity,Equality,Inclusion and Sport Specialist / Management and Team Coach.

Skype: diversitymanagementlcl

Myth 21: Charity Solicitor was objective

In late summer of 2018 the impending doom level stepped up a notch when they told me that the assistant coroner wanted us to put together 'witness statements' about the last three months of the young woman's life "... and not to worry, this is not a trial...".

I hope the charity solicitor team gets investigated and I am very curious whose idea was it to make me the scapegoat.

Very difficult period of time, my father passed away earlier in the year and my mother was mentally and physically unwell and a few of us were frantically trying to get her medically assessed, while others seemed to working against this, no assessments, just sucking my mother's finances clean while allowing her to get worse big time.

I was very very torn, *go home to the states to support my mother or support this charity who seemed to not want me to really tell the truth about anything* .

I told the charity solicitor and the charity early on that to not count on me at any coroner hearing because I was still actively trying to get to the states where possible...definitely like being 'stuck between a rock and a pile of crap'...none of my choices were any good.

I was very 'clear' that the charity and the solicitor were not to be trusted(they did not leave a very good 'first impression' on me) and that I need to be truthful in an written statements, even if being encouraged to 'water down' my statements by the charity solicitor.

I wrote the watered down and submitted a 'limited witness statement', but after experiencing the assistant coroners relentless attacks upon me, I knew he was never going to actually tell me what material evidence did he actually have from me(e.g. Witness statement, Exhibitions, etc.).

Begin forwarded message:

From: Eric Lawrence <<u>diversitymanagementlcl@btinternet.com</u>>
Date: 31 August 2018 at 15:49:11 BST
To: Julie Ford <<u>Julie.Ford@hilldickinson.com</u>>
Cc: Kate Fawell-Comley <<u>Kate.Fawell-Comley@hilldickinson.com</u>>
Subject: Re: Request for assistance concerning a coroner's inquiry. [HD-UKLive.12014150.1]

Good afternoon again,

Elly Jansen, has been in contact with me for several months via email asking for my 'recollection of history'.

I have tried my best to advise her honestly and professionally as I could. I have not yet seen how those several pages of emails have been used by the charity...if my comments have been incorporated into their draft statement for this matter, I am 100% ok with seeing their draft statement(and no need for the Board Meeting minutes)...this may be enough to help me to decide whether I would write a statement with the support of the charity.

I have a lot of respect for Elly's past work but I need evidence that it has not been wasted or missed used(re my various past detailed emails to Mrs Jansen).

I am not trying to be awkward, I just do not wish to be taken for granted.

I still have most of my emails and can forward these to you if they would be helpful.

Duncan

D.E.Lawrence:

Diversity, Equality, Inclusion and Sport Specialist/Management and Team Coach.

Please think of the environment – do you really need to print this email or its attachments?

Sent from my iPhone

On 31 Aug 2018, at 14:42, Julie Ford <Julie.Ford@hilldickinson.com> wrote:

Dear Mr Lawrence

Thank you for getting back to me so quickly. Would it be possible to speak to you briefly this afternoon or on Monday.

I appreciate your involvement was very limited but the coroner has requested a statement from you and so even if you were not supported by RPFI, you would still need to provide the coroner with a statement in due course.

I have requested a copy of the board meetings relevant to the period of time in question. I am not really sure however, why you would need to the board minutes 12 month prior to your employment and 12 months after your employment? Would you be able to explain the reason for me?

As mentioned, the coroner's inquiry is a fact finding inquiry to ascertain the circumstances leading to the death only. It is for that reason I am querying why you need so may board papers to provide such a statement.

Perhaps we could speak?

My office number is set out below or you can contact me on my mobile number – 07985588438.

I look forward to hearing from you.

With kind regards

Your sincerely

Julie Ford

Legal Director
Healthcare
Hill Dickinson LLP
Julie.Ford@hilldickinson.com

The Broadgate Tower, 20 Primrose Street, London, EC2A 2EW
TEL: +44 (0)20 7280 9338
FAX: +44 (0)20 7283 1144

<image003.jpg> <image004.jpg>
<image005.jpg>

From: Eric Lawrence [mailto:diversitymanagementlcl@btinternet.com]
Sent: 31 August 2018 14:28
To: Julie Ford
Cc: Kate Fawell-Comley
Subject: Re: Request for assistance concerning a coroner>s inquiry. [HD-UKLive.12014150.1]

CAUTION EXTERNAL EMAIL:This message originated outside the organisation. Do not click links or open attachments unless you recognise the sender and know the content is safe.

Good afternoon,

Re: the above mentioned email.

I was literally only involved with the Charity for a few weeks and was removed from my work by non mutual consent so am unsure how I can be of assistance in this matter.

With the charity's assistance I could consider writing a statement.

I would need to review documents such as:

1. Board Meeting minutes for period of 12 months before I was taken on.

1.1 Board Meeting minutes for the period that I was engaged by the charity.

1.2 Board Meeting minutes for the period of 12 months after I was let go by the charity.

Without these documents I will not even consider making a statement.

Respectfully submitted by,

Duncan Lawrence

D.E.Lawrence:

Diversity, Equality, Inclusion and Sport Specialist/Management and Team Coach.

Please think of the environment – do you really need to print this email or its attachments?

Sent from my iPhone

On 31 Aug 2018, at 15:01, Julie Ford <Julie.Ford@hilldickinson.com> wrote:

Dear Mr Lawrence

I am assisting a colleague, Kate Fawell-Cowley in a matter in which you have been asked to provide a statement for a Coroner's inquiry. Further details are set out in the letter attached which is password protected (password to follow).

I should be grateful if you would contact me to confirm receipt of the letter and your response the queries set out within it.

I look forward to hearing from you at your earliest convenience.

With kind regards

Your sincerely

Julie Ford

Legal Director
Healthcare
Hill Dickinson LLP
Julie.Ford@hilldickinson.com

The Broadgate Tower, 20 Primrose Street, London, EC2A 2EW
TEL: +44 (0)20 7280 9338
FAX: +44 (0)20 7283 1144

<image003.jpg> <image004.jpg>
<image005.jpg>

Hill Dickinson

<Letter to duncan Lawrence.doc>

Hill Dickinson

Email: diversitymanagementlcl@gmail.com or
duncan@considercelebratingdiversityandsport.com

Conclusion

I have a 'recurring pattern'(or recurring problems depending on how you look at it and or from who's perspective is looking at and 'considering my patterns', think that I am being 'respectfully discreet' when I hold other people's stuff rather than just blabbing it here and there, and this was generally true with my pattern whether a colleague said something directly to me, or whether someone said something 'indirectly' (*it's those 'indirect' things that will get you all the time!)* to me such as a 'suggestion', etc...especially when in 'threatening situations', I rarely 'spill the beans on others'. Even when the atmosphere might be moving towards becoming tense, even in situations where I might have ample written documentation to keep me 'out of harm's way'[23], my 'self-talk' seems to always say "... Duncan, no need to be a 'rat', just let the documentation do the talking ...".

Let me tell you ...it has rarely worked out, the people involved, the colleagues, the managers, the leaders etc, if I don't say anything about what they said to me or suggested to me...they 99% of the time keep quiet too "... I don't know where he('Duncan') got that idea or where he got that suggestionfrom..." and or by not saying anything at all, they(by omission), and by doing so ' the narrative changes'[24] and I am to being 'thrown under the bus' and the 'real toxic villain(s)' usually slither away with little or no consequence.

---

23 Or so I think!
24 Without 'truth no factual narrative can remain the same.

It gives me little joy whether a month 'after-the-fact' or years later if an ex-colleague that I was friendly with at the time might say something like "...you really should have told them everything you knew straight away...". In my head I am thinking, "... *you ass, why didn't you just say what you knew straight away too, even just for your own sense of honesty... your 'keeping quiet' has changed our relationship forever even if I never told you...*".

These recurring 'Duncan patterns' happen at least once during every year of my working life. In a very practical sense, ` nice guys can always seem to finish last' and there are so many around us who in their desperation and or within character flaws and patterns will gladly 'lead us down thelane of blame' . Ironically, too often as explained earlier 'others' often in key leadership positions or in 'hr' generally already knew the truth as well but seem to collude with keeping the truth silent and looking the other way...yes, Social Care and ` work relationships' at their worst.

Is this part of the` white male jealousy and or anger' at a black man appearing too cocky, too clever... maybe doing things that they never had the confidence or real natural talent to do, who knows, only 'the all-knowing universe' does...she knows us all even when we think no one is looking.

I remember Brother Martin Luther King Jr. and Brother Malcom X regularly saying profound thoughts that still resonated with me to this day such as "...if you think what I am writing is true, if you think what I am saying is correct... don't just listen or watch, why don't you just get up and do these things for yourself...they could encourage me and many many many others...step into the light brothers and sisters...the world is better with positive human actions and positive human reactions...".

Thought Questions:

? = What do you think about the state of the charity in 2015/16?

? =How does this chapter's emails/ information relate to what you read in the news and or social media, and or that you saw on television about Duncan?

? = Out of court, the rumour was that Duncan was a bit of an 'internal whistle blower' and that is why there was a lot of energy to silence and slander him and keep his emails 'hidden' (he could cost the charity loads of money if what he knew really came out during the coroner's inquest) ...what do you think?

?= Do you think D.Eric Lawrence's expectations of the charity solicitors were reasonable?

?=Why do you think that they were reluctant to provide him with any Trustee Board Meeting Minutes?

?= Were D.Eric Lawrence's written submissions and statements consistent throughout? Yes/No

7. Does Truth Really Matter?

Some Reflective thoughts from D.Eric Lawrence

Bamboozled Wisdom (Number 7) Liars come in all different shapes and sizes and like clumsy chameleons at times...trying to change shapes (lying) just to blend in and not be seen, although most of us that really want to see, we will always see you, although we might not be able to get out of your way quick enough and then "...slurp...", the lying tongue takes us with them...! Too slow Duncan

Bamboozled Wisdom (Number 7.1)What inquiry? The current Covid-19 UK inquiries are an example of holding white past/present males in position of power accountable for their own actions, my story is the opposite of that...my recent history is a road full of liars, bystanders, survivors, victims and a bamboozled public.

I feel envious every single time that I see transparent UK justice.

I have had to especially over the past few years, consider that I needed to 'pick and choose my fights carefully... toxic organisation and their senior management will get limited or no fight from me...I leave it to karma and the universe.

Of course however, if there are any 'group actions', I might then change my mind and jump directly into the fray!

I think this chapter is going to rattle a lot of people...it seems 'more real' than any of the memoirs text that have been presented thus far.

Only the universe knows the point of continuing to show me white senior managers taking what seems to be the easy and well-treaded path for them of 'blame and lies', again and again and again and again and again...don't they realise that they continue to 'be seen' by all of us,no one is fooled, their insecurities glare like a blazing sun...yes please please universe explain what you want me to learn from meeting so many toxic senior managers at this stage of my life...can't I skip this?

I am just trying to reduce my work load and put social care to rest (at least for me) and I keep meeting people, survivors and victims (of their senior managers) that have sad and heart wrenching stories.

If 'truth' is generally considered as ...the real things(not a 'pretend' thing), why does it seem so hard for our managers and leaders to regularly engage in it...and often choose the opposite, like an 'non truth addiction'.

Is it important to tell the truth...why? One of the focus group members says that she was a habitual liar at one stage in her life. "...For me, I felt more 'powerful' when I was able to be more in control within my various work commitments...I could move the organisation and situations totally by what I said and or did not say...amazing isn't it?...".

Lies are generally accepted as to making an untrue statement(s) with intent to deceive. In the social care area, where the work can be very daunting at times, and regular lies for some seems just as bad as blame although its consequences may be felt differently potentially because those around you might find it genuinely easy to assume that their long or short term senior managers ' have no reason to engage in this type of nasty behaviour, and maybe describe it as a 'strategy to cope with their work stress ' and could potentially go on to attribute more and more positive characteristics to their bosses...yes, those same liars.

I wonder how those that challenge their senior managers are perceived, are they automatically seen as 'liars', is it perhaps a race or culture thing, a gender thing... perhaps maybe having ' a chip on their shoulders' and maybe we (the workers) go onto ' attribute negative characteristics' to those of us that challenge their senior managers such as "...stressed out, don't know any better, feel trapped...easily led...". ...I wonder???

When someone unfairly blames others, I remember my grandmother telling me that this is worse than any lie and they would go on to say "... there are several lies within a blame..." and she'd rather have a 'blaming boss' than a lying one.

I think I agree with her sentiment at times but I wonder if it 'translates' ('the weighting') to the wider general public, to the justice systems and other UK institutions, when they don't scrutinize facts presented to them and find it easier to 'digest a lie', as in the memoir discussions on press and the media.

I was charged with 'withholding information', but yet prosecution, judge, press, media, etc. never actually let me take the stand to share what Information that I really had, bring witnesses to show what information that they knew and or had. With my four important court letters that were withheld by the court and never saw the light of day, maybe they and the press and media should have charged themselves for withholding information...society definitely needs a break from 'institutional liars'.

Part of my focus group thinks that they would prefer an out and out senior manager that is a blamer to a repeating senior manager that lies almost like they are breathing.

I think I would take a liar senior manager to a blamer any day...a blamer ramifications seem to travel throughout the organisation and potentially through your career.

Quite scary to think, that some senior managers, regardless of their race and or culture have some devastating options at their disposal, ones that can totally devastate and break spirits of individuals, families and teams.

Does the truth really matter?

Not many people over the years have ever asked me "... Duncan what happened? ..." I could have easily told them(I think) or referred them to my draft memoir manuscript, it is very long but it can be read in someone's own time and hopefully will have all that they need to know to be able to answer "...Duncan what happen...", legally and spiritually?

The court itself resisted very strongly to ask me "...in your own words and with your own evidence and witnesses, please tell us what happen...".

A lot of what's in this chapter I already knew, it helps to have experienced some very good people and some very wise and learned individuals from all over the world.

I am assuming that readers had explored these memoirs in ways that they could potentially answer the question "...Duncan what happen...". Was it difficult to see the truth or a bit easy? Who is responsible once problems are identified... should individuals always get their own private legal teams or should a local, regional and or national organisations get involved, say like the charity commission...they might be a potential great ally...I wonder.

Felt like I have been chasing truth for the past few years and when no one wanted to know...I think past and present emails helped me to put things together and see the big picture...the truth is not always nice, but it is what it is. I have survived some not so nice people, several past and present wounded organisations, a country full of dangerous institutions...I guess next I need to find how to make use of it, to make the truth really matter...and make it do some real good for legacy of the survivors and the victims...for me!

Because of the daily trauma of racism for people of colour in the UK, add that to the 'social care work atmosphere' and daily lies by their predominately white senior managers, most staff of colour could be going to work each and every day experiencing some level of daily trauma that might be experienced physically, emotionally, spiritually and or psychologically...on the way to work, at work and after work... for me this rings very true!

Thought Questions:

? = What do you think about this chapters 'topic'...does truth really matter...? Was it an honest and or interesting chapter? Y/N Explain

8. Father to Father Contact

Some Reflective thoughts from D.Eric Lawrence

> **Bamboozled Wisdom:** (Number 8) 'The vulnerable' will always be 'at risk' of those that need help to hide the truth and or are only used to help move the truth even farther and farther away from the sunlight...shame really, they could have worked hard to take responsibility for their own actions, or could they...I wonder.

I could not have imagined losing children regardless of the age or circumstances...my joy would have been snatched away for an awfully long time if I had experienced such a catastrophic loss that potentially took away 'my future purpose'.

I have unfortunately seen too many parents that lose their children for a variety of reasons such as cancer, stabbings, gun violence, police murders, gang violence drug and alcohol overdoses, accidents and in each case, whether the parents and families show 'grace under fire', or they unfortunately 'go down the low road' within their 'words and actions' ...this seems very random set of rationalities, but in most cases, it usually has something to do with the influence of those around them, people that either generate positive energies in and around us and those that do not. I can only be convinced that regarding the small RPFI charity of 2015/16, they were at times influenced by some that did not genuinely have their interests at heart, being an optimist in most cases myself, it is hard for me to think otherwise.

I tried to show respect and patience with them but as the family started to play to press and seemed to be manipulated by various stakeholders that had 'multi-layered interests' (those that hated the charity and wanted to bring it down, those that wanted to build a lawsuit leading to a large cash payment, etc) I quickly started to lose respect for them...this was well before the court hearings even began. They were heavily impacting upon me, my family and my daughters own father... 'crossing the line for general respect, patience and human understanding several times and sadly doing it so easily.

I remember in the Spring of 2019, there was a family that won a half million-pound award from a social care organisation that neglected a 14-year-old, leading to her taking her own life...incredibly sad.

This was the same time period, one where the Assistant Coroner was coming at me very hard. I am confident that negative stakeholders saw this news too and were putting negative energy into this unfortunate family with hopes of a very big public pay out too...I really do not know.

There are so many of the Lancaster unit (trustees, staff, past service users and parents and carers) that know about the real level of self-harm and suicide gestures that occurred weekly and that specifically knew the details for the service users and staff that were on that sad day in May 2016, but they chose to keep quiet with the truth. I wonder if the parents ever put energy looking into this and had any luck tracking down information in this area, I genuinely hope so. Even with my own personal grief and the miscarriage of justice that unfortunately that they were very much a part of, I still tried to be helpful.

The way my case was conducted, as if 'a dance between the Judge and the prosecutor, this led to misguided levels of public sympathy and I felt as if I had none, either as a grieving son that recently lost his parents or as an innocent victim of the premeditated scapegoating.

My youngest daughter that was at the last court hearing, she overheard them telling the press that they did not want for me to go to prison, being grieving parents and individual adults that let a non-factual narrative be generated 'in their names' (within the coroner process, within the court process and within the press/media), one that helped to send an innocent citizen to prison...very confusing and weak stance publicly and behind closed doors it appears.

I was always confused by them, how could the father that seemed so respectful early on could then turn into a toxic human being and seemingly very easily misrepresent me in the press and present themselves in court as if I had personally done something to them(when I had not)...when they had a 'victim impact statement' read out in court about me I wanted to punch him right in the mouth right there and then(I was partly a victim of their lives and conspiracy, where was 'my victim impact statement'?) ...I wanted them to feel some of what they were unfairly giving and projecting onto me, right back onto them. Not genuinely 'nice thoughts' from someone that is usually an optimist and very empathetic with humans generally and with 'those in need' specifically. I am very much aware that with regards to this family, that I am a 'walking contradiction'. If they had behaved better maybe I could have helped them more than I did.

They even 'kept it quiet' during the summer/autumn 2019 court hearings when I had sent them some 2015-16 emails that I had recently recovered from three old phones (that I sent to them via the court and via the assistant coroner...see the 'four unanswered court letters' that are later illustrated within this book), nor did they tell anyone that I responded to a 'father to father' email request(see below)...no, they just kept quiet and relentlessly continued to push a non-factual narrative that I did not care about them and that I continued to withhold crucial information from them...unfortunately, this was bamboozling too! The early memoir chapters that discuss 'does the truth really matter'...it becomes all too real again here too. What was 'their motivations' during this period, was there any differences between what was in 'their hearts' and in 'their heads'...did they want to be held accountable for what the court system was doing to me 'in their family's name' or perhaps they disassociated themselves from what was happening within the court processes?

I had to work hard (unsuccessfully it seems) to not let them take over my trying to get the case to be about the 'inappropriate charge' and not just their quest for closure about their adult daughter taking her own life. If was difficult for us all then *and it is still difficult now. Was my name, potentially losing my liberty and credibility worth nothing to them leading up to,during and after the court hearing? When they went to the hearings for the charity and the ex-CEO I wonder were they thinking of me then...were they thinking of the missing charity founder(Ellie/Nellie Jansen)...I wonder if they told that particular court about the emails that I gave to them...I am assuming that 'the low road' was taken again, where the 'positive attributes that could arise from family values' were still very much 'hidden in plain sight'.*

I can never imagine any apologies coming from them. I am sure this is not about a personality thing or a family being unsure of 'the truth'. I think at some point in time, I stopped being a 'human being' to them too (similarly to the Assistant Coroner and Judiciary) and maybe just an unworthy black man that deserved everything he gets, maybe in their minds and or as other toxic actors might be regularly putting 'in their heads', it was me, standing in their way of who they really wanted, Elly Jansen, the ex-CEO,etc... 'the goal' was emotional closure and potentially some financial closure, both that seem to be eluding them...did any of these things occur, I am sure that 'the universe' and 'karma' has a plan for us all and hope that this family can begin to move on from me sooner rather than later. As I said earlier in this book, please just leave me alone, I am nothing special and you have not proved to be worth so much toxicity to me and my family.

Once cleared, I will consider getting a restraining order out against them, being a willing and foolish co-conspirator, leading to me going to prison means that I struggle to find genuine sympathy and will not tolerate any further lies and or toxic harassment. They should read the book, it is very transparent and could be helpful for additional closure, please just respectfully leave me well alone.

Some people may think that I am too harsh on the father and his family, but if they wished me to have seen them as something 'different', they could have acted differently and or 'just changed' and taken the higher road. The world would not have judged them harshly for saying that they treated me very unreasonably.

I forgive them, but it is a daily struggle, and I will never forget.

---------- Forwarded message ---------

From: **Eric Lawrence** <<u>diversitymanagementlcl@btinternet.com</u>>
Date: Thu, 22 Aug 2019 at 11:24
Subject: Bennett Coroner
To: <<u>Louise.Smith@lbhf.gov.uk</u>>

Apologies for making contact this way(was not sure how to make contact any other way) and was trying to avoid the press.

I found some emails Wednesday am in a previous phone folder that I have not used in awhile. Inside were some random RPFI/RCI emails that yourself and Bennett family might find useful.

I have submitted these to the Court Officer and Prosecutor yesterday.

Unedited by me they illustrate directly some of 'the mood'(and activities that took up a lot of its time/limited resources of a very small charity) within the RPFI/RCI Charity and some of the internal thoughts and actions about the Lancaster unit as well as the other two units that comprised the charity.

I hope that this is enough to further demonstrate my seriousness of your role and process.

And hopefully you will now remove your focus off me and directly on to the charity, its founder/lead advisor, past and present CEO, Past and Present Trustees and past and present and present Lancaster Unit Managers and staff.I never received any payment what so ever once I ended with them.

The organisation originally was called the Richmond Fellowship decades ago and because of the financial irregularities the founder was struck off and she opened up RPFI/RCI.

Google this, this is very easy to confirm about Ms Elly Jansen.

We had meetings at her home, she owned and collected rent from all the charity properties and yet you pursue me(and I continued so many times to refer you to her, Ms Elly Jansen-Founder and Lead Advisor of RPFI/RCI).

There were service users trying to take their lives monthly (again I referred you to the founder and trustees to get exact numbers).My next court appearance I will let all know how many times that I referred this process to talk to the direct sources eg founder/lead advisor, ex-Trustees Chairs (some that had other social care business relations with the founder) and ex-CEO.

I was never the 'motherlode' of hidden information that I was built up to be. Crazy narratives about me in the varied news 2019 media did not produce yesterday's emails...I was very grateful and relieved to find them...more to show you that I never took your role lightly sir, your job can help patterns from being repeated in order to prevent deaths(although I think I have been more assistance to this process than ever credited).I just also wish you to go after the right people.

I have nothing else to add in terms of emails and hope that one day my previous recommendations and suggestions to you can actually reach the light of day, the Bennett family etc.,sooner than later...they are worthwhile if taken seriously.

Respectfully submitted,

Duncan Lawrence

D.E.Lawrence:

Diversity, Equality, Inclusion and Sport Specialist/Management and Team Coach.

Please think of the environment – do you really need to print this email or its attachments?

Sent from my iPhone

---------- Forwarded message ---------

From: **Duncan Lawrence**
	<duncan@considercelebratingdiversityandsport.com>
Date: Tue, 29 Dec 2020 at 18:46
Subject:
To: Diversity Management LCL <diversitymanagementlcl@ gmail.com>

Begin forwarded message:

On Sunday, February 3, 2019, 10:50 am, Eric Lawrence <diversitymanagementlcl@btinternet.com> wrote:

No disrespect to you or your family sir.

My family has been in crisis mode for several weeks. My father passed away of a preventable death and my mom has had pacemaker put in (although a heart operation due later this week)and is frail mentally and physically and could pass soon too(along with multiple family challenges alongside, which included recently being temporarily homeless).

I spent several hours preparing several dozen pages of evidence (that I hope you have seen by now)for the coroner with email evidence as back up, trying to be honest and open at the same time.

Please believe me sir, I am very sorry for your family loss and hope that the coroner's process adds closure.

I have to put my extended family first at this time and it is in no way saying that they are more important than your family loss.

There is learning to be had all around within the charity and the ways that it works, hopefully knowing this helps to.

Respectfully,

Duncan Lawrence

D.E.Lawrence:

Diversity, Equality, Inclusion and Sport Specialist/Management and Team Coach.

Please think of the environment – do you really need to print this email or its attachments?

Sent from my iPhone

On 3 Feb 2019, at 09:00, Ben Bennett <bpjbennett@gmail.com> wrote:

Dear Duncan

I am Sophie's father. Could you please have the common decency to explain to me why you have avoided giving evidence at the Inquest into her death? It is nearly 3 years since she died. I have fought to discover the truth of what happened and you are part of that truth. You could give evidence tomorrow and the family would appreciate that.

Ben Bennett

D.E.Lawrence:

Diversity, Equality, Inclusion and Sport Specialist/Management and Team Coach.

2020+ : Please only use diversitymanagementlcl@gmail.com and company emails relating to 'consider celebrating diversity and sport' to make contact in the future...thanks and be safe!

Please think of the environment – do you really need to print this email or its attachments?

Sent from my iPhone

Thought Questions:

? = Should the family get 'a free pass', regardless of how appalling their words and or actions have been towards D.Eric Lawrence in the court, in the press, in the media, etc.?

9. Court Process (including the Probation Service)

Some Reflective thoughts from D.Eric Lawrence

> **Bamboozled Wisdom:**(Number 9) The 'appearance' of a court building, one that houses potential criminals, victims, prosecution, and a judge...in the light of murky and toxic environments such as this, who can really tell 'who' is really 'who'?

My first time going to court for myself was not too scary initially. There were three magistrates at my first hearing and the entire 'introduction hearing' seemed quite straight forward. I had already given my guilty plea (with extenuating circumstances) via email to the MET hoping to get a reduced fine. Where things went a bit scary was when the family read out a letter to court talking about how I was hurting them with my silence and when the court did not seem to actually know about my plea that occurred a few days before the first hearing (so the court clerk read out an email copy of my plea...I happen to have had a copy with me at the time and alerted them about my first pre-court email effort).

The 'scariness level stepped' up to a crazy higher level when the prosecution stated that they were considering a custodial sentence! This was, when honestly there was none of us in that court room that really understood the charge including me, to now have the prosecutor state that they were thinking about a prison sentence...shocking!

The three magistrates visibly freaked out too and adjourned for a few weeks for 'consultation'...I was freaked out too!

It was after this session that I realised that I needed to step up my approach and seek advice, then write to the court accordingly in a very timely manner.

<u>Some of my friends and the press seemed taken aback by my initial guilty plea, but they could not understand that I initially was hoping for a fine as the MET initially suggested...</u>*I felt too knackered by the press, media and assistant coroner and had no wish to fight it out, just to prove a point to anyone.*

The press and the court are truly amazing...they can work closely together, especially if no one is making a fuss.

Even though I mentioned in court that the London Metropolitan police advised me that an ' early plea' would mean potential reduction of any fine, so I emailed my plea well in advance of my first court hearing. The court and the press were happy to let the narrative be that I foolishly pleaded guilty in court(where in reality I just corrected the court to say that I sent my plea via email) because I was asked to read it. I can almost guarantee that there is not one factual court transcript that reflects me reading my email, nor will there be any factual press accounts...the closest ' the truth comes to poking her head out ' is right here within my memoirs!

Was not sure what chapter to put these comments, sadly enough they easily fit into my reflections of the press and my reflections of the court...not one institution protected the truth or protected my Human Rights, especially as they related to Article 6.

The following week I sent out the first of my four letters to the court/prosecutor that were never actually mentioned in court and I was sentenced without ever giving evidence, without presenting witnesses and without giving my account of the charge.

The 'hidden court letters' were based upon the following areas:

1. *Change of Plea Application*
2. *Complaint about the Assistant Coroner*
3. *Additional emails given to the Bennet Family*
4. *Request to judge to suspend court process until they clarify if the 'charge period dates' actually reflect my charge*

I vigorously tried to get legal aid but was denied. I had a lovely advocate support me for one session and I was incredibly grateful for her support (could have been sentenced much earlier without her) ...wish I could have had her full time!

I tried to pay for a solicitor, but after one court session where my solicitor literally said nothing, I knew that he was out of his depth and so I tried my best to represent myself. **Important to note**, *I did have a very competent QC for one hearing but* *because of the judge refusal to address the four unanswered court letters, the Judge refused to hear or discuss my change of plea application25...British Justice, where were you then on that day?*

The court probation officer (whose job it was to create a pre-sentence report for the court) did not even seem to care about getting to the truth (via ample evidence and written statements that I provided to her), she was only focused on serving the prosecution and judge's expectations. It seemed like they were somewhat afraid of the judge and prosecutor too at times, I cannot be certain.

Even when I made a complaint to the probation service, the complaints management was not committed to answering my complaints either (probation officer wanted me to 'tow a line' in terms showing empathy and remorse to the family of the young woman that took her own life and disregard anything else, the truth did not matter and would not keep me from a custodial sentence it seemed...a total 'stitch up', and they were servants of clear white privilege whether they wanted to admit it or not).

---

25 It is important to note, this was not my 'change of plea application' that I had sent to the court a few days after the court hearings began. The barrister on this day unfortunately as talented and as confident as he was, my solicitor did not even tell him in advance about my four letters that were withheld by the court...he only heard about them 'on the day', not enough time to bring them up I guess. The toxic judge I am sure if had made a strong fuss that day, that this judge would have potentially stated that he was hearing my application then. This would have been impossible without speaking to me, the author generally and specifically following this up talking to me about any evidence and witnesses did I wish to submit...these discussions did not ever occur. Don't believe any incompetent judges potential spin.

My thoughts about the appeal process:

I thought that 'any reasonable appeal' would be one that allowed me to present witnesses, present evidence and would allow time to consider the 'legal implications' of the original court withholding my four court letters, that finally it would come to light about the various false narratives, lies and collusion by several stakeholders and actors...boy was I wrong, the Kingston Crown Court, clearly wanted to not rock the boat and simply fought very very very hard to not have to give a written opinion about the original court bias, lies and mistakes...read about them yourself below! They instead chose to fine me twice £330 with no explanation to put me off. Ironically, I am sure that it will eventually be the past and or a future 'appeal process' that leads to the clearing of my name.

I did not choose to either give up and or to let the assistant coroner and his toxic team of actors have their way, the universe it seemed wanted me to clear myself/distance myself from this craziness and move on with my life...no matter how long it takes.

My Initial Plea via email sent to the MET:

Sent from my iPhone

Begin forwarded message:

From: Eric Lawrence <<u>diversitymanagementlcl@btinternet.com</u>>
Date: 8 August 2019 at 05:19:13 BST
To: <u>tyrone.ward@met.police.uk</u>
Subject: Police investigation

Charge: Prevent Evidence /document production/provision of a thing for an investigation

I plead 100% guilty to the above charge.

By not answering all of the coroner process questions I can understand that they may have wrongly assumed that I did take the important coroners process seriously. I never lied or had any negative intentions either and I respectfully also want it officially noted (if possible alongside with my plea), my extenuating circumstances so that I am not misrepresented today within my plea:

1. Both parents were medically and psychologically fragile and nee= ded my care and attention as the eldest son (and hence from the beginning, initially through the charity solicitor I said that it may be difficult to do more than regular written submissions). My mother passed away in May 2019 and my father in Spring 2018.

2. The charity solicitors told us the coroner process only wanted written submission details from three months leading up to the young woman taking her life. I strongly

suggested that this could be misleading because animosity between the charity and the charity unit where she took her own life, goes back a few years and I made multiple related recommendations to founder/advisor,Chair of the Trustees etc to try to lessen the deep rooted animosity between all parties. I should have been more insistent, maybe I would not be here today.

3. I had wrongly assumed that by my regular written recommendations to coroner process would be objectively considered and checked out and and by doing so that he would change his views of my usefulness to the coroner process .

4. I wrongly assumed that I could support my parents/family and provide helpful useful written statements at the same time. The juggling attempts proved very difficult.I failed very badly on both accounts.

5. With the emerging news media and coroner process bias, intimidation and misrepresentation towards me (and the above four areas in combination) I was totally stressed out and I did not read and answer all of his questions as best as I should have. I tried my best, even tried using the full coroners own complaint procedures to review my efforts and actions (from me, to me and around me) .Although I never lied or sought to mislead,upon reflection more careful reading of his letters could have avoided me being here today, therefore I am guilty of the above charge.I have no further information to add.

Respectfully submitted:

Duncan E Lawrence

8.8.2019

Sent from my iPhone

On 2 Aug 2019, at 21:32, <Tyrone.Ward@met.police.uk> t;Tyrone.Ward@met.police.uk= > wrote:

Dear Mr Lawrence,

I hope you are well since we last met.

I am emailing to confirm that this case was referred to the CPS who have considered the evidence in the case. They have made the decision to charge you with one offence contrary to schedule 6 of the Coroners and Justice Act, 2009. Please find attached a postal charge and requisition (PCR) with the details of the offence for which you have been charged. You are now required to attend Wimbledon Magistrates Court on 16/08/19 at 10am to enter a plea. It is vitally important you attend on this date as failure to do so may make you liable to arrest.

Also attached is a means form for you to print off and fill out.

A hard copy of both the PCR and means form has also been posted to your home address.

Please do not hesitate to contact me if you have any questions around this.

Kind regards,

Tyrone

DC Tyrone Ward 1163SW
Safeguarding Team 3B
Mobile 07741702833
Email tyrone.ward@met.police.uk
Address Eagle House, Ram Passage, Kingston upon Thames, KT1 1HL

Probation Service Comments

The court probation staff are meant to work in partnership with the magistrates court by professionally assessing me via discussion, observations and then make a recommendation to the judge as to a type of sentence that could fit my level of risk and remorse.

My probation officer seemed very timid regarding challenging the judge. As polite and friendly as she was, 'she did not feel me' and my view of how I came to be in this legal mess.

She read my court letters and my emails that in 'another reality' would have easily illustrated my innocence, especially with regard to the inappropriate charge period dates.

All she was concerned with however was with me 'showing remorse' to the family of the young woman that took her own life(and nothing else).

She did not see herself as even partly 'a gate keeper for the truth' to come out.

From training probation staff for years I knew she was mistaken...she could have easily integrated my views e.g ."... Duncan has deep empathy and sympathy for this family's loss. He states that he tried to be as helpful as he could within his witness statement and exhibits. He also feels that the charge sheet for his potential sentence does not relate to a time that he ever knew the Assistant Coroner. Additionally he feels that his 'change of plea application' if considered by this court (where he could submit witnesses and evidence) would illustrate his innocence of this charge, while not downplaying this family's grief...".

The probation officer put forth 'a very weak' pre- sentencing report, one that basically' rubber stamped' for this Judge to give me a custodial sentence (even though I never had as much as a parking ticket my entire life and have given so much to the UK in the areas of social science, criminal justice, diversity and inclusion and social care).

10. Hidden in plain sight… documents withheld by the London Met, court, the prosecutor and the Judge

Some Reflective thoughts from D.Eric Lawrence

> **Bamboozled Wisdom:**(Number 10) You know that you are on to something when you submit something that only takes less than two-four hour sessions in total to write up and then those you sent it to[26], fight like Superman and Batman combined to 'deny its existence'. "…Up up and (a) hide!!!…".

For the longest time, no one in the Wimbledon Magistrates Court would ever admit to the existence of my four court letters (even though I received an email receipt from the court once I sent them).

The letters below include some ' running commentary' from those that helped with acknowledging that my court letters existed and those that hindered the court acknowledging their existence).

This overall illustrates somewhat some of the effort that I had to put out just to get some acknowledgement from Wimbledon Magistrates Court.

---

[26] Your writing,etc..66/*/

Quite a few messy email chains but all there!

Were they worth all the hassle, only time will tell!

Unanswered court letters from August and Oct 2019

From: Duncan Lawrence <<u>duncan@ considercelebratingdiversityandsport.com</u>>

Date: 15 April 2020 at 17:39:48 BST

To: HM Courts and Tribunals Service <<u>replies@optic.justice. gov.uk</u>>

Subject: Re: Complaint (ref: 3463020)

You are amazing Ms.Aedy, thanks for getting back to me so quick!

Re: Appeal Application

I think we are talking at 'cross purposes'. My solicitor sent one in 2019(and then cancelled it...I am not chasing this one) <u>and I sent a different one in January 2020...it is this one that I am chasing now.</u>

Thanks again for everything, I am grateful!

Duncan E.Lawrence

London SE26 5LB

D.E.Lawrence:

Diversity, Equality, Inclusion and Sport Specialist/Management and Team Coach.

<u>Please think of the environment</u> – do you really need to print this email or its attachments?

Sent from my iPhone

On 15 Apr 2020, at 16:59, HM Courts and Tribunals Service <replies@optic.justice.gov.uk> wrote:

Dear Duncan Lawrence

Thank you for your complaint of 15 April 2020 in relation to the handling of your case.

I have corresponded previously with you in relation to how your case was dealt with at Wimbledon Magistrates Court and **I assured you that the Judge had had sight of all the documents you submitted to the Court.**

In relation to your Appeal, I can confirm that this was submitted to Kingston Crown Court on the 25th November 2019. I can't understand why Kingston Crown Court are saying that they have not received the documentation as we have a sending receipt.

I have asked my team at the Magistraes Court to re-send the Appeal to the Crown Court using the previous digital notification we used for the documentation we sent on the 25th November 2019.

In the meantime, if you have any questions please call/email Alison Aedy, 0300 303 0645, or email alison.aedy@justice. gov.uk.

Regards,

Alison Aedy
Operations Manager

Wimbledon Magistrates', HM Courts and Tribunals Service | HMCTS | c/o SE London Magistrates' Courts Admin Centre, 1 London Road, Bromley, BR1 1RA
Phone: 0300 303 0645

 HM Courts & Tribunals Service

NOTE: Please do not edit the subject line when replying to this email.

From: Duncan Lawrence <duncan@ considercelebratingdiversityandsport.com>
Date: 20 August 2019 at 18:32:20 BST
To: southlondonmc@justice.gov.uk, swlondonmc@ hmcts.g-si.gov.uk
Subject: FOA: Court Officer and Prosecutor(Wimbledon Magistrates Court)
FOA: Court Officer and Prosecutor-Wimbledon Magistrates Court

20 August 2019

Wimbledon Magistrates Court
Wimbledon Magistrates & Court, The Court House, Alexandra Road, Wimbledon, London SW19 7JP

URN 01TW/00755/19
Duncan E.Lawrence
Date of birth 16/02/1959
Arrest summons number 19/01TW/02/44P

Charge:

1. Prevent evidence / document production / provision
    of a thing for an investigation

Between 10/06/2018 and 04/02/2019, within the jurisdiction
of the Central Criminal Court, Duncan Lawrence failed to
provide documentation as directed by the Coroner for the
purposes of an investigation, with the intention to have the
effect of preventing that evidence, document or other thing
from being given, produced or provided for the purposes
of such an investigation, contrary to paragraph 7(1)(b) of
Schedule 6 of the Coroners and Justice Act 2009.

Contrary to paragraph 7(1)(b) and (6) of Schedule 6 to the
Coroners and Justice Act 2009.H.O. - EWNI - 6 months
- CJ09018

**FOA: Court Officer and Prosecutor-Wimbledon Magistrates
Court**

20 August 2019

Wimbledon Magistrates Court

**Re:/ Related to Criminal Procedure Rules 24.10 Change of
Plea**

1. On 16.8.19, 10 am in Court 8, I pleaded guilty (with
    written extenuating circumstances) to the above
    charge.

1.1 At that time (and before) I was told it was a fine hearing and I was hoping to tell the truth, pay the fine and move on with grieving my parents that had recently passed away.

2. Unexpectedly in the hearing there was talk of a custodial sentence possibility

   (even though my MET charge papers did not refer to this, nor my MET financial statement papers...they regularly referred to be prepared to possibly pay a fine and the sooner a guilty plea the more of a fine reduction(I sent my plea on 6.8.19...you took my email copy at the hearing with email date stamped on it.).

2.1 Since the hearing legal goal posts have now changed/further developed within considering my charge, <u>I would be unfairly done by unless I too had a chance to change/further develop my plea statement and evidence to submit and based on the new additional possibilities that you yourselves are considering during the adjournment period.</u>

<u>FYI, my plea if accepted would be not guilty</u>, but I would be adding almost the same exact original extenuating circumstances' to explain myself(too add context).

3. <u>I would like to submit all correspondence to/from myself to the coroner as evidence</u>(electronically), in order to highlight **(a)** all of my recommendations about the charity (RPFI), **(b)** my specific recommendations to the coroner advising how he could confirm my written

statements and finally **(c)** show my recommendations that could have assisted lessons learned from the young woman taking her own life in 2016. These might provide family with some closure.

3.1 If possible, to would like to additionally add evidence of my attempts to see if I was being treated with bias by this coroner (although I would understand if this particular evidence is not acceptable, although I hope it is).

4. Finally is it possible for you to invite Ms Elly Jansen, The founder and lead advisor of the charity during the time of the death? She could provide further clarification about all of my statements and potentially answer any leftover questions from the coroner/family.

Respectfully submitted by:

Duncan E. Lawrence

London SE26 5LB

P.S:I am emailing this and posting it special delivery as well to you both at Wimbledon Magistrates Court.

From: Duncan   Lawrence   <duncan@ considercelebratingdiversityandsport.com>
Date: 20 August 2019 at 18:39:57 BST
To: southlondonmc@justice.gov.uk
Subject: FAO:Court Officer and Prosecutor

Good morning Court Officer/Prosecutor

Can you please forward this to magistrates that heard my case last Friday(10am) at Wimbledon Magistrates Court... thanks for your consideration.

The two complaints letter and form detail my related stress and concerns related to unfair bias with the coroner leading my charge.

The complaints also lay out an attempt to get a review body, someone to review our relationship to see if it has always been fair, professional and reasonable for an public official.

I wish now that you might add it to your considerations as well before I return on 27.8.19...I saw that a family member added a letter at the hearing which you took in, so hope me sending this to you is ok as well to take in as well.

I look forward to seeing you on the 27.8.19.

Respectfully Submitted:

Duncan Lawrence

London SE26 5LB

D.E.Lawrence:

Diversity, Equality, Inclusion and Sport Specialist/Management and Team Coach.

Please think of the environment – do you really need to print this email or its attachments?

D.Eric Lawrence

Local Government Ombudsman - Complaint Form

Which body (council, authority or care provider) are you complaining about?

West London Coroners Court

Have you complained to the body already? Usually, you should have completed all stages of the body's complaints process before we can look at your complaint.

Yes

Please say when you complained to the body. (We will need to see the letter from the body that confirms you have completed their complaints procedure – you will have the opportunity to upload this at the end of the form.)

If you don't have your letter and can't remember when you complained, put 'don't know' in the box

10 June 2019Your complaint to the Judicial Conduct

What do you think the body did wrong?

Please explain briefly what your complaint is about, including dates of any incidents and names of any officers or staff of the body complained about, if known. Please also explain why you are not happy with the response from the body concerned.

If your complaint involves a child it would be helpful if you could provide their full name and date of birth.

Regarding Complaint about:

C/o Louise Smith
Coroner's Office
West London Coroner's Office
25, Bagleys Lane,
Fulham SW6 2QA

I wish to formally complain about the above mentioned Coroner's treatment of me during/after the 'Sophie Bennett Coroner Inquiry '

I additionally formally express my dismay at his ongoing bias towards me .I have respectfully specifically summarised my reasons for this below.

I have also respectfully listed my expectations of this complaints process below as well.

Summary of events leading up to my formal complaint today:
For approximately three months in 2016 I was a consultant for a social care charity that had three homes.
(I supported all of them) and I ended up wearing 'other hats too' such as Interim Management Support, Clinical Lead ,etc. during this three month period.
The Charity had a pre-existing and difficult relationship with one of their two adult mental health homes over a few years (interpersonal problems between the founder, the charity board and the manager, ex-CEOs and mutual antagonism).
 After a difficult three months of advising this charity(although my suggestions for reducing animosity between the different stakeholders were usually often not taken up), I was released from my temporary contract in March 2016.
Three-four months after(the ending of my charity role) that , a woman resident of one of the homes sadly committed suicide.
The charity asked(with several months in advance notice) could I help with being involved with preparation for Coroners Inquiry (scheduled for winter 2018).
Simultaneously to this my elderly father was dying of cancer and my elderly fragile mother was mentally and physically

page 1 of 6

462

ill.

At that time I told the charity solicitors in writing and verbally that while I would provide a written statement submission, that because of my parent situation at the time I could not guarantee to attend and needed to support my immediate and extended family (but would keep everyone informed if I could).

Last spring of 2018 my father passed away and my extended family went into meltdown mode which included my mom being kicked out of the family home and being made homeless due to unpaid gas, electric and water bills.

With all of that going on, trying to work when I could to keep a roof over my head and help where I could with my mothers well-being) and being the eldest son, I could not have any face-to-face time for the Coroner inquiry and put my much needed physical time and action into supporting my mentally and physically fragile mother (I gave the charity and Coroner regularly written updates especially when regularly asked about my on going availability).

At the end of the initial inquiry in mid February 2019 I was slated and never a mention of sympathy for my fathers death and my mother's deterioration...it was like that did not matter and the Coroner misrepresented that I was not in regular contact, nor was I helping the process, both which were all untrue. Because of this misrepresentation , I 100 % expected the trial by media storm that followed and a fine. The media storms (Feb 2018 and May 2018) were awful and generally related to misrepresentations arising from the Coroner process.

At the same time, once my main agency employer heard about the case early February 2019, they ended my contact and I was unemployed until 19 April 2019.

The Coroner said they would decide a fine amount. Instead they asked me a few more follow up questions which I answered and to provide proof that I was unemployed.

It was then that I respectfully and specifically expressed my concerns about bias and complained about this over two Spring 2019 emails(as part of responding to him directly regarding his questions to me), he never even acknowledged my comments and concerns and inferred that I was rewriting history (rather than simply checking out my response validity [as I respectfully suggested]with the charity founder/advisor. and or the Trustee Chair and or the Trustees).I asked for the link to the complaint procedure.

The latest is the Coroner process recently rubbished my 1996 doctorate degree in Public Administration because it was not from an outstanding British College, University etc (though I got a UK student loan to pay for it) and inferred that I was acting like a medical doctor or psychiatrist or something similar , something that was very untrue(my degree, it has nothing what so ever to do with 'caring profession')...I was just fortunate to have a lot of experience in mental health, leadership , residential work , case work and interpersonal relationships since the late 1970s(US/UK/EU).

I recently found out that he unfairly complained about me to different professional bodies that I am part of for decades. such as the British Association for Counselling and Psychotherapy...I was never even in a counsellor role during my time with the charity connected to the Coroner Inquiry...so why did he do this? Does he feel disrespected by me in some way? If so, that was never my intention and I sincerely apologise.

I feel like he has some misguided thoughts about me and unfairly wants to embarrass me, discredit my credentials and he never wanted to acknowledge my real and regular contributions to the lessons learned pool ' from this Coroner process. I find it very hard to believe all of this hassle was just because I split my energies between my family and the Coroner process (rather than choosing one over the other), some would commend my efforts rather than disrespectfully misrepresent them over and over again.

I am sure another non biased professional would have no need to disregard my constructive written Coroner statements and recommendations, especially in the spirit of being transparent.

If he has never treated other stakeholders connected with this particular Coroner inquiry in the same way(with bias, unfair scrutiny etc), then I want a written apology and commitment that he will stop and leave me alone in the future.

I always told the truth to the Coroner and made regular recommendations (things that were never acknowledged by him) but I refused to give him proof that I was unemployed...did not wish for the media and future employers to get a hold of this information(in which they would have done so via his office).

I felt so much incredible onslaught of bias against me from the Coroner process at so many levels, race, privilege classismetc but I was never really sure of the root source and the negative motives /intentions.

There were several other senior stakeholders that never had their credentials regularly questioned... it seems it was just me that is getting regularly decimated within this Coroner process.

As a freelancer consultant , I never once ever fraudulently misrepresented myself as a medical doctor, I do not even know where this misrepresentation story came from.

I thought about making a complaint earlier about the Coroner process but in the end did not. I am 60 years old and did not wish my final career phase to be judged solely by my

Local Government Ombudsman - Complaint Form

developing dysfunctional relationship with this particular Coroner process .
I know 'different interests' are looking for a future payout from the charity in question and the successful belittling/discrediting of me helps their future cases. I honestly hope that I am not a 'pawn' being misused by this process.I was only on 'the side' of trying to tell the truth and be helpful.
I accepted the £650 fine for non attendance at the Coroner inquiry , but I 100% cooperated with any and all requests from the Coroner...at least 10 -13 thousand +word statements and constructive suggestions came willingly from me.
I am so so sad and horrified that now they wish to tear me down even further via my various professional fellowships and long British Association of Counselling and Psychotherapy membership.
I was never a counsellor or therapist for the charity in question(although the charity had details of my BACP Fellowship), and in my brief charity role I just mainly made several recommendations for improving standardisation across the charity, made practical suggestions to improve the poor interpersonal relationships and communications between the founder/advisor, past CEOs . Past-Present Unit managers and their staff teams, developed a new draft mission statement, a well-being and employability programme and attempted to demonstrate to staff how to facilitate it(although left the charity before this later task was actually implemented). These tasks, ones that are actually good for any social care or residential organisation, I am being accused of introducing 'change' too quickly (what the charity founder/advisor hired me for) , which stressed staff and long term residents out. Where in reality as mentioned earlier. I also provided a series of advice that if taken up would have improved the long term interpersonal problems and antagonism between the charity founder, old CEOs, Trustees, ex manager and their teams. So from earlier on I was 'mislabelled ' and my charity efforts misrepresented, something that the Coroner process seems to wished to keep me defined and limited to(even though the truth was that staff and residents resisted the ideas and never actually engaged in even one week of my ideas prior to me leaving). I even asked the charity to become an organisational member of the BACP to illustrate their emerging quality standards.
Ironically my mother finally passed away last weekend, we are burying her today and I am still not allowed to grieve (due to my less than three months work for a charity, one in which sadly a resident took her own life 3-4 after I had left). I told the Coroner several times, I was not there and can not give any specific opinion about her suicide .
The BACP register is open to public scrutiny but I hope that the BACP does not unfairly get involved here.I have been proud and ethical BAC/BACP member for decades .
The Coroner process only recently found out that I was a BACP Fellow (an honour since 2002) because in Spring 2019 he asked me to send copies of items that I would have given to the charity in 2016. Even though I was extremely concerned that he'd misuse whatever I sent him(which he did unfortunately),I sent him my various Fellowships, and my doctorate copy,2016 CRB etc anyway and he has tried to discredit (some within the press/media) every single item I sent and not missing out on any of them! Because he was hinting(indirect threat actually) to refer charity/me to the CPS, I was too frightened to not send him anything. Maybe I should have continued to resist his bullying threats and to not send him any details upon reflection last spring.Going after my BACP professional association is very low in a series of bias acts toward me.
What would I hope for from this complaints process
1.   Clarify if there have been any previous complaints about bias, bullying etc..from this office.
2.   That I am assisted with ensuring that this Complaint goes through in a timely manner and is not hindered because I am not an expert in your processes and procedures.
3.   That I will not be shown even more bias and or related media storms due to filing this formal complaint.
4.   Someone to review written comments to me, from me and about me to check if there was any unfair bias , say when compared to other similar experienced stakeholders involved within this particular Coroner Inquiry (I first started working in social care, education and criminal justice in the late 70s while still in university).
5.   If bias found or 'allowed ', provide explanation why I was singled out? I only worked for a few months within the charity in question and he goes after me as if I was a long term employee with maximum influence during my time (within the charity)...three months is only three months. 90 % of my daily/weekly instructions were from the charity founder/advisor ...the Coroner process seemed very unwilling to ask her was this actually true...why not?She could validate my claims in minutes.It was her charity and not mine.
5.1 Did any other stake holders have police sent around to their homes.
5.2 Did any other stake holders have rumours spread about them, directly from the coroners office e.g. that I hired someone (A white man...I am an African-american) to attend a coroner video hearing and had them act as if they were me.
5.3 Did any other stakeholders have any coroner related charges filed against them?

27.8.19

Local Government Ombudsman - Complaint Form

	6. 'Using privilege' because you can against me like he's done should never ever happen to anyone again...it feels absolutely horrible. 7. Consider if any collusion occurred within the Coroner process(related to myself directly and or indirectly) 8. Written apology, especially for lack of empathy shown for me and my family losses that were occurring simultaneously to the Coroner process, and for trying to cause unchecked havoc to my professional reputation and career 9. Put Coroner on an anti-bias course 10. Would like a full list of the organisations and individuals that he has written in connection to me(and detail who else knows of this eg, the family, their solicitor, CQC, particular press ,etc) 11. While I have no interest whatsoever for the results of this complaint to go public , I too would simply like a written commitment to stop this overt/ covert publicly bullying and harassment of me. It adds no value to any 'lesson learned ' for the family of the young woman that committed suicide...just seems such an unfair abuse of powers regularly coming after me in such a nasty , vicious, irresponsible and irrational manner(and all roads seem to lead on to unwarranted and unwanted media storms that are very embarrassing to me, to my family , to my friends and to my professional colleagues)...all emanating from this Coroner process. Thanks in advance for considering this complaint. Respectfully submitted by: Duncan Lawrence

How has this affected you?

	Please explain briefly what impact the problems you've described above have had on you.
	For example, has the body concerned failed to provide you with a service or a benefit you are entitled to? Was there a delay before you got the service or benefit? Have you suffered a financial loss? Have you been put to a lot of trouble or inconvenience? 1. My personal and professional reputation is regularly soiled in the media, directly after any interaction with the coroner(Feb ,May and August 2019) 1.1 Lost a good agency contract in Feb 2019 because of the coroner misrepresenting me in the press. 1.2. He has written to my various professional associations misrepresenting me(Spring-Summer 2019). 1.3 He has sent two policemen over to my home. I had to voluntarily present myself at the police station for a coroner related charge. I am being sentenced for a coroner related charge on 27.8.19 1.3 I am worried that I will lose my current job, especially after being unemployed from Feb 2019 to 19 April 2019 and have debts related to my mothers passing,31 May 2019. 1.4 I might get a criminal record

What do you think the body should do to put things right?

	1. Just a basic review to see if there has been any unfair bias to me, connected to me and have other similar stakeholders in this particular coroner process been treated exactly as I have. 2. See if there have been any other complaints to this coroner. 3. Publish your findings to all relevant stakeholders asap. I know it is too late for my 27.8.19 hearings, but it will assist my professional and personal associations to have a

page 4 of 6

	more clearer picture about myself and this coroner.

More help

	We are committed to making sure the way we work does not put anybody at a disadvantage. If you need any help or support to use our service, please tell us your request in the box below and we will consider what changes we can make.
	Please leave this box blank if you do not require help or support to use our service.

Contact Details (on Behalf)

Are you completing this form on behalf of someone else ?	No
	We will need you to provide written consent from the other person, or documents to show you can act on their behalf. We tell you how to give us that consent once you have submitted the complaint.

Local Government Ombudsman - Complaint Form

Name

Title	Mr
First Name	Duncan
Surname	Lawrence

Address

House number/name	18-C,Kenthouse Road
Address Line 2	Kenthouse Road
Address Line 3	
Town	London
Post code	SE26 5LB
Email Address	diversitymanagementcl@gmail.com
Confirm Email Address	diversitymanagementcl@gmail.com

Telephone

Daytime Contact Phone Number	07733130306
Mobile	07733130306

If you want to upload a file in support of your complaint you can do so below

	This complaint form will only accept one attachment and we have a maximum file size of 8MB.
	We allow the following file types: txt; pdf; doc; docx; ppt. xls; xlsx; wav. mp3; jpg; gif; tiff
	If your file is larger than 8MB, please do not attempt to send it, as your complaint may not get through to us.
	Please do not send any other documents at this stage. We will discuss with you what other documents we need to see.
File 1	31490-LAWRENCE-DISMISS.pdf

How did you find out about the Local Government Ombudsman?

	Internet website

page 6 of 6

467

**Judicial Conduct
nvestigations Office**

Judicial Conduct Investigations Office
81 & 82 Queers Building
Royal Courts of Justice
Strand
London
WC2A 2LL
DX44450 Strand

T 020 7073 0315
E hameera.chaudhry khan
@judicialconduct.gov.uk

http://judicialconduct.judiciary.gov.uk

Mr D Lawrence
Portal complaint

Our ref: 31490/2019

15 July 2019

Dear Mr Lawrence,

Out of time complaint

Thank you for your emails of 3, 6 and 8 July in response to my letter of 24 June.

In my letter I informed you that your complaint had been made outside of the three-month time limit, and that the Judicial Conduct Investigations Office (JCIO) may only accept a complaint outside of this time limit in exceptional circumstances.

I note you have not provided any reasons for the delay in making your complaint. I should explain that the JCIO does not regard a complainant choosing not to complain in time because the case was ongoing, as exceptional reasons for accepting a complaint.

Rule 12 of the Judicial Conduct (Judicial and other office holders) Rules 2014 stipulates that (subject to rule 14) the JCIO must not accept a complaint made outside the three-month time limit. Rule 14 permits the JCIO to extend the time limit "only in exceptional circumstances".

As you have not provided any reason for the delay in making your complaint, it is rejected in accordance with rule 12.

I should also explain that rule 15 states that the fact a complaint may contain an allegation of misconduct will not, by itself, be sufficient reason for the JCIO to accept a complaint outside of the three-month time limit.

I note that you also make a new complaint regarding the coroners conduct since the inquest ended on 7 February 2019. you have submitted several emails between yourself and the coroner's office to support your complaint.

We have now assessed the new part of your complaint. You are receiving this letter because the new part of your complaint is outside the JCIO's statutory remit. The 'Further information about our remit' appendix to this letter should help you to understand why we cannot accept the new part of your complaint.

It might help if I explain that coroners are constitutionally independent. This means that they are entitled to make decisions and manage hearings free from outside interference by officials (including this office), government ministers or other judges.

Further to the above information, you may wish to consider seeking legal advice. You may be able to obtain some advice free of charge from:

- a solicitor
- a local law centre
- Citizen's Advice - www.citizensadvice.org.uk
- Civil Legal Service - www.gov.uk/civil-legal-advice
- Bar Pro Bono Unit - www.barprobono.org.uk

If you do not understand the information contained in this letter you can speak to a member of the team by telephoning: 020 7073 4719.

Judicial Appointments and Conduct Ombudsman

You can complain to the Judicial Appointments and Conduct Ombudsman, Paul Kernaghan CBE QPM, if you believe that we have not handled your complaint properly. The Ombudsman does not have the power to investigate the complaint itself, but he can consider how we handled it. You should make your complaint within 28 days of receiving this letter. The Ombudsman is not required to consider complaints outside this period, and will only do so if he believes it is appropriate in all the circumstances.

The Ombudsman's office can be contacted:

In writing: 1.55, 1st Floor, The Tower, 102 Petty France, London, SW1H 9AJ
By e-mail: headofoffice@judicialombudsman.gov.uk
By phone: 020 3334 2900

You can find further information about the Ombudsman and complaint forms (including an easy-read version) at:

https://www.gov.uk/government/organisations/judicial-appointments-and-conduct-ombudsman

Your personal data

You can find information about how the JCIO collects and processes personal data in our Privacy Notice, which is available in the 'Making a Complaint – What you can expect from us' section of our website: https://judicialconduct.judiciary.gov.uk

With regards,

2

Hameera Chaudhry-Khan
Judicial Conduct Investigations Office

Further information about our remit

3

The statutory framework in which we operate

The JCIO is a statutory body which supports the Lord Chancellor and Lord Chief Justice in their joint responsibility for judicial discipline.

Our remit and procedures are governed by statutory rules and regulations, which can be found on our website at: https://judicialconduct.judiciary.gov.uk

Why we cannot accept your complaint

Our statutory remit is to deal with complaints of **misconduct** about coroners. This means how a coroner has behaved personally, e.g. making a racist remark, inappropriate use of social media, or falling asleep in court.

Rule 8 of the Judicial Conduct (Judicial and other office holders) Rules 2014 requires that a complaint must *"contain an allegation of misconduct"* about a named or identifiable person holding a relevant judicial office.

We assess all the complaints we receive carefully to decide whether a complaint contains an allegation of misconduct about a coroner.

A complaint does not contain an allegation of misconduct about a coroner simply because a person is unhappy about something a coroner has said or done.

We also cannot accept generalised complaints or complaints based on supposition, e.g. *"I think the coroner was rude because he would not allow me to present my evidence"*.

We can only accept complaints which contain a specific allegation of behaviour that, if true, could result in a finding of misconduct.

You can find information about the sorts of complaints we can accept by reading the disciplinary statements on our website.

The information below includes examples of some of the more common types of complaints we receive which are **outside our remit**.

Coroners' decisions and case management

We cannot accept complaints about:

- A coroner's decision to hold a post mortem examination or any other enquiries made whilst establishing cause of death; including an inquest
- Bias in a coroner's decision-making
- How a coroner has managed an inquest, e.g.

    ○ allowing one party to speak for longer than another
    ○ refusing to allow a witness to give evidence or admit certain documents
    ○ appearing to react more favourably to one person's evidence than another's

4

- A coroner saying that he or she does not believe a person's evidence, questioning a person's credibility or criticising a person's actions

We cannot accept these sorts of complaints because coroners are independent. Judicial independence is a vital and long-established feature of our system of justice. It means that coroners must be free to manage cases and make decisions without interference from external agencies, including from this office, from politicians, or from Government ministers. For the same reason, we cannot intervene in inquests or ask a coroner to explain why they have made a decision.

If you believe that a coroner's decision or the way a coroner has managed an inquest was incorrect or unfair, the only way to challenge the decision is via the coroner directly and/or by judicial review. You should consider seeking advice about your options from a solicitor, law centre or the Citizens Advice Bureau. You can find information about sources of free legal advice at:
http://www.lawcentres.org.uk/other-sources-of-advice

Coroner's officers

We cannot accept complaints about coroner's officers because they are not judicial office holders. Coroner's officers are managed by either the local authority or the police, depending on the area. You will need to write to the appropriate body if you wish to complain about a coroner's officer.

The police

We cannot consider complaints about the police. You can find out how to complain about the police at https://policeconduct.gov.uk/

You can find more information about our remit and view the rules and regulation which govern our remit and procedures at https://judicialconduct.judiciary.gov.uk

Information about time limits

The statutory time limit for making a complaint to the JCIO is **three months.**

We can only extend the time limit in exceptional circumstances. If a complaint is made outside the time limit and we assess it as being within our remit, we will invite the complainant to tell us about any exceptional reasons they have for doing so. However, this does not apply to complaints we reject because they are outside our remit.

FOA: Court Officer and Prosecutor,

Wimbledon Magistrates Court

Re:Related to Criminal Procedure Rules 24.10

In preparation for my 27.8.19 hearing, I have sent you very important email bundles earlier in the week.

For your convenience,I have sent in total:

1. Date: 20.8.19 Change of plea / additional evidence request(I will provide Magistrates a memory stick with all of my Jan -May 2019 Coroner communication)

2. Date: 20 .8.19 Request that you look at my attempts to get various bodies to look at my complaints of bias against the coroner.

3. Date: 21.8.19. Found a few dozen 'new' emails that morning and they could be useful to Coroner/family and for court to see a little of what it was like and the inner workings of the small charity RPFI/RCI during Jan-March 2016.

I promise not to send any more emails and will bring a memory stick with total email content for your review and comments .

Enjoy your bank holiday weekend and I look forward to seeing you all Tuesday at 9:30 am.

Duncan Lawrence

Respectfully submitted by:

Duncan E. Lawrence

London SE26 5LB
27.8.19

From: **Duncan** **Lawrence**<<u>duncan@</u>
<u>considercelebratingdiversityandsport.com</u>>
Date: Sat, 17 Aug 2019 at 11:07
Subject: Fwd: FYI Only
To: <<u>swglondonmc@hmcts.gsi.gov.uk</u>>

Good morning,

Can you please forward this to magistrates that heard my case last Friday(10am) at Wimbledon Magistrates Court... thanks for your consideration.

The two complaints letter and form detail my related stress and concerns related to unfair bias with the coroner leading my charge.

The complaints also lay out an attempt to get a review body, someone to review our relationship to see if it has always been fair, professional and reasonable for an public official.

I wish now that you might add it to your considerations as well before I return on 27.8.19...I saw that a family member added a letter, so hope me sending this to you is ok as well.

I look forward to seeing you on the 27.8.19.

Respectfully Submitted:

Duncan Lawrence

London SE26 5LB

D.E.Lawrence:

Diversity, Equality, Inclusion and Sport Specialist/Management and Team Coach.

Please think of the environment – do you really need to print this email or its attachments?

Sent from my iPhone

From: Duncan Lawrence <duncan@ considercelebratingdiversityandsport.com>
Date: 23 August 2019 at 06:48:13 BST
To: southlondonmc@justice.gov.uk, swglondonmc@hmcts. gsi.gov.uk, swlondonmc@hmcts.g-si.gov.uk
Subject: FAO: Court Officer Prosecutor

D.E.Lawrence:

Diversity, Equality, Inclusion and Sport Specialist/Management and Team Coach.

Please think of the environment – do you really need to print this email or its attachments?

Dear Court Officer and Prosecutor

Wimbledon Magistrates Court
Wimbledon Magistrates & Court, The Court House, Alexandra Road, Wimbledon, London SW19 7JP

URN 01TW/00755/19
Duncan E.Lawrence
Date of birth 16/02/1959
Arrest summons number 19/01TW/02/44P

Charge:

1. Prevent evidence / document production / provision of a thing for an investigation

Between 10/06/2018 and 04/02/2019, within the jurisdiction of the Central Criminal Court, Duncan Lawrence failed to provide documentation as directed by the Coroner for the purposes of an investigation, with the intention to have the effect of preventing that evidence, document or other thing from being given, produced or provided for the purposes of such an investigation, contrary to paragraph 7(1)(b) of Schedule 6 of the Coroners and Justice Act 2009.

Contrary to paragraph 7(1)(b) and (6) of Schedule 6 to the Coroners and Justice Act 2009.H.O. - EWNI - 6 months - CJ09018

Dear Court Officer and Prosecutor

1. *On 21 August 2019(today), I found some old RPFI/RCI Emails in a mislabelled file that I missed for several months.*

2. *I have voluntarily submitted them to the court so that they could be forwarded on to the Coroner in question.*

2.1 *I have only added details on what the email subject is, but have not edited any emails.*

3. *I hope innocent people listed within these emails do not get hurt in the media what so ever. I have sent the hurful and disgusting levels people are open to.*

The emails were random but can print a picture of Jan – March 2016 across the charity and can be grouped by topics such as:

1. **HR** related emails from across the charity...some to do with the Lancaster Unit staff and ex-Manager

2. **Some frank conversation** between myself, the founder/lead advisor and Chair of The Trustees about the state of the charity and sometime the Lancaster Unit specifically.

3. **Various emails** related to training, responding to Lancaster Unit residents parents, attempting to prepare for a respectful Lancaster Unit Manager departure etc..

4. Some directly related **to trying to honestly explain our short comings** to CQC, parents and professionals.

5. Some to do with **on-going audits**I just am glad and grateful to have been guided this morning to look through some more folders on my mobile phone.

Also expect coroner, the media and the rest of us to use my data in a respectful manner to those not involved with these procedures.

Now I hope that I can now be released from this very disappointing and hurtful process as well.

Respectfully Submitted by:

Duncan Lawrence

London SE26 5LB
21 August 2019

1) CEO and DL Discussion Strategic Plan Need/CEO Support

From: diversitymanagementlcl
Date: 7 March 2016at 04:21:38 GMT
To: Peggy J, Peggy Jhugroo, Elly Jansen, Elly Jansen,
Subject: Fwd: Peggy Support

Good morning Peggy,

Regarding your early am text instructions today (to me for LL), until I see a written strategic plan that I can buy into I am not stepping into LL.

I have always provided a steady flow of verbal and written RPFI/RPI strategic ideas(for at least short and medium term progression opportunities)...these contributions were before and after recent LL CQC inspections.

As recent as the second day of CQC being around and they did not get 'my letter idea',I put in writing to the entire RPFI/RCI SMT and its Board Chair that I would not support any plan that involved you coming into LL as the CEO/Anyone's Boss.

I came in this past weekend only because I genuinely wanted you to have a few hours of rest to enjoy Mother's Day.

It is now Monday. I have to do David's WH complaint hearing this am. I am 100% open and ready to support you today even without a written LL plan, but from outside the LL house only.

I am sure Colin has told you several times that an RPFI/RCI SM has never yet been given the power and authority to actually strategically lead and manage their own houses(and you recently heard from some LL residents that they were told to not comply with me...as were the staff...M,B and R were the only fit for purpose LL staff that were ready to engage the residents and to give the Enhanced TC a chance,etc.)...not a good and secure position ever to be for an organisation that is trying to be strategic in its thinking (rather than as it is now e.g. day-to-day assessing, day-to-day planning and hourly and day-to-day instructions from the CEO).

I am not currently willing to be 'LL on-paper SM', or 'your LL Deputy' waiting to receive your hourly and or daily instructions and or a LL short notice Bank Staff...a total waste of my talents,plus LL's current situation crosses so many of my 'ethical and leadership red lines'(on an hourly and weekly basis).

I am not trying to be obstructive Peggy and I did give advance written notice last week of my intentions...e.g that to not assume that I would cooperate without a plan.

Without a plan(at least this week...I will assess my RPFI/RCI options each week until the end of my current March 2016 contract), I will however be open to assist the wider charity and LL indirectly (without ever entering the LL building) with interviews, staff and leadership training, assisting with inductions,developing paperwork systems,do HR hearings for LL and beyond, attend professional external meetings,doing 1-1 and group therapy, staff supervision, etc...but no 'LL SM' role, no LL Deputy to you, no more on-call and definitely no LL bank worker role.

I am willing and able to revise my current stance once I have seen and considered a written LL strategy.

Without this I think the charity continues to be very veryvery vulnerable and open to CQC issues, local government issues, local resident issues and potential for growth in LL resident and staff non compliance movement, residents being unwell,staffshortages,etc..

Duncan

Sent from my iPad

From: Diversity Management LCL <<u>diversitymanagementlcl@btinternet.com</u>>
Date: 5 March 2016 at 19:05:36 GMT
To: Geoff Benton <<u>bentongeoff@gmail.com</u>>
Subject: Peggy Support

Good evening Geoff,

Peggy is really investing a lot of herself into Transforming LL but I worry that she is leaving herself vulnerable to staff spite and criticism, and residents accusations of her putting too much upon them(and potentially use RPFI as an excuse to stay unwell).

I am not sure of what her short and medium term vision is, my preference is still to restructure LL. Is there a 'plan b'?

Staff and residents in a community meeting yesterday abused Peggy something terrible.

I have to chair a grievance hearing at 9am Monday at WH,but will leave and work away from there soon afterwards.

Have difficulty being with staff that do not even check to see that Peggy was ok .

Duncan

D.E.Lawrence: Diversity,Equality,Inclusion and Sport Specialist / Management and Team Coach.

Sent from my iPhone

2) HR Related Items

From: "Jhugroo, Peggy"
Date: **1 March 2016**at 09:32:17 GMT
To: 'diversitymanagementlcl'
Subject: B

Hi Duncan,

I have added date to B'sletter, it needs to go on headed note paper with her correct address and yellow colour removed. Once you are happy with it, please send to Heather for final confirmation and then sign and send off registered post.

Thanks,Peggy

3) HR Related

From: "Jhugroo, Peggy"
Date: 1 March 2016 at 09:32:17 GMT
To: 'diversitymanagementlcl'
Subject: B

Hi Duncan,

I have added date to Bletter, it needs to go on headed note paper with her correct address and yellow colour removed. Once you are happy with it, please send to Heather for final confirmation and then sign and send off registered post.

Thanks,

Peggy

4) HR Related

From: Oi
Date: 29 February 2016at 09:45:08 GMT
To: Diversity Management LCL
Subject: Re: S Hearing

Will do

Kind Regards,

O

From: Diversity Management LCL
Sent: 29 February 2016 09:05

To: O

Subject: S Hearing

Hi O,

I hope that you are well.

If anyone mistakenly

Shows up the WH this am, please refer them to LL...I will wait.

Thanks,

Duncan

D.E.Lawrence: Diversity,Equality,Inclusion and Sport Specialist / Management and Team
Coach.

Skype: diversitymanagementlcl

Sent from my iPhone

4)HR Related

From: Peggy J
Date: **28 February 2016**at 21:00:58 GMT
To: "colin_newatlantis@hotmail.com"
Cc: "diversitymanagementlcl@btinternet.com"
Subject: FW: S Appeal Hearing

Hi Colin,

Please note that Hearing meeting is at Lancaster Lodge and as mentioned we would like you to take minutes.

Please liaise with Duncan.

Peggy

From: @hotmail.com
To: peggwegg@hotmail.com;   diversitymanagementlcl@btinternet.com
Subject: SN Appeal Hearing
Date: Sun, 28 Feb 2016 19:03:23 +0000

Hello,

Please find attached S's Hearing letter and Disciplinary minutes.

Kind Regards,

Ope

5)Reminder from DL to Board,CEO and Founder/Lead Advisor about my ideas of a monthly blog to sell charity new vision to staff and service users and to add family members and staff to Trustees Board

From: Diversity Management LCL
Date: 9 February 2016at 06:39:56 GMT
To: EllyJansen,Elly Jansen, «<u>peggwegg@hotmail.com</u>", Peggy Jhugroo
Cc: Geoff Benton
Subject: RPFI/RCI Board Composition

Good morning to us all,

Just a reminder of my ideas have a monthly or quarterly charity blog/news letter to alert staff and service users to the 'vision' and to consider expanding the board to include staff member rep and a service user/parent-carer rep... because we always have so much to do when we all meet I am aware that these ideas might gotten lost.

Every day when doing this charity's work, I am reminded that each month we may be stepping over a great opportunity to bring the charity together more efficiently.

Have a great day!

Duncan

D.E.Lawrence: Diversity,Equality,and Inclusion Specialist / Management and Team Coach.

Skype: diversitymanagementlcl

Sent from my iPhone

6) HR Related

From: Heather Grant
Date: **4 February 2016**at 13:20:57 GMT
To: Peggy J, "diversitymanagementlcl@btinternet.com"
Cc: Elly Jansen
Subject: RE: Disciplinary/Investigations

Dear All

Please see attached my comments. I haven't repeated all the advice given to Peggy yesterday, but where I've spotted that you are waiting on me (I'm assuming I'm "HR") I've indicated my current understanding of the position.

Kind regards

Heather

Heather Grant
Senior Employment Law Adviser
Ellis Whittam Limited
Tel: 0845 226 8393
Web: www.elliswhittam.com

From: Peggy J [mailto:peggwegg@hotmail.com]
Sent: 03 February 2016 21:53
To: diversitymanagementlcl@btinternet.com
Cc: Heather Grant; Elly Jansen
    Subject: Disciplinary/Investigations

Hi Duncan,

Please see attached update on staffing issues. I would like to get dates set for investigations/hearings.

Peggy

7) HR related, including Lancaster Unit staff

From: Peggy J
Date: 3 February 2016 at 21:53:21 GMT
To: "diversitymanagementlcl@btinternet.com"
Cc: "heathergrant@elliswhittam.com", Elly Jansen
Subject: Disciplinary/Investigations

Hi Duncan,

Please see attached update on staffing issues. I would like to get dates set for investigations/hearings.

Peggy

Staffing Issues

Staff	Issues	Action so far	Outstanding Action	Update from HR
Vincent Hill	Resigned but may bring constructive dismissal case. He is also in touch with residents and may be encouraging them to act against RPFI.	Resignation received and offers to deal with his issue through grievance procedures rather than resignation - declined. VH met with residents last week and may help fuel them complaints.	PJ to establish facts around VH's meeting with residents and email HR.	
	Investigation into leaving staff member alone despite concerns about residents.	Conclusion from hearing is to draw a line as insufficient evidence to cast blame.	HR to draft a post-hearing letter.	

...

[Message clipped] <u>View entire message</u>

Begin forwarded message:

From: Eric Lawrence <<u>diversitymanagementlcl@btinternet.com</u>>

Date: 28 October 2019 at 10:05:17 GMT

Cc: Wimbledon Magistrates Court 1 <<u>swlondonmc@hmcts.g-si.gov.uk</u>>, "Wimbledon Mag.Court 2"

<swglondonmc@hmcts.gsi.gov.uk>, Wimbledon Mag Court 3 <southlondonmc@justice.gov.uk>

Subject: Duncan Lawrence's coroner's'first contact' letter/ evidence in full

FAO: Court Clerk and Prosecutor
Wimbledon Magistrates Court

27.10.19

Re:Request to delay 30.10.19 sentencing of Duncan E.Lawrence

On the charge of:

Dear Court Clerk and Prosecutor,

For quite a few weeks I have been trying to get someone to take serious my claims that my charge date periods do not relate to me factually.

I have been charged with withholding information from a coroner over a six month period(see charge sheet above/ below). The problem is that a charity solicitor (connected to my old work place)only wrote to me on 31.8.18 informing about an upcoming coroner inquiry and the charge period covers most of June, July and August 2018(right up through 4.2.19).

I have provided the 31.10.18 RPFI charity Solicitor email evidence and the related RPFI Solicitor letter inviting me to develop a witness statement (see below as an attachment) for the coroner which I did.

Three months may seem insignificant, but it is half of the total charge period when I didn't even know that the coroner existed.

I am due to be sentenced at Wimbledon Magistrates Court on 30.10.19 on a charge that is factually incorrect.

I have written to several officials including the officer that actually wrote the charge sheet to no avail initially although recently the following are looking into my claims/have looked into my claims about the factually inaccurate charge period :

*London Magistrates CPS
* Judicial Conduct Investigations Office CRM:0055535
* CPS:London South Magistrates Team
* London North CCET(CPS)
*Original Met Officer that wrote the charge sheet.

I am respectfully asking that you delay or adjourn the sentencing hearing until you see the findings from the above mentioned names and CPS section. If you are truly trying to administer justice, then scrutinising an inaccurate charge sheet should be important priority to you too.

I am 60 and have never committed a crime and have given my entire life to helping children, families and communities.

All I wish is for someone to scrutinise my charge and correct/ amend it or drop it before any sentencing.

If you scroll down this email you will see the Charge Sheet, Some discussions between myself and the MET officer that actually wrote the charge sheet, 31.8.18 RPFI Charity Solicitor and their 31.8.18 attachment letter to me(**the attachment password is hdnhs)**

Respectfully submitted:

Duncan Lawrence

18-C, Kenthouse Road
London SE26 5LB

D.E.Lawrence:

Diversity, Equality, Inclusion and Sport Specialist/Management and Team Coach.

Please think of the environment – do you really need to print this email or its attachments?

Sent from my iPhone

Begin forwarded message:

From: Eric Lawrence <diversitymanagementlcl@btinternet.com>

Date: 21 October 2019 at 06:09:40 BST

To: Mr Tyrone Ward <tyrone.ward@met.police.uk>

Subject: Duncan Lawrence's coroner's'first contact' letter/ evidence in full

Mr.Ward,

I am resending my first RPFI Charity Solicitors letter with its attachment(I previously did not send the letter's attachment (...the password is **hdnhs).**

I hope any CPS 'review' decisions about if my charge should stand or be dropped(or 'something else') happens quite quickly.

We are talking about *half* the charge period being inappropriately given to me sir.

The charge dates have been very stressful and confusing throughout my legal journey and the prosecutor at one time was talking about 'custodial sentence' because of them.I want my life back, ideally today sir.

I pray for a timely and full reply Mr.Ward.

Duncan Lawrence

London SE26 5LB

D.E.Lawrence:

Diversity, Equality, Inclusion and Sport Specialist/Management and Team Coach.

Please think of the environment *- do you really need to print this email or its attachments?*

Sent from my iPhone

Begin forwarded message:

From: Julie Ford <Julie.Ford@hilldickinson.com>
Date: 31 August 2018 at 14:01:24 BST
To: "diversitymanagementlcl@btinternet.com"
<diversitymanagementlcl@btinternet.com>
Cc: Kate Fawell-Comley <Kate.Fawell-Comley@hilldickinson. com>
Subject: Request for assistance concerning a coroner's inquiry. [HD-UKLive.12014150.1]

Dear Mr Lawrence

I am assisting a colleague, Kate Fawell-Cowley in a matter in which you have been asked to provide a statement for a Coroner's inquiry. Further details are set out in the letter attached which is password protected (password to follow).

I should be grateful if you would contact me to confirm receipt of the letter and your response the queries set out within it.

I look forward to hearing from you at your earliest convenience.

With kind regards

Your sincerely

Julie Ford
Legal Director
Healthcare

Hill Dickinson LLP
Julie.Ford@hilldickinson.com
The Broadgate Tower, 20 Primrose Street, London, EC2A 2EW
TEL: +44 (0)20 7280 9338
FAX: +44 (0)20 7283 1144

Error! Filename not specified.

Error! Filename not specified.

Error! Filename not specified.

Hill Dickinson
www.hilldickinson.com

This email and its contents, together with any attachments, are confidential to the sender and the intended recipient(s) and may be covered by legal professional privilege. If you are not the intended recipient of this email and its attachments (if any), you must take no action based upon them, nor must you copy them or show them to anyone. Please contact the sender if you believe you have received this email in error. Hill Dickinson LLP is a firm of lawyers authorised and regulated by the Solicitors Regulation Authority under registration number 424853. It is a limited liability partnership registered in England and Wales No. OC314079. Its registered office is at No.1 St. Paul's Square, Liverpool L3 9SJ.

This e-mail and any attachments is intended only for the attention of the addressee(s). Its unauthorised use, disclosure, storage or copying is not permitted. If you are not the intended recipient, please destroy all copies and inform the sender by return e-mail. Internet e-mail is not a secure medium. Any reply to this message could be intercepted and read by someone else. Please bear that in mind when deciding whether to send material in response to this message by e-mail. This e-mail (whether you are the sender or the recipient) may be monitored, recorded and retained by the Ministry of Justice. Monitoring / blocking software may be used, and e-mail content may be read at any time. You have a responsibility to ensure laws are not broken when composing or forwarding e-mails and their contents.

diversitymanagementlcl@btinternet.com

Your Ref:
Our Ref: 12014150.1.JDF.JDF
Doc Ref: 1539414119.1
Date: 31 August 2010

Direct Line: +44(0)20 7200 9333
julie.ford@hilldickinson.com

Dear Mr Lawrence

The Inquest touching the death of Ms SB

I act on behalf of RPFI in relation to the inquest concerning the death of SB. As part of the Coroner's investigation he has asked RPFI to provide statements concerning the care provided to SB from April 2015 up to and including her death in May 2016. The Coroner has indicated that he will be focusing on the period from December 2015 onwards and, in particular, he intends to investigate:

- The new management regime at Lancaster Lodge after April 2015;
- Details concerning the turnover in staff at Lancaster Lodge;
- the number of residents leaving Lancaster Lodge during the key period;
- Steps taken to arrange the transfer of SB to an alternative residential setting.

The coroner has specifically requested that you provide a statement as part of his investigation into the death of SB. You are just one of a number of individuals who has been asked to provide such evidence. As such, I should be very grateful if you would contact me upon receipt of this letter so that I may discuss the steps that need to be taken in order to provide the requested statement with you.

I do appreciate that this letter may have arrived 'somewhat out of the blue'. I wish to reassure you that a Coroner's inquiry is simply that. It is not a trial and it is not a court of blame. The Coroner, assisted by a Jury in this case, is required to answer four questions, namely: who, where when, how (and in what circumstances) SB came by her death.

It would be very helpful to understand what aspects of the queries raised by the Coroner that you can assist with in the form of a statement. In order to complete your statement, you will obviously need to review some RPFI documentation which I can assist you with.

Hill Dickinson LLP
No. 1 St Paul's Square
Liverpool L3 9SJ
Tel: +44 (0)151 600 8000
Fax: +44 (0)151 600 8001

hilldickinson.com

The Hill Dickinson Legal Services Group has offices in Liverpool, Leeds, Manchester, London, Piraeus, Singapore, Monaco and Hong Kong.

Hill Dickinson LLP is a limited liability partnership registered in England and Wales with registered number OC314079. Its registered office is at No. 1 St Paul's Square, Liverpool L3 9SJ.
Hill Dickinson LLP is authorised and regulated by the Solicitors Regulation Authority

I do however appreciate that you no longer work for RPFI and that you may not wish to accept the support offered. This is entirely a matter for you. In the event that you do not wish to be supported by RPFI, I should be grateful if you would notify me accordingly.

If you do not wish to be supported by RPFI, it does not mean that you may avoid providing a statement for the Coroner as requested. Instead, the Coroner may contact you directly through his officers or you may choose to obtain your own legal representation who can liaise directly with the Coroner with regard to your statement on your behalf.

I should also mention that the Inquest Hearing has provisionally been listed for three weeks in January 2019(specific dates to be confirmed). The Coroner has not made a final decision on which witnesses he proposes to call to give oral evidence at the Hearing. I recommend that you keep January free to attend the Inquest, albeit I doubt you will be required to attend for the full three week period. As soon as we are in a position to confirm the dates we will of course do so.

If you already have holiday commitments or will be outside of the London area during this time please do let me know, when you respond to this letter. In the event that you choose not to be supported by RPFI you will need to draw this to the Coroner's attention as soon as possible either in person or through your legal representative.

In the first place however, I should be grateful if you could respond to me directly to confirm whether you:

- Wish to be supported by RPFI in the lead up to the Inquest and at the Inquest if you are called to give evidence;
- If you do, then I should be grateful if we could speak directly to arrange a time that I may talk to you about the extent of your involvement and what documents you will require in order to complete your statement.
- If you do not wish to be supported by RPFI, please would you contact me to confirm the position. I will then notify the Coroner that he (or his officers) will need to contact you directly to obtain a statement from you in the event that you have not instructed separate legal representatives to support you in the meantime.

I look forward to hearing from you.

Yours sincerely

pp

Kate Fawell-comley

Hill Dickinson LLP

11. Appeal...and 'the journey around the houses'

Some Reflective thoughts from D.Eric Lawrence

> **Bamboozled Wisdom:** (Number 12) "...Why hide from someone else's mistakes...doing so makes you smell like the stink of the original skunk, although you never actually met them...just tried to protect them because you were both skunks...!)

The appeals process was rather 'easy' and 'hard' at the same time. I did not realise that the UK had developed such an accessible appeal application form (one that could be completed with or without legal support). Initial 'hiccup' was when Kingston Crown initially cancelled my application because it was thought to be related to a previous application that was 'mutually cancelled' Oct/Nov 2019 between myself and a solicitor that was engaged in my behalf 'for a minute'(I think we both had no confidence in each other's ability to 'create a legal pathway to success'). I had to convince the Crown Court that my own initiated application was never withdrawn.

The even harder part was very 'similar' to trying getting the London Met Police to admit they made a dangerous and grossly unfair choice when the allowed the CPS and courts to make legal movements based upon inaccurate charge dates...where via emails to me they blamed it on others and told me to sort it myself legally.

All I wanted was for the Crown Court to give a written opinion about the 'four withheld magistrates court letters' from me...*either they would be heard as part of my appeal, or they would not be*. The Court acted like I was obstructing the appeals process and regularly 'clouded the main issues' with excuses...I was not going to agree to an appeal that I initiated without written discussion on the status on my four withheld letters and this needed to be done upfront and in a transparent manner.

This particular Crown Court was not a fan of *Article 6 of the Human Rights Act* either, she just fined me twice(the same amount each time), gave no written clarity about the four withheld magistrate court letters, cancelled the appeal(although continued to blame me) and that was that!

She too was not going to 'demonstrate courage by doing something that the London Met would not do, that the CPS and the Wimbledon Magistrates Court would not do either... *acknowledge the fact that the four withheld letters did exist and that there is some legal confusion around the 'charge period dates'*.

She did however 'acknowledge' that she had inside knowledge about me and my behaviour (but never elaborated what she specifically was talking about).

Conclusion

I was assertive, consistent, persistent and courageous in my own right during this period of time although simultaneously I was ready just in case the press was alerted and 'restarted' its negative false narratives again. I was also concerned on how current and future employers would view my appeal if it proceeded. Some at interview staged voiced their satisfaction and seemingly admiration that I was continuing to try and clear my name, but I equally wondered how supportive they would actually be if the press/public/social media knew that I was working for them...my natural optimism was slowly being replace with the persistent reality of thoughts and self-talk "...most leaders often do not show bravery and courage if it means 'being the first' to take a stand and or to question something that was done by others 'in your profession', all with the spectre of press and social media impact if you do 'take the high road'...".

APPEALING AGAINST A MAGISTRATES' COURT DECISION[1]

SECTION 1

Important information you need to know before filling in this form.

You can use this form if you are appealing against a magistrates' court decision.

If you pleaded **not guilty** you can appeal against your conviction or sentence or both.

If you pleaded **guilty** you can usually only appeal against your sentence.

You should send in the form within **21 days** of the date you were sentenced. If you miss this deadline you will have to ask the court for permission before you can appeal.

---

[1] Criminal Procedure Rules, rule 34.2.

If you **win** your appeal against **conviction** that is the same as being found not guilty and the sentence will not apply.

If you **win** your appeal against **sentence** the court may reduce or change your sentence.

You may be able to claim some costs.

If you **lose** your appeal the **Crown Court can increase your sentence.** But, not more than the magistrates' court could have sentenced you to.

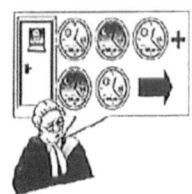

If you **lose** your appeal you may have to pay costs.

SECTION 2

This section asks you for details about you and your case.

What is your name? DUNCAN ERIC LAWRENCE

What is your address? 18-C, KENT HOUSE ROAD, LONDON SE26 5LB

What is your phone number? 07733 13 0306

What is your e-mail address? diversity management kel @ gmail. com

If you are in prison, what is the name of the prison you are in?

Wandsworth HMP

What is your prison number? A01 08 EL

What crime(s) were you convicted of? Prevent evidence / document production / provesion of a thing for an investigation

What was the name of the magistrates' court where you were convicted? (for example Hull Magistrates' Court)

Wimbledon Magistrates Court

What date were you sentenced?

_30. 11. 2019_

What is your magistrates' court case reference number? (**this can be found on letters you have received from the court about your case and will look something like this 1400006746**)

SECTION 3

Your Appeal

If you miss the **21 day deadline** to appeal you have to ask the Crown Court for permission to appeal. If you are appealing late, explain why here. If you have any documents or letters to help explain why your appeal is late please include them with this form.

1. I am appealing late because I did not have enough written evidence from the other stakeholders (eg court clerk, prosecutor, judge, probation officer, MET officer, CPS, etc) that the charge date (and the charge) did not reflect me.

1.1 Following on, I need to find out what happen to my email letters to court clerk/prosecutor from August 2019 and Oct 2019.

1.2 Needed time to go through various stakeholder complaints procedures (as part of gathering written fact)

2. I was in prison on the charge.

Key: ** = Related to Human Rights Act, specifically Article 6

SECTION 4

Information about why you are appealing

Tell us here why you do not agree with your **conviction**. Please give the facts about the situation and what you think is wrong. You can use extra paper if you need to.

1. Charge dates did not reflect me and my actual contact and or knowledge of the Assistant Coroner.
1.1 None of my letters to the court clerk and prosecutor were actually responded to even though I got email confirmations
1.2 This especially relates to my first email letter where I asked to change my plea, ask to have witnesss and submit evidence, all based upon criminal Procedure Rules 24.10.
1.3 Was being unfairly pushed by probation officer to ignore my own views and just agree with prosecuter and family for a lighter sentence.
2. My Human Rights (specifically Article 6) were violated and nothing in my case was clear or transparent especially decision making process.
3. Related to above, all stake holders did not try to get and or give a fair trial.

Write here why you do not agree with your **sentence**. Please give the facts about the situation and what you think is wrong. You can use extra paper if you need to.

1. Sentence is much too heavy for a 60y/o with no history of offending, one that gave his entire adult life to supporting vulnerable members of society.
2. Judge, prosecutor (Asst. Coroner Gill) not being forthcoming about what information that I actually did provide to the Assistant Coroner from 13.Jan.2018 to Spring 2019 and in August 2019.
3. Probation officer felt too intimidated by high profile case and did not offer her normal recommendation of conditional discharge, etc.
4. No opportunity to present witness or evidence
4.1 No opportunity to debate or discuss process
4.2 No explanation for charge date rationale
4.3 July 2019 Judge seemed visably angry by me standing up for myself at last hearing. Sentence seemed personal.

Appeals Against Conviction

You only need to fill in this section if you are **appealing against your conviction.**

How long did the trial last in the magistrates' court (for example 5 hours)?

_____

Write here the names of any witnesses who gave evidence for the prosecution who you might want to be questioned as part of your appeal in court.

1. Judge

2. Original three magistrates

3. Prosecutor

4. Assistant Coroner

SECTION 5

Other Applications

Disqualification and Bail

Are you asking the court to suspend your disqualification (for example your disqualification from driving)?

Please tick ✔

Yes ☐   No ☑

If you have ticked yes, explain your reasons here.

....

....

Are you asking the court to release you on bail before your appeal is heard?

Please tick ✔

Yes ☐   'No ☑

If yes, explain your reasons here

....

....

I want my application(s) to be considered by

Please tick ✔

The magistrates' court ☑   The Crown Court ☑

(you can apply to both)

∴ Because of the high profile of of this case and

Past disrepectful media storms', Can this 7 be
Considered away from Wimbledon area? D.57

505

SECTION 6

What Happens Next.

Sign this form below and send a copy to the **magistrates' court where you were convicted <u>and</u> to the prosecutor** (you can find the address of the prosecutor by contacting the magistrates' court where you were convicted).

Signature ....

Date .....20.1.2020...................

The Court hearing

Your appeal will be heard at the Crown Court.

The Crown Court will contact you about your appeal.

The Crown Court may ask you to come to a hearing where the date for the appeal will be decided and other arrangements for the appeal will be made.

Human Rights Article 6 Explanation

Article 6 protects your right to a fair trial

You have the right to a fair and public trial or hearing if:

- you are charged with a criminal offence and have to go to court, or

- a public authority is making a decision that has a impact upon your civil rights or obligations.

In this context, your civil rights and obligations are those recognised in areas of UK law such as property law, planning law, family law, contract law and employment law.

It is a good idea to get <u>further advice</u> if you think the right to a fair and public hearing might apply to your case.

What is a fair and public hearing?

You have the right to a fair and public hearing that:

- is held within a reasonable time

- is heard by an independent and impartial decision-maker

- gives you all the relevant information

- is open to the public (although the press and public can be excluded for highly sensitive cases)

- allows you representation and an interpreter where appropriate, and

- is followed by a public decision.

You also have the right to an explanation of how the court or decision-making authority reached its decision.

What rights do you have at a criminal trial?

You have the right to:

- be presumed innocent until you are proven guilty

- be told as early as possible what you are accused of

- remain silent

- have enough time to prepare your case

- legal aid (funding) for a lawyer if you cannot afford one and this is needed for justice to be served

- attend your trial

- access all the relevant information

- put forward your side of the case at trial

- question the main witness against you and call other witnesses, and

- have an interpreter, if you need one.

Everybody must have equal access to the courts under the Human Rights Act. This includes a right to bring a civil case (a case between individuals or organisations), although this right can be restricted in some situations (see below).

See also the right to <u>no punishment without law.</u>

Are there any restrictions to this right?

The right to a fair and public hearing does not always apply to cases involving:

- immigration law

- extradition

- tax, and

- voting rights.

There is also no automatic right to an appeal (an application to a higher court for the reversal of the decision of a lower court).

The right of access to the courts can be restricted, for example, if you:

- keep bringing cases without merit

- miss the time-limit for bringing a case.

There are times when the public and press are denied access to a hearing. This can happen in the interests of protecting:

- morals

- public order or national security

- children and young people, or

- privacy.

The courts might also decide to exclude the public or press if they think that their presence is not in the interests of justice.

What the law says

Article 6: Right to a fair and public hearing

1. In the determination of his civil rights and obligations or of any criminal charge against him, everyone is entitled to a fair and public hearing within a reasonable time by an independent and impartial tribunal established by law. Judgment shall be pronounced publicly but the press and public may be excluded from all or part of the trial in the interest of morals, public order or national security in a democratic society, where the interests of juveniles or the protection of the private life of the parties so require, or to the extent strictly necessary in the opinion of the court in special

circumstances where publicity would prejudice the interests of justice.

2. Everyone charged with a criminal offence shall be presumed innocent until proved guilty according to law.

3. Everyone charged with a criminal offence has the following minimum rights:

- to be informed promptly, in a language which he understands and in detail, of the nature and cause of the accusation against him

- to have adequate time and facilities for the preparation of his defence

- to defend himself in person or through legal assistance of his own choosing or, if he has not sufficient means to pay for legal assistance, to be given it free when the interests of justice so require

- to examine or have examined witnesses against him and to obtain the attendance and examination of witnesses on his behalf under the same conditions as witnesses against him

- to have the free assistance of an interpreter if he cannot understand or speak the language used in court.

Example case - DG v Secretary of State for Work and Pensions (ESA) [2010]

DG appealed against a decision to refuse him Employment and Support Allowance (ESA), which was taken after a medical examination. Even though DG requested Jobcentre Plus to contact his GP (also his nominated representative), neither the GP nor DG's social worker were approached for evidence. At the first stage of the independent tribunal process (the First Tier Tribunal), DG waived his right to put his case in person at an oral hearing. This decision was based on advice from Jobcentre Plus. The appeal was dealt with on paper and dismissed.

When DG appealed this decision, the Upper Tribunal found that DG did not have a fair hearing of his appeal as required by Article 6. This decision took into account the bad advice from Jobcentre Plus, the claimant's mental health problems and the failure of both the Department for Work and Pensions and the tribunal to communicate with his GP.

(Case summary taken from 'Human rights, human lives: a guide to the Human Rights Act for public authorities'. Download the publication for more examples and legal case studies that show how human rights work in practice.)

Last updated: 15 Nov 2018

DL letters and complaints to Kingston Crown Court and copies to CPS

CROWN PROSECUTION SERVICE FEEDBACK AND COMPLAINTS FORM

CPS

*You must complete the sections marked ***

What is your name?
* (Mr, Mrs, Miss, Ms, Dr)

Mr. Duncan E. Lawrence

*What is your date of birth?

16.02.1959

*What is your address?

18-C, Kenthouse Road London SE26 5LB

What is your telephone number?

07733 130306

What is your personal email

diversitymanagementcl @ gmail.com

How would you prefer to be contacted?

Email ☑

Letter ☐

Phone ☐

Are there any restrictions on when or how we can contact you? no

1/4

U

Do you know which part of the Crown Prosecution Service you are contacting us about?   Crown Court Admin Team - London South

Please select the CPS Area, Police Force or Investigating Authority that dealt with the issue, or provided the service that you are contacting us about. You can leave this blank if you are unsure.

Please enter a URN (Unique Reference Number) and Defendant(s) name here (if known):

*How are you related to the case (tick one):

Victim ☐

Victim ☐
(Bereaved family member)

Witness ☐

Defendant ☑

Other (please specify) [   ]

If you are a Nominated Representative, what is your relationship to the person you are representing?

Please specify here: [   ]

Note: If you are making a complaint on behalf of someone else you must provide **written permission** to act for them.

*Full name (Mr, Mrs, Miss, ~~Ms, Dr, other~~): [   ]

2/4

*Postal address:

Telephone number:

Email address:

*Type of comment (tick one): ☐ Complaint ☑
　　　　　　Feedback

* Enquiry Details

**Please tell us what happened. Only provide information that
is relevant to your complaint or feedback.**

I was sent an email from O, Adeoye -CPS
London South, Crown Court AdMin Team Re:
Complaint Cref: 5484 279) on 7 Aug 2020.
I responded and sent attachments too but I
have heard nothing back. I have sent
several follow up emails and no reply
what so ever.
① Why no response ???
(1.1) IS it possible to get a full response
　　to my email?　　　　　　　　　3/4
(1.2) Clarify that I am not part of a 'coverup'!

Please return to the relevant CPS office by post or email. All contact details are available on our website via the following link: https://www.cps.gov.uk/cps-areas-and-cps-direct.

Thanks in advance,
Duncan E, Lawrence
18-C, kenthouse Road
London SE26 5LB

diversity management1c1@
gmail.com
23, 9, 2020

4/4

From: Duncan Lawrence <<u>duncan@</u>
<u>considercelebratingdiversityandsport.com</u>>
Date: 7 August 2020 at 12:35:05 BST
To: London Crown Court <<u>London.Crowncourt@cps.gov.uk</u>>
Cc: <u>cpsdirect.vrrandcomplaints@cps.gov.uk</u>, Cps <<u>info@cps.</u>
<u>gov.uk</u>>
Subject:Complaint (ref: 5484279)

Sent from my iPhone

On 7 Aug 2020, at 11:24, London Crown Court <<u>London.</u>
<u>Crowncourt@cps.gov.uk</u>> wrote:

FAO:

O. ADEOYE.
Crown Prosecution Service,
London South
Crown Court Admin Team
2nd Floor,
102 Petty France,
London.
SW1H 9AJ.
DX : 161330,
Westminster 11.

Good Morning,GOOD MORNING

We are writing to you, for more information; concerning
the above case.FYI, THE EMAIL FROM THE JUDGE BELOW
IS FACTUALLY INCORRECT...I HAVE ALWAYS ONLY ASKED
KINGSTON CROWN COURT TO EXPLAIN HOW THEY WILL

CONSIDER OR NOT CONSIDER THE FOUR UNANSWERED COURT LETTERS DURING MY FIRST TRIAL AT WIMBLEDON MAGISTRATES COURT...PLEASE SEE MY LAST TWO LETTERS TO THEM BELOW.

IS THERE A NAMED PERSON THAT I CAN SEND COPIES OF ALL MY LETTERS AND EMAILS TO KINGSTON CROWN COURT? THE JUDGE UNLAWFULLY FINED ME ON 23.7.2020 AND 28.7.2020,WHEN I AS THE INITIATOR OF MY APPEAL CONSISTENTLY TOLD KINGSTONCROWNCOURT THAT I WAS NOT READY TO START AN APPEAL PROCESS THAT I DID NOT KNOW WHERE MY UNANSWERED LAST COURT LETTERS STOOD IN ANY APPEAL PROCESS. FINING ME FOR A PROCESS THAT I INITIATED, IS TOTAL UNFAIR AND A CONTINUING VIOLATION OF MY HUMAN RIGHTS, ESPECIALLY ARTICLE 6 RIGHTS.CAN YOU PLEASE GET THIS FINED WIPED OFF?

THIS JUDGE SHOULD NOT BE ABLE TO GET AWAY WITH MISREPRESENTATION OF ME AND SOMEONE SHOULD LOOK INTO IT ASAP.

Respectfully submitted by: Duncan Lawrence, London SE26 5LB

Please, can you give us the following details below:

   i)   Case Name.DUNCAN ERIC LAWRENCE

   ii) The URN.See below

   iii) Offence date.See below

   iv) Offence.

v) Last hearing date at the Magistrate Court30.10.19.

vi) The Magistrate Court, the case was last heard. WIMBLEDON MAGISTRATES COURT

vii) Also, if you know the Crown Court the case will be heard.KINGSTON CROWN COURT WAS WHERE THE APPEAL WAS TO BE HEARD

viii)   Also, if you know the Crown Court the case was last heard.

ix) And if you have, the Magistrate Court "MEMORANDUM OF CONVICTION" can you provide us.

x)

Also, if the Magistrate Court can provide us with "MEMORANDUM OF CONVICTION".

We await your response.

Thanks-so-much.

O. ADEOYE.
Crown Prosecution Service,
London South
Crown Court Admin Team
2nd Floor,
102 Petty France,
London.
SW1H 9AJ.
DX : 161330,

Westminster 11.

Last summer I was charged with a crime that I did not commit (connected to not showing a up to coroner's inquest in Jan 2019.

MG4D WRITTEN CHARGE
ATTENDANCE REQUIRED Duncan Lawrence
18C, Kent House Road
London
SE26 5LB URN 01TW/00755/19 Date of birth 16/02/1959 Arrest summons number 19/01TW/02/44P POSTAL REQUISITION You are charged with the offence below: On 16/08/2019 at 09:30 you must appear at the courthouse at Wimbledon Magistrates' Court, The Court House, Alexandra Road, Wimbledon, London SW19 7JP to answer the charge. Warning If you do not reply to the charge or attend court, the court may hear the case in your absence and may issue a warrant for your arrest. If a warrant is issued for your arrest, you may be held in custody until you are brought before the court. Police Bail If you are on police bail for the offence, you do not have to return to the police station and your police bail has been cancelled. Advice and help If you need advice about what to do you should get help from a solicitor or advice agency at once. If you cannot afford a solicitor you may be able to get free advice about your plea, or how to apply to the court for a representation order so that you can have a solicitor at the hearing. Do not wait until you first come to court. If you need any general advice about the court, contact the court office at Wimbledon Magistrates' Court, The Court House, Alexandra Road, Wimbledon, London SW19

7JP. CHARGE Charge authorised by Detective Constable Tyrone Ward Prosecution contact details Metropolitan Police Service a: EAGLE HOUSE, RAM PASSAGE, KINGSTON UPON THAMES t: 101 e: tyrone.ward@met.police.uk Date 1. Prevent evidence / document production / provision of a thing for an investigation Between 10/06/2018 and 04/02/2019, within the jurisdiction of the Central Criminal Court, Duncan Lawrence failed to provide documentation as directed by the Coroner for the purposes of an investigation, with the intention to have the effect of preventing that evidence, document or other thing from being given, produced or provided for the purposes of such an investigation, contrary to paragraph 7(1) (b) of Schedule 6 of the Coroners and Justice Act 2009.

Contrary to paragraph 7(1)(b) and (6) of Schedule 6 to the Coroners and Justice Act 2009.

H.O. - EWNI - 6 months - CJ09018 Charge authorised by Detective Constable Tyrone Ward Prosecution contact details Metropolitan Police Service a: EAGLE HOUSE, RAM PASSAGE, KINGSTON UPON THAMES t: 101 e: tyrone.ward@met.police. uk Date Statement of means If you are found guilty, you may be fined for this offence. The court will expect you to pay on the day. Please fill in and bring the enclosed statement of means when you come to court. If you do not provide this information, you may be ordered to pay a fine which is more than you can afford. Discount for early plea of guilty The court, when passing sentence on you, will consider giving you a lower penalty if you enter an early guilty plea.

The amount of any discount will depend on how early you indicate your plea, as well as the circumstances that made you plead guilty.

If you wish, you can write to the prosecutor and the court as soon as you have been charged and are sure that you want to plead guilty. If you intend to see a solicitor you should speak to your solicitor first.

You can tell the court how you will be pleading at any hearing of your case, even if your case may have to be heard at the Crown Court. Nothing stated here is intended to persuade you to plead guilty. Page of 01TW/00755/19 Page 1 of 2

From: HM Courts and Tribunals Service [mailto:replies@optic.justice.gov.uk]
Sent: 06 August 2020 12:06
To: duncan@considercelebratingdiversityandsport.com
Cc: London Crown Court
Subject: Complaint (ref: 5484279)

Dear Mr Lawrence,

This has been referred to HHJ Brown who your appeal was listed before on the 23rd July2020.

She has confirmed the Court considered the recent correspondence from you in which you made it plain you did not want to, nor intend to, participate in the appeal process to the Crown Court as provided by Parliament. Since that is the only process available to the Court, your correspondence was treated as notice of abandonment. The Court noted you had not attended and you had been warned by the Court that if you did not attend, given the history of the case, then the Court was likely to conclude you had abandoned your appeal. The Court therefore determined that you had abandoned your appeal which concluded the matter.

The Court cannot enter into any further correspondence about this case.

Yours sincerely,

Emma Smith
Delivery Manager
Kingston Upon Thames Crown, HM Courts and Tribunals Service | HMCTS | Kingston Crown Court <u>6-8 Penrhyn Road, Kingston upon Thames KT1 2BB</u>
Phone: <u>020 8240 2500</u>

<image001.jpg>

No disrespect, but the judge either was misinformed and or was neglecting his duties with me.I am putting my confidence in him, once I step into his court and he seems to take my views for granted.

How can I be part of an appeal and have so much outstanding issues related to 24.10,an English Law Code that was ignored in my last court hearings and seems to wished to be ignored by the Judge that could probably state his opinion in less than a few minutes should he so choose.

I do not wish to proceed to an appeal, similar to my last case... where I am not explained why I can't change my plea, why I can't present evidence or why I can't have witnesses.

Can I get a second opinion?

I feel like my Human Rights, especially Article 6 are being trampled again without getting what the court, Judge, etc. say checked out by an objective legal body.

My appeal needs to be transparent and above board and I am just looking for assurance that I will be treated fairly, in a transparent manner and not have to do so much chasing over several weeks just to get a straight legal answer.

Respectfully submitted by:

Duncan Lawrence
London SE26 5LB

D.E.Lawrence:

Diversity, Equality, Inclusion and Sport Specialist/Management and Team Coach.

2020+ : Please only use diversitymanagementlcl@gmail.com and company emails relating to 'consider celebrating diversity and sport' to make contact in the future...thanks and be safe!

Please think of the environment - do you really need to print this email or its attachments?

Sent from my iPhone

On 17 Jul 2020, at 17:53, HM Courts and Tribunals Service <replies@optic.justice.gov.uk> wrote:

Dear Mr Lawrence

Further to receiving your correspondence, this has been referred to HHJ Barklem.

The Judge has directed that it is not the role of this Court either to provide legal advice or to explain the actions of other Courts. You were told that any representations could be made at the hearing to mention and fix. That hearing took place in your absence, and a date has been fixed for the hearing of the full appeal. If you fail to attend that hearing it is likely to be treated as abandoned.

The date of your appeal is the 23 rd July 2020 with a time estimate of 1 hour.

Should you require legal advice you should contact a solicitor or the Citizens Advice Bureau.

Yours sincerely,

<~WRD000.jpg>

Emma Smith
Delivery Manager
Kingston Upon Thames Crown, HM Courts and Tribunals Service | HMCTS | Kingston Crown Court 6-8 Penrhyn Road, Kingston upon Thames KT1 2BB
Phone: 020 8240 2500

<image001.jpg>

NOTE: Please do not edit the subject line when replying to this email.

<~WRD000.jpg>

This e-mail and any attachments is intended only for the attention of the addressee(s). Its unauthorised use, disclosure, storage or copying is not permitted. If you are not the intended recipient, please destroy all copies and inform the sender by return e-mail. Internet e-mail is not a secure medium. Any reply to this message could be intercepted and read by someone else. Please bear that in mind when deciding whether to send material in response to this message by e-mail. This e-mail (whether you are the sender or the recipient) may be monitored, recorded and retained by the Ministry of Justice. Monitoring / blocking software may be used, and e-mail content may be read at any time. You have a responsibility to ensure laws are not broken when composing or forwarding e-mails and their contents.

<~WRD000.jpg>

This email has been scanned by the Symantec Email Security.cloud service.
For more information please visit http://www.symanteccloud.com

----

Key Letters to refer to:

From: Duncan Lawrence <duncan@considercelebratingdiversityandsport.com>

Date: 17 July 2020 at 18:15:09 BST

To: HM Courts and Tribunals Service <replies@optic.justice.gov.uk>

Cc: London Crown Court <London.Crowncourt@cps.gov.uk>

Subject: URN 01TW/00755/19 A20200063 Complaint – A20200063 (ref: 5484279)

No disrespect, but the judge either was misinformed and or was neglecting his duties with me.I am putting my confidence in him, once I step into his court and he seems to take my views for granted.

How can I be part of an appeal and have so much outstanding issues related to 24.10,an English Law Code that was ignored in my last court hearings and seems to wished to be ignored by the Judge that could probably state his opinion in less than a few minutes should he so choose.

I do not wish to proceed to an appeal, similar to my last case... where I am not explained why I can't change my plea, why I can't present evidence or why I can't have witnesses.

Can I get a second opinion?

I feel like my Human Rights, especially Article 6 are being trampled again without getting what the court, Judge, etc. say checked out by an objective legal body.

My appeal needs to be transparent and above board and I am just looking for assurance that I will be treated fairly, in a transparent manner and not have to do so much chasing over several weeks just to get a straight legal answer.

Respectfully submitted by:

Duncan Lawrence
London SE26 5LB

D.E.Lawrence:

Diversity, Equality, Inclusion and Sport Specialist/Management and Team Coach.

2020+ : Please only use diversitymanagementlcl@gmail.com and company emails relating to 'consider celebrating diversity and sport' to make contact in the future...thanks and be safe!

Please think of the environment – do you really need to print this email or its attachments?

Sent from my iPhone

On 17 Jul 2020, at 17:53, HM Courts and Tribunals Service <replies@optic.justice.gov.uk> wrote:

Dear Mr Lawrence

Further to receiving your correspondence, this has been referred to HHJ Barklem.

The Judge has directed that it is not the role of this Court either to provide legal advice or to explain the actions of other Courts. You were told that any representations could be made at the hearing to mention and fix. That hearing took place in your absence, and a date has been fixed for the hearing of the full appeal. If you fail to attend that hearing it is likely to be treated as abandoned.

The date of your appeal is the 23rd July 2020 with a time estimate of 1 hour.

Should you require legal advice you should contact a solicitor or the Citizens Advice Bureau.

Yours sincerely,

Error! Filename not specified.

Emma Smith
Delivery Manager
Kingston Upon Thames Crown, HM Courts and Tribunals Service | HMCTS |
Kingston Crown Court 6-8 Penrhyn Road, Kingston upon Thames KT1 2BB
Phone: 020 8240 2500

Error! Filename not specified.
The Crown Court
At Kingston-U-Thames
FAO : Clerk to Justices
FAO:Crown Court
Case Number:
A202000073
Court Code: 427

Dear Crown Court,

I was sent a letter dated 13 July 2020 regarding a ` notice of appeal hearing'. I am attaching my original appeal application for your review.

Even though I have sent several email letters to this court well in advance, nothing in my Kingston Crown Court process(emails and letters written to me by this court) thus far, reflect any advance court resolutions related to any of these advance email letters nor my original appeal application and I am not yet confident that my human rights are being respected (especially Article 6 of the Human Rights Act) because the decision making processes are not transparent and I have not been helped to be included within them.

My appeal and appeal planning would definitely take some time for this court with advance preparation time (more than an hour), especially with the outstanding issues;

1: Legal Code 24.10. Was this still relevant in August 2019? I applied for a 'change of plea' using this legal code and have had no response to this day.'Application to withdraw a guilty plea'

24.10.– (1) This rule applies where the defendant wants to withdraw a guilty plea.

(2) The defendant must apply to do so—

    (a) as soon as practicable after becoming aware of the reasons for doing so; and

(b) before sentence.

(3) Unless the court otherwise directs, the application must be in writing and the defendant must serve it on—

(a) the court officer; and

(b) the prosecutor.

(4) The application must—

(a) explain why it would be unjust not to allow the defendant to withdraw the guilty plea;

(b) identify—

(i) any witness that the defendant wants to call, and

(ii) any other proposed evidence; and

(c) say whether the defendant waives legal professional privilege, giving any relevant name and date.

I also asked to submit evidence and have a witness within this same application ...again no response.

Question: I have written several email letters to this court wishing written clarification on how and if these four 'non responded to letters' from Wimbledon Magistrates's Court if and or will they reflect on any appeal eg.;

* Was this action legal and or does it reflect good court/ legal practice by Wimbledon Magistrates's Court generally,

the Magistrates (there were three initially), the prosecutor and the judge???

* If so, how does it or should it impact upon any appeal???

1.1 Can I now submit evidence and witnesses for any appeal???

2. Can the appeal be held 'behind closed doors' due to the high profile nature?

For several months I have been advised by several legal professionals that any particular appeal court is best placed to provide written clarification (in advance of any appeal process that would begin in their own court) and that I should focus my energy there.

I found my first experience of the criminal justice system very bias, racist and led by white male privilege throughout, with my human rights being trampled throughout(especially article 6 of the Human Rights Act).

I am just being an assertive citizen and want to know up front where this particular court stands on the outstanding issues, having a 'closed court', and will they transparently respect my article 6 Rights (of the Human Rights Act) from the outset.

With this information, I can proceed with confidence in any appeal process. Without it, I am respectfully still declining to even get started.

I am representing myself and I have repeated my stance several times now and do not wish anyone to waste their valuable time, especially during these extraordinary times related to covid-19.

I respectfully have no transparent and or written reason to attend any appeal within this court on the date that you have currently set.

If this goes to the press(and I genuinely hope that it does not), I hope that my full intentions will not be misrepresented in any way.

I have been trying to move this appeal related situation forward since Jan 2020 and would have never imagined it would come down to 'last minute' continued lack of 'start up clarity', that hinders any appeal process to start upon a transparent and fair basis.

Respectfully submitted by:

Duncan Lawrence
London SE26 5LB
16.7.19

London Collection and Compliance Centre
Enforcement Team Contact Details   Phone 0300 123 9252
Email: LCCCComplianceUnit@justice.gov.uk
Post: PO Box 75667 London WC1A 9QD

Mr DUNCAN LAWRENCE
18C KENT HOUSE ROAD
LONDON
SE26 5LB

Division: 077
New account number: **20075310R CG**
Born: 16 February 1959

Notice of transfer of fine

The financial penalties shown below have been transferred to this court for enforcement from Kingston upon Thames Crown Ct.. The total amount to be paid is £ **660.00**

Date of Transfer: 28 July 2020
Date of Sentence: 23 July 2020

See reverse for details on how to pay and use your **new** account number whenever you make a payment or contact the court.

Date: 28 July 2020

Designated Officer

Offences and penalties

Date	Offences and Impositions		Amount £
23 Jul 2020	/ Appeal against administrative decision.	Costs	330.00
		Costs	330.00
		Total: £	**660.00**

You must pay: The total amount on or before **23 October 2020**

28 July 2020/FINOT_45_0/47582.100/1

Mr DUNCAN LAWRENCE

Thought Questions:

?= Do you /should you expect a high degree of professionalism within a court proceeding(or should you just accept what you are presented with)?

12. Prison

Some Reflective thoughts from D.Eric Lawrence

> **Bamboozled Wisdom:**(Number 13) Prisons are great opportunities to crush human spirits and remind bystanders and colluders alike who has the real power and the intent to silence voices of truth.

"...wow I saw you on tv tonight, what did you do, rob a bank ?..."

I told my youngest daughter who came to court with me on 30 Oct 2019 that "...I had to get everything out in the last court hearing..." or I could not bring something new up later in any appeal...I thought it was important for her to understand that I had to be very clear and assertive with the judge and prosecution, whether they liked it or not. I had prepared the judge a binder full of email evidence illustrating that I did not know the Assistant Coroner for most of the charge period, copies of my 2015-16 CPD awards/diplomas and some letters of professional support27.Even though he had this for at least one hour prior to coming into the court (the clerk confirmed this fact) he never fully used its contents nor his court room to support my Human Rights(especially those related to Article 6).

---

27 Ironically, there were none from my ex-RPFI colleagues, they were terrified that they too would be drawn in whatever 'toxic whirlpool that I was clearly very deeply drowning in. I do not blame any of them, I might have been a bit frightened too If I was in their shoes.

I knew I was going to prison once the judge stopped listening to me defending myself and telling him that he has the wrong person and that I am being set up...he got visibly red in his face and if looks could have killed, I definitely would have been dead. He then left the court for several minutes and then two private security staff came and sat by me.

I think if I did not have family, I would have made a very big fuss...specifically to get media attention but because my daughter was there, I just kept quiet.

The court staff continued to be genuinely nice, they let my daughter collect my binder, my keys/bag from the security staff and they allowed me to send out a variety of emails before taking away my phone. It was moments like these that I was very grateful for and reminded me that not everyone was toxic and that some were and are beautiful human beings.

Ironically, I had been to most prisons in the UK (and some in EU) as a senior researcher at Goldsmiths College, University of London in the early 90s and it was quite strange feeling coming in as an inmate number.

I often have a lot of questions asked by me and or to me around my prison experiences. For example, a few days into my sentence I was assessed in writing as being a very very low risk and could have been moved straight to an open prison, why didn't this happen? Definitely felt like tangible but shadowy energy to keep me inside and learn my lesson in the most disturbing manner.

I was approved for Home Detention as well, even after several unanswered letters to the governor trying to chase this up, and after several false starts such as being given provisional home detention start dates, this programme was denied to me as well for reasons unknown to me (even though I followed every process as required and was even offered a verbal provisional date to go home).

I am not normally a paranoid person, but I genuinely felt that 'some individuals higher up were having discussions about keeping me inside'(and that is exactly what they did). Hopefully my future legal team can get some answers in this area.

Several inmates come to think of prison as their 'home' and regularly 'check themselves in' (get arrested, etc) in order to get off the streets for a while, get food, collect a small prison payment, especially in the winter months.

There were some very lovely individuals, then there were some that were deeply vulnerable, damaged and clearly some of the men so very psychologically dangerous characters too that could and did at times cause physical and emotional damage to staff and other inmates.

Self-harm and suicide attempts were daily occurrences. I would not always blame any one person or organisation for this, prisons are very complicated circumstances.

Some men seemed to live for the rather large two meals a day, their prison friends and associates, nicotine patches and or tea leaf smokes and any available drugs(mainly things like 'spice' that were readily available), others like me that 'lived past the confines of the prison walls' and I just kept my mind and soul connected to issues solely to 'life outside'...we all had different hopes, dreams and inspirations although all locked up in the very same place.

My parents, grandparents, my great grandparents, and their ancestors worked very hard to overcome...I remember. I have worked hard generally and within this period specifically ... hopefully my family and my ancestors will remember me too!

I will write a book about this period of time but for now I will just say, I was very fortunate to have roommates that looked after me and I in turned supported them in a 'big brother mentoring role'...I only felt sorry for myself for a week or so and then went on to straight 24/7 planning how I could clear my name (I used the hallway lights and usually worked until I fell asleep). My roommates seemed to get a kick out of me organising myself every day in the early morning alongside my early morning exercising.

Prison is not a good place, there are loads of vulnerable inmates and vulnerable staff that 'get hooked' on being there.

Thought Questions:

?= Have you ever been locked up against your will?

Why didn't those around you come forth and tell the truth?

13. Journey to Clear My Name: Gratitude, Hindrances, and Bystanders

Bamboozled Wisdom:

(Number 14) Watch out...watch out...watch out...When working hard, fighting and climbing up a mountain on your own, then on the way down a 'crowd' suddenly appears and says that they all have been there all of the time and are now there to help you down 'your mountain'...and then say that they were always there 'with you' (but were trying not to get in your way).

Some Reflective thoughts from D.Eric Lawrence

I am incredibly grateful for my friends, my past clients and associates, all that gave me opportunities to give and receive support, opportunities, adventures and friendship.

Even though the coroner process, press and the courts tried to decimate me and my past experiences, I am clear...I lived...I loved...I have shared...I have created...I have achieved...I have learned and struggled with real people and even if I never see them again or never communicate with them ever again (or they with me), no one can take away the memories and or 'the lived experiences'.

One long-term friend thinks my case will never be resolved, primarily because he thinks that there are forces well beyond my control such as the Free Masons, Illuminati etc.

I grew up Pentecostal and then progressed as a young adult on the path to being more of a Buddhist thinker. Where I am very sure that there are 'positive energies' in the subjective and objective realms of the universe, I also can believe that there are negative energies there too.

I believe these energies are and can be influenced overtly and covertly by individuals, family, groups, nations, worldly and outer worldly associations...but why did they come after me at that time? This toxic resistance cloud seems to have gotten a hold of me and does not want to let go.

On the other hand, my mother used to say that sometimes things that we experience have nothing whatsoever to do with us and that all we need to do is to get out of our own way at times and 'not take ownership of other people's stuff' (as part of not making things worse).

I attribute a lot of what has happened and what will happen to the fact that often people have blind loyalty and those same people often that cover up for each other too. White men and their foot soldiers convicted me and sent me to prison. Sure, there were people of colour 'in the outskirts', but none of them had any real institutional and or financial and or real legal clout to have planned and then 'influence in plain sight' my conviction, sentencing and my imprisonment.

I was always a 'thinker' and going to prison only helped to create an enhanced opportunity for me to consider and reconsider 24/7.

I clarified and reclarified who I thought I was angry with and or who was responsible for putting me in this situation and went through this process several times a day.

I clarified and reclarified what steps I might need to take to clear my name via prayer, meditation, and daily focus.

I committed myself in prison to leave friends and associates alone that were currently leaving me alone and to solely dedicate my energy and focus on to my immediate family and to the steps and actions that could assist clearing my name.

Gratitude

Since being out, literally several dozen old friends and associates have been sniffing around primarily via social media...I am currently not really interested to encourage them to continue to do so.

To me I have a lot to be grateful during this period. I have a strong tradition of volunteering, activism and of being observant of things around me.

All of the above helped me to gain experience, confidence and curiosity about a lot a things at a very young age and have been fortunate that various people have been very generous with their time and wisdom over the years, often making themselves available to me on a 24/7 basis...I am forever grateful for this, it has helped me to focus during this period...their energy and practical lessons helped me to get up when I might be in a slump or be at risk of feeling sorry for myself and or losing my focus.

Leading up to being sentenced I felt I had more 'inquisitive friends and associates' get in touch about something that they might have read and or heard in the press and or on social media...their curiosity...not mine, not much to feel grateful for there.

I had some friends and associates offer me financial assistance, what little that they had...I was genuinely touched by these moments especially when I really needed it.

I also had loads of people that said that they were 'praying for me'...to this day I am not sure how I feel about this expression. I was always taught that 'faith without works (action) means nothing' so where I am sure these people were very well meaning, I think I would have felt more grateful for example if they had asked if they could help me on a practical basis and really mean it (in addition to their potential powerful prayers).

In some ways while the covid-19 pandemic provided an 'ironic distraction', I am grateful for those friends, associates and family that gave me 'space'. To a lot of people this might have felt and sounded like a strange thing for me to say and or that why was I not even depressed by them or made angry by them. For me, honestly the more 'space' that I received, then the more 'focus' opportunities there were for me and the more time for me to get physically and mentally ready for my next steps whatever they might be.

For this I am also very grateful because with the vast emails, the legal applications and this book, these acts would never have come together without this 'space' and 'focus' from these friends, family and associates.

I had people that brought me food, wine and offered to jog with me...I am incredibly grateful for these moments, I enjoyed their fellowship and conversation.

I had my long-time friend, and music partner say "...yes..." to a monthly online jazz and blues nightclub...I hated the UK so much at that time (and still do) and the music and hanging out kept me alive, gave me regular opportunities to channel my frustrations and kept me less hateful to myself and others, I am tremendously grateful for this and will always continue to be by this. I cannot imagine to not have my music as a healer.

Although once the pandemic started, I stopped some of my regular new habits. I had begun to only keep a few dozen people updated with my legal adventures, those whose opinions and respect that I genuinely valued ...often some wrote back to me to say thanks for sharing during my busy moments...I was very touched and grateful that someone took the time to read my very often long notes and then write a meaningful note back to me... I am forever grateful for these moments.

There has been some humour along the way too. I had some women friends and associates during this period that seemed to only care about me as a man...like they felt inspired to look after me (the 'man' that could not look after himself currently), I was grateful for these moments too (although thinking about them always brings a smile to my face).

I am incredibly grateful for those employers that gave me interviews (and employment offers) even after I had explained what happened within the courts and press/media. I felt that they were very brave and, in most cases, seem to appreciate me more for telling the truth to them. There were others that interviewed me several times (after I came clean about my legal situation) and then for some reason broke off their contact with me, with no explanation.

Finally, even though I only mainly saw them initially via WhatsApp video, zoom and Thursday evening yoga fusion class taught by my youngest daughter, I am deeply grateful to my daughters Nicole, Akosua and Lildonia for allowing me to be me, while quietly getting on with my legal adventures away from them. My two lovely and clever granddaughters only wanted me to be granddad and nothing else...this kept me young, happy and hopeful about being part of their futures.

I am not blaming here, most people have always seen me as someone that lands on their feet and that can generally sort out my own shit (and this matter while very very confusing on the surface and made even more complex,more unfair,more sad and more toxic by the various press, television and social media accounts), several said that is why they gave me space...they hoped that 'I would be Duncan soon' and get through.

Hindrances

I see these as individuals and organisations that usually lied to protect others, lied to protect themselves, ran away and did nothing whatsoever (because it all seemed so overwhelming to them at the time), blocked efforts to finding and or unearthing the truth and or moments of bias, racism, misrepresentations, white privilege, white male privilege, classism etc... obstruction and standing in the way is very much a choice that we each need to stand accountable for.

Some of these people did not know each other personally but seemed to be part of some kind of 'unwritten law' to unconditionally back up those in your profession (coroner, police, prosecutors, judges, and magistrates, etc.) and or those in your social status and or your race and or your white male club or those you would hope to earn a higher status from and 15 minutes of fame from.

I had written thousands of words trying to get support. Those that I found either useless, and or out and out committed to covering up bad practices/actions include:

2019/Present **British association for Counselling and Psychotherapy**

Outcomes;

- *From my perspective, they have been one of my major hindrances to clear my name. It seems like they thought that they were doing their civic duty by trying to kick me out of the association and the more 'publicly' the better.*

I have given years to this organisation, and they wished get me away from them as if I was shit. I can imagine the panel composition of the panel members assigned to get me out. Crazily enough they would not even let me resign, they only wanted to let me out on their terms e.g., more public decimation, misrepresentation and never once attempting a public challenge of what they were reading or hearing about me.

I will later in this book's Volume II share some of my example energetic responses that I used trying to get them to be fair and for them to critically research anything they saw in the press and review anything from the coroner process in order make sure that it was fair, accurate and just.

In some ways I have not been proud of how I have been treated by the BACP and felt that they should have offered me 'supportive pathways' rather than coming across as 'dangerous judge and jury'. I cannot imagine them ever apologising and or trying to make things right with me.

2019/2020 **Wimbledon Magistrates Court Complaint Procedure**

Outcomes:

- *After several emails, they confirmed that the judge read all four of my letters to the court (refer to my emails in this application)*

- *referred me to the Crown Prosecution Service regarding the judge's behaviour*

2019/2020 **Crown Prosecution Complaint Procedure**

Outcomes:

- *sent dozens of emails*

- *would never explain the legal ramifications for the 'charge period dates'*

- *they often blamed me for pleading guilty*

- *summer 202 allowed Kingston Crown Court Appeal Judge to fine me twice with no explanation (I have sent several complaint email follow up to no avail)*

Oct 2020 **Head of the Department for Public Prosecutions (UK)**

Outcomes:

- *never came back to me*

2019/2020 **London Metropolitan Police**

Outcomes:

- *. Wrote several times*

- *they blamed the CPS Lawyer and the Assistant Coroner for "...expanding..." the charge period dates*

2019/2020 **Chief Coroner(UK)**

Outcomes:

- *referred me to Senior Coroner*

2019 **Assistant Coroner**

Outcomes:

— *never responded to reasonable questions*

2020 **Local Member of Parliament** *(Ms.Reeves)*

Outcomes:

— *Never passed on my complaints about CPS, Courts, etc. in a practical manner. Every place that they referred me to said that they could not assist me. Did not seem to really care that a miscarriage occurred, even after seeing loads of information.*

2019 **Judicial Conduct Investigation Office:**

Outcomes:

— *Same... it was out of the remit because Coroners are meant to be not hindered with their activities when carrying out their work*

2019 **Local Government Ombudsman:** *See above*

I found 'a pattern of resistance' about 90% of the time and was very grateful and surprised when I experienced any positive cooperation...quite sad and shameful really.

Bystanders

Bystander apathy was one of the worst experiences in my adult life, I had seen similar growing up in the 60s ... you and your friends see horrendous things on the television and in your neighbourhoods but then go to school the next day with white friends, and your white teachers and they act as if they did not really see these same violent examples of racism, discrimination, and unfairness...crazy crazy crazy!

Some people and organisations see the potential human rights violations, the racism, the white male privilege that occur daily...these are all very stressful and totally unfair environments and yet do nothing to intervene...regardless of whether you knew me or not, there were enough past and present UK miscarriages of justice to at least ask for facts... at least ask for human rights to be respected...nope.

The expression "...do unto others as you like to be done to you...", this totally had no examples in my case unless our society only wanted lies, bias and b#s to bloom and blossom.

I must admit I also had battles in my head and in my heart with those that I thought had let me down as 'bystanders' e.g., by not offering to be a witness in court, not being open to provide detailed professional references, those that did not challenge the press and media, those that did not ask me if I needed any help (I could have used legal funds, help with living expenses, jogging and pub partners, help me to keep my existing work, etc.).The founder of the charity, one that gave us our main work assignments and had a lot of secrets of her own was 'protected' and did nothing to assist me. I even had one very close friend that ran away from our friendship quicker that Usain Bolt!

So far, the 'helpful energy' has come from my daughters, my builder friends, a long-term colleague from a counselling/ psychotherapy training center, an ex-student and new friend, an ex-manager/CEO from a group of London children's homes, a long-time school friend, a long-time music partner/ co-worker, a long-time co-worker and friend that actually tracked me down in prison, and some very new friends and associates from a 2019 job that I had...they clearly were not bystanders and I will forever be grateful for their friendship, respect and time.

Even though in past and present history, the bystanders are often whitewashed out, I will do my best to name some my own feelings and be clear about what I saw as 'bystanders' and 'bystander apathy'.

Thought Questions:

?= What do you think kept some individuals and or organisations 'on the fence' when they could have shown support in a variety of ways?

?= Would more support (for/of D.Eric Lawrence)potentially have made a difference in the final court outcome? Y/N

?= Should D.Eric Lawrence have asked more vocally for support from friends, associates and organisations(and or could each of them 'stepped up' more on their own initiatives)?

Where are you now?

14. Final Reflections

> **Bamboozled Wisdom:** (Number 15) Looking back to go forward...hey, stay out of your own way!

Thoughts from the foreword Author:

Whew...the past two years have been like a crazy rollercoaster ride for Duncan and his lovely family ...one that goes up ...then goes down ...it moves back and forth and then over the same area of track that it started from...one where the rules and track directions change with no warning...stops for long periods of time with no explanation. When you look to the left and then to the right, there are several bystanders... some whose faces are hidden in the shadows... some standing right there with their chests pushed out as if they really have something to be proud about...some old and new friends and even some recent associates just all standing and gawking... still bystanders none the less.

Oprah often says "...say thanks for the opportunity...", Duncan has changed so much of his life because of this 2015-16 situation and is very much still evolving, so thanks very very very much for this opportunity!

Those toxic and often criminal actors together and or alone are the only ones that could explain their motivations for lying directly and or indirectly, for colluding with and protecting others that have lied and or provided obstacles and roadblocks and or hindered the truth from coming out... this book was not written for them...karma will get each of them in its own time and in their own way.

No, this book was very much more for their friends, their husbands, their wives, their siblings, the police, the coroners etc....maybe they can act as 'the conscious' every time they see their loved ones and those they respect and or those that they look up to...ask them "...why did you lie about Duncan and or protect those that lied about Duncan???...how did that work out for you?..."

Final thoughts from Duncan:

1. Here I lay it out as best as I can within these memoirs. Some will definitely recognise themselves in my memoirs...there are significant individuals and loads of toxic actors. I have not triumphed over the institutions, the press and the public's bamboozling in plain sight. I am just an ordinary guy that loves his family, his new and old friends and generally tries not to bother anyone. As my memoirs illustrate, especially from 2015 and beyond I have experienced some of the best that the UK can offer and some of the worst and nastiness from people that ever came out of the UK. These memoir years have impacted upon all areas of my life and will continue to do. Hopefully even without reading the following rambling but sincere(and hopefully even useful) conclusion, you can get a taste of what it was like for me during this period, one

person...dear readers there are thousands of others out there that are working in Health and Social Care and or have worked in Health and Care or have quit, been fired or have retired early from Social Care.... they have stories and experiences too. Please, get to know them and their stories too!

2. Writing my memoirs, about a certain period of my life...was easier and more difficult than I could have imagined. I have been reminded recently however, that when I had written previous articles and chapters, and that I had always been 'sharing parts of myself' for many years. I hope that readers of this book can get a 'flavour' of what it might have been for me 'working while black' in 2015-2016 as well as how it felt trying to return to work in 2019,2020 and 2021. I also genuinely hope that readers find this book interesting, and that you can 'selfishly get something for yourselves' too, such as increased hope that things can get better for you whatever your situation is, that you (and I) can now make better use of opportunities that the universe presents us with, the strength and continued bravery to walk away from toxic relationships, etc... the list could be endless, just live our best lives.

Initially when I was just organising myself in September-December of 2018 for my coroner's witness statement and later when trying to help organise my charity legal team, I was getting very very frustrated that "... no one will ever hear my side of the story...". It was then that my youngest daughter said something like "... don't worry about it Dad, put it all in your memoirs...".

I am not a 'tech guy' and did not realise that my emails from my iPhone were being stored 'on the cloud' unless I deleted them...wow! Additionally, various RPFI ex-senior managers sent me copies of their relevant RPFI emails and wondered if they could be helpful to me...again wow!

I think my parents would have been saddened to have seen me in this position arising from 2016 and would have expected more of a public protest, although they would not have been surprised by my persistence to clear my name, nor my desire to take some time away from London to reflect and energise, rather than continue on as if nothing serious really happen.

I think most of the toxic actors within this book would be surprised with how many emails that I now have access to and that this is only Volume 1!

I like several others[28] will continue to firmly believe, that my experiences of 2016 and beyond would have occurred 'in a different way' had I been a blond haired blue eyed consultant...most people acknowledge that I potentially would not have even entered the criminal justice system whatsoever...potentially would have been financially compensated for my being scapegoated...my humanity definitely would have stayed 'front and centred' in the press and social media...being treated like a non-person in front of millions was so surreal...in front of some of my past and

---

[28] People that had got in touch via social media.

present professional associations...and in front of my friends and family.

Several individuals and groups will have 'splits' about my views, but I will let the emails themselves 'name names' and 'speak for themselves'. I did not have the 'institutional power' to help myself, so race, racism, white privilege, and white male privilege has spun its weblike toxic features quite comprehensively throughout this period. This is a clear example of how black people really can't be racist. What the Assistant Coroner initiated in 2018 as a result of me putting my recently deceased father and my soon to be deceased mother in front of him, even with good intentions and writing what I thought was a helpful inquest witness statement ... what he saw was someone being cocky enough to say "... no..." to him. And with that, he, along with several colluders, with several people rising to his privileged position that he did not earn, they set out to 'teach me a lesson' and 'keep me in my lane'.

As mentioned above Black people rarely have the 'institutional power' to do something like what he's started with me. White potential and actual employers soon move away like he asked them to, like Moses parting the Red Sea...strange really...this man will stay in his lane, and that will teach him and anyone like him to never say 'no' (to him) again.

He's never really put my mind 'in my lane', but in terms of work and professional opportunities like opportunities to write 'opinion pieces' in the press, he sure has, getting and keeping work sure has been very hard and new paper editors rarely come back to me. I think this is one of the things that disturbs me most about this period, that he got me so wrong and the 'toxic perfect storm actors' joined up to keep me down ever since.

When I do have moments of work, some around me act like (without ever really saying it to me directly), "...at least it is over now and back to normal for Duncan...".

To me, and the 'pandemic space' helped, 'my new normal' is when I can have ideas to follow up as I like and not have to afraid to go after them and or expect to have to take crap from less qualified asses that do not have a clue about what range of immense talent, skill and generosity that comes with me. A new normal means choices about where I live and how I live. A new normal is when I can exhale and truly believe that I can offer things to myself and others without feeling 'less than'. I am not sure my new normal will occur in London, my recent memories might be too big for me to really 'lighten up'.

It's quite unsettling that potential employers and potential business clients keep trying to vet me on social media like LinkedIn...I do not update any social media because it is the same place where toxic actors trying to threaten me go and thinking that they can get more information to come after me with.

It has been very tempting to update my social media for legitimate employers and businesses to check me out, but I really do not (yet) want to explain to each and every business opportunity about the status and or progress about how close or far away that I am from clearing my name.

Quite a frustrating position to be in, on one hand I want people to take me as they find me and if they like what they see then they should respectfully 'come and get me' and if they have 'concerns' then they should quietly go away, no explanation required.

Very frustrating position to be in, in 'my world I wanted people to be brave', forget what they might have heard and hire me anyway...I had mixed results and reviews in 'my world'.

People and organisations that have tried to pressure me for information while dangling the chance of a real or non-existent job don't seem to realise, that regardless of their 'motivation'(for making direct and indirect contact with me) I will never really trust them now and will genuinely have felt ' victimised' by them...not based upon logic, that's just me being honest about how I feel. That is why ideally, I'd rather be outside of London/UK during this period...the 'space' would feel like much needed fresh air and much less of an intense environment to wake up to each morning, then feeling the spectre of the Assistant Coroner still having a grip on all aspects of my life.

As long as it takes to clear my name, it feels like I have had to take any work that I can get until then.

Legally I have been advised that my memoirs being published before any final legal settlement, that this could have a negative impact...hence I have had no choice but to keep my memoirs unpublished and on hold for the time being.

One common feature about this period of time was the 'reoccurring theme' of individuals and organisations lying or covering up theirs and other people's messes, the glaring misrepresentations and unfair bias in plain sight and then like clockwork act like it was a 'normal everyday process' and that it's me that overreacting...serious 'gaslighting'.

I often wondered if the first time that anyone ever saw 'the truth' about my legal situation will be via my memoirs that you are reading right now although there will have been so many legal opportunities to 'say and do the right thing' that will have come and gone.

The 'energy' to Bamboozle the public in plain sight continues to be so intense, I only hope that we can keep this book very accessible to anyone wishing to read it(before any legal efforts to keep it off the shelves).

If we don't talk about it now, nothing will ever change.

People need to know that given the 'perfect storm situation', that anyone will lie and cover up and or allow themselves to be used and manipulated by others. Even though it is happening to me, it is still a very fascinating phenomenon to consider. In a Star Trek movie (for example) you might have an 'energy' that goes from body to body, making them do its bidding. My situation, at least to me seems very similar, wherever I go, 'the energy' to lie and downplay the series of event seems to already have been there...it beats me to the punch time and time again.

3. 'Positive and non-serious things' came out of 2015 and 2016 period for me as well; I began a serious keep fit program and lost a load of weight, survived a cancer scare, started coaching college and university level sports, made SEN training a CPD priority, continued to let my hair grow, started collecting art more seriously and began to perform on the keyboards[29] to a world class level again.

4. There are so many more people on the planet that deserve our time, our consideration, and our prayers. I am nothing special and did not wish publicity then, nor do I want it now. Just want to be given privacy and respectful space to move on from these series of tragic miscarriages.

5. My family deserves a break too.

6. People have said to me over the years "...slow down, you do too much, no one will ever say...thank you Duncan, you always give us more than we ask for, I wish we could pay you more...". **Being generous and hardworking should not be 'the gateway' to exploitation,** or having to always set the stage for insecurity, jealousy and potential crazy acts that can then be followed up by irrational thoughts and 'collective' acts such as e.g., falsehoods being

---

[29] Jazz, gospel, blues, and funk mainly.

perpetuated and or unfair complaints initiated, withholding of evidence/your work, not giving you public and financial credit/awards...the list is endless. Several readers are probably nodding their heads when reading this paragraph and saying "...Duncan, you are a clever nice person, but pretty stupid too... you always leave yourself exposed with these horrible ### people, seems like you'll never learn...".

From my point of view, most are right I think, and I hope that I am not too old to learn new ways to protect myself when working with others. So many of us around the world get caught up at times, not a new phenomenon just one pattern that many of us fall into (and for me it clearly was a pattern, all too familiar at times).

7. When thinking about ex-employers, I have been told by several reputable colleagues that I should sue anyone that let me go based on something that they read in the paper. I think I have moved on from that idea and needed to pick and choose my fights carefully, right now I will be led by my legal advice and my family.

8. When recent job opportunities hear about my 'legal situation'(after being cleared and or going to court to finally present evidence and witnesses), I am concerned that they might say something like "... that's why he (Duncan) seemed so passionate about helping us to organise 'risk assessments' for all the suicide gestures that we experienced ...this is why he wanted us to be so nice to service users..."putting 2+2

together and getting 78. I just simply wanted the best within my work environment and not that I was now somehow 'damaged' and or now too 'over sensitive'.

9. Some forward-thinking companies[30] around the world 'celebrate ideas by its members' in real time like with applause, with team time off, with non-scheduled promotions and the like...**white managers and senior managers is this you?** This is a great transformation opportunity, to change and improve from an insecure and oppressive management style to one of the celebration of success, regardless of where the ideas, the suggestions and the creativity come from within your teams and organisations...**be the earth moving positiveness that might be / has been lacking in you**... maybe even try to **make amends where you might have screwed up** a person of colour's professional and or personal life.

Or stay where you are...continue to 'oppress and or discipline your team member(s) 'back into their lanes'...think about it, I definitely will. **Senior Management, Trustees and Board Members** should take note, **you are responsible for all bad management practices on 'your watch'.**

10. I like the quote "...when someone shows you who they are...believe them...". Sometimes it's not clear why certain social care organisations exist but then on other

---

[30] Where 'success within the team is valued' where ever it comes from, and managers are judge by how well they can cultivate this type of positive and productive environment (or identifying their management style patterns when they might repeatedly screw it up).

occasions, with other organisations you can see the tremendous amounts of quality care and the amazing love that oozes out of certain organisations, where in these moments it's 100% clear why certain health and social care organisations exist ... you can easily see why certain teams exist...can easily see why certain individuals are there, you can easily see where there are those that can and do make a real difference... like the differences between night and day.

One thing that could also possibly be assumed, with so many vacancies,across so many large and small Social Care charities and related organisations, the pool of ethical and 'genuinely big hearted ' human beings that 'just wanted to work hard' is shrinking. I think these human beings should be 'protected'(from any toxicity and or from 'passive bystanders')supported, encouraged, inspired, and carefully recognised for their contributions (while understanding that some of these wonderful individuals and groups that might be in paid or unpaid roles, they might not wish public praise or any attention that might attract trolls and haters).

In recent years, especially during the 'living crisis periods', I have seen some very interesting, creative gestures that can sustain these 'added value angels', and help them to do what they do just a little bit longer.

These initiatives and actions include;

- providing live in posts or other types of accommodation

- free meals while on duty

- Choice of extra leave time as incentives

- Free and well-rounded well-being activities (some of these could be made available within work breaks and integrated into substantial team building activities).

- Provide amazing staff centric CPD opportunities (although these can be 'encouraged 'and not always made mandatory. I have seen cool opportunities to improve reading comprehension, writing support, book and film clubs, etc. all at work...amazing! Where there are 'mandatory implications' for CPD opportunities is because are part of legislation/good practice and they add to the protection and improvement of support of vulnerable individuals, families and those that support them. Additionally, there are those in leadership and management roles that often have little or no quality experience or qualifications in the area of leadership and management. In my own self-reflection and talking to others while developing my memoirs, it was dysfunctional leadership and management (individual moments or cumulative ' drip drip drip effect') that caused many of them/us to leave, to get booted out, to change careers, to taking up drinking, to get ill with hypertension, back pain, migraines, cancer, stress... the by-products of poor leadership and management is vast. These roles carry a lot of stress and pressure in them, and all the more reason to get 'role specific' CPD.

— Even though this can be tricky and needs careful monitoring; why not allow 'focus groups and support groups' to exist in social care more often. These can include assessing ' organisational health' and having the teeth to 'name and support' those areas of the organisation that might be 'at-risk' of toxicity, this includes opening support across the organisation including those at voluntary and casual levels, and to those at leadership and management levels...an honest acknowledgement that whether you are 'at risk' in toxic workplaces,regardless of whether you are *a victim, a victimiser and or a bystander* to and from the roots and the perpetuation of toxicity in the work place. Allies of this type of initiative understand that it takes bravery(at all levels within the organisation)to name and root out toxicity by creative and non-blaming activities (*it is often hard to be exact in establishing which came first a toxic personality and or something about ' the work')*. Others publicly and behind closed doors might consider this 'a bit cultish'. Other ' non fans' of these types of initiatives say these can be 'behaviour courts', where you have to 'toe the line' or you are out. I personally believe with a commitment to ' weeding out the roots of toxicity', while taking ' bravery leads' from leaders and managers to show support in their transparent governance, is well worth the efforts. There are potentially staff and volunteers that 'physically and spiritually die at work'.

— Letting staff peer assess across the organisation grades, so potentially a carer could peer assess a CEO...amazing possibilities here!

11. Past and present white male line managers, senior managers, politicians etc should be made to voluntarily swear that they have never colluded with or directed the screwing over of a black colleague and or of a black citizen, one that you knew was fully innocent or partly innocent...in the past 5 years...in the past 10 years...in the past 20-30 years???

12. The editors of the press, the social media, the senior staff of charities, professional associations, judiciary, police etc should also consider making this type of public oath too!

13. Most of the acts against me were perpetuated under the protection of white privilege although being a bystander or a colluder knows no race, colour, creed, gender or status...still wrong and shows the state of our society where they are the majority (bystanders).

14. Some people say 'my first problem' was working for an unethical charity founded by Elly Jansen...one that would throw me under the bus at the first sign of danger. I understand this perspective, but when we look around, how many of us can concisely know who will really act unethically and or graciously when

'challenged' with stress and strife? I wished I did have this sort of gift for seeing the future.

15. Not getting to know much about me professionally... my 'lived' and 'work experiences' that 'made me me'...my annual CPD patterns and history[31]...all areas that RPFI/Elly Jansen could have supplied at the initial and continuing coroner process, to the Charities Commission, and to the press, it could have potentially taken 'the toxic wind' out of the 'clinical lead bamboozle games'.

16. Even trying to get back to work now to save for my 'Plan B Funds' (get away and chill as soon as possible), I see the pressure that it can still create for other managers and entry level staff. In an ideal world I might not work at all and just keep a low profile. With 'work pressures', other 'not so positive', but very very 'familiar' patterns can emerge (work/life balance can go haywire, pressure to 'cheat' on your results increases, oppressing work colleagues becomes so much easier to do, being less 'service user centred focused' and more 'what's best for me focused'... hopefully I am protecting myself and those working with me better, in a wiser manner).

---

[31] In 2014-16 I took my annual CPD courses at Level 3-7 etc. that 'added value' in any of my work settings such as diversity, equality and inclusion management in organisations, health and fitness, nutrition, group boot camps, SEN, managing stress and aggressive situations, etc. and was at Fellow level in Management and Leadership, Education, Sport, Counselling, etc..

17. Some potential employers when they found out that I now had a criminal record, they either saw this as a cool or trendy 'extra value' from this 'new lived experience' or they saw it as something to then treat me 'as less than' and write and or talk to me anyway that they wished, definitely not in the same way as 'their initial vibe' e.g. treating me as 'an equal' or as an experienced senior practitioner/consultant ...quite amazing 'the difference' to how and which 'Duncan' that they are speaking to and or reacting to.

18. Even in 'low risk' jobs, where local people are the 'service users', actions such as self-harm, suicide gestures etc can potentially still occur daily(inside and outside of the workplace). In these difficult and sad situations, considering 'who is generally liable' in times of self-harm and suicide will continue to be a 'grey area' ...staff/shift that are on duty, the key workers, the senior management, new/past consultants, societies, family, cultural centres etc we are all potentially able to be held liable. In my case, I seemed to have held more responsibility (or assigned 'after thought responsibility') for the service user that took her own life in 2016, say more than the staff on 'suicide watch/observations' during that sad day... more than the family, more than the local authorities... were there 'smokers' on the 'suicide watch' shift, did this contribute to a 'lapse of concentration'...I will never know, this type of information was kept away from my trial...Bamboozled 101!

19. I often have up and down levels of motivation and inspiration since returning to work opportunities. Believe me, I am not trying to be a senior manager or consultant at present and definitely do not want the attention in the workplace, just want to do a good job, keep a low profile as a team player and save a bit of cash to travel, at least until my legal pursuits have ended. Bit awkward at times though. I have said for several months that I would be loyal to any employer that would take me on. It is difficult when you see moments of incompetence and lack of rigor in some managers, where they seem to not even try to add value or inspiration with their presence, some don't even try to 'fake it'...definitely part of the white privileged domain (although some managers are absolutely amazing with their care of their staff and their service users...I have seen and experienced this first hand!) . I am usually the oldest and or the most experienced team member and this must influence my work experiences and how others may 'value' and or 'feel very threatened' by 'the same very Duncan'. Trying to stay loyal to an employer in situations such as these is very very difficult although I still have tried to keep my word and show regular gratitude where I can to my employers, regardless of whether they deserve it or not.

20. Someone once asked in court if could they read an 'impact statement' about me and how it made them feel about me withholding information...my how karma

works, now I can consider doing a 'tell all' Impact Statement about them, regardless of their rationale and excuses for lying and or playing to the public with their regular use of false narratives.

21. Not sure why the press, media, court etc. ignored the fact that I had multiple roles across the charity in 2016 and only focused on the 'clinical lead' role (and make 'absurd connects' in this instance to 'a medical' setting and me and to my 'personal development' degree). The 2016 charity Trustees wrote this job description not me, they tried to put all my roles into one title...good intention...poor outcome, one that caused me, my credentials, my experience, my gifts my talents, and my ethics to all get slammed.

22. Some toxic actors clearly wanted me to assist them to make some personal cash from a morally corrupt social care organisation...I often wonder (too much I think) how did that work out for them?

23. I will get through this. I have always tried to take the high road in these events, even when it became crystal clear that there were individuals and organisations that were quite happy with taking the low road of lies, bias, make believe, racism, cover up and make regular violations of my human rights (especially Article 6 rights) just to support their false narratives and or get their 'fifteen minutes of fame'(directly or indirectly... through trying to continuously keep my evidence and witnesses out of the public eye).

24. I am also very clear; the courts and the press/media would have seen me in a different light in each court hearing had the prosecution and judge been courageous enough to not have colluded to keep my four court letters from seeing the light of day in court...bamboozled!

25. I hate having the following charge hanging over me, when unfairly being falsely linked to a young woman that took her own life, especially when she unfortunately resided in a social care facility where suicide gestures and self-harm were often daily occurrences...something that I genuinely tried to support the staff team and organisation to reduce.

**Prevent evidence / document production /
provision of a thing for an investigation.**

Having this on my record, it means nothing to me except a true reflection and constant reminder of the scapegoating, lies, bias, misrepresentation, white male privilege, racism and the risk of 'working while black'...bamboozled. I was always innocent and never withheld evidence from this crazy, obsessive, and toxic Assistant Coroner, especially during a charge period when I did not even know that he existed.

White people get fines, 'temporary black while working people' go to prison and get decimated in the press/media... 'no questions asked' from within the media and within the wider public.

Racism, white privilege generally and white male privilege specifically is real and at times can be a 'real and present danger' to individuals, families, and society...ignore it our peril!

26. One thing that I am also clear about regarding my case, is that not every stakeholder's motivation started out with negative intentions...I am sure too that some individuals and organisations started out really wanting to know if the RPFI charity's service delivery, their 'quality and their competence' in 2016 had anything to do with a young woman taking her life in 2016.

They[32] seemed to however only 'stopped at the hearsay level' and seemed to not expect to receive a further factual/explanation basis, one to clearly explore and see the truth from.

They also naively probably assumed that actors such as coroners, police, charity founders, charity trustees, charity commission, CQC, CPS, etc. would <u>always</u> and steadfastly be 'the leaders' for true justice when gathering and disseminating facts, rather than being the leaders for creating and sustaining false narratives, bias, lies and covering up true examples of poor social care practice. Unfortunately, there have been several examples of the latter and if you have not seen this for yourself yet, then you really should read this book again (especially Chapter 2 and 3) and get a copy of Volume 2.

---

[32] The press, social media, criminal justice system,etc.

Coroner processes can serve a great function in society but in a small number of occasions it can go very very wrong. I followed up several individuals and families that felt like me, that some coroners have way too much power and are very unsafe at times. Without any quality assurance and anti-bias procedures in place (within current UK law), they can basically do whatever they wish. **I challenge the Chief Coroner of the UK (he knows me and my case very well) to put some quality assurance systems in place this year,** one with 'anti-bias strategy fully integrated within it. I am not even sure that the coroner process in my case will ever come back and make things right with me.

27. I will clear my name and then quickly leave London for a while to reflect and energise myself...I would have left London several months ago had things worked out differently with regards to my initial court proceedings.

28. As of this month, November 2021, I think I am hopefully concluding my final large legal manoeuvre...I have not recently heard of any other timely action(s) that I could take to clear my name any further. The outcome is where I am only semi-hopeful. I have a recent history of 'legal professional' only repeating what they have read from magistrate's court (for example) and not being brave enough to ask for proof, facts for any evidence that any court have given then. My premise has always been that courts have lied, misrepresented me shown bias to me, why just take their word for everything without question and or challenge...

without this you are indirectly saying that the dozens of email evidence from me is useless to you, that it has been not enough for you to fight on my behalf for.

29. The toxic press and social media stories reached out to my extensive network of personal and professional relationships (which included vulnerable children, young people, and their families/carers) that I have had my entire adult life...then quickly moved on as if nothing ever really happened.

I am not even thinking at present about trying to 'reset' my previous professional and personal associations here in the UK...just need time away to reflect and to recharge. This nasty business has caused some 'non replaceable and non-repairable' damages to positive memories that I will grow old with. The universe will repair itself the best way that it can, I am sure of that.

30. Having no boundaries, having the confidence to say or do anything without fear of condemnation, this is currently the domain of the press, the social media, the white privileged generally and the white male privileged specifically that is for sure...this will not change until our society changes and then begins to expect more from those around us, especially those that are in positions of power and authority.

31. Some stakeholders already planned well before the January 2019 coroner's inquest had even started, about who they thought were guilty of 'neglect' from

the charity and or who they had wanted to be guilty of negligence from the RPFI charity...whispers of conspiracy!

32. Without factual evidence such as work emails, written reports and video evidence etc ` the truth' will have always been very difficult to 'find and stay in focus' regarding the RPFI Charity (at the beginning, throughout the coroner and legal processes and upon conclusion of the process and which can safely form the basis of any consequence, sentences and other judgments). An 'attention spectacle'... a 'narrative'(and or a variety of narratives that were around including those floating around on social media and the press) that attracted the Assistant Coroner and became his own...'the family's own' ... and owned by those with a beef against the charity...these all had 'consequences', regardless of their roots and or regardless of which side(s) that any one of us seemed to have latched on to.

33. Those professionals along with family members and carers with a stake in the Coroner/RPFI Process...with 'good intentions'(initially), somewhere in their process must have had their 'doubts' along the way e.g. when the evidence did not at times support the crazy and unfair narratives being put around at times and or if and when I put in any written evidence that was hidden, and or written complaints that were hidden and or maybe even when one of your friends, family, and or associates questioned your 'lack of following up' areas of this process that troubled you...believe

me you too are now very tainted ...passing the blame on to others should not free your conscious and on the contrary if a legal process does not catch up with you, then karma will in its universal pursuit of balance if it has not already done so. It is never too late to stand up and do the right thing.

34. I am sure, even after viewing my many many emails, some will still not accept me being cleared and or not guilty, whichever happens first...I am not trying to change their minds, just hoping that they will no longer hassle me personally or professionally. I am not sure if future versions of this book will retain actor names generally and or retain any names within emails specifically...they (several guilty actors) might then unfortunately miss out on any public justice or scrutiny.

35. I am only one person, a quiet introvert that has seen the benefits of diligently and quietly working in a focused manner and collecting evidence along the way ("... without evidence it is not true and or does not exist...not necessarily a lie though...").I estimate that I have spent at least a .75 permanent post (equivalent) amount of 'energy 'since January 2018 just trying to clear my name, and or fending off real and or perceived toxic actors trying persecute me within my professional associations, misuse the judicial and criminal justice system to drag me unfairly through the muck. One of my respected colleagues mentioned that in law school they will probably

'name' a procedure after me... 'The Duncan Lawrence manoeuvre' ...where you can say or do anything within the law, within the press and within the workplace, especially if no one holds you accountable for your actions. I have not used all the instances (within this book) in recent years that I have been threatened, even within work interviews and work generation activities, people want me until I mentioned that I am trying to clear my name from an unfair sentence. It is usually then that one of two things will happen, they stop communications with me altogether, or they find some reason to blame me somehow (for them not being able to use me).

36. I am not sure if it is because I am a black man and or because I now have a 'sensational criminal record'...I really am not sure. I am sure that white men are less afraid of me (and my counter-actions) and are very emboldened after my criminal conviction to go on to trying similar toxic acts if it serves theirs and or others purpose(s).

37. What about those citizens who don't know how to stand up for themselves and or have not seen the benefits of being assertive, not seen the benefits for not automatically believing everything you read and or hear (even if from a public and or senior charitable official and or from someone from within the legal system), have not seen the benefits from doing your own research in order to be able and capable of pointing out lies, bias, unfairness and or collusion and

conspiracies...you are definitely at the mercy of those around you(and their 'intentions') within the coroner process and within the entire legal process itself at times. It is crucial to get to know 'the intentions' of those around you, especially those claiming to be offering support to you.

38. A Personal Warning: Once you start turning in on yourself then you are done for...depression sets in, self-doubt sets in, and then self-victimising of yourself can become 'your jailer'...then you and any liars and or bystanders are unknowingly on the same energy track and moving towards keeping you and or me guilty, keeping personal and professional reputation decimated in the press, public ...within certain past/present/future employment opportunities created fear about taking on someone like you and I e.g."... the press...the media...the Assistant Coroner...they would not write something untrue, why should we take the risks...you seem competent, you seem very ethical etc but we read and hear differently in the press, your DBS says something different...there is no smoke without fire...".

39. It is still very very true "...I am not responsible for anyone but myself and how I respond to situations and my own life events...".

40. I choose not to sanitise my story, the public needs a true glimpse of my experiences, I have not tried to glamourise them either, they are what they are.

41. I will continue to not comment in social media...I have enough trolls already in my daily life.

42. It would be a disaster for me to 'get cleared' and then the emails within my memoirs never actually 'go public'. My memoirs do not illustrate 'legal technicalities', they do however illustrate regular and systematic harm done by toxic actors within all sections of society, ones that would go to any lengths to 'weaponize' the press, the courts, and other UK institutions to meet theirs and other's needs.

43. Either way this book and any follow up interviews and or any related 'Op Ed's' that I might be fortunate to write (on white male privilege, the power of action and bystanders, etc) will start to help a 'reset'...facts often make resistors look very much 'alone' in their manipulations, bias and 'creative rewriting of history'.

44. I made very good use of the pandemic and am now a lot clearer about what works for me (personally and professionally) 'upfront' and can take more 'smart risks'. 2015 and 2016 ended up being very problematic years but are still not enough to put me off working with others, maybe just not in London and just not in England.

45. Some individuals and organisations have now become obsessed with me, and I am clear that there is nothing that I can do to change this, nor do I wish to give them further 'oxygen' every time that they threaten to put

me into the press yet again...certain people have no boundaries whatsoever and will not stop until society stops giving them 'oxygen' too. Personally, I need to find a way to be more resilient in this area, especially when the public seem very 'okay' with 'how things have turned out for the black man'.

46. I just want actors 'named' and for them to receive 'suitable consequences' ... a positive justice.

47. I love and or respect the thousands of individuals, families, couples, children, young people, associations and the like over from my decades of work and life, but honestly I have been feeling that until I have some quality time away from London (and because I am satisfied that I am and was a very blessed and grateful soul to have had these past experiences and encounters), that I will not be trying to rebuild/ restart these relationships and nor will I spend time trying to help people understand what happened to me over the past few years. My thoughts may change in a few years' time but this is how I feel now, in these moments . Someone set out to tamper with the fabric of my past and present relationships and to ' cancel out' my contributions to the UK, EU and the Caribbean...I have accepted this and have started to move on to the next phase of my life....wherever that may lead me. Let us all live our best lives!

48. Education, social care, counselling, equality and diversity, human rights, criminal justice, management

and leadership etc. these fields did not assist me during my 2018/2021 legal challenges and adventures and I have no unconditional loyalty to them as I might have had in the past.. Music, Sport and the Arts got me though 2019-present. Some organisations told me that once cleared that they would try to get me back in to their organisations. Right now I can't even see any circumstances where I would want to 're-join' any organisation at present.

49. I felt like 'a laughing pure evil energy' had crossed my path for reasons only known to him during 2016-2021. With karma always running true, I wonder if it has worked out well for all of those in 'the toxic actors club' and it's collection of bystanders and rabble rousers.

50. I have not done much differently in my recent writing (when, say compared to my past writings) except to temporarily (hopefully) 'becoming a national and international story' myself), that my 'lived experiences' have increased my self-awareness and ability to empathise with others

51. There were so many things done in plain sight, yet 'hidden' from those that matter and or especially those that could have made a difference such as a 'clean court', a 'clean Metropolitan Police Department', a 'clean Crown Prosecution Service', courageous law firms, brave and open minded employers, an ethical and non-bias press and media, brave professional

associations, brave and ethical standard bearers such as the CQC, Charities Commission, Chief Coroner, Probation Service, etc. ...the list goes on and on.

52. Most were at least given email evidence of at least half of these areas listed below and yet still did nothing.

53. Told the charity solicitor the truth and they downplayed my witness statement to set the stage for me to take the blame/downplay my contributions as a consultant. Thank goodness for all of my emails.

54. Told the London Met Police the truth about how I was feeling during Spring/ early Summer of 2019 (grieving about my father who passed away a few months earlier and my mother that was gravely ill) and they manipulated what I said in order that they/ the CPS charged me for a 'different time period' altogether mainly comprising 2018 when I hadn't even heard of the Assistant Coroner.

55. Told the Court, the Judge and the Prosecution at Wimbledon Magistrates Court about their miscarriages and they buried my four letters to them...they were never heard in court ever.

56. Repeatedly told the CPS of their mistakes and they repeatedly said I was just trying to get off my sentence and ignored my email allegations. The Met said it was the CPS solicitor that set the charge period dates for me (but she would never respond to my email/letters to her at the CPS HQ). There was no 'open and public'

written statement rationalising her charge dates that was ever presented.

57. Did not seem to matter to them that I was interviewed about one period of time and then charged about another period of time altogether.

58. Regularly told my 'out of their depth' legal teams that they had their emphasis wrong(they were terrified it seemed with the 'emotional narrative' that was pushed in the court and in the press/media) and that they should focused on themselves, the Charity, the Met, The Assistant Coroner, etc..

59. Told the probation service to stop trying to get me to apologise to the parents of the young women that took her own life in May 2016 and to focused on my factual narrative and to not be so overwhelmed by the 'false emotional narratives' that were pushed by press, Prosecution, Judge, family, CPS,etc..

60. The judge/prosecutors were happy to keep me from making statements, presenting evidence and or presenting witnesses and never once mentioned in an open hearing about my four withheld letters that any of them on their own would have made a big difference and that each of them collectively probably would have cleared me.

61. The parents were happy go with non-facts, lies, racial bias and ignore their own past/ previous factual contacts with me. They have never once even made an

attempt at an apology to me afterwards. Like they felt that due to their very sad daughter's passing, that this gave them 'a never ending free pass' to ruin my life. I kept so many things quiet out of respect for their loss.

62. Various government watchdogs that I complained to over several months, they in their own way all told me how they could not help because "...Assistant Coroners in the UK had no legal boundaries..." to be externally scrutinised.

63. The charity founder/lead advisor refused to support me financially or professionally, even after repeated requests .She allowed me to unfairly take heat in court and in the press. She avoided lawsuits by saying that her real name was ' Nelly Jansen' and not ' Elly Jansen', the name used in all of the lawsuits against her.

64. There was so much energy to allow her to keep her honours and awards out of the court process...some of my professional associations seemed very happy to collude with press and Assistant Coroner to take away/give away my honours and awards.

65. The Assistant Coroner charged me/fined me in May 2019 and the Judge convicted and sentenced me in October 2019 and to this day, no one has ever explained what the difference was between the two charges.

66. Summer of 2021: Court fined the Charity £40K and ex-CEO £7k . I, the temporary consultant while black was sent to prison...with no questions asked from the press or courts about bias.

67. I sent my story to all major UK television companies and all major news outlets(at least twice)...there was no takers. This was very surprising considering the role that they all took in their bias towards me in 2019.

68. Only one publisher (out of 78) wanted to pay their own costs to have my memoirs published. The majority wanted me to pay them to 'self-publish'.

69. Difficulty getting quality jobs if I told the truth about my conviction and or if the DBS certificate arrived.

70. Chief Coroner said he had no power to help. I never knew how to ever check if this was ever really true or not. When he finally did try to help he referred me to a timid Senior Coroner to investigate my claims... this useless actor could not even bring himself to specifically admit that I provided him with enough email/factual evidence to show that the Assistant Coroner treatment of me was ' unsafe' in the least and grossly unfair at best. He stated that he found no fault in the way that the Assistant Coroner treated me...he, the Senior Coroner should be stripped of his right to practice in the UK.

71. The press/social media never challenged what they were actually being fed...they eventually became

'self-feeders' and perpetuated their own toxic content.

72. The judge was ` a complete ass' and seemed to hate my defiance with him. I can imagine the amount of people that he gave unfair sentences to if they made him feel insecure and or had actually pissed him off. He should have all of his cases reviewed, especially mine and be suspended from the bench.

73. I qualified for an open prison after my first week but was never told about it until my last three weeks.I am sure there was collusion to keep me locked up.

74. Director of Prosecution never responded to my letters.

75. Key CPS complaints procedure staff stopped acknowledging my emails/letters and just whitewashed the magistrates court process. I think they thought that I was a nuisance.

76. The appeal court fined me twice rather than rule in writing about the status of my four withheld magistrates court letters (in any appeal hearing process). Those involved should be fined and sanctioned.

77. Government watchdog took well over a year to say they could find no fault in how I was treated at the magistrates and or at the Crown Court Levels. I know they were short staff during the pandemic and I have some empathy for their attempts at searching out

miscarriages of justice. They would have been better off temporarily closing down until they were once again fit for practice.

78. My employers and professional associations showed no courage or respect in 2019-2021.

79. Took dozens of letters back and forth to Wimbledon Magistrates Court for them to admit that all four of my letters to them were seen by the judiciary.

80. Regardless of whether or not I get legally cleared or not and or I can get any compensation to use, especially to clean up my name on the internet, this is definitely not 'the end', I expect to have future periods of creativity, moments of joy and hope, experiences of giving and receiving diverse moments of love, more travel, meeting new and interesting people, more grandchildren, seeing my grandchildren graduate, dunk a basketball again, do a solo piano gig, grow more hair(might even cut it all off), become a publisher, live and work in another country...yes, the universe still has more plans for me.

81. In Volume II I will further reflect upon my relationships with the larger institutions within the UK, the ones that should have known that they would be found out sooner than later.

82. **If I had a 'wish list' for the next year or so it would be something like:**

- ✓ To have all the actors that helped to get me into this UK legal system be 'named and shamed', sanctioned and re-trained within their own professional associations.

- ✓ Related to the above, to have my memoirs published using primarily original emails between myself and the various toxic legal and non-legal actors.

- ✓ Write an 'Op Ed' on 'White Male Privilege'

- ✓ Support older people and those with SEN via sport, music and wellbeing activities in paid and non-paid roles.

- ✓ Publish several unfinished books this year.

- ✓ Consider which parts of the UK are 'worth salvaging' for me (if at all), in terms of any 'past' or 'emerging' personal and or professional relationships.

- ✓ Spend quality time away from the UK.

Some Practical Recommendations

1. For **Bystanders**

   - Take your brave and courageous first steps to be a 'helper'

2. For **friends and families**

   - Please look after yourselves, while never stop living your best life. If a friend or family member is in an unfair legal bind, find a way to be there at times too. Challenges can bring relationships together or break them apart...choose wisely, nothing stays the same.

3. Work **Colleagues and Peers**

Work can be beautiful, fun, worthwhile and a self-fulfilling series of opportunities...please do not take yourself and those around for granted...it may be difficult to fix organisations that 'get wonky' later.

- When differences and agreements occur always fight fair...always try to tell the truth even when egos and insecurities may be involved.

- Don't unfairly bring in line managers (especially if you might be one yourself) ...this could unfairly give someone an unfair advantage in a fight, research has shown time and time again that white line managers 'win' most complaints about them or initiated by them.

Line managers:

- I can go down a very long list of organisations since my early young adult job history, organisations where I have witnessed and or have personally experienced unfair employers, either for allowing their senior staff to 'fight unfair fights' where certain employees would have been better off not even trying to defend themselves and when personnel departments blatantly overlook incidents of racism, discrimination, white privilege, bias, low numbers of black people at senior management level, etc..

People of colour, seem to be 'easy prey' at times for ambitious white colleagues to walk over their black peers in order to make others look bad, to 'justify their own existence for keeping power and or for continuing to move up the power rung' within their organisations.

Other influential white and non-white colleagues simply look on and rarely challenged (for various reasons) this nasty behaviour, no matter how blatant and no matter how bad 'the team' motivational spirit was and can be further impacted ... "...they just keep on doing what they do...".

From my experience counselling, education and social care are some of the worst offenders for creating and or adding to the ever growing 'toxic workplace' at times...where their 'PR and marketing machines' say one thing but on 'the ground' it can be a much much much more of a 'different world' for staff, potential staff and their service users.

As long as this type of 'work environment' is present then managers and senior management will almost never really have the genuine respect of those around them and they will only see our 'working while black at work persona'(jumping through foolish hoops, fighting each other just to get ahead, not backing colleagues where we could, limited key promotions, limited professional development opportunities, keeping quiet to any rude and or mouthy and or immature line managers, when in reality 'a good kick in the ass' would have been the best course of action, etc.).White managers that have earned respect at work(rather than fear) must be amazing and beautiful people aside from work generally...the world is truly blessed to have them in it.

It is important to honestly note here, 'on-the-ground' I have been challenged by some of my 'non male' allies, I am challenged to get readers of my limited memoirs to understand, to further explore, to start 'the resistance rather than just the blaming' of white men, because this is truly not enough to make a real difference in the area of 'social care'. Social care middle manager levels can often be overly populated by white women, where racism and internalised sexism can run rife too...how do you explain this phenomenon?

Just look at the types of 'medical issues' (but very much 'stress related') connected to 'working while being a black woman' such as several types of cancers, diabetes type I/II, asthma, hypertension, obesity, stress, anaemia, relationship breakdowns, etc..

Having three daughters that are senior level practitioners, these areas very much concern me daily.

So many of my respected colleagues, associates and friends say things like "...unfortunately we will probably pass away before 'the roles switch', ..." e.g.where supremely qualified and talented women of colour are directly supervising the current crop of social care, criminal justice, education and health white senior management teams and board members that are providing services to a large number of multi-cultural, multi-racial and diverse range of service users.

Limited access to power sharing, hesitation with the enlarging of 'white senior management and board level club' has been a continuing theme throughout these memoirs and or mentioned in my other written publications going back to the 80s.

They say my experiences from 2015-2019 would have been much worse had I been a black woman. Like me, most women that I am an ally to often are a bit like me in their thinking,for example, we think (and will often say)we "...could do racism in our sleep, but it is the internalised racism(the things that we do to each other)that we spiritually and morally have a difficulty with...".My women allies say that at work, some of them actually treat each other like their worst enemy and competitors that they need to protect themselves from even though they really don't know each other well enough to have such 'passionate stances'. White work colleagues must think we're crazy when they see this acted out right in front of them. My black women allies think and often state to me that "...personnel departments should take internalised racism seriously too ..." and not just think of it as 'just a problem for the black community to sort out'.

Lastly my black women allies see internalised sexism as one of the most toxic barriers within the workplaces... where women go after each other for a variety of historical reasons. For example, your body shape, your clothes, the number of children you might have, the state of your marital relationships, these could all be reasons for you to be 'talked about behind your back' and or viewed as being a 'threat to other women because of your 'unspoken level of attractiveness to men'.

Growing up with an activist mother that continuously did some amazing things in her community until her passing, 'I have always seen them' and will try to be a much more 'public ally' because their fight is my fight and my fight is and was always their fight.

February 2022 Note: I am aware of the ever-increasing number of daily local, regional and international violent conflicts. I challenge any respected and ethical researchers to record the development (and 'diversity compositions') of senior management teams and board levels of charity organisations and NGOs that support individuals and families from these conflicts...**would anyone be surprised by the tangible results?**

- Fight fair

- Understand that not everything can be attributed to 'having a chip on one's shoulders', sometimes 'the toxic monster' does exist and is out causing havoc within diverse workplaces.

- Sometimes bad behaviours can happen...don't be afraid to 'name it' wherever it occurs (in general staff and or line manager levels)

- Allow others to fight fair (never be tempted to allow 'one sided evidence' or allow 'one side perspectives' to be the basis of your 'judgements') and or simply delay any 'disciplinary actions/talks', etc. until you have enough 'balanced evidence'...be brave and courageous during these situations.

- Present all evidence to all parties (never omit or only disclose to the most senior staff) ...total transparency should always be the goal.

- Never 'over-kill' by letting another senior manager get involved...a total 'imbalance' occurs here and then there is no chance of a fair fight.

- **Let your presence always be inspiring, fair, as a resource provider, as a mentor, as a leader and be that of a problem solver(not a problem maker)...be brave and courageous** and ask your senior level peers and your teams if this is how they see you.

If these simple steps do not occur, then toxic acts and attitudes may occur such as;

- Unsafe and unfair disciplinary actions may occur... some that will be far reaching and impact upon current and future careers.

- Racism or racist bias

- Misrepresentations

- Rude and or disrespectful language moments from the 'senior staff' where the junior staff' are not equally allowed to be rude and disrespectful (without severe disciplinary process being enforced upon them).

- Lies/mistruths can build up quickly within individuals, teams and often 'rumours' can create their own narratives.

- Misuse of HR policy and procedures

4. For those **going before a judge or magistrate**:

- Make sure that your charge sheet is factually correct (including the charge period dates)!

- Make sure that you and your legal representative are 'on the same page'!

- Get someone (or yourself) to ask 'the questions in your head and or those that might be within your 'heart' to the court...it will always be extremely hard to ask them later.

- Consider your human rights, especially your Article 6 rights.

5. For **magistrates and judges**:

- See above.

- Do not just rubber stamp the 'evidence' and 'recommendations' of other professionals...take time to read your papers and be prepared to be objective and non-bias, even during busy periods for the court.

- Do not violate any one's human rights (especially regarding article 6)

- Be aware of your verbal and nonverbal interactions with the prosecutors ...people are always watching and could assume bias and or a conspiracy on your part otherwise.

- Never supress a defendant's evidence.

- Get someone (or yourself) to ask 'the questions in your head and or those that might be within your 'heart' to the court...it will always be extremely hard to ask them later and could lead to miscarriages of justice and the ruining of your professional reputation.

- Admit when you and or others around you have gotten things wrong...take the time to 'make things right'.

6. For **police**:

- Do not collude with other professionals or keep quiet!

- Use 'best practices' when making referrals to the Crown Prosecution Service

- Be open and transparent and involve others where possible to keep the process fair and honest!

- Never supress evidence.

- Get someone (or yourself) to ask 'the questions in your head and or those that might be within your 'heart' to the court...it will always be extremely hard to ask them later and could lead to miscarriages of justice and the ruining of your professional reputation.

- Admit when you and or others around you have gotten things wrong....take the time to 'make things right'.

7. For **politicians** and **political appointments**:

- Do not promise something that you go on to never do!

- Listen carefully and show empathy.

- Be transparent, non-bias and respect human rights always (especially regarding article 6)

- Show courage and honesty even during busy periods and or when dealing with a high- profile cases.

- Never supress evidence.

- Get someone (or yourself) to ask 'the questions in your head and or those that might be within your 'heart' to the court...it will always be extremely hard to ask them later and could lead to miscarriages of justice and the ruining of your professional reputation.

- Admit when you and or others around you have gotten things wrong....take the time to 'make things right'.

Thought Questions:

?= After reading this book, have your thoughts changed regarding D.Eric Lawrence and or his case? Y/N Explain:

?: Will you do anything as a result of reading this book e.g. write to your MP, challenge the press and or news media, start a social campaign, etc. ? Y/N Explain:

Volume II will explore a few of Duncan's substantial communications with:

- The CPS

- Probation Service

- London Metropolitan Police

- Chief Coroner (UK)

- Kingston Crown Court

- RPFI

- Elly Jansen

- Ex-employers

This will be presented in 'case study' format, still using unedited emails as the basis for consideration and discussion.

Tentative Publication Date: Spring 2027

Epilogue

- *Who are you?*

- Why you?

- Where was the truth?

- Why didn't those around you come forth and tell the truth?

- Where are you now?

Who are you?

As you have heard by now, even after several hundred hours of trying to clear his name, Duncan may be free in his heart and soul but has not yet been cleared by any United Kingdom Legal Standard.

- *The charity that he worked for less than four months over 2015/16 was fined by the courts in the summer of 2021.*

- *The ex-charity CEO was fined by the courts in the summer of 2021.*

- *The social care charity founder who was also the lead advisor during Duncan's 3 months + time was never presented in any court and kept her Queens Awards.*

- *Duncan, a Black man, a temporary consultant/ trainer/staff and management mentor was hounded and decimated by the press (as recently as the summer of 2021), disrespected by several professional associations, convicted and sent to prison in 2019.*

https://www.thirdsector.co.uk/charity-fined-40000-death-teenager-its-care/management/article/1709412

https://eminetra.co.uk/the-chaotic-care-home-fined-40000-for-the-judges-failure-to-protect-the-patient-who-hung-his-neck/332261/

- Why you?

All of these court actions were 'carried out in plain sight' and not one reporter, not one criminal justice organisation and or individual politicians asked for Duncan's case to be reviewed...not a one.

Not one ex-employer has come back to Duncan hoping to review their stance taken with him...not a one.

Why you?

Not much 'real care' (or fairness) in social care, counselling and education organisations, and local-National politics, and it seems the number one action is to 'cover your ass, and even better if no one gives you a hassle for doing so'.

Those that scapegoated him from day one, those that withheld facts and emails from ever being presented in court, belatedly most of these same people will only be highlighted, named, and uncovered when you the readers read this book and see the damning mountain of email evidence yourselves.

His last hope for a 2021 miracle was a very weak report that was submitted by a very pivotal organisation that could have done so much better (see related correspondence below), the CCRC, an organisation with such a magnificent history at times, that even after almost a year of assessments took a very lazy and less than courageous route in this instance. Even after he complained, 'their response' ironically was always more substantial than their original report to Duncan ever was.

Where was the truth?

I wonder where your reading of these memoirs will lead your views...'Duncan is guilty' or 'Duncan is not guilty', or maybe something else?

*Judge for yourself, **what did the various legal professionals get right...what did they get wrong...what could the various coroner processes have actually brought to the legal table** that was left out here(from the Chief Coroner, to the Senior Coroner to the CPS, to his local politician), **were they as helpless as they presented** themselves at times or are they **just part of toxic process that was just protecting itself by directly and or indirectly allowing the 'weaponising of the coroner process'** to fit the individual coroner personalities, to reflect the individual coroner integrity levels,etc..?*

*What about the 'non legal organisations'...the professional associations, the employers and potential employers, the reporters, the press... the list is vast of those that could have shown courage and say "...**no, something is not right here...we will be brave and at least fair in this matter...".** 'Kicking the can down the road', the blaming of 'the court' as an excuse for not challenging and or when you are being **afraid of the press finding out that you had been brave or weak** (whatever the case might have been) ...clear examples of taking the well-worn out low road.*

Duncan's evidence that the courts withheld was generally more substantial than the evidence than the court and press ever tried to present against him.

Why didn't those around you come forth and tell the truth?

In all of these instances have we observed the very best that Britain could offer in situations like this or is it that sadly once someone decided to 'attach' an unfortunate suicide to him, one that he never really had a chance to detangle himself from, in this case any action(s) would have been too late or would never be enough?

Where are you now?

People that know Duncan will probably tell him to "...just leave it now Duncan, your conviction is spent... now go after the jobs that you really want and put all this behind you... then, get away when you can...".

I have no clue what Duncan will now do, but if he sticks to his word, his path will be very different than his previous days were within the UK.

If he sticks to his word, he will continue to pray each day for the world, himself and for his past and present family, friends, and associates. He says that he wants to get away and I am sure that spiritually he has already left.

Peace to us all and thanks for reading these memoirs!

33

Duncan gigging for a homeless shelter fundraiser.

www.ingramcontent.com/pod-product-compliance
Lightning Source LLC
Chambersburg PA
CBHW030904120626
46554CB00001B/5